W9-DFW-537

August, 1962

# INTRODUCTORY
## SOCIOLOGY

# INTRODUCTORY SOCIOLOGY

BY

## WILLIAM E. COLE

PROFESSOR AND HEAD,
DEPARTMENT OF SOCIOLOGY
THE UNIVERSITY OF TENNESSEE

DAVID McKAY COMPANY, INC.    New York

1962

INTRODUCTORY SOCIOLOGY

LIBRARY OF CONGRESS CATALOG CARD NUMBER: 61-5093

MANUFACTURED IN THE UNITED STATES OF AMERICA

# PREFACE

THIS BOOK is designed to help the student and teacher develop learning situations in the introductory college sociology course which will accomplish five objectives:

1. To help the student develop a meaningful concept of the field of sociology, the value of it, and some of the common methods employed in the study of sociology (Introduction).

2. To help the student acquire an over-all perspective of how society developed (Part I).

3. To show how society and its component parts are structured (Part II).

4. To help the student find out how society functions and what goes on within it (Part III).

5. Finally, to show some of the major products coming out of society (Part IV).

The above objectives constitute a large order for a beginning college text, thus space permits only sketchy treatment of important topics in some instances. However, questions for further study and annotated references are given at the end of every chapter to guide the teacher and student toward developing greater depth of knowledge about the topics presented.

The volume takes the position that sociology is the study of social systems. This approach to the field appears to be not only logical but the one most productive of empirical sociological data. The book has a normative approach, except for some chapters in Part IV. This volume will soon be followed by a second on social problems.

In view of the encyclopedic, disorderly, and complicated organization of many introductory textbooks in sociology, particularly confusing to freshman and sophomore students, we have placed emphasis upon simplicity of outline and readability of the text. The outline is the result of the author's thirty years of experience in teaching introductory sociology courses at the universities of Tennessee and North Carolina, Cornell University and George Peabody College for Teachers. Illustrations—graphic and pictorial—have been carefully selected to supplement and illustrate points made in the text.

The author is indebted to his editors, colleagues, and many students who gave suggestions guiding the preparation of the book, to Mrs. Margaret Garrett for her careful work in the preparation of the manuscript, and to Jerry W. Combs of the U.S. Bureau of the Census, who kindly read and checked on the facts in Chapter 6, "Demographic Structures."

WILLIAM E. COLE

*v*

# CONTENTS

# ILLUSTRATIONS

# FIGURES

# INTRODUCTORY
# SOCIOLOGY

# 1. INTRODUCTION: SOCIOLOGY AS A FIELD OF STUDY

CONCEPTS of the nature and scope of the field of sociology vary, but for our purposes it may be defined as a study of social systems. Other commonly used definitions call it the study of plural behavior or social interaction. More will be said about these concepts later in the chapter after a word about the popularity of sociology in this country.

Although the roots of sociology are strongly embedded in European origins, the subject has enjoyed unequaled popularity in the United States. High schools enroll a half million pupils in this area every year. Small colleges usually offer from three to twelve courses, while large universities may offer as many as fifty. Altogether, Odum listed some 3,000 courses in sociology in 1951.[1]

The reasons for the rapid growth of sociology in the United States are fairly clear. For one thing, Americans have always had easy access to the work of European scholars. Thus, early American sociologists studied the works of Herbert Spencer, Auguste Comte, and Emile Durkheim. A later generation studied the extensive writings of the German sociologist, Max Weber. Such foundation writings of European origin helped to establish sociology in the United States.

Social reform movements developed in the United States as they did in Europe. In fact many American reform movements had their European antecedents. Industrialization and urbanization brought their own core of social problems in America, as did the heavy influx of immigrants. Out of slavery and emancipation came many problems unique to the American continent.

The social reform movements, and the social problems that developed out of the establishment and growth of a new nation, created a demand for empirical research in sociology which has grown by leaps and bounds since the depression of the 1930's and the period following World War II in the late 1940's.[2]

[1] Howard W. Odum, *American Sociology* (New York: Longmans, Green and Co., 1951).

[2] For a brief and concise statement on the development of sociology in the United States, *see* Roscoe C. Hinkle, Jr. and Gisela J. Hinkle, *The Development of Modern Sociology* (New York: Random House, 1954).

## THE SOCIAL SCIENCES

Sociology as a separate discipline grew out of generalized courses in social science in the United States. Around the turn of the century early American sociologists belonged to a large organization known as the National Social Science Association, but in 1906 they broke away from the parent organization to form the American Sociological Society, which currently has a membership of around 7,000. The Society was formed at just about the time that American colleges and universities began to offer courses in sociology.

As set up for teaching purposes in the colleges and universities of the United States, the social sciences are usually designated as follows:

1.  History (often classed as a humanity)
2.  Economics
3.  Political science
4.  Geography, in its human and economic aspects
5.  Anthropology, especially social and cultural
6.  Psychology
7.  Sociology

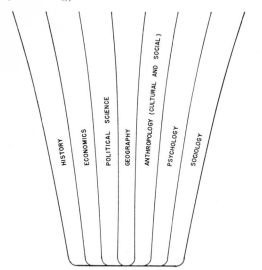

FIG. 1. SCHEMATIC DIAGRAM OF THE SOCIAL SCIENCES

This diagram shows how the social sciences are fused at the base and how each has developed into a distinctive specialty.

As the accompanying diagram (Fig. 1) shows, the social sciences are fused at their base. This means that there is much overlapping of subject matter between them and that there are many common elements among them, yet each stands out as a distinctive field from the other.

### History

History is the oldest of the social sciences. History is primarily a systematic, often chronological, account of past events, particularly as these relate to the human race. History is not just a record of past events but part of a continuing process. While much of history has to do with political organization and reorganization of governments, and with diplomacy and wars, the social and cultural history of a people is a proper concern of sociology. Many good sociological studies also have their historical background.

Many of the more capable historians do not accept history as a social science but prefer to classify it, along with literature, philosophy, and the languages, as a humanity. For our purpose we accept history as a social science.

### Economics

Economics is concerned with wealth getting and wealth spending, and the economic institutions concerned with these processes are among the most important of social institutions. Economics is greatly concerned with social trends because they influence economic trends. Many economic analysts concern themselves with population data, especially as these data relate to growth and composition of population. In many areas of research and teaching the economist and the sociologist may work profitably together.

### Political Science

Political science is the science of politics or government, an important phase of which is public administration, the latter having to do with governmental administration. Much of the subject matter of political science developed out of history and the general social science movement. Many political scientists do not like the term "political science" but prefer the more inclusive term "government" in speaking of their field of endeavor.

Many phases of political science are closely related to sociology. For example, the struggle for power in politics cannot be understood apart from its psychological and sociological aspects. Much of the basic work in social power has been done by sociologists.[3]

Much use of sociological data and literature is made by students studying public administration, and by persons actively engaged in administering governments. For example, at least one course in urban sociology and in rural sociology may be taken by students of local government. A person preparing to become a city planner is likely to have at least one basic course in urban sociology and one in urban ecology. City planners, welfare directors, and public safety directors often have background training in sociology.

## Geography

Geography, apart from physical geography, which is a study of the physical differentiation of the earth's surface, has many social aspects. Economic geography has to do with the development and growth of economic pursuits in various parts of the world. The distribution of peoples and their technologies under different climatic, topographic, and resource conditions, and their adjustment to differentiated conditions, approaches a phase of sociology known as human ecology. More recently, courses in urban geography have come into being. Thus it is that the geographer and the sociologist may work together to the mutual benefit of

each, the areas of study being fused at the base, as indicated in Figure 1.

## Anthropology

Anthropology is the science of the origin and development of mankind. Physical anthropology has to do with man's physical development and appearance. Cultural anthropology deals with the development of man's cultural items and social forms. Sociology thus depends heavily upon cultural anthropology to supply it with information needed on cultural development. The nature of such information is indicated in Chapter 3, The Structure, Growth, and Impact of Culture. Also, where the sociologist is concerned with giving a picture of the characteristics and culture of early man, he depends upon the anthropologist rather than the sociologist for his information.

## Psychology

Psychology has been variously defined as the science of the mind or the science of the mental states and processes.

While psychology has to do with mental development, with mental measurements (psychometrics), and with individual behavior, it is concerned with the relation of the individual to the group and often with altering individual-group relations where better adjustment of the individual to his groups is needed.

Perhaps it is in courses in social psychology that the subject matter of sociology and psychology are brought most closely together. Such courses are taught in departments of both sociology and psychology and often are part of the training of both sociologists and psychologists.

## Sociology

Sociology, which we have defined as the study of social systems, emphasizes individual to individual interaction, group to individual interaction, and group to group interaction, as contrasted to psychology, which is more concerned with motivation and individual behavior.

---

[3] For example, Floyd Hunter's *Community Power Structure* (Chapel Hill, N. C.: University of North Carolina Press, 1953). *See also* Dorwin Cartwright (ed.), *Studies in Social Power* (Ann Arbor: University of Michigan, Research Center for Group Dynamics, 1959).

SOME CONCEPTS OF SOCIOLOGY

Definitions of the field of sociology vary both with time and with individual scholars. Therefore we may do well to consider some of the concepts of sociology as defined by certain of the leaders in the field.

1. Vilfredo Pareto: "Human society is the subject of many researches. Some of them constitute specialized disciplines: law, political economy, political history, the history of religions, and the like. Others have not yet been distinguished by special names. To the synthesis of them all, which aims at studying human society in general, we may give the name of sociology." [4]

2. Pitirim A. Sorokin: Sociology is "a study, first, of the relationship and correlations be-

tween various classes of social phenomena (correlations between economic and religious; family and moral; juridical and economic; mobility and political phenomena, and so on); second, that between the social and the nonsocial (geographic, biological, etc.,) phenomena; third, the study of the general characteristics common to all classes of social phenomena." [5]

3. Max Weber: Sociology is "a science which attempts the interpretative understanding of social action in order thereby to arrive at a causal explanation of its cause and effects." [6]

[4] *The Mind and Society* (New York: Harcourt, Brace and Co., 1935), I, 3.

[5] *Contemporary Sociological Theories* (New York: Harper and Bros., 1928), p. 760-61.

[6] *The Theory of Social and Economic Organization* (New York: Oxford University Press, 1947), p. 88.

# PHYSICS   BIOLOGY  SOCIOLOGY

MATTER   ORGANISM   SOCIETY

MOLECULE   TISSUE   GROUP

ATOM   CELL   INTER-RELATION

*John B. Knox*

4. Henry Pratt Fairchild: Sociology is "the scientific study of the phenomena arising out of the group relations of human beings. The study of man and his environment in their relations to each other." [7]

In general there are three approaches to defining the subject matter of sociology: (1) as the scientific study of society; (2) as the study of plurality patterns and plural behavior, and (3) as the study of social systems. We shall discuss the first two briefly but will emphasize the third approach, which is being used in this text.

Many sociologists define sociology as the scientific and systematic study of society. This emphasis is good. However, society in mass is too extensive and complicated a unit for sociologists to study except through mass observation and critical appraisal which may also be scientific and systematic. The study of society becomes much more meaningful when we break it down into its component parts for scientific analysis. We shall attempt this presently.

A common concept of sociology is that it is the study of plurality patterns. A plurality pat-

[7] *Dictionary of Sociology* (New York: Philosophical Library, 1944), p. 302.

tern is composed of two or more persons. Since most behavior is plural, it takes place with others or it is in some way related to others. The behavioral interplay between persons, even though it may be largely psychic and not overt, is called *social interaction*. This is one of the key terms in sociology, and the process of interaction is the basic social process in all societies and in all plurality patterns.

Social interaction is less complicated than it may seem. A couple in love with each other constitutes an interaction pattern. Courtship partners usually have contact with each other. The contact may be bodily or it may be through the mail, via telephone, or in memory of happy moments spent together. Two people in love stimulate and influence each other. The stimulus of one influences the response of the other. *Social interaction, then, is the way in which one person influences the behavior, the thoughts, and the attitudes of another person.* It comes about as a result of contact, stimulus, and response between two or more persons. Interaction patterns may be simple in a small group like the family, but complicated in a more complex plurality pattern like a rioting mob. A simple and a more complicated interaction pattern is indicated by the accompanying diagrams (Fig. 2).

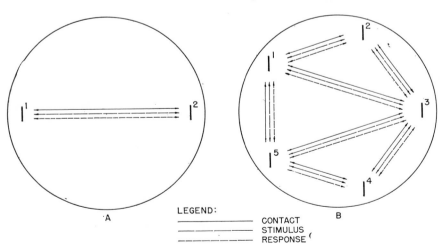

LEGEND:
_____ CONTACT
_ _ _ _ _ _ _ STIMULUS
_ . _ . _ . _ RESPONSE

FIG. 2. DIAGRAMMATIC SKETCH SHOWING TWO INTERACTION PATTERNS, ONE SIMPLE (A) AND THE OTHER COMPLEX (B)

Social interaction is the basic social process in all societies. At times it may make for unity and cooperaton between and within groups. At other times the interaction process is such as to develop hostility and conflict between the members of a group or between groups.

## A WORKING DEFINITION OF SOCIOLOGY

In two or three previous books the author has defined sociology as *the study of social systems.* This concept is rather closely related to the one we have just discussed above, but calls for more analysis.

*A social system is basically a system of interacting personalities plus the physical environmental base and the cultural base which support and sustain the system.* As Loomis and Beegle say: "Social systems, whether studied as going concerns in the present or from a historical point of view, are composed of social interactions and the cultural factors which structure these interactions." [8]

Parsons indicates the nature of a social system in the following language: "Thus conceived, a social system is only one of three aspects of the structuring of a completely concrete system of social action. The other two are the personality systems of the individual actors and the cultural system which is built into their action." [9] What Parsons means is that interaction in a social system, say a family, would be influenced not only by the structure and make-up of the system itself, but also by the personalities of the members of the family and the cultural base which supports the system. For instance, the Navajo culture requires an obedience in its children which would not be required in most non-Indian cultures. The role of a Hindu upper-class wife may be considerably different from the role of an American upper-class wife. One culture supports a state, also a social system, developed and organized according to the culture of a democracy, while another state is developed and planned according to communistic or socialistic ideologies and may be ruled by a dictator or by a small political clique.

What, then, are the major social systems found in a society? A society itself, say a state, national, or a community society, is a social system. Within this system, as in other social systems, are found groups, audiences and crowds, social classes and sometimes castes, social institutions and locality social systems, such as neighborhoods, communities, and regions.

If sociology is a study of social systems, what is it that sociologists study about social systems? They may study their origin and development, analyze their structure, determine what is going on within them and what is coming out of them. Such are the major purposes of this book.

Let us now look more minutely at the make-up of a social system. We shall use as an illustration the elements of a Protestant church, a church being an illustration of a social system known as a social institution.

These elements, discussed below, are interrelated. Many of them are in use at the same time. When the elements are added together and the matrix given a time factor, the unit becomes a social system.

Sociology is a social science. In general there are two requisites for a science: one is that there be a subject-matter field somewhat distinctive from other fields; the other requisite is that this field of subject matter be such that it may be studied by systematic and scientific

[8] Charles P. Loomis and J. Allen Beegle, *Rural Sociology: The Strategy of Change* (Englewood Cliffs, N. J.: Prentice-Hall, 1957), p. 2. *See also* Charles P. Loomis, *Social Systems: Essays on Their Persistence and Change* (Princeton, N. J.: D. Van Nostrand Co., Inc. (1960), *and* Talcott Parsons, *et al., Theories of Society* (2 vols.; Glencoe, Ill.: Free Press, 1961).

[9] Talcott Parsons, *The Social System* (Glencoe, Ill.: Free Press, 1951), p. 6. *See also* Frederick L. Bates, "Position, Role and Status: A Reformation of Concepts," *Social Forces,* 34:313-21, May, 1956.

ELEMENTS OF A SOCIAL INSTITUTION FOUND IN A CHURCH

| *Elements of a Social System* | *Examples* |
|---|---|
| 1. People, or actors | Pastor, ministers of education and music, elders, deacons, teachers, members of congregation, and maintenance personnel. |
| 2. Interaction, acts, or behavior | Worship, teaching, preaching, singing, prayers, fund-raising, and informal visitation. |
| 3. Ends or objectives sought by the system | Personal salvation, religious teaching, social improvement, church extension, and personal satisfaction and improvement. |
| 4. Social norms, or rules and regulations, controlling conduct or behavior in the system | Conduct codes for pastors, Sunday-school teachers and officers of the church, and more general conduct norms for members. |
| 5. Beliefs which are part of the system | Belief in a Supreme God and a basic belief in the teachings of the Bible. |
| 6. Statuses and status relationships of the actors in the system | Status hierarchy in the church organization, and the fact that only men may serve as elders and deacons in the church. |
| 7. Role relationships and role expectations of persons in different status positions | The role of the pastor as leader of his flock, the role of the elders as spiritual leaders, and the deacons as the financial and business leaders of the church. |
| 8. Authority or power of some to influence the behavior of others | The elders may accept or reject prospective members and may remove members from the church, whereas the deacons have authority to spend funds and administer property of the church, and church bodies, of which the church is a part, may examine and accept, reject, or remove ministers. |
| 9. Instruments and other cultural items which are symbolic of the system | The Book of Church Order, the altar, the Cross, the Sacrament, religious songs, and religious pictures. |
| 10. Nonsymbolic facilities and cultural items which aid the system to achieve its ends | Physical equipment, financial and property resources, church records, and teaching aids. |
| 11. Habitat and territory | The church edifice and supporting properties, and a vaguely defined service area. |

means. Sociology fulfills these two requisites. The field is distinctive and separate from other fields, and the data may be studied by techniques used in other sciences, as well as by means developed as appropriate tools for study in sociology itself.

## METHODS IN SOCIOLOGICAL RESEARCH AND STUDY

The sociologist tries to obtain knowledge from carefully prepared research. When this is not possible or impractical, he may resort to another source of knowledge which is that of empirical observation derived from existing knowledge and experience. The teacher of sociology seeks valid information, as should also the policy maker who deals with social problems or social issues.

Whatever the method used in research in the social sciences, the steps are very often much the same. With some variations, depending upon the nature of the problem and the data available, the steps in scientific method follow

STEPS IN SCIENTIFIC METHOD

| *Steps* | *Example* |
|---|---|
| 1. A statement of the problem to be solved | 1. "The Effect of World War II upon Juvenile Delinquency in a City of 100,000." |
| 2. Hypothesis | 2. During wartime the juvenile delinquency rate is expected to increase in a city. |
| 3. Review of literature | 3. Studies dealing with delinquency in the city and with the more general subject of the impact of war upon delinquency. |
| 4. Collection of data | 4. From juvenile court records the number and kinds of juvenile offenses were obtained for the prewar, wartime, and postwar periods in the city. |
| 5. Tabulation and arrangement of the data | 5. Simple statistical tables were made, showing amount of delinquency, its rates and composition for prewar, wartime, and the postwar period. Some data were graphically presented. |
| 6. Controls | 6. The only control possible was to compare the delinquency rates during the wartime period with those of the prewar and postwar period. |
| 7. Interpretation of the data | 7. Since this study was a standard master's thesis, the interpretation of the data and the report had to conform to standard university form. Interpretation centered about the testing of the hypothesis. |
| 8. Conclusion | 8. In testing the hypothesis (step 2 above), the data did not bear out the fact that delinquency rates increased in the city during World War II, or that its composition changed materially. |

closely the above illustrated sequence. Historical research does not always follow this pattern.

One of the tests of science is its predictability. Under the same set of conditions an experiment in science should yield the same results. Predictability is easier to establish in the physical and biological sciences than in the social sciences where predictability is more difficult.

Research ways and methods in sociology vary greatly in scope or range of study. Many studies are "microscopic" or "molecular" in scope; that is, they cover a small number of subjects or a small sampling of sociological data. Such studies tend to be more factual and objective and scientific than do "macroscopic" studies, which cover a vast range of data. Both kinds of studies have their usefulness and their

merits.[10] American sociologists perhaps neglect studies of macroscopic scope and lay stress upon those of microscopic scope. This neglect of studies of greater scope has been voiced by Znaniecki. He says:

. . . a laboratory, a clinic, a hospital, a place where a small number of people regularly congregate, a kindergarten, a school building with or without its neighborhood, a classroom within a college or a whole college campus, a prison, a summer camp, a military center, a section of a factory or an entire factory, sometimes also the area where workers live, a village, a town, the habitat of a tribal or rural community or an ecological part of a city. . . . [Such a focus of study ignores] the enormous multiplicity and complexity of social phenomena developing on

[10] *See* James A. Schellenberg, "Divisions of General Sociology," *American Sociological Review,* **22**:660-63, December, 1957.

the national scale, the continental scale, and the world-wide scale, as well as the historical background of these phenomena.[11]

In developing or obtaining new valid knowledge in sociology, the sociologist may make use of one or more of the following methods.

1. *Observation.* Careful observation must be a valid method of study in any science. The chemist uses it in his laboratory, as does also the biologist. The sociologist gains much knowledge of social conditions and situations through observation. Community sociologists and social and cultural anthropologists have a technique they use in community and cultural studies which is known as *participative observation.* Using this method, the investigator lives in a community and becomes acquainted with its culture, its institutions, and its people to a point where he can give an adequate picture of the community, its culture, and its people. He may supplement this method of study with any data he can find on the community.

2. *The case-study method.* The case-study method is an intensive study of one or more subjects. In sociology the subjects may be individuals, groups, or some other social system. Pioneer users of the case-study method in American sociology were W. I. Thomas and Florian Znaniecki, who used life-history materials in a famous piece of research on the Polish peasant.[12] The case-study method has

[11] Florian Znaniecki, "Basic Problems of Contemporary Sociology," *American Sociological Review,* **19**:519, October, 1954.

[12] William I. Thomas and Florian Znaniecki, *The Polish Peasant in Europe and America* (New York: Alfred A. Knopf, 1927).

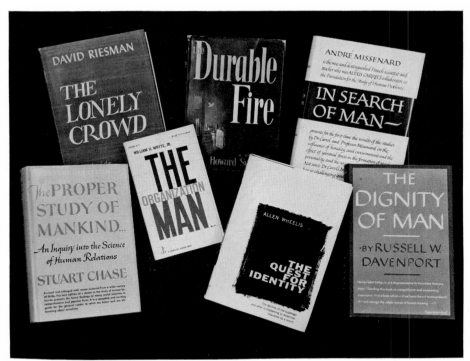

E. I. du Pont de Nemours & Co., Inc.

*Increasingly mankind is turning his research techniques to the study of man himself.*

been admirably applied also to the study of individual juvenile delinquents and adult offenders.[13] Depth studies, which are detailed studies of a small sample, are frequently made of individual families or communities using the case-study method. Some of these studies are very detailed in scope.[14] The case-study method may also be applied to an institution, such as a church, or to a newspaper. One of the most common uses of it is made by social workers who study individual clients or families. For some purposes, then, the case-study method is a useful one to use in sociology and related fields. Its value lies in the depth of study.

3. *Statistical methods.* Statistical methods in social science research are often referred to as quantitative methods. Stouffer points to some developments in mathematics and mathematical statistics which have considerable promise for research in sociology.[15]

Methods of testing hypotheses in sociological research have improved greatly. One technique that has proven useful is the obtaining of considerable information relative to a problem before an hypothesis is established. Particularly valuable is sampling in which only that size sample is used which approves or disapproves a hypothesis in contrast to fixed-size and much larger samples. Improved sampling of data may cut down greatly the size of sample, yet gives as good results as a larger sample.

Many statistical studies involve surveys and questionnaire techniques. Here the problem of sampling invariably arises.[16] What universe, or scope of study, to use becomes a practical problem to the researcher. The methods range from getting a 100 per cent sample to highly random methods of selecting a small sample. The more systematic methods of sampling emphasize a careful examination of the universe to be studied and a drawing of the sample.

In a study of adoption practices and attitudes in a city of 125,000, a very careful telephone directory sample of 2,500 names was selected. The sample was so well chosen that perhaps 2,500 more names would have given little information that the original sample did not give.

In studying attitudes, well-accepted scaling techniques have been developed.[17]

Correlations between certain characteristics and behavior, or between certain conditions and characteristics, are common. For instance, one may study the relation between various family background factors and happiness or nonhappiness in marriage.

Many sociological studies use simple statistical procedures like gross statistics, medians, averages, per capita data, and rates expressed in terms of ratios. The *U.S. Census of Population* or the *Statistical Abstract of the United States* contains a wealth of fairly simple statistical data which the college sociology student will find useful. *The Demographic Yearbook* of the United Nations is also a rich source of world population data yielding comparative population data.

While the hand compilation of statistics is still the practice and is most useful to students of sociology, electronic computers are being installed in many research laboratories. These, of course, vastly increase the speed of research

[13] Clifford R. Shaw, *The Jack-Roller* (Chicago: University of Chicago Press, 1931), and *The Natural History of a Delinquent Career* (Chicago: University of Chicago Press, 1931). *Also* Irving Shulman, *The Amboy Dukes* (New York: Doubleday and Co., 1947).

[14] Such studies as Robert S. and Helen M. Lynd, *Middletown* (New York: Harcourt, Brace and Co., 1929), and *Middletown in Transition* (New York: Harcourt, Brace and Co., 1931). *Also* W. L. Warner, *Democracy in Jonesville* (New York: Harper and Bros., 1949), and A. B. Hollingshead, *Elmtown's Youth* (New York: John Wiley and Sons, 1949).

[15] *See* Samuel A. Stouffer, "Quantitative Methods," in *Review of Sociology: Analysis of a Decade*, ed. Joseph G. Gittler (New York: John Wiley and Sons, 1957), pp. 25-55. *See also* John H. Mueller and Karl F. Schuessler, *Statistical Reasoning in Sociology* (Boston: Houghton Mifflin Co., 1961).

[16] *See* Frederick F. Stephan and Philip J. McCarthy, *Sampling Opinions* (New York: John Wiley and Sons, 1958).

[17] *See* Warren S. Targeson, *Theory and Methods of Scaling* (New York: John Wiley and Sons, 1958).

*U.S. Bureau of the Census*

*Electronic computers are now found in some of the more outstanding social science research organizations. This particular machine was developed to make the 1960 census tabulations.*

and greatly widen its scope. Perhaps in a first course in sociology only a generalized knowledge of quantitative methods, plus ability to interpret simple statistics, is needed.

4. *The laboratory method.* Laboratory research situations are not as easy to establish in sociology as in the natural sciences. Not only are experiments in social research more difficult than experiments with plants and animals, but controlled conditions are especially difficult to establish and maintain. Controls are, of course, a major problem to the investigator working in chemistry, with microorganisms in bacteriology, with white rats in a foods laboratory, or with pigeons in learning situations in a psychological laboratory.

Laboratory situations, with adequate controls, are possible in sociological research. The industrial sociologist may select two groups of

workers and equate them as to age, past production records, and personal or work-condition factors. The two groups may then be put to work under different conditions and with different types of supervision, with one group acting as a control against the other. Later their production records may be compared. Such research situations have yielded valuable information to industry and to the field of industrial sociology.[18]

Two carefully selected samples of juvenile delinquents may be matched with each other so that each sample is roughly equivalent in age, sex, and previous juvenile record according to number and kinds of offenses committed. Supervision in the form of counselors may be supplied to one group, whereas the

18 *See* John B. Knox, *Human Relations in Industry* (New York: Random House, 1955).

other group may have only the usual services of busy probation officers from the juvenile court. The two samples continue for a period of time while the number and kinds of offenses in the two samples are compared. In this instance, the group supplied with counselors is the experimental group, the other the control group. The experimental situation is roughly akin to a controlled laboratory research situation.

5. *Logical inquiry.* Logical inquiry has its place as a method in sociology. The much-maligned armchair sociology has its place. There is great need for the person who can critically evaluate sociological research techniques and assess the research results of the application of these techniques—for the scholar who can distill and synthesize the research of hundreds of studies in the many branches of sociology and critically present his findings. In the social sciences, as in physics or chemistry, there is need for the investigator with the critical, inquiring mind who can see the sociological forest and its problems, as well as the individual trees of the forest. This is another reason why we say that critical inquiry and evaluation has its place in sociological research and study.

## SOME DIFFICULTIES IN SOCIOLOGICAL RESEARCH AND ITS APPLICATION

The data in sociology are complicated. People and their problems are complicated. Social behavior is complicated. In spite of this complexity, sociology is rapidly maturing as a social science. Sociology as a field of study and investigation is only about 50 years old, whereas some of the natural sciences are several hundred years old. The amount of money now being spent on research in the social sciences is infinitesimal compared to that being spent on research in the natural sciences. For instance, in 1954 federal research support was divided as follows: physical sciences, 87 per cent; biological sciences, 11 per cent, and social sciences, 2 per cent. This situation exists in spite of the fact that the great problems of the United States and the world are largely social—the problem of peace and war; the problems of relationship between races and groups; problems of the use of leisure; the problems of poverty and deficiency in an age of abundance in many lands; the problems of the stress diseases and increasing personal disorganization. Too little attention is directed by the sociologists to these problems, much of their research and study time being devoted to theoretical formulas and to problems of small significance rather than to the realistic problems of the community, state, and nation.

There are some difficulties peculiar to the application of research data in social sciences, especially sociology. First of all there are lags between the progress and development of knowledge and its application. For instance, in the field of juvenile and adult corrections we have ample knowledge to push forward progress in corrections possibly 50 years; yet in many states the administration of correctional institutions is in the hands of incompetent political hacks who operate antiquated penal programs in obsolete structures.

Vested interests constitute a major difficulty in applying knowledge in the sociological field. For instance, public river valley development is fought vigorously by private electric utilities which are fearful of public electric power projects. Slum clearance and urban renewal in many communities have been retarded because of the opposition of owners of slum housing or the agents of rental property. The application of the social gospel is often retarded in churches by sincere church members who have little social concern for their fellow men or the environments in which they live. The use of school facilities for recreation is frequently not permitted because school board members hold to the narrow view that school facilities are for education only.

Another difficulty in sociological research and in applying sociological knowledge is what we may term "the one-cause fallacy," which is the fallacy that social problems have single, and often simple, causes. Juvenile delinquency may be explained on the single ground of poor inheritance, inadequate home situation, or bad companions. Most social problems are multiple in causation. For this reason remedial programs are often ineffective because they are of single-track character. Research designed to get at the causes of problems is often neither basic enough nor wide enough in scope to get at the roots of social problems. Because the public adheres to the one-cause fallacy, it is unwilling to support adequately sociological research on a broad enough scale or at adequate depth to get at causes. Neither is it willing to support adequate remedial programs to get rid of acute problems or to reduce them substantially.

## THE CONTRIBUTIONS OF SOCIOLOGY

There are many contributions which courses in sociology may make to the college student while he is in college and after he graduates.

1. Sociology helps us to understand ourselves. We can hardly know too much about ourselves. Sociology aids in helping us to understand why we behave as we do in social situations, and why we react to others as we do.

2. Sociology helps us to understand others. We have already spoken of our continued contacts and relationships with other people. Many college graduates will be in managerial positions when they complete their degrees; others will be salesmen. Others will be professional men in law, teaching, or medicine, where success may depend as much upon the quality of human relationships maintained as upon the technical knowledge acquired in professional training.

3. Sociology is of vocational value. Some students will become sociologists and use sociological knowledge in their vocation. Here the contribution is obvious and direct and needs no elaboration.

4. Sociology contributes to citizenship knowledge. After college, students are likely to occupy positions of importance in their communities. Some will take over leadership in various community movements. Others will head social or welfare agencies or serve on agency boards. In their citizen roles and in their leadership positions sociology will serve them well.

5. Sociology helps to clarify major social issues and to give guidance to their solution. First of all, sociology helps to show the origin of many of our social issues. For example, it is pretty clear to anyone who has studied population trends over a period of years that one of the emergent social issues of our time is the employment and care of the aged. Not only does a knowledge of sociology fill in a background to this issue, it also points to some solutions.

Sociologists assess the impact of scientific knowledge and technology. Many major social issues of our time have their origin in scientific and technological development and change. A good illustration of this is the control of the use of atomic weapons and other radiation dangers. Another example is the social control of fumes, smog, and dust which plague certain of our fast-growing cities. Soil conservation, resource development, and resource utilization are among the important social issues of our time calling for social decisions and policies.

The author has taught a number of young men who have studied later for the ministry. Almost invariably they attest to the richness of understanding that sociology has given them. A number of doctors from these same classes point to the value of sociology as their major before they entered their technical training in medical schools. They feel that sociology gave them a perspective of people's problems and an understanding of behavior which they never had an opportunity to acquire in medical school. Perhaps it is well to remember that one may be well trained in a specialized field and be illiterate in others.

## SUMMARY

In this chapter we have shown what the major social sciences are and something of the content of each and its relationship to sociology. We have defined sociology as the study of social systems, have shown the characteristics of such a system, and have pointed out the major social systems. We have taken the position that sociology is a science, and have given some reasons for this. We have also indicated five methods by which sociology is studied, namely, observation, the case-study method, statistical methods, the laboratory method, and critical inquiry. Following this we have attempted to show some contributions that sociology may make to the student. About 75 per cent of sociologists teach, whereas others work largely in government service, in the welfare services, and in business. We have, finally, taken the position that a college course does not have to be of direct vocational use in order to be valuable, and that sociology may add significance to one's life and work in many ways.

Sociology is about man, his culture, his roles and relationships. These subjects we shall explore in succeeding chapters.

### THINGS TO DO AND TO DISCUSS

1. Based on your critical inquiry, compare three concepts of sociology. Which one do you accept? Why?

2. From your friends collect a sampling of their concepts of sociology and what its study is worth. Compare these in class.

3. What are some reasons for the popularity of sociology in the United States?

4. What are the major social sciences and what relation has each to sociology? In your institution is history classed as a social science or one of the humanities? Why?

5. Why do we say that the social sciences are fused at the base?

6. Do you or do you not agree that sociology has all the requisites of a science?

7. What are the major social systems found in your community?

8. Select one of them and analyze them against the scheme developed on page 7.

9. What are the essential steps in scientific method?

10. What methods of investigation are particularly appropriate to the field of sociology?

11. What are the major difficulties in sociological research and its application?

12. Would you say that too little emphasis is placed upon the support of research in the social sciences?

13. What are some of the major contributions which sociology may make to the student while in college and after graduation?

FOR FURTHER STUDY

BAIN, READ. "Sociology as a Natural Science," *American Journal of Sociology,* 53:9-16, July, 1947. A critical treatment of the attempts to classify sociology as a natural science.

BERNARD, L. L., and BERNARD, JESSIE. *Origins of American Sociology.* New York: Thomas Y. Crowell Co., 1943. A good source book on the development of sociology in the United States.

CHASE, STUART. *The Proper Study of Mankind.* (2nd ed.) New York: Harper and Bros., 1956. A popular treatment of the application of research to a variety of human and social problems.

CLAUSEN, JOHN A. *Sociology in the Field of Mental Health.* New York: Russell Sage Foundation, 1956. How sociological research is being developed and used in the field of mental health.

DAVIS, KINGSLEY. *Human Society.* New York: The Macmillan Co., 1949. Contains a very good analysis of the elements of a social system.

GITTLER, JOSEPH B. *Review of Sociology: Analysis of A Decade.* New York: John Wiley and Sons, 1957. A synthesis of the status of sociology at mid-century.

HINKLE, ROSCOE C., JR., and HINKLE, GISELA J. *The Development of Modern Sociology.* New York: Random House, 1954. A brief account of the development of sociology, especially in the United States.

IGGERS, GEORGE G. "Further Remarks About Early Uses of the Term 'Social Science,'" *Journal of the History of Ideas,* 20:433-36, June-September, 1959. An excellent treatment of the early use of the term "social science."

LOOMIS, CHARLES P., and BEEGLE, J. ALLEN. *Rural Sociology: The Strategy of Change.* Englewood Cliffs, N. J.: Prentice-Hall, 1957.

MYRDAL, GUNNAR. *An American Dilemma.* New York: Harper and Bros., 1944. Appendix 2, Section 2, contains some enlightening remarks about the conflict between scientific methods and existing value systems.

NEET, ROBERT, and HETZLER, STANLEY A. *An Introduction to Electronic Data Processing.* Glencoe, Ill.: Free Press, 1959. A readable text on this important subject.

ODUM, HOWARD W. *American Sociology.* New York: Longmans, Green and Co., 1951. A good treatment of some of the major American sociologists and their contributions.

OHLIN, LLOYD E. *Sociology in the Field of Corrections.* New York: Russell Sage Foundation, 1956. The application of sociology in the field of corrections.

PARSONS, TALCOTT. *The Social System.* Glencoe, Ill.: Free Press, 1951. A leading treatment and analysis of the social system concept.

SCHELLENBERG, JAMES A. "Division of General Sociology," *American Sociological Review,* 22:660-63, December, 1957. Some of the major areas now appearing in courses in general sociology.

SIMMONS, LEO W., and WOLFF, HAROLD G. *Social Science in Medicine.* New York: Russell Sage Foundation, 1954. The application of the social sciences in the field of medicine.

*Sociology and Your Career.* Tallahassee: Florida State University, Department of Sociology, n. d. Career opportunities in sociology.

WARNER, WELLMAN. "The Roles of the Sociologist," *Bulletin of the American Sociological Society,* September, 1951. Some of the major tasks at which sociologists are employed.

WILLIAMS, ROBIN M., JR. *American Society* (2nd ed.) New York: Alfred A. Knopf, 1960. An excellent sociological analysis of American society.

ZETTERBERG, HANS L. *Sociology in the United States, A Trend Report.* Paris: UNESCO, 1956. Major trends in sociology in the United States.

| # THE DEVELOPMENT OF SOCIETY

To UNDERSTAND the significance of sociology as a field of study, the student of sociology must know the meaning of sociology, the relation of sociology to the other social sciences, some of the more important methods employed in sociological research, and some of the values of sociology. These topics were treated in Chapter 1.

A logical and comprehensive treatment of sociology cannot neglect the subject of how society developed. Such is the objective of Part I.

Chapter 2 presents the latest information on the development of man, his racial divisions, and the significance of these divisions.

Chapter 3 traces the growth and impact of culture.

Chapter 4 explains how culture varies, why it varies, and the significance of cultural variations, and Chapter 5 shows the nature of society and how societies developed.

# 2. EARLY MAN AND HIS RACIAL DIVISIONS

THE DEVELOPMENT of culture parallels the development of man in the prehistoric period. During the historic period, dating back some 6000 years, no great changes have occurred in man's biology even though revolutionary changes have been made in his culture. To understand culture development and the development of man's society, we must understand something of the development of man himself.

## THE QUEST FOR ORIGINS

Problems of time and origin have troubled man for centuries. He has long gazed into the heavens and wondered what was there. He has developed lore and religions to help explain his origins, and has created systems of magic and science to help regulate the forces of nature over which he has little control. Only since the development of modern astronomy have we been able to move close enough to the planets to tell much about them. Having seen the planets and sampled the outer space around them with man-made satellites, most of us still wonder about their movement in space. Man continues to ask what is there in outer space and how did it all happen? Being earthbound and used to definite distances, it is not easy for him to conceive of the infinite, or millions of miles in space. With modern machines in his culture for negotiating distance, and with modern instruments for measuring distance, man's time and space senses have been greatly extended.

Man is still concerned over problems of origin. The phenomena of life and death are unsatisfactorily explained to most men even though they are universal in nature. Man has long wondered how he originated and who his ancestors were. He has developed complicated theories about his own origin and the origin of his races. He has speculated upon the nature of death and life beyond the grave, and has developed theories and religions to explain these phenomena. These concerns and explanations are of significance to the sociologist because of the effect they have upon man's behavior in his social systems and also because of the way that they influence the structure and function of these systems.

### Back of man, the earth

Man's habitat is the earth. It is the stage upon which he is born, on which he acts, and on which he dies. He leaves behind upon the earth the cultural accumulation of his intelligence. We do not know that other planets are not inhabited. There has been almost as much speculation about the origin of the earth as there has been about the origin of man. The Brahmans of ancient India taught that the earth was eternal, and the Chaldean priests claimed that it emerged from chaos 2 million years ago. The Christian lay concept is based largely upon the acceptance of early Hebrew writings.

No one knows exactly the age of the earth. Zoroaster of ancient Persia said that the earth was 12,000 years old and that it would last another 3000 years. At that time a new prophet, Zor, would be born, the dead would come to life, and a state of incorruptible existence would begin.[1]

Competent authorities would not agree with Zoroaster. The earth may be 4 billion years old. The oldest rocks are 2 billion years of age. Rocks 1 hundred million years old are common, whereas "young rocks" have an age of 10 million years.[2] As one geologic timetable shows (Table 1), simple forms of life appeared millions of years before higher forms developed. Trilobites so common in sedimentary deposits go back a half billion years, whereas dinosaurs are less than 200 million years of

age. At the most man is less than 1 million years old in the biological scheme of things.

### How the scientist computes time

Back of historical time lies geological, anthropological, and archeological time. The scientist, in reckoning the time element in man's biological and cultural development, makes use of the following methods:

1. *Geologic time scales.* Geologic time scales (Table 1), based largely upon the kinds of fossils found in sedimentary rocks, form a basis for computing time; this field is known as geochronology. For instance, should the bones of a human being be found along with the

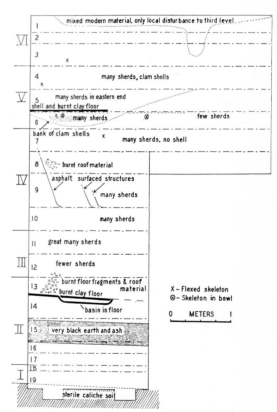

*Profile of Pavon Site Excavation, Mexico, as seen from the north*

---

[1] *See* Chester R. Longwell and Richard Foster Flint, *Introduction to Physical Geology* (New York: John Wiley and Sons, 1955), Chapter 4, "Geologic Time." *See also* W. K. C. Guthrie, *In the Beginning: Some Greek Views on the Origin of Life and the Early State of Man* (Ithaca, N. Y.: Cornell University Press, 1957).

[2] Longwell and Flint, *loc. cit.*

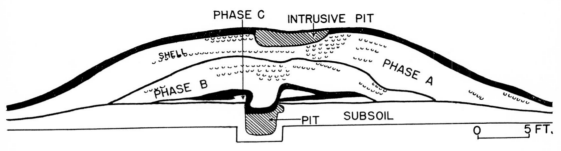

*The stratigraphic method of studying the culture strata of a burial mound is shown here in both photograph and cross-section drawing.*

SOURCE: Thomas M. N. Lewis and Madeline Kneberg, *Hiwassee Island* (Knoxville, Tenn.: University of Tennessee Press, 1946), Plate 1, Figure 1, and Plate 29, Figure 2. Reproduced by permission of the publisher.

bones of the earliest known horse in a sedimentary rock, one would have to say that the human remains were possibly 70 million years old. Actually, according to the geologic column used by us, man appeared not over a million years ago. As Table 1 shows, the dates established by geologic columns are relative and not absolute.

2. *Stratigraphy*. Prehistoric peoples had a strong tendency to build their houses upon sites previously occupied. Often the mound builders would bury their dead upon the mound where previous occupants had buried their dead. Mound building was common among American Indians. Thus several cultures would be evident in the stratification of the same mound, with the bottom strata being the oldest.

The anthropologist or archaeologist, who systematically studies prehistoric cultures, removes the material from a stratified mound, layer by layer, sometimes doing a cross section of the mound to show different culture layers. In many instances sea shells or river shells are found in these mounds. Relative chronology is established by the size of the mounds, the number of layers, and amount of shell food consumed, as measured by the amount of shells in relation to the number of burials found in and near the mounds. Charcoal or pieces of

*Table 1*

### STANDARD GEOLOGIC COLUMN AND SCALE OF TIME

(Ages increase from top downward, as in a sequence of sedimentary rocks)

| System and Period | Series and Epoch | Distinctive Records of Life | Dates in Years * |
|---|---|---|---|
| | | *Cenozoic Era* | |
| | Pleistocene | Appearance and development of man | 1,000,000 |
| | Pliocene | Dominance of elephants, horses, large carnivores | 12,000,000 |
| Cenozoic | Miocene | Development of whales, bats, monkeys | (*17,000,000*) 25,000,000 |
| | Oligocene | | 35,000,000 |
| | Eocene | Development of primitive mammals | (*58,000,000*) 60,000,000 |
| | Paleocene | Earliest horses | 70,000,000 |
| | | *Mesozoic Era* | |
| Cretaceous | | Development of flowering plants | 130,000,000 |
| | | Extinction of dinosaurs | |
| Jurassic | | Climax of dinosaurs | |
| | | First birds | 165,000,000 |
| Triassic | | First dinosaurs | |
| | | First primitive mammals | 200,000,000 |
| | | *Paleozoic Era* | |
| Permian | | Conifers abundant | (*230,000,000*) |
| | | Reptiles developed | 235,000,000 |
| Pennsylvanian | | First reptiles | |
| | | Great coal forests | 260,000,000 |
| | | Abundant insects | |
| Mississippian | | Echinoderms abundant | 285,000,000 |
| Devonian | | First amphibians | |
| | | Earliest forests | 325,000,000 |
| Silurian | | First land plants and animals | 350,000,000 |
| Ordovician | | Earliest primitive fishes | 410,000,000 |
| Cambrian | | Large invertebrate faunas | (*440,000,000*) |
| | | Trilobites predominant | 500,000,000 |
| | | *Precambrian Time* | |
| | | Earliest known records of simple organisms | (*620,000,000*) (*1,420,000,000*) (*1,800,000,000*) (*2,200,000,000*) |
| | | (No known base) | |

* Plain figures give estimated dates at start of corresponding time units; italicized figures in parentheses are the most reliable determinations from radioactive minerals found in rocks known to belong in the time division indicated.

wood found in such mounds may be tested by radioactive carbon methods to give dates with less error than formerly when stratigraphic methods were used.[3] More about this later.

3. *Fossil pollen.* In northern Europe, where there are many peat bogs, much attention has been given to the study of fossil pollen found in peat bogs in association with archaeological and anthropological materials. The sources of the pollen are known—much of it came from trees—and the approximate dates of the plants that bore the pollen are also known. The pollen grains, therefore, may be of interest to either the paleobotanist or to the anthropologist or archaeologist, and serve a function in the relative dating of archaeological remains. By archaeological remains we mean such items as stone tools and weapons, pottery, and parts of structures. By anthropological remains we mean skeletal remains or other human remains. Often, of course, the two kinds of items are found together.

4. *Dendrochronology.* Dendrochronology is the study of the annual ring growth of trees, and has been of much use in the dating of cultures. One usually works backwards, using trees of known date and comparing the ring growth with that of trees found in structures. Certain sites in the Southwest have been dated as early as A.D. 1, according to Shapiro.[4] De Witt Clinton, as early as 1811, used the growth of tree rings to date certain earthworks at Canandaigua, New York.

5. *Radiocarbon dating.* Dr. W. F. Libby and his colleagues are responsible for a method of dating archaeological and anthropological remains known as radiocarbon dating. There are now some twenty-five laboratories where specimens may be sent for dating, half of which are in Europe. Radiocarbon dating is effective for dates up to about 70,000 years.

The theory of radiocarbon dating is described by Longwell and Flint:

Tissues of living organisms incorporate carbon, and durable tissues such as wood retain measurable quantities of radiocarbon long after death of the organism, though the activity declines at a known rate. By concentrating carbon from a piece of ancient wood and measuring the *specific* activity, we can determine closely the length of time since the wood grew.

Accuracy of the method has been checked against samples of known date, such as corn and wooden beams from ancient tombs and pieces from the heart of a large redwood tree. One of the most significant investigations by the technique used wood from trees pushed over by the ice sheet the last time it invaded northeastern Wisconsin. The age determined for this wood dated the glacial invasion as only 11,000 to 12,000 years ago.[5]

Some examples of radiocarbon dating of man's cultural remains will show its usefulness. The interested student may want to pursue the subject in more detail.[6]

Indian sandals made of bark found in a cave in Oregon were woven 9,000 years ago according to the dating. Charcoal taken from an ancient hearth in New York State indicates that it was left 4,930 ± 260 years ago. A boat carried in a funeral procession following the death of a pharaoh and then sealed in his tomb was dated at 1850 B.C. Marine-life shells found in an Indian mound in Kentucky were estimated to be 5,149 ± 300 years old. A burned bison bone from Lubbock, Texas, where the Folsom flint points of early Folsom Man have been found, is dated at 9,883 ± 350 years. Ap-

[3] For a good discussion of stratigraphy and pollen dating, *see* Harry L. Shapiro, *Man, Culture, and Society* (New York: Oxford University Press, 1956), Chapter II, "The Study of Early Cultures." *See also* F. E. Zeuner, *Dating the Past* (4th ed.; New York: Longmans, Green and Co., 1958).

[4] Shapiro, *op. cit.,* p. 42.

[5] Chester R. Longwell and Richard Foster Flint, *op. cit.,* p. 53.

[6] The literature on the subject is extensive; *see* Willard F. Libby, *Radiocarbon Dating* (Chicago: University of Chicago Press, 1951).

Source: Chester R. Longwell and Richard Foster Flint, *Introduction to Physical Geology* (New York: John Wiley and Sons, 1955), p. 55.

parently the ancient bison, from which the bone came, was one of the favorite sources of food of Folsom Man. Charcoal-bearing dirt from the charcoal beds of the Cochise Indian culture in Arizona, dated by radiocarbon methods, is estimated at $7,756 \pm 370$ years.[7] Charcoal obtained from a campfire site of an early American inhabitant at Tule Springs, Nevada, is dated at 23,000 years. Charcoal remains from Sandia Cave, New Mexico, are dated at 26,000 years, evidently from fire used by Neanderthal Man.[8] Deep in Iraq's Zagros Mountains, in a cave used for hundreds of years by Kurdish goat herders, was found the skull of a Neanderthal Man, an old Stone Age cousin of modern man. Radiocarbon dating revealed the skull to be 45,000 years old.

Since the practicality of radiocarbon dating is at present limited to dates under 70,000 years, it will be of more significance to archaeology and to recent anthropology than to the anthropology of earlier dates. The point is that it is a very useful and exact method of dating archaeological and anthropological remains, especially in America, where they may not extend back more than 35,000 years.

6. *The artifacts of excavation.* Artifacts are the tools, weapons, and other culture items which have been left by past generations. Many such items are found in burial mounds or excavations of the habitation sites of early man where they were placed as possessions or might be useful in the future life.

Archaeologists are able to arrange these materials in sequential fashion and to assign approximate dates to them. We will say more about this in the next chapter. The archaeologist knows that rough stone artifacts came earlier than polished stone artifacts. He knows, also, that the use of metal took precedence over polished stone implements to set up an entirely new series of artifacts. Artifacts may be found in conjunction with human or animal skeletal remains and also with charcoal from fires. In such finds several methods may be used in dating the materials, including radiocarbon dating. The ability to date artifacts approximately by the anthropologists, the archaeologists, or the geologists is of great importance to the sociologist in studying the development and diffusion of culture and social systems.

## MAN DISCOVERS EARLY MAN

### The first man

The similarity of man's skeleton to extinct apes or even to the skeleton of higher apes now living has caused much difficulty in separating man from the apes. As an illustration, in South China there lived an extinct apelike creature called by some *Giantopithecus,* or giant ape, and by others *Giantanthropus,* or giant man. This creature had great height—up to 12 feet —and lived in caves or rock shelters where these were available. The discovery of an

ancient jawbone, reported in 1957, led Dr. Pei Wen-chung, a Chinese anthropologist, to classify this creature, which lived between 400,000 and 600,000 years ago, as definitely an ape.[9] The presence of charcoal in the caves has caused other anthropolgists to take an equally strong view that this early creature belonged to the human race. They reason that apes would not have had the intelligence to use fire.[10]

Capable anthropologists recognize that early man had apelike characteristics, but they usually take the position that man did not

[7] The examples are all taken from *ibid.*, pp. 66-96. *See also* H. R. Crane and James B. Griffin, "University of Michigan Radio-carbon Dates III," *Science,* 128:1117-22, November 7, 1958.

[8] Marjorie Van De Water, "Extinct Uncle Gave Us Fire," *Science News Letter,* 67:122-23, February 19, 1955.

[9] "Find Man-Like Ape," *Science News Letter,* October 5, 1957, p. 213.

[10] *See* the discussion in this text on Peking Man on page 26, in which we quote from Shapiro, *op. cit.*

develop from the ape stem but from a different stem, and that there has been development in both stems. The point is that man is here. He is nature's noblest creature. How he got here we may sometime know or we may never know. This does not mean that the sociologist should lose interest in his origin.

Perhaps 1 or 2 million years ago, in what we call the Pleistocene period, the curtain arose on early man (see the geologic timetable earlier in the chapter).

It was in Java, on the Solo River, in 1891 and 1892, that a young Dutch scientist-surgeon, Eugene Dubois, employed in the Netherlands Colonial Service, discovered a skull cap, a femur bone, and teeth of an early human being who may have lived from 750,000 to a million years ago.[11]

[11] Charles R. Knight, *Prehistoric Man* (New York: Appleton-Century-Crofts, 1949).

Dubois called his discovery *Pithecanthropus erectus,* which means "erect ape man." More commonly, this ancient man is referred to as Java Man. The stature of *Pithecanthropus* was erect. His skull was thick and his brain case somewhat intermediary in size between that of modern man and that of the higher apes. The skull was thicker than modern man's and the chin was receded, an anthropoid characteristic. These characteristics are indicated by the accompanying photograph of the reproduction of this ancient "uncle" of modern man.

Dubois' discovery has been criticized because of its meager evidence. In 1937 and 1938 another Dutch anthropologist, Von Koenigswold, and his colleagues, discovered several parts of skull cases, some other bones, and a well-preserved jaw in the same area in Java where Dubois had worked. These finds authenticated Dubois' discovery, so *Pithecanthropus* is now

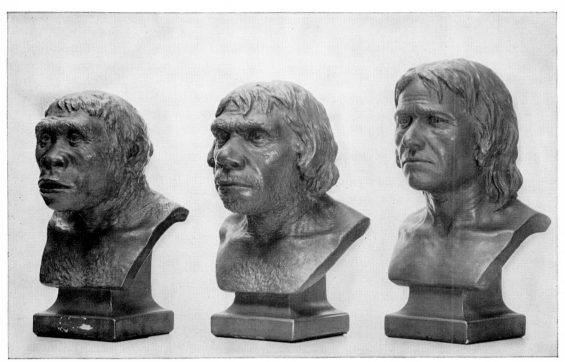

*Courtesy of the American Museum of Natural History*

PITHECANTHROPUS ERECTUS        NEANDERTHAL MAN        CRO-MAGNON MAN

*Restorations of Early Man*

accorded a place in the chronology of early man.

## Peking Man

At Choukoutien, near Peiping in South China, have been found fragments of an early man not unlike those of *Pithecanthropus*. From 1903 until World War II, remains representing some 40 individuals were unearthed. The name given this early man is *Sinanthropus,* and he may have lived from 600,000 to 400,000 years ago. His brain was larger than that of Java Man, indicating somewhat greater development. His forehead was more developed. He stood erect, and he had human-like teeth. In speaking of his hominoid status, Shapiro says:

If any further evidence of Sinathropus's claim to a hominoid status were required, their way of life would be ample. These people lived in caves, the floors of which they littered with the skeletal debris of animals they hunted and consumed. They used fire and employed stone tools of a primitive kind. Any additional attributes of culture can only be inferred, but it seems likely that people as advanced as this in technology must have also had a language. But of its nature we can only guess.[12]

12 Shapiro, *op. cit.,* p. 12.

*Courtesy of the American Museum of Natural History*

*Jawbone of Heidelberg Man*

In Africa skulls almost as old as those of Peking Man have been found. These finds point to the possibility that man may have originated in Asia or Africa.

## Heidelberg Man

We now go to Europe for the next record of early man. This is Heidelberg Man, who is estimated to have lived 450,000 years ago in the first interglacial period in Europe.

The reproduction of Heidelberg Man (see the accompanying photograph) is based on the finding of a massive but definitely human jaw in an 80-foot sand and gravel pit near Heidelberg, Germany, in 1907. Dating was made from fossil remains found in the pit.

Heidelberg Man had a prominent jaw. He was massive and heavily built and had a protruding face. The teeth were rather small but definitely humanlike. Had a skull case been found, we would know much more about Heidelberg Man than we do.

Mention should be made of a well-documented human fossil skull found at Swanscombe, England, in the Thames Valley. The human being who possessed this skull lived during the Second Interglacial period 250,000 years ago. Except for its extreme thickness, the skull was not unlike that of Neanderthal Man. From the succeeding interglacial period another skull, known as the Fontechevade skull, was found in France. It may be dated at about 125,000 years ago.

## Neanderthal Man

During the fourth and last glacial period, as Europe warmed, it is assumed that Neanderthal Man arrived in Europe. Where he arrived from we are not sure, because a large number of skeletons have been found in Europe, North Africa, and parts of Asia.

Shapiro discusses the Neanderthal type (see photograph, p. 25):

The so-called "classic" Neanderthal type has a heavily constructed skull, with a large projecting horizontal ridge of bone between the eye sockets and the forehead, another bony ridge stretching horizontally across the occiput, a massive but not especially prognathic face, a mandible still lacking a chin, a cranial vault fully as large as in modern man but of a form still reminiscent of the more primitive *Pithecanthropus* and *Sinanthropus*.[13]

Knight describes Neanderthal Man as a short, stocky individual, some five feet, four inches in height, with a big head, a short neck, a clumsy gait, big hands and feet, a long torso, and shorter than modern man below the knee.[14]

Even today, Europe's climate is rigorous. Neanderthal Man had to make an adjustment to a much colder climate as the last interglacial period began. For protection he relied upon caves and rock shelters. In these protective locations he built fires to keep him warm, to cook his meat, and to repel wild animals. He apparently wore clothing made from the hides which he skinned and fleshed. To kill game and to protect himself against enemies, he used rough, heavy flint tools and hand axes. Smaller tools were used for boring, skinning, and scraping.

The ultimate fate of Neanderthal Man is not known. More intelligent Cro-Magnon Man, with superior weapons, especially the lance and spear, may have killed him off. Perhaps driven from his caves by Cro-Magnon Man, he may have succumbed to exposure and death from wild beasts. Vestiges of his type may have amalgamated with the Cro-Magnon people. More than one type of Neanderthal Man has been found; for instance, in Israel a hybrid type existed.

Apparently Neanderthal Man dominated most of the Old World between 75,000 B.C. and 40,000 B.C. Recent finds of Neanderthal remains in Iraq suggest that the birthplace of this prehistoric human, which is not now known, may have been in western Asia.[15]

13 Shapiro, *op. cit.*, p. 14.
14 Knight, *op. cit.*, p. 154.
15 "The Historic Skull of Shanidar Cave," *Life,* November 4, 1957.

*Courtesy of the American Museum of Natural History*

*Engraving from the Wall of the Galerie des Fresques, Font-de-Gaume, France*

### Cro-Magnon Man

We arrive now at a discussion of ancient Cro-Magnon Man, who lived recently enough and in such a way that we know much about him. Like Neanderthal Man, Cro-Magnon Man was a cave and rock-shelter dweller. He was a great artist, and on the walls of widely scattered caves in Europe, especially France, he left many murals and drawings (see the accompanying photograph) to tell us much about his life. Cro-Magnon Man is associated with the Upper Paleolithic period, which may extend back to about 25,000 B.C. and up to about 8,000 B.C.

Cro-Magnon Man had improved stone tools and weapons made from flint, bone, and horn. These materials were used for spear points, lance points, and borers and scrapers. He used these weapons to hunt the woolly mammoth and rhinoceros, the reindeer, the cave bear, and the wild horse. He trapped game. Various types of heavy rock weapons were used to crack the large bones of the kill for bone marrow, an apparent delicacy. Beautiful carvings and ornaments were made from ivory and the antlers of animals. Cro-Magnon Man left behind many well-defined camp and hearth sites. In Europe, however, he did not reach a

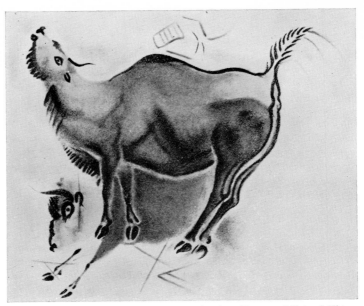

*Courtesy of the American Museum of Natural History*

*Roaring and Galloping Bison from Cave Drawings, Altamira, Spain*

stage in advancement where he engaged in weaving and potterymaking. These cultural pursuits had to wait for a later people. There is evidence that Cro-Magnon Man may have had some form of religion. He buried his dead.

The earliest American inhabitants do not go back to Cro-Magnon Man. We believe that they came from Asia. As the glaciers receded, they migrated to ice-free areas. The earliest skeletal finds have been those of Folsom Man discovered at Folsom, New Mexico. He may have lived as much as 15,000 to 17,000 years ago, although some authorities date him around 13,000 years ago.

### . . . and he shall have dominion

The Bible says that man shall have dominion over the beasts of the field and the fowls of the air. Certainly to date man has demonstrated his superiority. Wherein lies this dominance?

We must recognize in setting forth these traits that many of them are relative and are of degree rather than of kind. We must also recognize that the significance of some of these traits is tied in with mass culture and can hardly be divorced from this culture. Speech is a good example in that the quality and tone of speech is shaped by the culture. Many skills which man uses are the result of training and not just a result of his superior physical equipment.

1. *The large well-developed brain.* Man's mental capacity sets him apart from the animals. His brain in relation to his size is much larger than that of most animals; it is more developed than the primates'. The large well-developed brain, the basis for man's intelligence, not only gives him the ability to adjust to relatively new or novel situations, but combined with his experience in using it, enables him to develop insights or to analyze situations quickly.

2. *Erect stature and use of the hand.* Man's erect stature frees the front limbs for use with weapons and tools and for carrying items. It

HARVESTING WITH A FLINT SICKLE

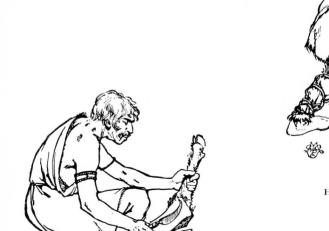

CUTTING MEAT WITH AN IRON
KNIFE

SMELTING IRON

SHAVING WITH
A BRONZE RAZOR

*Courtesy of the American Museum of Natural History*

*While primates possess a hand with an opposable thumb, man's intelligence enables him to use his hands to make tools and implements and to fashion many aspects of a complex culture.*

has been one of the factors in developing the generalized use of the hand and in developing the specialized use of the foot for standing and locomotion.

The opposable thumb, highly developed in man, and the generalized use of the hand, plus man's binocular vision and intelligence, serve as a fundamental base for his culture-building ability. Such ability solidly separates man from the animals. Of course, a chimpanzee may use a stick for punching or striking, but he does not sharpen a steel and fasten it to the end of the stick. He does not make a bow to propel the stick. The chimpanzee may do a variety of finger paintings or clay models, but he does not do a mural on canvas or strike a sculpture out of marble.

There are other physical and physiological traits which are distinctive to man which we will not discuss. We are concerned primarily with those traits which give man a culture-building power and dominance over other animals.

3. *Speech*. Without a doubt man's superior mental capacity is one of the reasons why he has developed speech. Memory is necessary for the development of speech and language. Apes apparently have vocal equipment which would enable them to speak if they had sufficient mental capacity.

Man's culture-building power is greatly enhanced by speech, which enables him to tell wherein he has succeeded or failed, and to transmit culture from one person to another and from one generation to another with speed and accuracy. Of course, speech is only one form of communication, sounds and gestures being others.

4. *Versatile voice box*. The voice box of man is versatile, as we have hinted above. It changes with maturity and is responsive to training in such a way that it develops great variation in variety of sounds, volume, and tonal pitch. Having such versatility, the voice is a great asset in culture building and in interaction between persons and groups.

5. *Bifocal vision*. Bifocal, or binocular, vision, which is the ability to focus simultaneously upon an object at the same time with both eyes, is highly developed in man. Such visual development, plus his intelligence, makes him visually oriented. He is able to gain impressions through sight, and to form symbols and images. Such visual acuity serves man well in his powers to communicate and to develop and transmit a culture, as well as to transform meanings into objects.

As they are used by man in action, there is continued reciprocal reaction among the foregoing five traits. For example, some anthropologists think that hand skill developed the brain rather than the other way around. Man's erect stature raised the vision to include far horizons and starry skies, with interesting reciprocal effects upon the mind, the speech, the skillful hand, and behavior. Thus it is, in these reciprocal relationships, that cause becomes effect and effect cause.

## MAN DIVIDES MANKIND INTO RACES

Without a doubt clans, tribes, families, and place groupings have long recognized the fact that they are different from other groupings. Behavior was often related to these differences. Skeletal remains, which extend our knowledge back into prehistory, contain evidence of violence. Whether people fought because they were physically different, or because other people invaded their occupied territory, we do not always know. There is evidence that man, even in prehistory, divided himself into recognizable categories. As cultural differences between people developed—religious and property differences for example—such differentiation tended to separate people into categories and classes.

*Bases for racial classification*

Krogman defines race as follows:

A race is a subgroup of people, possessing a definite combination of physical characters, of genetic origin; this combination serves, in varying degree, to distinguish the sub-group from other sub-groups of mankind and the combination is transmitted in descent, providing all conditions which originally gave rise to the definite combination remain relatively unaltered; as a rule the sub-group inhabits, or did inhabit, a more or less restricted geographical region.[16]

Such a concept of race is a physical one, in which the traits are transmitted from parent to offspring. Only physical traits are reliable ones to be used in classifying races, and even then the task is difficult enough. While there are many variations within races, most anthropologists agree on three—the Caucasoid, or white; the Mongoloid, or yellow; and the Negroid, or black. Difficulties which have arisen in classifying the native peoples of Australia have caused some authorities to recognize a fourth race, Australoid.[17] We shall confine our attention to the first three.

The physical characteristics used in the classification are shown in the accompanying table. Principal ones are skin color, head form, hair color and texture, eye color and eye fold, and nasal index.

We see, from the list of racial characteristics (Table 2), outstanding observable features of the three races. Of course, each race has mixed with the others to the point where there are many variations in types within races. There are no pure races, only segments of races with widely varying differences. Also, many physical characteristics are common to all races. This holds true for the organs of the body, the circulatory system, muscles, and many details of skeleton structure.

16 W. M. Krogman, "What We Do Not Know about Race," *Scientific Monthly*, **57**:97-104, 1943.

17 W. W. Howells, *Mankind So Far* (New York: Doubleday and Co., 1944).

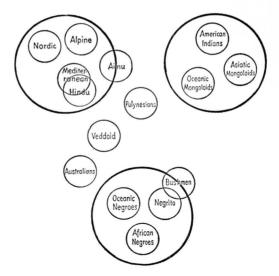

*The Major Races and Subraces*

SOURCE: A. L. Kroeber, *Anthropology* (New York: Harcourt, Brace and Co., Inc., 1948), p. 140. Reproduced by permission of the publisher.

*The problem of race quality*

The problem of race quality needs some discussion at this point. As we shall see in later chapters, racial lines and marked cultural differences between peoples constitute a basis for differentiation, class stratification, and, sometimes, segregation. It is not so much the racial differences per se that are important as it is the cultural interpretations that are placed upon them and the social situations that develop around them. Obviously, each race believes itself superior. This belief is the result of social conditioning and ethnocentric thinking rather than the result of objective comparison and the application of empirical knowledge about race quality.

Various approaches have been taken to try to prove the superiority or inferiority of one race over another, or to vest the qualities of one race against those of another race. These are indicated below.

1. *The culture contributions approach.* Some anthropologists and writers have tried

*Table 2*

PHYSICAL CHARACTERISTICS OF THE THREE STOCKS OF MANKIND

| Trait | White | Yellow | Black |
|-------|-------|--------|-------|
| Skin color | Pale reddish white to olive-brown | Saffron to yellow-brown; some reddish-brown | Brown to brown-black; some yellow-brown |
| Stature | Medium to tall | Medium tall to medium short | Tall to very short |
| Head form | Long to broad and short; medium high to very high | Predominantly broad; height medium | Predominantly long; height low to medium |
| Face | Narrow to medium broad; tends to high; no prognathism | Medium broad to very broad; malars "high" and flat; tends to medium high | Medium broad to narrow; tends to medium high; strong prognathism |
| Hair | Head hair: color light blond to dark brown; texture fine to medium; form straight to wavy; body hair moderate to profuse | Head hair: color brown to brown-black; texture coarse; form straight; body hair sparse | Head hair: color brown-black; texture, coarse; form light curl to wooly or frizzly; body hair slight |
| Eye | Color light blue to dark brown; lateral; eye-fold occasional | Color brown to dark brown; medial epicanthic fold very common | Color brown to brown-black; vertical eye-fold common |
| Nose | Bridge usually high; form narrow to medium broad | Bridge usually low to medium; form medium broad | Bridge usually low; form medium broad to very broad |
| Body build | Linear to lateral; slender to rugged | Tends to be lateral; some linearity evident | Tends to be lateral and muscular, but some linearity evident |

Source: Wilton Marion Krogman, "The Concept of Race," in *The Science of Man in the World Crisis,* ed. Ralph Linton (New York: Columbia University Press, 1945), p. 50.

to show that one race has made more contributions to the culture of the human race than any other. For instance, there grew up in the latter part of the nineteenth century the theory of Nordic superiority, namely, that the greatest contributions to civilization had been made by the fair-skinned and blond-haired peoples of northern Europe, especially the Scandinavians and the northern Germans. This is an example of *racism,* which is the theory that one race is by nature superior to all other races.

Prior to World War II Hitler whipped to white heat his theory of Aryan superiority. Hitler proclaimed that the Aryan race, which was no race at all but at its best a segment of the white race, had brought to the main streams of civilization the greatest contributions. So superior were the Aryans, in fact, that other races should move over and make room for "the chosen people." In the Hitler Youth Organization a generation of German youth who believed in this type of thinking was brought up. Hitler and his leaders tried progressively to decimate the Jews of Germany because, as he said, they had polluted the superiority of the German people with their "inferior" qualities.

The cultural approach to proving race superiority is beset with many difficulties. By what standards is the superiority of one culture to be measured against another? At what time did the culture develop and under what circumstances? The Chinese, for instance, were living in a stage of advanced culture at a time that Europeans were largely uncivilized. What advantages did one spot on the world's surface afford for cultural development as compared to other localities? These questions make it impossible to isolate other factors that enter into the development of a culture and to prove that a given culture develops to high state because of the innate superiority of its people, while another does not because its people are innately inferior. Let us suppose, for instance, that the Negroes had originally inhabited the United States, had brought in the whites as slaves, and had kept them in enslavement until the Emancipation. The chances are that the whites would not today be as advanced as they are and the Negroes would be more advanced.

2. *The physical characteristics approach.* Another approach to the attempt to determine superior and inferior traits in races is through the cataloguing of racial characteristics of contrasting races. For instance, whites are often compared with Negroes. The long arms and the rounded forehead of the Negro are often called "anthropoidal," a mark of "inferiority." Actually the Negro's lack of body hair and dark skin are nonanthropoidal. Incidentally, two of the beauty traits admired today in Hollywood are full lips and a well-tanned skin. Pigmentation of skin may be explained by natural forces and selective factors. There is a fair chance that the ancestors of present races were pretty uniformly yellow or brown.[18] The reaction to skin color is strongly a cultural response. In the eyes of the Indians "the pale face" was inferior. The missionary, David Livingstone, testified to the fact that, after he had lived with the blacks in Africa, a white skin looked to him unhealthy. In the eyes of a white person who associates white with purity and black with impurity, a black or dark brown skin may be a mark of inferiority. While the comparison of physical characteristics is interesting, it yields few clues to so-called racial inferiority or superiority.

3. *The intelligence test approach.* With the development of intelligence tests sociologists and psychologists were sure they had an adequate tool to test the ability of races and to make adequate comparisons. Pretty soon it became clear that intelligence tests measured not just innate capacity but also learning. A superior person brought up in a superior culture with many opportunities for learning may rate superior in I.Q. tests in comparison with a person brought up in a less well-developed culture. Another problem has been to get test results from an adequate cross section of the population. Tests administered to draftees in World War I furnished some opportunity for adult comparisons, as did those administered in World War II. The general use of intelligence testing in school systems also offered a wide range of studies for comparison. What did the studies show?

In World War I the I.Q. test scores made on army alpha tests by whites from the southern states were little different from the scores made by Negroes from northern states. Northern whites made scores superior to southern whites, and southern whites had higher median scores than southern Negroes. State by state medians were lower for Negroes than whites. Selection through migration may have been one reason Negroes of the North made higher grades than southern Negroes, an opinion doubted by some investigators, but the greater

[18] Franz Boas (ed.), *General Anthropology* (New York: D. C. Heath and Co., 1938), pp. 95-123.

opportunity for schooling probably accounts for much of the difference in test scores. It must also be pointed out that most army tests were administered by whites, as is true of most other test programs. We cannot assume that the rapport established with Negroes would be the same had the tests been administered by Negroes.

Test scores with school children in biracial test comparisons show so much overlap in results that conclusions with respect to racial superiority-inferiority are difficult to establish. In a well-planned study of 8,400 Negro school children in Chicago, 512 were classed as exceptionally bright; 103 had Stanford Binet I.Q. scores of 120 or higher, and one girl tested 200. These superior children showed the traits characteristic of superior white children.[19]

Klineberg has summarized many tests of race and nationality comparisons as measured by I.Q. tests. Using a score of 100 as the "American" norm in these tests, American Negroes had median scores of 86 in all the studies. However, in Los Angeles they scored above the norm, having a median I.Q. of 105. Among Americans of foreign background, the Italians scored 85, the Portuguese, 84, the Mexicans, 83.4, while American Indians scored 80.5. People with Scotch, German, Jewish, Chinese, and Japanese family backgrounds scored near the all-over American norm of 100.[20]

These studies indicate something of the interplay between man's biology and his culture, and the fact that intelligence tests measure elements of both. Many of the studies attest strongly to the fact that learning aptitudes of persons of different races are similar when educational inequalities have been eliminated. The ability to adjust to relatively new and novel situations is present in all races.[21] Years ago, Boas remarked:

Careful tests reveal a marked dependence of mental reactions upon conditions of life and that all racial differences which have been established thus far are so much subject to outer circumstances that no proof can be given of innate racial differences.[22]

With regard to the use of mental tests in searching for the position of the races in the hierarchy of mental abilities, Klineberg concludes:

This method, like the others previously discussed, is open to so much criticism that in this case also the conclusion must be that racial differences in psychology have not been—and perhaps cannot be—demonstrated.[23]

Klineberg goes ahead to relate that there are significant psychological differences between ethnic groups but that these are the product of historical, cultural, and environmental factors rather than genetic factors.

A survey made by *Fortune* in 1939 showed that 60 to 77 per cent of people believed Negroes inferior to whites. From 28.7 to 54.8 per cent of the people interviewed attributed this inferiority to innate factors. Whatever the facts, the belief in racial inferiority and superiority still exists. The problem of desegregation in the South has whipped the issue of race differences to high heat, as we shall see in a succeeding chapter. This gap between belief and science is well described by Myrdal. He says:

Hardly anywhere else or on any other issue is there—in spite of intensive and laudable efforts to popularize the new results of research—such a wide gap between scientific thought and popular belief.[24]

[19] P. A. Witty and M. D. Jenkins, "The Educational Achievement of Gifted Negro Children," *Journal of Educational Psychology,* **25**:585-97, 1936.

[20] Otto Klineberg, "Racial Psychology," in *The Science of Man in the World Crisis,* ed. Ralph Linton (New York: Columbia University Press, 1945), pp. 63-77.

[21] L. C. Dunn and Thomas Dobzhansky, *Heredity, Race and Society* (Rev. ed.; New York: American Library of World Literature, 1952).

[22] Franz Boas, "Race," *Encyclopaedia of the Social Sciences* (New York: The Macmillan Co., 1934), XIII, 34.

[23] Klineberg, *op. cit.,* p. 77.

[24] Gunnar Myrdal, *The American Dilemma* (New York: Harper and Bros., 1944), p. 93.

## *The cleavages are more sociocultural than biological*

The most important thing about racial differences is the fact that they serve as the basis for social cleavages. There are significant physical and physiological differences between races. Skin color is one of the least significant differences physiologically, though socially it is grimly important. Every race believes itself superior and builds up in its people a cluster of ethnocentric racial beliefs which are expressed in their attitudes toward other races. Another fact is that there are no pure races, only representatives of the races that run true to type. We shall say that, when the evidence is all in, the cleavages between races are more social than biological. On the other hand, one keen student of the subject of racial differences says that we have not, and may never have, evidence to prove the equality or inequality of races.

### THINGS TO DO AND TO DISCUSS

1. Why have the problems of origin troubled man? In what ways has he sought to explain his origins? Why is the problem socially significant?
2. What are the most reliable ways developed by scientists to compute time? What methods are used in your institution? Have one or more of these explained and illustrated in class.
3. In what geologic era did the development of man probably take place? Characterize this era.
4. Develop a dramatic sketch depicting the discovery of the remains of *Pithecanthropus erectus.*
5. Prepare a brief research report on Folsom Man. If possible obtain for exhibit one or more Folsom points.
6. Characterize the culture of Cro-magnon Man.
7. What characteristics give man dominance or superiority over other creatures?
8. What indices are used in making racial differentiations?
9. In the attempt to measure the superiority of one race over another what methods are used? To what conclusions do you come relative to the outcome of such measurement?
10. To what conclusions does psychological testing lead in the comparisons of capacities of races? Gather evidence from your community or the press to show how thought and action about races do not often correspond to the facts.
11. Why are the cleavages between races more sociocultural than biological?
12. Internationally, why are racial cleavages important?

### FOR FURTHER STUDY

BARRON, MILTON (ed) . *American Minorities.* New York: Alfred A. Knopf, 1957. Standard text material on racial and other minorities.

BEALS, RALPH L., and HOIJER, HARRY. *An Introduction to Anthropology.* New York: The Macmillan Co., 1953. Good basic source material on races.

CLELLAND, H. F. *Our Primitive Ancestors.* New York: Coward-McCann, 1928. A readable, semipopular account of contemporary man's ancestors.

DAVIS, KINGSLEY. *Human Society*. New York: The Macmillan Co., 1949. Some good comparisons between human and animal societies.

HEIZER, ROBERT F. *The Archaeologist at Work*. New York: Harper and Bros., 1959. An authoritative statement on how the anthropologist goes about his work.

HONIGMANN, JOHN J. *Culture and Personality*. New York: Harper and Bros., 1954. The way in which culture shapes the personality of people.

KEPHART, CALVIN I. *Races of Mankind: Their Origin and Migration*. New York: Philosophical Library, 1958. How races developed and migrated.

KLINEBERG, OTTO. *Social Psychology*. (Rev. ed.) New York: Henry Holt and Co., 1954. Contains an excellent chapter, summarizing much research data, on ethnic differences.

LE GROS CLARK, W. E. *History of the Primates: An Introduction to the Study of Fossil Man*. London: British Museum Guide, 1949. Standard guide on fossil man.

LIBBY, WILLARD F. *Radiocarbon Dating*. Chicago: University of Chicago Press, 1951. Standard work by a pioneer in this field.

LINTON, RALPH. *The Tree of Culture*. New York: Alfred A. Knopf, 1955. Popular standard work on the growth of culture.

LONGWELL, CHESTER R., and FLINT, RICHARD FOSTER. *Introduction to Physical Geology*. New York: John Wiley and Sons, 1955. Excellent treatment of the subject of geologic time.

McGREGOR, JOHN C. *Southwestern Archaeology*. New York: John Wiley and Sons, 1941. Some good descriptions of the culture of early man in southwestern United States.

*Scientific American, The* (Vol. 203, No. 3). This issue (September, 1960) is devoted to human origins and distribution. The origin of speech and society and the origin of cities.

SHAPIRO, HARRY L. *Man, Culture, and Society*. New York: Oxford University Press, 1956. A variety of good chapters on early man, his races, and his cultures.

SIMPSON, GEORGE E., and YINGER, J. MILTON. *Racial and Cultural Minorities*. New York: Harper and Bros., 1953. One of the better texts on minorities.

UNDERHILL, RUTH MURRAY. *Red Man's America: A History of Indians in the United States*. Chicago: University of Chicago Press, 1953. Good treatment of Indian cultures in the United States.

WAGNER, PHILIP L. *The Human Use of the Earth*. Glencoe, Ill.: Free Press, 1961. A good statement of how the earth's surface is occupied and used.

WEAVER, F. KENNETH. "How Old Is It?" *The National Geographic Magazine*, 114:233-55, August, 1958. Mostly about radiocarbon dating.

ZEUNER, F. E. *Dating the Past*. (4th ed.) . New York: Longmans, Green and Co., 1958. A standard work on the dating of fossil remains and cultural items.

# 3. THE STRUCTURE, GROWTH, AND IMPACT OF CULTURE

A CONCEPT OF CULTURE is essential to the understanding of human behavior. When people think and behave differently than we do, it may be because they have been reared in a culture or subculture that is different from ours. We discussed in the last chapter the development of early man, such discussion being essential for an understanding of man's behavior in the present. We have already seen something of early man's culture, especially that of both Neanderthal Man and Cro-Magnon Man. The earliest human remains were not accompanied by stone implements or any other evidence of culture. Peking Man left charcoal hearths to indicate that he used fire. It was not until the time of Cro-Magnon Man that any considerable knowledge of the culture of early man developed. Cro-Magnon Man left well-defined charcoal hearths, as well as cave drawings and carvings. Burial remains and his art work tell us something of how he lived, something of what was in his mind, and something of what he thought about death and the hereafter.

## WHAT IS CULTURE?

We have already used the word "culture" several times in the two previous chapters. Culture, in an educational sense, is often used to refer to a person of refinement or to a person who has knowledge of "great" books, art, or music.

*Sociologically, culture refers to the man-made aspects of the environment—the things, the attitudes and ideas, the values, and the so-cial systems developed by man and transmitted to each new generation by man.* This is an inclusive concept of culture. In the sense we use the term, all people have culture; all people are "cultured." Let us now look at three other concepts of culture.

In 1871, the English anthropologist Tylor defined culture as "that complex whole which includes knowledge, belief, art, law, morals,

*37*

customs, and any other capabilities and habits acquired by man as a member of society." [1] This concept is inclusive and good.

Seventy-five years later (1944) another Englishman, Bronislaw Malinowski, gave his generalized concept of culture in the following language:

It is the integral whole consisting of implements and consumers' goods, of constitutional charters for the various social groupings, of human ideas and crafts, beliefs and customs. [2]

A year later Kluckhohn and Kelly described their concept of culture in the following language:

Culture in general as a descriptive concept means the accumulated treasury of human creation: books, paintings, buildings and the like; the knowledge of ways of adjusting to our surroundings, both human and physical; language, customs, and systems of etiquette, ethics, religion and morals that have been built up through the ages. [3]

Our own concept of culture, and the three other concepts indicated above, are generalized references to a total culture. This may be the total culture of a nation or community. It may refer to the culture of a people at a given time, say the Navajo or Hopi Indian culture. By this we mean that the Navajo culture has certain characteristics which are distinctive to it and which separate it from the Hopi culture, even though the two tribes are located in southwestern United States. A major line of separation would be the emphasis the Navajos place upon sheep herding and the emphasis which the Hopis place upon the growing of corn. Out of these two practices grow many differences in culture.

[1] E. B. Tylor, *Primitive Culture* (London: John Murray, 1871), p. 1.
[2] Bronislaw Malinowski, *A Scientific Theory of Culture and Other Essays* (Chapel Hill, N. C.: University of North Carolina Press, 1944), p. 36.
[3] Clyde Kluckhohn and W. H. Kelly, "The Concept of Culture," in *The Science of Man in the World Crisis,* ed. Ralph Linton (New York: Columbia University Press, 1945), p. 96.

## Levels of culture

Rather arbitrarily, culture may be divided into three large categories of items, sometimes called "levels" or "orders" of culture: (1) material culture objects often referred to as artifacts; (2) culture concepts,* and (3) the behaviors.

*Table 3*

### THE ASPECTS OF CULTURE

1. Speech
   Languages, writing systems, etc.

2. Material traits
   a. Food habits
   b. Shelter
   c. Transportation and travel
   d. Dress
   e. Utensils, tools, etc.
   f. Weapons
   g. Occupations and industries

3. Art, carving, painting, drawing, music, etc.

4. Mythology and scientific knowledge

5. Religious practices
   a. Ritualistic forms
   b. Treatment of the sick
   c. Treatment of the dead

6. Family and social systems
   a. The forms of marriage
   b. Methods of reckoning relationships
   c. Inheritance
   d. Social control
   e. Sports and games

7. Property
   a. Real and personal
   b. Standards of value and exchange
   c. Trade

8. Government
   a. Political forms
   b. Judicial and legal procedures

9. War

Source: Clark Wissler, *Man and Culture* (New York: Thomas Y. Crowell Co., 1923), p. 74.

* Such cultural concepts are often referred to as "mentifacts."

E. I. du Pont de Nemours & Co., Inc.

*Media of exchange are to be found in all cultures. The stone disc is from Yap, the shell money from New Caledonia, the copper cross and the six-foot spear money from the Congo, and the copper shield-like symbol from the Alaskan Indians.*

A stone ax, an arrow point, a ritual mask, or an automobile steering wheel are material culture elements, often called artifacts. How a ritual mask shall be used is a concept, whereas its actual use in a pattern of interaction is a behavior. Money is a material culture object, the value placed upon it a concept, and the spending, saving, giving or banking of it a behavior.

The followers of many religions believe in a Supreme Being, a monotheistic belief, which is a culture concept. The worship of such a Being is a behavioral element in a culture.

Material culture objects may be utilitarian or symbolic. Symbolism is conceptual. A cross in a church is first of all a material culture object. However, it is more than an object; it is a symbol. It is often said that American culture is materialistic, which means that we place a lot of emphasis upon material culture objects.

Social behavior patterns are related to concepts because concepts influence acceptance, avoidance, cooperation, and hostility. Both the concepts and patterns of behavior are developed through learning. As concepts and behavior patterns develop, they may also be related to material culture objects. Verbal behavior depends, as we have seen, upon both vocal equipment and mentality.

For a more detailed picture of the content of culture see Table 3.

## *The organization of culture*

The smallest unit of culture is called a *trait*. Again, traits may be material or nonmaterial. A cigarette is a material trait. Monogamy, the belief in marriage to a single mate at a given time, is a nonmaterial trait; so also is the concept of fidelity in marriage.

Two or more culture traits used together to perform a function are called a *culture complex*. The smoking of a cigarette, involving several traits, such as cigarettes, matches or lighter, perhaps a cigarette holder, and various methods of handling the cigarette while smoking, is an example. A marriage ceremony is a culture complex made up of a number of culture traits, some of which are symbolic.

Culture complexes are then constellations of traits designed to achieve given ends.

More complicated than culture complexes are *culture patterns*. These are the dominant characteristics or "themes" of a culture. For example, the dominant culture pattern of the Mississippi Delta is cotton farming. The dominant economic pattern around the Great Lakes is industrial, the dominant pattern in Iowa is agricultural. Monogamy is the dominant pattern in American marriage. The striving for success is also a dominant American pattern.

Sutherland, Woodward, and Maxwell give a good characterization of the organization of the units of a culture by contrasting two Indian cultures with the non-Indian cultures of the United States (Table 4).

*E. I. du Pont de Nemours & Co., Inc.*

*Striving for success is an important pattern of American culture, as these Horatio Alger books, widely read a generation ago, indicate.*

Sometimes a geographical area has a definite culture pattern or set of patterns which sets it apart from other areas. Such areas are called *culture areas.* Herskovits, for instance, has identified the culture areas of Africa. Where these areas are large they have also been referred to as *culture regions.* An example would be the industrial East. Small areas with a definite culture complex or occupied by a people making use of distinctive culture complexes which set the small area culture apart from that of the surrounding area are sometimes called *culture islands.* The idea of the culture island is that there is a distinctive cluster of culture traits, characteristic of a small area, in a larger "sea" of culture. For instance, on one small southern mountain range there are two German settlements and a Swiss settlement with ways of life sufficiently different to mark them as cultural islands. A compact Chinatown in a city is a culture island, as are Amish settlements in Ohio and Pennsylvania.

The customary culture traits and complexes of a people are known as *folkways.* For instance, in this country we have lunch around

*The whole continent of Africa can be divided into culture areas.*

SOURCE: Melville J. Herskovits, *Backgrounds of African Art* (Denver, Colo.: Denver Art Museum, 1946), p. 9. Reproduced by permission of the publisher.

*Table 4*

UNITS USED IN DESCRIBING THE CULTURE OF A PEOPLE

| | Level of Cultural Integration | Illustrative Examples | | |
| --- | --- | --- | --- | --- |
| Units | | *The Kwakiutl Indian* | *The Crowe Indian* | *The United States Today* |
| The culture pattern | Brief characterization of the dominant themes in the culture as a whole | Sedentary but non-agricultural people. Great emphasis on individual prestige based on property distribution and nobility titles | Nomadic hunters, living in small bands. Emphasis on individual exploits and on the power of visions | A machine culture. Emphasis on competition and the profit motive, on democracy and humanitarianism. A highly mobile and generally "urbanized" population. Belief in progress |
| The culture complex | Clusters of functionally associated traits | Potlatch complex. Salmon-fishing complex | Tobacco complex. Guardian-spirit religion. Buffalo complex | School complex. Touring complex. Sports complex. Political party-election complex |
| The culture trait | Individual folkways and culture objects | Totem poles, plank houses, cannibal dance society, blankets as media of exchange, shamans | Tipi dwelling, sweat lodge, "counting coup," tobacco society, sun dance | Textbooks, automobiles, baseball, voting machines, honeymoons, banquets, policemen, tuxedos |

Source: Robert L. Sutherland, Julian L. Woodward, and Milton A. Maxwell, *Introductory Sociology* (4th ed.; Chicago: J. B. Lippincott Co., 1952), p. 31.

noon. This is a folkway. In Mexico the siesta at noon is a folkway. In some of the more remote rural sections of the Ozarks and the Appalachians, the different phases of the moon guide the timing of many agricultural activities, including planting, harvesting, and slaughtering. These are local folkways.

Folk beliefs or behavior standards which influence the ethical conduct and behavior of people are called *mores*. These are sometimes called moral customs. The distinction between mores and folkways is often slight. A key to the difference is that conformance to mores is held to be more vital to the welfare of the group or society than conformance to folkways. Monogamy, in the eyes of Christians, denotes con-

formity to the mores of Christianity. Christians believe that its practice is necessary for the welfare of society. On the other hand, polygyny (more than one wife) has been permitted under some religions, for example, the Moslem religion. In South Korea it is a folkway that mature children take care of their parents. It is also an obligation to the mores that they do so.

As societies have developed there has been a trend toward many mores and some folkways becoming the basis for many laws. In a community where it is a folkway to close down all businesses at 12 o'clock on Saturday night, the time may come, as the community grows, when a law enforcing closing is necessary. Many

Sunday Blue Laws have originated in this way because of the belief that Sunday business conflicted with the mores. At one time the support of children by their parents in this country was pretty well determined by the folkways and the mores. Today there are laws regulating such matters. The laws are enforced because they are supported by the mores. Even today, the strongest support for monogamous marriage comes from the mores of the people and not from the laws.

### Other characteristics of culture

Culture has certain characteristics, some of which have been indicated in our concept of culture. The major characteristics we shall discuss only briefly:

1. *Culture is learned.* The concept of culture which we have used indicates that it is learned. *Learning,* as a process, is a way of acquiring specific behavior patterns with which we were not born. Products of learning are the acquired patterns. Each new generation must be taught the culture. This is one of the reasons why the task of learning a culture is much more complicated in complex societies than in simple ones. In simple societies, cultural material items are fewer, as are adult role expectations and goals. A child growing up in a simple society is likely to know what he will be doing as an adult and is prepared by his family groups for these tasks.[4] In a complicated society the child may have no idea of where he will be living or what he will be doing when he grows up.

We have no reason to assume that the human ability to learn is greater today than it was 20,000 years ago. Yet, in culture development this period of time just about spans the gap between the New Stone Age culture and the period of the technological revolution.

2. *Culture is transmitted.* By culture transmission we mean that culture is passed from person to person and from one generation to

*Skeet Tallent Studio, Knoxville, Tenn.*

*An important part of culture transfer takes place when the young meet the old.*

another. We might more correctly say that it is selectively passed from one generation to another. The process of learning or internalizing the elements of a culture is called *enculturation.* A person is enculturated when he conforms generally to the culture and makes use of its culture traits and complexes. This means that he makes use of the culture objects and concepts of his culture and conforms to its behaviors.

The transmitting agencies of a culture are largely made up of adults and the institutions they dominate. Peer groups, however, may transmit culture to their members. In transmitting the culture of a mass society the school plays a leading role. In transmitting the culture of subgroups, the family, play group,

[4] *See* Margaret Mead, *Coming of Age in Samoa* (New York: New American Library, 1949).

cliques, and gangs have great influence. The transmitting roles of government, the church, and the economic institutions are usually more specialized in the transmitting process, although not entirely so.

Animals learn. They differ from man in the rate, extent, and method of learning. A significant difference between man and other animals is the extent to which man transmits what he has learned, through language, and the extent to which he uses tools. Gestures and sounds often serve purposes similar to language in communication. Man has a remarkable power of memory whereby he can envelop the past in his thought and actions and then transmit his experiences and his impressions.

3. *Culture is functional.* Culture traits and complexes develop and exist to serve human needs and desires. This statement needs some modification. Just as an attic accumulates a certain amount of useless plunder, some cultural traits and complexes become vestigial or useless or accumulate in the cultural attics of societies. As we walk down the street with a lady, we shift our position to the curb side of the sidewalk. In years past this was done apparently to protect milady's dress from the mud spattered by horses in the street. Some individuals and groups have vested interests in the continuation of outmoded cultural traits and complexes, whereas the masses may not have.

If a culture element does not function in the lives of people they tend to change it, modify it, or reduce it to a position of secondary importance. Culture traits, complexes, and patterns are not likely to be given up by people so long as they function in their lives. Some continue to exist where they have no apparent usefulness. Where new desires develop, sooner or later culture changes to meet these desires are likely to take place, but there may be major cultural lags in putting new changes into practice. For instance, knowledge of health, technology, the science of government, and approved welfare practices may be well in advance of their widespread application.

4. *Culture has an integrative tendency.*[5] Culture traits, complexes, and patterns in a society are interrelated. As an example, the basic theories of democracy, Christianity, and capitalism are interrelated. Each places an emphasis upon the development of the individual, upon an element of freedom, upon individual success, and upon the accumulation and disposal of property under approved means. Of course, many political, civic, religious, intergroup and economic practices are out of character with the theories of approved practices.

Other examples will show the interrelationship of culture. The automobile has influenced greatly the culture of the family and the recreation and leisure-time habits of the people. The oribiting of men in space by the Russians and by the Americans has spurred on new research and education in the sciences. One's motivations may be influenced by the social class to which he belongs. One's patterns of aggression in a group or in a social situation, or his tendency to withdraw from a group or social situation, or to identify himself with certain groups bears a relation to the cultural and social groups he grows up in. The integrative tendencies in cultures are usually gradual and incomplete.

5. *Culture is adaptive.* The most obvious illustrations of culture adaptation occur in material traits and complexes. A good knife is adaptive to many uses. In articles of clothing and items of diet one makes an adaptation to geographical features, such as rainfall, sunshine, and temperature. One type of agriculture may be followed where the rainfall is sparse and another where the rainfall is heavy. It is not just an accident that most big cities of the world, those of over a million population, are found in areas ranging in temperature from 50 to 80 degrees Fahrenheit. Light metals may be used for thousands of purposes. Like-

[5] For a good discussion of cultural integration, *see* Melville J. Herskovits, *Man and His Works* (New York: Alfred A. Knopf, 1948), Chap. 14, "The Integration of Culture."

wise, there are many ways of preparing and serving the same foods. Men living in Little America do not make marked physical adaptations to living there; they make their adaptation to an antagonistic environment through the use of culture items.

6. *Other characteristics of culture.* The previous discussion indicates the obvious social quality of culture. In the first place all culture is produced in groups or in response to social demands of one type or another. Social systems, made up of more than one individual, are the only culture transmitting media. The culture value systems held by individuals, and supported by the social systems of which they are a part, are those which the mass society holds in high esteem usually. For example, if the groups and institutions of a society place a high value upon leisure, then leisure has a high value in the lives of individuals. Economic institutions are likely to cultivate, feature, and exploit this emphasis.

## HOW CULTURE DEVELOPS

What, then, are the sources of culture? The question needs no great elaboration. In general, there are five sources of culture or ways in which it develops.

### Biological factors

One of the sources of culture lies in the biological make-up of men. People must eat and therefore they must develop ways of obtaining food, so food technology becomes a part of the culture. People have certain sex urges which may be sublimated by one culture and exaggerated by another. Ways of satisfying and regulating these urges are developed in the culture. Culture ways of caring for the young have to be developed, and ways and means of socializing the young are present in all cultures. These culture ways, of course, are highly variable from culture to culture.

### Invention and discovery

The development of a new culture trait or complex is called invention or discovery. The terms are best applied to what we call invention and discovery in scientific fields. A scientist discovers, while looking for something else in his laboratory, that a green penicillin mold has an antibiotic or bactericidal quality and a whole new science of antibiotics gets under way. A man discovers that a certain clay deposit is rich in bauxite and from this develops a way of producing aluminum metal from clay. The terms "invention" and "discovery" are not mutually exclusive. The need element is not likely to be as important in discovery as in invention, although the discovered culture element may be fully as important. By definition there is an element of chance in discovery as contrasted to the element of planning so important in invention. The key role of the inventor in invention is emphasized. This is not always true in discovery, where the role of the discoverer may be incidental to what he discovers. Invention is never pure originally. It is always a new combination of old culture elements. An inquisitive and inventive man assembles a complicated machine made up largely of items already known and calls it a motor car. Thus begins the dawn of the Motor Age. There are enough new elements of invention in it so that some features may be patentable. Thus he protects certain phases of his invention through a patent issued to him by the U.S. Patent Office.

### Innovation

New uses for old culture traits and complexes are called innovations. Many culture complexes are the result of combinations of traits and complexes. For example, hundreds of culture items may grow out of a basic invention in plastics or synthetic fibers. A new dance may develop and have several characteristics of other well-known dances. A new religion may combine certain elements of other religions. A substance used largely in explosives, nitroglycerine, may be used as a drug to relieve a form of heart ailment. These are all examples of innovations.

### Diffusion and borrowing

Culture develops through diffusion and borrowing. By cultural diffusion we mean the spread of a culture trait, complex, or pattern from its place of origin. A good example is the spread of the use of tobacco, especially cigarettes. Christianity, which began with a small group of persecuted people, has spread around the world. Other movements, as shown in the chapter on social movements, have had similar growth.

Culture diffusion and borrowing may be spasmodic or planned and methodical. Much modern advertising is directed toward encouraging the spread of trade items. The supermarket, which had its origin in the United States, is now widespread in other countries. The United States Government may plan definite steps to "sell" democracy to the people of another country. We float balloons, which have attached to them printed tracts on democracy and its merits and accomplishments, into Iron Curtain countries. This is an attempt at planned diffusion. We send missionaries overseas to diffuse our religions among other peoples. The United States has a group of crop and livestock specialists who search the world for new kinds of plants and animals which appear to have promise to American agriculture.

In the diffusion and borrowing processes, the rate of culture flow is materially greater from more complex to lower cultures. To put it another way, a social class is likely to imitate the class above it rather than the one below it. Preliterates are likely to borrow more culture traits and complexes from literates than literates will borrow from them. The reason for this is that we tend to imitate the superior and not the inferior. We learn less from the savage than he learns from us. In a college class the superior student does not imitate the inferior, as a rule.

The rate and amount of culture diffusion is speeded up by modern means of communication and transportation. News originating in Manila may reach an American farmer at his dinner table minutes later. Iceberg lettuce, picked one day in California, may reach the Chicago market the next day. Lobster tails from the African coast may be flown directly to New York. An increase in income of a middle-class population may cause them to buy culture items, say television sets, previously enjoyed largely by upper-class people. Good examples of rapid acculturation are furnished by the experiences of military occupation on islands in the Pacific especially. Here, within a few years, cultural patterns and values have been changed by the impact of military occupation at a speed formerly thought impossible.[6]

### Accumulation

Culture develops through accumulation. Knowledge is a good example. At one time, if a young man wanted to study medicine, he attached himself to a practicing physician and "rode" with him. After a period of time he was ready to practice medicine. Today, medical training may require up to ten years of training, so extensive has been the accumulation of medical knowledge.

Even culture traits and complexes which have outgrown their usefulness we preserve in our behavior, our institutions, and in our museums and culture depositories of one kind or another.

[6] *See* Margaret Mead, *New Lives for Old: A Cultural Transformation—Manus, 1928-1953* (New York: William Morrow, 1956).

## THE STAGES IN CULTURE DEVELOPMENT

The early growth of culture has to date been best charted in the Middle East and in Europe, especially in France. There are several reasons for this: one is the active interest in archaeology and anthropology which developed in Europe; another is that the remains of ancient man have been found in considerable quantity and in a good state of preservation there.

Studies in the development of culture in Europe parallel those in the development of early man studied in the last chapter.

Owing to its perishable nature, much of the culture of early man has disappeared. Prior to the use of stone for implements, no doubt primitive man used wood, which is perishable, as is also true of skeletal remains. Except for the human bones enveloped in landslides or glacial deposits, we know little of early man's religion or his family life prior to the time that he buried his dead or left some record of his experiences on the walls of the caves of Europe.

### The Old Stone Age

This stage in culture development is scientifically known as the Paleolithic period. It is divided into the Lower, Middle, and Upper periods.

Man may have lived upon the earth for a million years. Perhaps 49/50ths of this time was spent in what we call the Old Stone Age —the Paleolithic and Mesolithic culture periods. During the Old Stone Age man was almost exclusively a food gatherer and hunter, living from the land, the streams, and the ocean.

The only stone implements of this period were flat, sharp-edged tools, evidently used for scraping, and crude hand axes. Many resemble stones found in nature. Since many of these crude implements have been found in valleys and near cave entrances, we assume they were made by early man.

As we go from the Lower Paleolithic culture

toward the upper periods, many superior stone tools are found. Although they were essentially crude, they were the product of human skills.

The Middle Paleolithic period was the age of Neanderthal Man. Implements belonging to this stage of culture show greatly improved flint flaking techniques.[7] There is evidence of

[7] For evidence of this, *see* H. L. Movius, "The Old Stone Age," in *Man, Culture and Society*, ed. Harry L. Shapiro (New York: Oxford University Press, 1952), pp. 62-64.

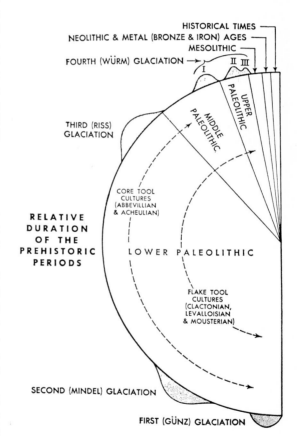

*Prehistoric Periods in Culture Development*

FROM *Man, Culture, and Society*, ed. Harry L. Shapiro. Copyright 1956 by Oxford University Press, Inc. Reprinted by permission.

*(at left) Bone Implements from Dordogne, France*

*(below) Implements and Or-naments of the Upper Paleo-lithic Period*

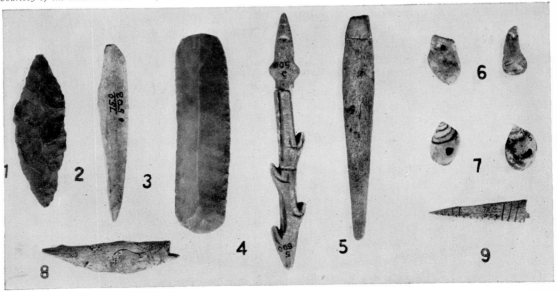

the use of bone and antler for implements. Chopping techniques are more in evidence—some of the large bones of mammoths being used as anvils for chopping.

The Middle Paleolithic period shows abundant use of caves for shelter. Well-defined hearths, with evidence of charcoal, indicate the use of fire. People of this period buried their dead. In the Upper Paleolithic period implements, a term used collectively for both tools and weapons, became more specialized, with well-defined blades. Much use was made of antler, bone, and ivory. Apparently man's earliest dwellings appeared during this period.[8] Upper Paleolithic men, who evidently belonged to modern races, engaged in collective hunting and apparently owned some private property in the form of movable items.

The Upper Paleolithic period parallels the period of Cro-Magnon Man. We have spoken of his skill as an artist, evidenced by murals, sculpturing, and engraving on the walls of caves. Some art work reflects certain beliefs about religion, fertility, and reproduction.[9]

Cro-Magnon Man wore skins for clothing and gave attention to personal adornment. Bones found near where he lived indicate that he subsisted largely upon the woolly mammoth, the woolly rhinoceros, the reindeer, cave lion, and wild horse.

[8] *Ibid.*, p. 64.

[9] *See* Gertrude Rachel Levy, *The Gate of Horn* (London: Faber and Faber, 1948).

*"Sure, we're bigger and stronger and know how to live better—but I say they're catching up with us and may even be ahead of us!"*

SOURCE: *Look Magazine*, January 20, 1959, p. 79. Reproduced by permission of the artist.

## The Mesolithic Period

The Mesolithic period of culture development in Europe is something of a transition period between the Old Stone Age culture and the New Stone Age period. The Mesolithic period was short, perhaps not more than 6,000 years long. It came in early postglacial time but continued the basic Old Stone Age economy of food collecting, hunting, fishing, and fowling.

As Movius indicates:

... the Mesolithic defines a stage in cultural development, basically founded on the economy of the Upper Paleolithic, but profoundly modified by the changes in environment induced by the recession of the ice sheets at the close of the Glacial period. It is in this sense that the term (Mesolithic) is used here, since with the coming-in of the new food producing Neolithic civilization, bringing its associated elements—pottery, domestication of animals, agriculture, and the art of polishing stone—there is a fundamental break in the sequence. Admittedly certain elements from the earlier phase continued in use, as no new forms replaced them, but these cannot be regarded as evolutionary. Instead they represent the survival of types of implements for which there was still a need, and in place of which no innovations were introduced by the new culture.[10]

## The New Stone Age

With the recession of the glaciers and the rapid changes in the flora and fauna which followed, man was able to make the new adjustments indicated above. After this came the slow transition to what is called the New Stone Age, or the Neolithic stage of culture development.[11]

The New Stone Age cultures began at different dates in various parts of the world. In general we say they came after 6000 B.C. in Europe. During the Mesolithic period there was a settling down of peoples, some domesti-

cation of animals, an increase in hunting and fishing techniques, and the beginning of pottery. These arts were extended and improved as the New Stone Age developed.

In addition to improved implements, many of which were characterized by highly polished surfaces, New Stone Age cultures show a great revolution in food supply characterized by the domestication of plants and animals. The domestication of cereals—wheat and barley especially—from wild forms found in the Middle East, opened the door to revolution in agriculture. This was followed by irrigation agriculture and dry-land farming, in which dry lands were planted every other year.

As Childe says:

Food production constituted a real economic and technical revolution. Firstly, it put society potentially in control of its own food supply. Paleolithic and Mesolithic societies, like contemporary savages, had to rely entirely on what nature obligingly provided in the way of plant, animal, fish, or insect food. The supply was always limited, and the human population was limited by it. But, at least in theory, cultivators can augment the food supply by simply tilling more land, and so can provide for the support of a growing population. The herdsman has only to abstain from eating lamb and veal and to clear fresh pasture to obtain a like result—again of course in theory. Secondly, plant cultivation and stockbreeding for the first time put men in control of sources of energy other than human muscle-power. The latter was the only force, apart from fire heat used in cooking and for hardening spears, available to earlier societies, unless perhaps the harnessing of dogs to pull sleighs by Mesolithic hunter-fishers in the North precedes the Neolithic revolution in time; sails certainly come later.[12]

The pounding of grain for food was a New Stone Age achievement, as was the cultivation of plants other than cereals. In the Mediterranean, Middle East, and Balkan areas, olive, fruit, and date trees were cultivated. In Europe the apple tree was planted for its fruit.

Potterymaking reached a high state of per-

10 Movius, *op. cit.*, p. 75.
11 For a more comprehensive account of the New Stone Age culture, *see* Shapiro, *op. cit.*, pp. 94-110.

12 V. Gordon Childe, "The New Stone Age," in Shapiro, *op. cit.*, pp. 98-99.

fection among New Stone Age peoples, with extremely wide variations in the quality and decoration of pottery. The making of fabrics from flax and wool, accomplished by spinning and weaving, was carried to a high state of development, with vegetable dyes being used in coloring.[13] Net and basketmaking were common in Mesolithic communities, but were carried to a higher state of perfection during the New Stone Age.

Improved houses—made of adobe, split saplings, and intertwined brush—have been found in the remains of Neolithic sites. Farming village sites in the Middle East date back as early as 4500 B.C. Sites have been found in Europe which show as many as 50 houses.[14] With the division of people into households evidently there was a shift from community ownership and use of equipment to more household ownership and use, although much community property still existed.

Neolithic excavations show evidence of a wide range of exchange of articles. Chief among the articles exchanged were sea shells. Whether these shells served as a media of exchange, were prized objects of beauty, or served a dual purpose, we do not know.

We now need to say something about the New Stone Age in America.[15] Without a doubt, the earliest immigrants to America, apparently from Asia, were hunters and food gatherers, who migrated to this continent 15,000 or 20,000 years ago. The earliest culture we know in America is the culture of Folsom Man. The dating of his culture is currently placed at something less than 15,000 years ago.

The most characteristic artifact of Folsom Man's culture was the fluted flint spear points, known as Folsom points, which he fashioned and used to kill the woolly mammoth, the mastodon, and smaller animals. Wherever possible, he lived in caves or under rock shelters. Central, South, and North America have yielded Folsom points. Scrapers, hammers of stone, and articles of bone were used as implements. The spear thrower perhaps antedated the bow and arrow. Charcoal deposits evidence the use of fire.

From these early human beginnings in the Americas developed the people named "Indians" by Columbus, who thought he had discovered the East Indies. So variable were their New Stone Age cultures that we shall not attempt to characterize them at this time. We shall say more about them in the next chapter.

### The Metal Ages

Toward the end of the New Stone Age man discovered minerals on the earth's surface. No doubt the use of fire was one factor that led man to experiment in using minerals. Three metal ages followed: The Copper Age, the Bronze Age, and the Iron Age.[16]

Copper implements were found in use in Mesopotamia as early as 4000 B.C. and in Egypt around 3500 B.C. After this date, work in metal became very important in Egypt. In America the earliest use of metals was apparently made by the Incas in the Andes at a period around 1493 to 1527.

Because of its low melting point, the smelting of copper was more easily achieved than the smelting of most other metals. Once man learned to smelt copper he began to experiment with the fusion of metals.

The fusion of copper and tin resulted in the very important Bronze Age. Because alloys of bronze were more durable than those of copper, revolutionary changes in the development, molding, and sharpening of implements were made. Even fairly sharp cutting edges and penetrating points could be made in the molding process. Where necessary, grinding wheels could be used to make sharper blades. From

---

[13] *Ibid.,* p. 104, indicates three types of looms in use in Egypt and temperate Europe after 3000 B.C.

[14] *Ibid.,* p. 105.

[15] For more details on the New Stone Age in America, *see* L. S. Cressman, "Man in the New World," in Shapiro, *op. cit.,* pp. 139-67, and William Smith Fowler, *Ten Thousand Years in America* (New York: Vantage Press, 1957).

[16] J. O. Brew, "The Metal Ages: Copper, Bronze, and Iron," in Shapiro, *op. cit.,* pp. 111-38.

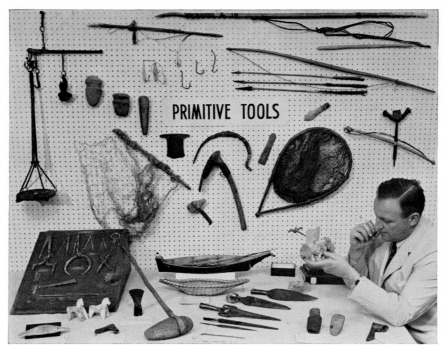

E. I. du Pont de Nemours & Co., Inc.

*Primitive Tools Made of Stone, Wood, and Metal*

bronze came superior axes, spears, knives, shields, ornaments, containers, metal coins, arrow points, plow points, and metal wheels, including potter's wheels.

The great Bronze Age inventions and discoveries led Childe to characterize the period between 4000 and 3000 B.C. in Egypt, Mesopotamia, and the Mediterranean region as the urban revolution.[17] Metallurgy gave rise to craftsmen and trade, and was a factor in the development of compact settlements. The improvements of agriculture furnished an improved food supply for people who lived away from the soil. The sail was perfected to encourage water transportation. Methods of counting and the alphabet were developed. The metal wheel stimulated land transport and led to the development of charioteering.

[17] V. Gordon Childe, *Man Makes Himself* (London: Watts and Co., 1936; also, New American Library, 1951). *Also,* by the same author, *What Happened in History* (New York: Penguin Books, 1942).

The commercial ceramic and metal pottery arts and crafts grew in prominence. Armies with superior weapons conquered armies with more men but poorer equipment. The use of metals in building ornamentation received great stimulus. Villages and towns developed into cities. Empire cities grew to power. Metal implements stimulated the diffusion of culture and the barter system gave way to trading with metal coins as the media of exchange. Weights and measures became a part of the trading culture, and the lunar and solar calendars came into use.

The Bronze and Iron ages overlap. In the Middle East iron appears to have been known as early as 3000 B.C. By 1000 B.C. tools and weapons of iron were fairly common in Egypt, southern and central Europe, and parts of Asia.

It is difficult to date exactly the beginnings of the Iron Age in Europe but 650 B.C. is an approximate time. After the smelting of iron was discovered, knowledge of smelting and the use of iron spread rapidly. Negro blacksmiths of Africa became famous. Europe's industrial beginnings date from the widespread application of iron. Knowledge of ironworking became widespread in its application.

As Brew indicates, following the dawn of the Iron Age,

political changes were varied and uneven. In Asia, the Bronze Age traditions of monarchy continued; but in the West, particularly in Athens, governments of definitely republican character were built up. Universal suffrage was unknown and slavery continued, but the ruling class operated upon a truly democratic basis. The new ruling classes were broadened to include craftsmen and merchants as well as priests and great land holders. Their governments produced public works and free dramatic performances, and they generally devoted at least part of their efforts to the benefit of the populace rather than merely of their own treasuries.

The developments in social organization, philosophy, science, and religion were numerous and rapid after the Iron Age got underway. The "natural philosophers" laid the foundations for the theory of organic evolution and the theory of music. The study of mathematics made great strides forward, particularly in Greece where the mathematicians of the Iron Age developed the theorem of Pythagoras and learned to solve quadratic equations. Astronomers in Mesopotamia and Greece learned to predict eclipses. Medicine was greatly freed from magic (or, at least, from demons) and the work of Hippocrates is still well known today. Growing knowledge of how men think, of how our brains work, culminated in the logical systems of Aristotle. Religion became more of an individual matter as in the Greek mystical cults; monotheism (the theory of a single god) arose and the teachings of the Jewish prophets, Buddha, Lao-tse, and Confucius formed the basis for many of our important modern religions.[18]

[18] Brew, *op. cit.*, pp. 137-38.

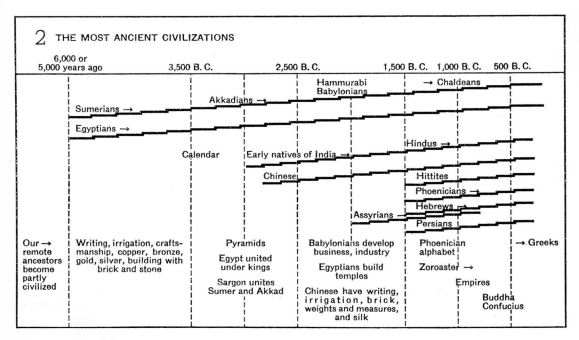

2  THE MOST ANCIENT CIVILIZATIONS

SOURCE: Carl Becker and Frederic D. Metcalf, *Story of Civilization* (Morristown, N.J.: Silver Burdett Co., 1944), p. 68. Reproduced by permission of the publisher.

### The Scientific Revolution and its impact

From the Iron Age developed the Steel Age. Out of the Iron and Steel ages came the steam engine and the internal combustion engine. The steam engine made possible the Industrial Revolution. The internal combustion engine led to the Motor Age, and to jet-propelled airplanes. Today we have a mixture of many types of culture. The Industrial Revolution continues. The motor and the jet have made possible the Air Age. We are now coming into a period of guided missiles and man-launched satellites. Other aspects of culture have changed as the material traits and complexes have changed. The present stage of scientific discoveries and technological development is the outgrowth of what we might call the Scientific Revolution.

As societies have progressed in the use of chemicals, electricity, and metals, with recent emphasis upon the light metals, such as aluminum and titanium, and upon the use of alloys with high temperature and failure strength, the wider use of motors, electronic devices, and surface and air-borne vehicles have developed. The combination of developments in chemical, electronic, and metallurgical technologies, coupled with the growth of large research centers, has given the world a scientific revolution much more spectacular than the Industrial Revolution, and with about as many problems. Whereas man, in the past, was physically earthbound, this is no longer true.

There are many ways in which this scientific revolution has affected people.

1. *The acceleration of scientific activity.* The permeation of the culture with more scientific activity is one of the results of the Scientific Revolution. In 1930 the expenditures for scientific research were less than $200 million. By 1958 these had increased to about $7 billion. In 1930 the number of scientists in the United States was fewer than 50,000; today there are about 300,000. Next to expanding military activity and expenditures for military purposes, the second most expanding activity in our social structure has been in the growth of the sciences.

2. *The increased use of scientific knowledge.* As new scientific activity has developed in cultures, it has released a constant stream of scientific knowledge, much of which is available and is being widely used by the population. New knowledge in chemistry moves quickly from the test tube and pilot plant into the fabricating plant and spinning mill, and then into the market place, as plastics and synthetic yarns have done. From the plant and the market place, these move rapidly into the automobiles, the homes, and the offices of people. New knowledge from aerodynamics laboratories flows freely into plants making military aircraft, civilian aircraft, and air-borne missiles. Faster and more comfortable civilian and soldier mobility result in new words like "jet" and "turbojet." "Emplaning" and "air-borne" become commonplace. New weapons receive consideration in the legislative assemblies.

From new developments in pharmacy and microbiology come new drugs which reduce sickness and lengthen life. The citizen buys radio sets which are the outgrowth of transistor electronics. Picture and sound are brought into his home by television. Microwave techniques play an important role in daily life. Electronic computers may even figure the citizen's tax and write his salary check. The increased use of scientific and technological advances has created a strong demand for these services. Public interest in science has been increased and science is featured in the mass media of communication.

3. *New industries have been created.* The gap between laboratory research and industry and agriculture has been greatly decreased as the Scientific Revolution has progressed. Not only has research in industry become more commonplace, but industries are becoming more readily adaptable to change and new techniques. They also search widely for applicable knowledge in the physical, biological, and social sciences. They frequently subsidize

university research. Field-scale and farm-scale research in agriculture has done much to narrow the gap between research in the agricultural sciences and the farmer. Some comparatively new industries which have been created by the Scientific Revolution include the chemical, electronic, nuclear energy, and biological and pharmaceutical industries.

4. *Higher standard of living.* Many reasons may be given for the explanation of the standard of living of a people (the people of the United States, for example)—the kind of government, the availability of capital goods, and state of technology among them.

Ogburn shows that the rise in the standard of living of the American people has resulted mainly from improvements in technology. By using three independent sets of data—per capita income, per family income, and per capita national income—he holds that, in terms of what money will buy, the standard of living of the American people doubled in the first half of the twentieth century. During this same period the mechanical energy for all purposes supplied per member of the labor force increased 116 per cent. The net national product per member of the labor force doubled in 52 years. During the same period poverty declined 50 per cent.[19] Not only has the standard of living been increased by the Scientific Revolution, but this increase has been widespread among the masses.

An important concern of many students of society in America today is whether or not man is the conqueror or the pawn of the mass culture. A favorite theme is that the individual is swamped by mass culture and that his individuality is swallowed up by it.

One writer in discussing the "human condition," by which he means the conditions of life within our modern culture, points out that American mass culture has been the most successful in history in providing a high standard of living for a large proportion of the population.[20] This within itself is a great achievement. The same writer hastens to argue that in modern mass culture man exists for the sake of the economy and not the economy for the sake of the man. Man does not own the machine, the machine owns the man. The people, collectively, become the captive audience of the communications industries. In spite of all its kindness, generosity, prosperity, and goodness, life as it is lived by a large proportion of the population is shallow, superficial, and vulgar, with much tawdriness and lack of dignity. The question of "What is the good life?" plays a minor chord in the mass culture in contrast to "How can we raise the standard of living?" This theme to be sure is a pessimistic one but one worth considering, to say the least.

Many of those who say that the individual is submerged by the mass culture advocate an escape to a Thoreau-like existence. While this may be a good solution for many people in the high-income brackets, the fact is that for the masses there are not enough Walden Ponds. Perhaps the real solution is for a type of education that will better equip individuals for living in a society that is complex in most of its phases.

5. *Increased mobility.* A very real impact of the revolution in science and technology has been the increase in the mobility of people. The railroad, the motor vehicle, with its wide use and flexibility, the airplane, and the helicopter have been the major forms of transportation adding to the mobility made possible by improved transportation.

Between March, 1957, and March, 1958, of the 168 million persons in the United States one year of age and older, about one-fifth moved, i.e., 33 million were living in a different house in March, 1958, than a year previous. Twenty-two million had changed residence within the same county, 11 million had moved from one county to another, and in 5.6 million instances the movers had changed

[19] William F. Ogburn, "Technology and the Standard of Living of the United States," *The American Journal of Sociology,* **60**:380-86, January, 1955.

[20] Joseph Wood Krutch, *Human Nature and the Human Condition* (New York: Random House, 1959).

states.[21] Other impressive aspects of mobility are the daily journey to work and to shop, and tourism and the trip to recreation and vacation areas.

6. *New groups of problems.* The scientific and technological revolution has brought to the fore new groups of problems, some of which we have indicated. The extent to which many peoples give emphasis to material items causes some concern among the students of value systems, especially the philosophers, the theologians, and the sociologists. Congestion of people and traffic is almost a universal problem in cities, as is air pollution. Mechanization and improved production practices have created surpluses of population in many agricultural areas. Automation poses a threat to employment. The growth in the use of machines for purposes of inventory and other

calculations, for perception and decision, is especially likely to displace workers in the clerical and consumers' goods fields.[22] Safety on the highways is a major national, state, and local problem. Atomic energy industries create problems of fallout, whereas air-borne missiles and atomic weapons are powerful enough to decimate the population. There are also problems of personal adjustment and disorganization that have a sociocultural setting. Some of these we will consider in Part IV of the text, where we shall also consider the impact of culture upon the development of personality and also personality deviation and its origin.

In future chapters we shall see that culture is the basis for thought, that our beliefs have cultural bases, and that most of our behavior is in response to cultural expectations and values.

## SUMMARY

A basic understanding of culture is necessary to an understanding of human behavior. We have defined culture as essentially the man-made aspects of the environment. It is man-made, is transmitted by man, and is made up of artifacts, mentifacts, skills, and various combinations of the three. Although there is a lot of luck in culture, it is not completely haphazard and random; it has organization. From traits, the smallest units of culture, develop culture complexes and culture patterns, which constitute the dominant structure and characteristics of culture. Culture also has a spatial characteristic. Thus we find culture areas and smaller culture clusters known as culture islands.

Within every culture there are customary traits and complexes known as folkways. If these have acquired an ethical character and particularly regulate the conduct of people, we call these behavior traits and standards mores.

Culture is learned. It is transmitted from one generation to another. Transmission depends largely upon culture traits and complexes continuing to function in the lives of people, but obsolete traits, complexes, and culture lags may contine to be transmitted along with more usable ones for long periods of time.

One aspect of culture is usually related to another so that, inherently, it has some integration. The degree of integration is not uniform in a given culture and may vary from time to time.

Finally, another characteristic of culture is its adaptiveness, many culture traits and complexes being used for more than one purpose.

Culture grows out of the biological characteristics and drives of men, and through invention, innovation, cultural borrowing, and diffusion. Through these means man has developed in his culture from a period when no culture was found with his remains, through the Stone and Metal ages into the modern periods of science and technology.

21 U.S. Bureau of the Census, "Mobility of the Population of the United States, March 1957 to 1958," *Current Population Reports, Population Characteristics,* Series P-20, No. 85, October 13, 1958.

22 A. Albu, "Automation," *Political Quarterly,* **27:**250-59, July-September, 1956.

THINGS TO DO AND TO DISCUSS

1. Do an inventory of various concepts of culture, after which develop what is to you a satisfactory concept.
2. What are the three major elements of culture?
3. What is the distinction between culture trait, culture complex, and culture pattern?
4. Analyze your community and indicate major culture traits, complexes, and patterns.
5. What are the more important characteristics of culture?
6. How does culture develop? Give examples.
7. What were some of the leading culture traits, complexes, and patterns of the Upper Paleolithic period?
8. What was the earliest culture stage found in America? Describe it.
9. Characterize the Neolithic period of culture development.
10. Bring to the class for discussion any New Stone Age items you may have from the Indian cultures.
11. What great cultural developments took place during the Metal Ages?
12. What have been some of the important impacts of the scientific revolution upon American culture? Do you agree that most Americans are swamped by mass culture? If so, how can this dominance be eased?

FOR FURTHER STUDY

BENEDICT, RUTH. *Patterns of Culture*. New York: Penguin Books, 1946. The generalized role of culture in both primitive and advanced societies.

BOAS, FRANZ. *The Mind of Primitive Man*. New York: The Macmillan Co., 1938. How the mind of primitive man functioned.

BOWEN, ELENORE. *Return to Laughter*. New York: Harper and Bros., 1954. An anthropologist describes her experiences in Africa.

FIRTH, RAYMOND. *Social Change in Tikopia*. New York: The Macmillan Co., 1959. An excellent restudy showing the changes made in a Polynesian community after the lapse of a generation.

GASTER, THEODOR H., ed. *The New Golden Bough*. New York: Criterion Books, 1959. An abridgement of the classic work on unusual customs by Sir James George Frazer.

HERSKOVITS, MELVILLE J. *Man and His Works*. New York: Alfred A. Knopf, 1948. Solid discussion of the culture development, the similarities of different cultures, and the techniques of cultural research.

HOEBEL, E. ADAMSON. *Man in the Primitive World*. New York: McGraw-Hill Book Co., 1956. Description of primitive man and his culture.

KLUCKHOHN, CLYDE. *Mirror for Man*. New York: McGraw-Hill Book Co., 1949, reproduced by Fawcett World Library, New York, 1957. The relationship of anthropology to modern life.

KROEBER, A. L., and KLUCKHOHN, CLYDE. *Culture: A Critical Review of Concepts and Definitions*. Cambridge, Mass.: Peabody Museum of American Archaeology and Ethnology, Harvard University, 1952. Exhaustive review of the concepts and definitions of culture and related terms.

KRUTCH, JOSEPH WOOD. *Human Nature and the Human Condition*. New York: Random House, 1959. How mass culture runs counter to human nature.

LINTON, RALPH. *The Study of Man*. New York: Appleton-Century-Crofts, 1936. One of the best of the studies of the impact of culture upon man.

————. *The Tree of Culture*. New York. Alfred A. Knopf, 1955. The development of culture and culture complexes in various parts of the world.

MEAD, MARGARET. *An Anthropologist at Work: Writings of Ruth Benedict*. Boston, Houghton Mifflin Co., 1959. Eight published articles and five unpublished articles of Ruth Benedict.

MEAD, MARGARET, and COLAS, NICHOLAS. *Primitive Heritage*. New York: Random House, 1953. What we inherited from the primitives.

MERRILL, FRANCIS E. *Society and Culture*. Englewood Cliffs, N. J.: Prentice-Hall, 1957. Contains a good discussion of the American culture pattern.

SHAPIRO, HARRY L. *Man, Culture, and Society*. New York: Oxford University Press, 1956. An especially good series of chapters on culture stages, as well as on a variety of topics on culture.

SUMNER, WILLIAM G. *Folkways*. Boston: Ginn and Co., 1906. The classic study on folkways.

TITER, MISCHA. *Cultural Anthropology*. New York: Henry Holt and Co., 1959. General text for cultural anthropology courses.

WARNER, W. LLOYD. *The Living and the Dead: A Study of the Symbolic Life of Americans*. New Haven, Conn.: Yale University Press, 1959. The final volume of the "Yankee City Series," devoted to symbols and symbolism in American Life.

WHITE, LESLIE A. *The Evolution of Culture*. New York: McGraw-Hill Book Co., 1959. Culture development from civilization to the fall of Rome.

# 4. CULTURE VARIATION AND ITS CAUSES

IN THE LAST CHAPTER we discussed the nature, structure, and development of culture. We did not discuss in detail characteristics of the Metal Age cultures as we did previous stages in cultural development for the reason that the student of sociology gets from history and other sources much knowledge of recent stages or epochs in culture development. He knows, for instance, that the steam engine was the forerunner of the Industrial Revolution, and that the gasoline motor sparked the Motor Age. We did discuss, however, the impact of the revolution in scientific discovery and its application and some of the problems associated with the impact of science and its technological applications.

## CULTURE VARIATION AS A FACT

The term "culture variation" is used here in a broad sense. It is logical, but a bit unusual, for sociologists to speak of variations within a culture. Culture variation usually refers to differences between or among cultures, whereas such terms as "subculture" and "culture conflicts" may be used in referring to variations within a culture. In this chapter we have followed the logical course of not confining culture variations to differences between or among cultures. This simplifies the treatment of culture variation.

Anyone who has traveled is impressed with the differences in the cultural items of people, the differences in the technology of occupations and customs, behavior patterns, and value systems. One may leave a small town, which is used as a trade and service center, and drive 20 miles into the country where the basic occupation is agriculture. Most towns have their "gold coast" or best section, with its superior dwellings and other advantages, and an "across the tracks" section where the houses are of slum standard.

Patterns of settlement of people vary. Settlement patterns influence visitation and cooperation. The Mormon farmer in Utah lives in a compact village where he has his home, his

*Philip Gendreau, N.Y.*

*Patterns of settlement are cultural responses to a set of factors influencing settlement. Woodstock, Vermont, and a farm in Wisconsin, upper left and right,* ⟶

*Wide World Photos*

*J. I. Case Co., Racine, Wis.*

*have different cultural responses from those of New York and Los Angeles, lower left and right.*

*Wide World Photos*

storage facilities, and his tools. He assists his needy neighbors. The land he farms may be some distance from where he lives. In Iowa, the homestead and the farm are part of the same plot of earth. In Kansas, the wheat farms are large; in the Appalachian area they are small. The physical appearance of some cities is dense and compact; others are sprawling. Each pattern of settlement is a cultural response to a set of conditions influencing the pattern.

A rather simple culture gesture, usually a culture complex, is the way in which we extend a greeting to a friend or to a stranger. While the variations in our own culture are fairly obvious to us, the large number of variations in this commonplace behavior is described by Hiller.

Among the Wanyika, people meet by grasping hands and pressing their thumbs together; dwellers in the region of the Niger join their right hands and separate them with a pull so that a snapping noise is made by thumb and fingers. The handshake of the Arab seems to be a scuffle in which each tries to raise to his lips the hand of the other. The Ainus draw their hands from the shoulders and down the arms to the fingertips of the person greeted [in greeting a woman], or they rub their hands together. . . . Polynesians stroke their own faces with the other person's hands. . . . The Fuegians in saluting friends hug "like the grip of a bear." Some peoples greet by placing one arm around the neck of the person saluted and chucking him under the chin, or encircling his neck with their arms. . . . [Among the Ainus a distinction is made] in the manner of greeting appropriate for men and women . . . men rub their hands together, raise them to the forehead (palms up) and then rub the upper lip with the first finger of the right hand. . . . In some Eskimo tribes . . . the courteous way of greeting a stranger is to lick one's own hands, draw them first over one's own face and then over that of the visitor. . . . Among the Polynesians, Malays, Burmese, Mongols, the Lapps, and others—a usual salute is that of smelling each other's cheeks.[1]

[1] E. T. Hiller, *Principles of Sociology* (New York: Harper and Bros., 1933), pp. 101-2, 119.

Culture variation is reflected in the religions. The major religious faiths in the United States are Protestantism, Catholicism, and Judaism. There are, of course, followers of Buddhism, Confucianism, and other faiths. In the United States there are more than 265 different religious denominations, most of these within the Protestant faith. Perhaps these different denominations reflect greater differences in religious ideologies than they do in religious behavior. On some traits the denominations have almost a common ideology. For instance, most believe in a single Supreme God. This is called monotheism. Most of them will hold that Christ lived, that he died and rose from the dead, but on other points there will be wide variation. Some religious followers will not bear arms in military service, whereas most denominations permit their followers to do so. Interesting variations in baptismal and worship services also exist. Some denominations do not permit the use of musical instruments in their churches.

### Some variable features of culture universals

There are some culture traits and complexes which occur in all cultures. These are called *culture universals.*

No simple explanation of culture universals exists; however, the theories have been well explored.[2] One source of universal culture traits and complexes lies in the basic physical impulses or drives common to all people. Since these physical needs are common to people everywhere, ways and means of meeting them are similar. This leads to the satisfaction of the drives through certain acts or culture ways. If the culture ways give satisfaction to the physical impulse, then the culture ways tend to be repeated and thus become established.

Bronislaw Malinowski shows how the universal physical impulses in people lead to acts

[2] *See* George Peter Murdock, "The Common Denominator of Cultures," in *The Science of Man in the World Crisis,* ed. Ralph Linton (New York: Columbia University Press, 1945), pp. 123-42.

*Variations in Worship among Protestants. The snake handlers at the top belong to a Protestant sect. The Episcopal church choir in the lower picture shows wide variation in behavior from that of the chanters above.*

*Table 5*

PERMANENT VITAL SEQUENCES INCORPORATED
IN ALL CULTURES

| Impulse | Act | Satisfaction |
|---------|-----|--------------|
| Drive to breathe; gasping for air | Intake of oxygen | Elimination of $CO_2$ in tissues |
| Hunger | Ingestion of food | Satiation |
| Thirst | Absorption of liquid | Quenching |
| Sex appetite | Conjugation | Detumescence |
| Fatigue | Rest | Restoration of muscular and nervous energy |
| Restlessness | Activity | Satisfaction of fatigue |
| Somnolence | Sleep | Awakening with restored energy |
| Bladder pressure | Micturition | Removal of tension |
| Colon pressure | Defecation | Abdominal relaxation |
| Fright | Escape from danger | Relaxation |
| Pain | Avoidance by effective act | Return to normal state |

Source: Bronislaw Malinowski, *A Scientific Theory of Culture and Other Essays* (Chapel Hill, N. C.: University of North Carolina Press, 1944), p. 77.

which satisfy these impulses (Table 5). The impulses isolated by Malinowski furnish a kind of biological basis for culture which we briefly mentioned in the last chapter. A man has to eat, so he develops culture ways of satisfying his desire for food. He becomes fatigued, so he develops culture ways of getting rest.

The most extensive cataloguing in this country of the characteristics of different cultures is the *Cross Cultural Index* at Yale University. The characteristics of all known cultures are closely analyzed and an intricate system of cross indexing has been established.

One of the problems that George Peter Murdock, an anthropologist, has given attention to to is the subject of culture universals. On the basis of his examination of the *Cross Cultural Index* files, he arrives at a partial list of cultural universals. He says:

The following is a partial list of items, arranged in alphabetical order to emphasize their variety, which occur, so far as the author's knowledge goes, in every culture known to history or ethnography; age-grading, athletic sports, bodily adornment, calendar, cleanliness training, community organization, cooking, cooperative labor, cosmology, courtship, dancing, decorative art, divination, division of labor, dream interpretation, education, eschatology,* ethics, ethnobotany,† etiquette, faith healing, family, feasting, fire making, folklore, food taboos, funeral rites, games, gestures, gift giving, government, greetings, hair styles, hospitality, housing, hygiene, incest taboos, inheritance rules, joking, kin-groups, kinship nomenclature, language, law, luck superstitions, magic, marriage, mealtimes, medicine, modesty concerning natural functions,

* Theory of death and the future state after death.
† The belief that certain plants are peculiarly identified with the welfare of the group.

mourning, music, mythology, numerals, obstetrics, penal sanctions, personal names, population policy, postnatal care, pregnancy usages, property rights, propitiation of supernatural beings, puberty customs, religious ritual, residence rules, sexual restrictions, soul concepts, status differentiation, surgery, tool making, trade, visiting, weaning, and weather control.[3]

Let us examine one or two of the basic needs of man and also some of the culture universals designed to satisfy these needs and variable features. A technology for obtaining food is a human requirement. Cooking is a universal complex, according to Murdock; so are food taboos, certain established times for meals, and a division of labor to prepare the meals. Food-producing and -preserving techniques vary greatly. Some people follow the grazing of herds; others grow farm crops. People who work in urban industries exchange their labor for money, which they in turn exchange for food. There is wide variation in cooking. As a rule women prepare food. This is the age of French fry, or deep fry, in America. The French sauté or shallow fry their foods. Food taboos, although universal, admit of great variations. Some people are vegetarians. Some cultures do not eat pork, only poultry, fish, and beef. Some groups enforce their food taboos throughout the year, while others enforce them only on special days of the year.

Drinking patterns vary greatly from culture to culture. American visitors to France and Italy often speak of the prevalence of drinking, especially the consumption of wines at meals, yet they almost invariably point out the scarcity of drunkards. Among the Russian Aleuts the drinking of *piva,* a form of home brew, is common. Drinking is usually indulged in at parties rather than in solitude. Much of it is done to "celebrate," and often with the intention of becoming intoxicated, which obviously is not the case with the French or Italians.[4]

Among the Galla of East Africa the native religion is based on animism with some concept of the hereafter. Funeral festivals are elaborate, and the mourning of the dead may be extended up to four months after the deceased has departed.[5]

Another interesting culture universal is *status differentiation.* All cultures have a rank and status system. A simple community may have an upper class, and a lower class that works for the upper class. Industrial or complex urban communities are likely to have from three to six classes. In general, the middle class in a society expands with industrialization.

For many centuries a caste system was an integral part of the Indian culture. One was born into his or her caste position and could escape from it only with great difficulty. The system was endorsed and reinforced by the prevailing mores and laws. Caste position entered strongly into friendship and economic patterns in some Hindu tribes.[6] Although some legal disabilities of caste were abolished by the new national constitution in 1946, and caste as a requirement for a valid marriage was abolished in 1955, it is still socially effective, being perhaps most noticeable in the division of labor and marriage.

On the other hand, the United States, in the founding documents establishing its form of government, abolished any system of caste, royalties, and titles. Some hold that the American Negro is a victim of an American caste system, is discriminated against, and is denied certain privileges solely because he is a Negro. These are earmarks of a caste system, although the Negro's lower-status position is not supported by the mores, such as equality of opportunity, or by such legal documents as the Bill of Rights. In the deep South subculture

[3] *Ibid.,* p. 124.
[4] Gerald D. Berreman, "Drinking Patterns of the Aleuts," *Quarterly Journal of Studies on Alcohol,* 17:503-14, 1956.
[5] Cornelius J. Jaenen, "The Galla or Oromo of East Africa," *Southwestern Journal of Anthropology,* 12:171-90, 1956.
[6] B. N. Bandhopadhyay, "Ceremonial Friendship among the Bhumji of Manbhum," *Man in India,* 35:274-86, October-December, 1955. *See also* the chapter on Stratification.

the mores do support the inferior status of the Negro, as do Jim Crow laws.

### The development of culture ethnocentrism

Cultures vary widely not only in material traits and behavior patterns, but also in the importance they attach to their own culture and other cultures. For instance, Alaskans and Texans are kidded a lot about their states. The absence of ethnocentrism is not a trait of either. A humorous sketch of how a Texan views his state in relation to others is shown below. The tendency to scale or evaluate other cultures in terms of the characteristics of one's own culture or to overrate one's culture in comparison to others is called *culture ethnocentrism*. This tendency to view one's

own culture as the center of everything is common in preliterate as well as literate societies. When Caribs were asked whence they came, they answered, "We alone are people." The meaning of the name "Kiowa" is "real or principal people." The Lapps call themselves "men" or "human beings." The Greenland Eskimos think that Europeans have been sent to Greenland to learn virtues and good manners from the Greenlanders. Their highest form of praise for a European is that he is, or soon will be, as good as a Greenlander. The Tunguses call themselves "men." As a rule it is found that nature people call themselves "men." Others are something else—perhaps not defined, but not real men.[7]

[7] William G. Sumner, *Folkways* (Boston: Ginn and Co., 1906), pp. 13-14.

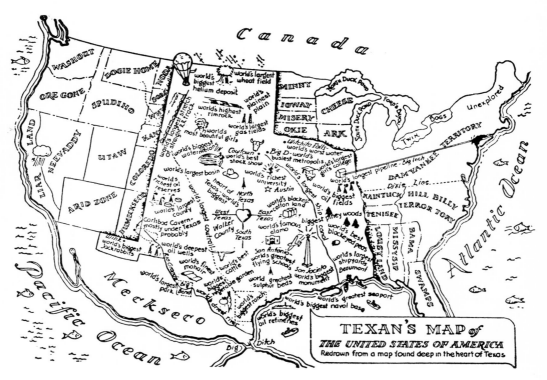

*A Texan's View of Texas and the Rest of the U.S.*

SOURCE: Robert L. Sutherland, Julian L. Woodward, and Milton A. Maxwell, *Introductory Sociology* (4th ed.; Philadelphia: J. B. Lippincott Co., 1952), p. 19. Reproduced by permission of the publisher.

*How the American tourist abroad looks to the British cartoonist Ronald Searle.*

SOURCE: Robert Coughlaw, "How We Appear to Others," *Life*, 43:152, December 23, 1957. Reproduced by permission of the artist.

All cultures are ethnocentric. Ethnocentrism is usually one outgrowth of socialization. A moderate degree of ethnocentrism gives an element of stability and integration to a culture. Pride in one's culture, unless carried to excess, is a good thing because it tends to strengthen identification of people with their culture and with those who share the culture.

The empirical student of sociology seeks to avoid excessive ethnocentrism. Just because a culture is different from our own is no reason for us to hold that it is inferior. Ethnocentrism is even worse when it holds other people in a caste or class position, or limits their opportunity to develop and function in education, economic life, politics, religion, and recreation.

Ethnocentric tendencies develop naturally. We are taught to believe in a culture by people who also believe in it. These same people may have developed a high degree of ethnocentrism. The Englishman may have been taught that he is superior to the Scotch and to the Irish. The white man may have been taught that he is superior to nonwhites, and the nonwhites that they are superior to the whites. These beliefs are then transmitted through learning from aduts to children and from one peer group to another.

A culture that has gained its dominance under a given set of conditions may continue its ethnocentric beliefs, which are invariably a part of dominance, after conditions change. Slavery in the South is an example of this. Ethnocentrism, and many of the patterns of behavior associated with slavery, such as segregation and discrimination, have continued to exist in the subculture of the South for more than 90 years after the abolishment of slavery. This is a good illustration of how social lags may continue long after legal corrections have been instituted in the basic laws.

Ignorance of a culture may be a cause of ethnocentric attitudes. We may judge a whole culture by a single contact with it or with a representative of it. For instance, when the author was served a poor meal in a Georgia town, he found himself expressing the opinion that the place was a "lousy" town. A mountain man stopped cutting corn for a moment to exclaim to the author "You know what's wrong with the world—Catholics." Actually there were no Catholics in the community, and it is doubtful if the man had ever known a Catholic. He had perhaps read some attack on Catholics in one of the religious tracts of the sect of which he was a member. These, then, are some of the ways in which we develop culture ethnocentrism.

## SOME CAUSES OF CULTURE VARIABILITY

It is not necessary in a sociology text to list all the causes of culture variation; therefore, we shall be content with only a few.

### Biological causes

Within a race or within a culture, a community, or even a group like a family, biological differences in people account for culture variations. First of all, we might mention *sex* differences. Among all people there are divisions of labor between the sexes. In all cultures women bear children and attend to them after birth. Another basis for culture differences is *age*. The young will play more than the aged and at different games. In most sports the young and the middle-aged excel. There are also wide differences in the potential and developed capacities of a population. Idiots cannot master a language, whereas those of high I.Q. may master the technical details of complicated sciences or highly theoretical systems of thought. We do not know as much as we should about the hereditarily oriented aptitude differences of races. We do know that there are differences in the aptitudes of representatives of races. Whether these are culturally acquired or have a firm biological base we are not sure. Controlled experiments to determine the facts are difficult to establish.

## Geographic influences and natural resources

There was at one time a theory that geography determined culture. This theory was known as *geographical determinism* and was advanced especially by the human geographers. A more acceptable position is that geographical factors influence or condition the culture of a people. As an illustration, the soil of Idaho, plus rainfall and temperature factors, would not necessarily make it a potato-producing state. Men would finally determine what would be grown there. The soil of Idaho is rich enough to produce cotton, but the climate is too cold. On the other hand, the Mississippi Delta, while excellent for cotton, would not produce good apples or pears.

The faulting of iron-ore deposits, limestone, and coal at the end of the Appalachian Range greatly increased the chance that Birmingham, Alabama, might become an iron-producing and steel-manufacturing center, but would not necessarily determine it. Men had finally to make the decision, which they did. So above the city of Birmingham stands the iron statue of Vulcan as a symbol of the city's metal industry.

Climate affects what we wear. It also influences sports and recreation. The sunshine cities of Florida would naturally develop water sports, whereas Lake Placid, New York, would go in strongly for winter sports.

Geographical factors, especially temperatures, rainfall, soil, topography, and wind currents, influence the plant and animal life of an area. Man, of course, later disturbed the flora and fauna as he felled the forests and killed the game.

The Plains Indians developed their culture largely around the hunting of the buffalo, which lived on the lush grass of the prairies. Buffalo hides became standard material in the construction of tepees and clothing. As the horse became available it was widely used in buffalo hunts.

The Northwest Coast Indians lived in the forests and along the streams. They utilized tree trunks for totem poles and canoes, and made houses of bark and slabs of timber. They fished streams and lived on game from the forests. They had a rich ceremonial life, aided, in part, by the mystery and solitude of the forests. They worshiped the totem animals which had been friendly and useful to them.

Across Canada ranged the caribou herds, hunted by the Caribou Indians. The Indians moved as the herds moved. They roasted their meat in boxes improvised from birch bark. The caribou was fairly easily domesticated, and was commonly used to drag wooden sleds along the ground. To the north lived the Eskimo in ice houses, collecting his food from the ice packs and from open water.

Finally, in the Southeast, where there was adequate rainfall, the Woodlands Indians developed a culture around hunting and fishing and the use of maize. Large shell deposits indicate the use of river mussels. Evidence of stockade structures used for ceremonies and protection is found today in archaeological excavations.

## Time factors

Time factors are important in culture variation. As we said earlier, culture tends to accumulate. All things considered, traditions and customs tend to pile up as a culture becomes older. This perhaps is one reason why European cultures and older churches have a richer ritual and ceremonial life than newer cultures like those of the United States and Canada.

Changing moods of the times reflect variations in culture. During the depression of the 1930's, when some 12 million men were out of work, there was an avalanche of social legislation, spearheaded by passage of the Social Security Act and the entrance of the federal government into the field of public housing and regional development.

Changing moods of a people also are reflected in their music tastes. Prior to World War II and for sometime during the war, military music was at its peak. As the war

*Examples of Culture Variation in Housing Developed by Different Indian Tribes——→*

*Courtesy of the American Museum of Natural History*

*Courtesy of the American Museum of Natural History*

*(upper left) Northern Arapaho tepee; (lower left) Ojibway Indian bark house; (upper right) Walpi Pueblo; (lower right) Seminole Indian thatched-roof house.*

ended, soft romantic songs and ballads seemed to take over. By 1947, country songs and ballads became popular, and in the 1950's rock 'n' roll developed under the gyrating hips and the thumbed guitar of a young Memphian named Elvis Presley.

## Cultural factors

Culture produces culture. Variations in cultural attitudes cannot be separated from the time factors. Important is the attitude toward inventors and innovators. If inventors were imprisoned and innovators burned at the stake, culture variability would lessen under the impact of a stalemated culture. Even under these conditions it would not disappear. Where the culture encourages, accepts, and rewards the inventor and the innovator, culture tends to grow in volume and amount of variability.

We feel that our democratic ideology is conducive to the development of new and variable culture traits and complexes. This is so because we put much emphasis upon each individual's contribution to the total American culture. Our ideology stresses individual development and, as a rule, rewards individual contributions. The nation is also large and has variable resources from which to develop a variable culture. We have people of many races and religions who contribute to this culture.

Within the American culture there are plenty of illustrations of communities, groups, and institutions where some new culture traits, complexes, and patterns are not wanted and are not welcome. Tradition and precedent hang heavy in such situations. Community and institutional lag is a fact. Even the lags make for variability because all groups and institutions do not stand still.

One of the most interesting subcultures which has been able to maintain many of its peculiar characteristics in spite of the rapidly changing surrounding cultures is that of the Old Order Amish. Although there are Amish subcultures in Ohio, Illinois, Indiana, Michigan, and Pennsylvania, we shall limit our discussion to that of the Old Order Amish of Lancaster County, Pennsylvania.[8]

The Old Order Amish date back to the Swiss Brethren, who came into existence during the Zwinglian Reformation after 1520. Since that time, because of their nonconforming beliefs and customs, such as opposition to war, slavery, and interest in money, they have been threatened, imprisoned, murdered, and dispossessed of their lands. The ancestors of the Pennsylvania Amish of course came to this country to escape religious persecution and to find farm lands suitable for settlement. They were settled in Pennsylvania prior to 1757. The Old Order Amish are by tradition and religious devotion tied to the land, and it is only in a rural life setting that their nonconforming beliefs and practices can be maintained.

Culturally, the Old Order Amish are considered peculiar by themselves and by others. They take pride in this peculiarity. Their nonconformity is based on their belief that God's people are peculiar and that they are nonconformists (Tit. 2:11-14 and Rom. 12:2).

The Amish men have long hair, with bangs across the forehead. They part their hair in the middle. The unmarried men shave. Married men wear beards but no mustache, since the mustache in Europe was often worn by soldiers and the Amish do not believe in service in the armed forces. Much of the outer clothing is homemade. Men wear simple trousers held in place by plain suspenders. Buttons are not worn on coats since they, too, were the mark of the soldier's uniform. Men's dress coats have no lapels or outer pockets. They wear broad, flat, black hats in winter and flat straw hats in summer.

The dress of Amish women is likewise simple. They wear solid-color clothing. Aprons are worn; those of the married women match their dresses, and those of unmarried women

8 Walter M. Kollmorgen, *Culture of a Contemporary Rural Community: The Old Order Amish of Lancaster County, Pennsylvania*, Rural Life Series No. 4 (Washington, D.C.: U.S. Department of Agriculture, September, 1952).

*The preservation of the old and interesting in a culture is important. Obsolete things still have their beauty and their value.*

are white. The cutting and curling of hair is taboo, as are hair ornaments. Braided hair is the favorite hairdo of the unmarried girls. Jewelry and perfumes may not be worn. Girls and women wear head coverings which have a religious, devotional significance, and also homemade bonnets. A cardinal sin is pride, however it may be manifested.

Although these restrictions are now relaxed to some degree, the Amish are forbidden to own automobiles, telephones, radios, television sets, musical instruments, and storybooks of non-Biblical character. Tractors may be owned but for years their use was limited to belt-power operations. The buggy and wagon are the favorite means of transportation. The young men drive open-top buggies and married men closed-top buggies. The use of buggy whips is forbidden. Invariably the buggies are painted black or dark gray. The rationalization on forbidding the home use of telephones

is interesting. It is based largely on the fact that the men say the women of the home would waste time talking to neighbors about what they were going to do and what they were going to wear. Such conversation is worldly and such waste of time is sinful. To facilitate the use of the telephone, especially for business purposes, pay stations are provided in communities.

Schools are simple, with school consolidation receiving much resistance. School programs are simple, with strong belief in the three R's. The morals of the young are supposed to be injured by exposure to higher education.

One may vote but there are limitations to the public offices one may hold. One must refuse to bear arms or to go to war.

Weddings are social events with elaborate feasts. After marriage one may not continue to participate in the Sunday night singings of the young people. Families are becoming smaller, which is some indication that the present-day Amish practice birth control. Separation and divorce are unknown. Marriage with outsiders is prohibited.

Unlike non-Amish communities with their large number of organizations, the Amish tend to limit organization both within and outside their church. Business partnerships are usually limited to the Amish.

In the church, bishops, ministers, and deacons are chosen by lot. Footwashing is prescribed and observed. Pictures and photographs are forbidden in admonition to Exodus 20:4: "Thou shalt not make unto thee any graven image." Even in death there is nonconformity in that simple funerals and simple caskets, many of them homemade, honor the dead. There are no funeral flowers. The gravestones of the Amish are as simple as their funeral services.

Commercial recreation is frowned upon by the Amish and is prohibited by the church. The visitation of relatives with each other is a favorite form of recreation. The young people attend singings on Sunday evenings, which give them a much-sought opportunity for pairing. The Sabbath is strictly observed, with only chores being done. Other work is prohibited. Business transactions on Sunday are also prohibited.

Mutual aid in time of stress or need reaches a high order among the Amish, who generally oppose insurance. The people also aid each other during the planting and harvesting season. Barnbuilding is a community activity in which the wives prepare the food while the men work to build a barn. It is not unusual for a barn to be constructed in a day or so.

One may ask how the Amish are able to maintain their distinctiveness surrounded by other cultures. There is a long historical and traditional basis for their differences, and pride in their nonconformity. Such nonconformity also has a religious basis. There is careful training or socialization in nonconformity from birth. Until recently Amish communities were pretty much self-contained and had limited contact with non-Amish communities. This isolation aided them in maintaining their peculiarities. Contact now, especially of the young, is much greater than formerly. There is, finally, the fear and threat of being excommunicated by the church if one fails to conform. John Umble gives an account of an Amish meeting in Union County, Pennsylvania, in which several members were excommunicated. He says of the meeting:

The excommunication of members was an awful and a solemn procedure. The members to be expelled had been notified in advance and were absent. An air of tenseness filled the house. Sad-faced women wept quietly; stern men sat with faces drawn. The bishop arose; with trembling voice and with tears on his cheeks he announced that the guilty parties had confessed their sin, that they were cast off from the fellowship of the church and committed to the devil and all of his angels.[9]

## SOME FEATURES OF THE AMERICAN CULTURE AS AN EXAMPLE OF VARIABILITY

The factors which influence variability in the American culture, or any other culture, we have just discussed. We have said that the American culture is favorable to the development of new and variable culture ways and wide sharing in the culture.

The impact of the total geographical setting of the United States, the way the country was settled, the principles under which it was founded, and the recentness of the centuries in which it has developed, have collectively meshed to give us a culture unlike any other in degree of emphasis upon certain culture traits, complexes, and patterns. These we shall now discuss.

[9] John Umble, "The Amish Mennonites of Union County, Pennsylvania," *Mennonite Quarterly Review,* 7:92, 1933.

Authorities are not in agreement on the major features of the American culture—some saying that we do not have a single culture but many cultures. Robert S. Lynd characterizes the American culture as follows: [10]

1. It is casual.
2. It is uneven.
3. It is unequal.
4. The pattern is basically urban.
5. It is oriented toward the future.
6. It is youth-centered.
7. It is increasingly a mass pattern.

Other scholars indicate that the American culture places a great emphasis upon conformity; that most Americans operate on the principle that human nature is good and is capable of being improved; that on the whole people believe man and nature in America are in cooperation with each other. In the end we believe that nature can be mastered. American culture has a practical rather than a theoretical orientation. Its time dimension is oriented to the future. It places much emphasis upon personality and physical comfort, and lays stress upon individual initiative, independence, and freedom.[11]

In addition to the traits, complexes, and cultural orientation, or emphasis, indicated above, the mobility of the American people is certainly one of the features of their culture. This mobility is of two kinds: movement from place to place, which we discussed briefly in the last chapter, and mobility up and down the social scale. A similar characteristic is the great emphasis upon communication and the prevalence of mass media of communication. Only one in every four Americans reads books. The Englishman is likely to read more widely, although the American is likely to have more reading materials readily available. He also has available more telephones, television sets, and radios per unit of population than any other major country in the world.

Any culture oriented to a democratic ideology is likely to place much emphasis upon the freedoms associated with this ideology. This we do in the American culture. We attach much importance to freedom of religion, freedom of speech, freedom of the press, and freedom to engage in economic activity. Many culture traits and complexes revolve around these ideologies.

The cultural characteristics of a society influence the decision-making of the people. Especially do the value systems supported by the people and espoused by the society influence their decisions. While decision-making, even by representative bodies of the people, reflects many conflicts and contradictions, the following elements in the value systems of Americans are likely to be reflected in their decisions: (1) the recognition of an individual's worth; (2) the quest for economic well being; (3) the improvement of education and physical and mental health; (4) cooperation in the solution of problems, and (5) an emphasis upon spiritual and moral guidance.

## SUMMARY

The central purpose of this chapter has been to discuss certain uniformities in culture, to show how these develop, and to indicate some major causes and forms of variations in culture. Attention has been given to the development of ethnocentrism as a cause and example of cultural variability. We have discussed in some detail the causes of cultural variability. Finally, we have discussed some of the outstanding features of the American culture as an example of how the major orientations of one culture may differ from those of another.

[10] Robert S. Lynd, *Knowledge for What?* (Princeton, N. J.: Princeton University Press, 1939), Chap. 3.
[11] *See* Arnold Green, *Sociology* (New York: McGraw-Hill Book Co., 1956), pp. 97-105.

THINGS TO DO AND TO DISCUSS

1.  What are some of the more important subcultures showing variations in the national culture of the United States?
2.  What are culture universals? How do you account for them?
3.  Within certain universal culture complexes, show how cultural differences exist.
4.  What is meant by culture ethnocentrism? Give examples.
5.  How do ethnocentric tendencies develop? Give examples of ethnocentrism in your community. Is ethnocentrism always bad?
6.  What are some of the major causes of culture variations?
7.  What would you say are some of the major culture orientations or characteristics of the American culture?
8.  How do cultural characteristics influence the decisions made by people?

FOR FURTHER STUDY

BEALS, RALPH L., and HOIJER, HARRY. *An Introduction to Anthropology.* New York: The Macmillan Co., 1959. Contains many excellent illustrations of culture variability.

BENEDICT, RUTH. *Patterns of Culture.* Boston: Houghton Mifflin Co., 1934. Excellent examples of culture variability.

BIERSTEDT, ROBERT. *The Social Order.* New York: McGraw-Hill Book Co., 1957. Good basic treatment of culture and its variations.

GERTH, HANS, and MILLS, C. WRIGHT. *Character and Social Structure.* New York: Harcourt, Brace and Co., 1953. The impact of social structure upon personality development.

HONIGMANN, JOHN J. *Culture and Personality.* New York: Harper and Bros., 1954. How culture influences personality.

LINTON, RALPH. *The Tree of Culture.* New York: Alfred A. Knopf, 1955. Excellent treatment of cultural variability and its causes.

MALINOWSKI, BRONISLAW. *A Scientific Theory of Culture and Other Essays.* Chapel Hill, N. C.: University of North Carolina Press, 1944. Excellent treatment of cultural universals.

MURDOCK, GEORGE PETER. "The Common Denominator of Cultures." *The Science of Man in the World Crisis,* ed. RALPH LINTON. New York: Columbia University Press, 1944. Culture universals common to all societies.

PIDDINGTON, RALPH. *An Introduction to Social Anthropology.* New York: The Macmillan Co., Vol. I, 1950; Vol. II, 1957. Excellent general treatment of culture.

SERVICE, ELMAN R. *A Profile of Primitive Culture.* New York: Harper and Bros., 1958. Content and variability in primitive cultures.

SHAPIRO, HARRY L. *Man, Culture, and Society.* New York: Oxford University Press, 1956. Good chapters on culture and its variabilities.

UNDERHILL, RUTH MURRAY. *Red Man's America.* Chicago: University of Chicago Press, 1953. Variability in America's Indian cultures and discussion of the major ones.

# 5. THE DEVELOPMENT OF SOCIETIES

FOUR BASIC CONCEPTS in sociology are inter-action, society, culture, and personality. The concepts of interaction and culture we have already considered in some detail. At this point we shall give attention to the concept of society and how societies developed. In later chapters we shall discuss personality development.

## THE MEANING OF SOCIETY

Our concern in this chapter is primarily with human societies, although the characteristics of insect and mammalian societies have some similarities to human societies.

The *human aggregation* is a collection of individuals brought together and maintained because of some external stimulus or condition. A bright light may attract and maintain an aggregation of insects. When the light is extinguished the aggregation disperses. All societies, as Davis indicates, have certain things in common which differentiate them from aggregations.[1] Societies involve levels of associa-tion and interaction which are closer and more intricate than mere aggregations. In aggregations responses are made to outside stimuli. When responses begin to be made by the individual units in the animal or human grouping to each other, and one helps the other to satisfy his drives and desires, the basis for a society begins. For example, in wasp societies the wasp larvae secrete a sweet fluid sucked by feeder wasps who feed the larvae. Mutual stimulation alone in a grouping does not within itself constitute a society. This might exist in a mob. A system of relationships which has durability is a characteristic of a society. In human societies the system of relationships recognizes individual units as persons rather than just as units. In this relationship the per-

[1] Kingsley Davis, *Human Society* (New York: The Macmillan Co., 1949), pp. 24-51. *See also* Marshall D. Sahlins, "The Origin of Society," *Scientific American*, **203**: 76, 1960.

son has a status and a responding personality to which the other units are responsive.

Animal aggregations and animal societies are held together by biological drives and inherited mechanisms, altered to some degree by the food supply and learned adaptation associated with obtaining food. Human societies have essentially cultural and psychological bases. Status and authority in such society is culturally and not biologically based.

In human societies sexuality and constant association of the sexes is present, which is not generally true in animal societies. The role of symbolism and social norms controlling behavior is strong in human societies and not in animal societies. As Davis points out, normative control in human societies is possible because individuals are responsive to others.

Another characteristic of human societies is the extent to which the members cooperate in maintaining themselves, in perpetuating their society, and in providing for their continuity. In composition, human societies are made up of men, women, and children. Societal groupings are basically large-scale, the size being determined by whether the society is community, state, national, and so on.

The territory occupied by a society is recognized and the people have a sense of belonging to it. The limits of territory may be only generally defined. National, state, community, and neighborhood societies have rather definite territories. Culture societies, such as the Navajo, may cut across two or more states, sometimes across national boundary lines, and their consciousness of kind may create international problems. The French world is not all under the French flag; neither is the Arab culture society limited to a single nation.

A society also has a web of culture common traits, values, complexes, and patterns running through it to give it added unity. We discussed some of the common elements in the previous chapter. This alone again is not a test of a society; the United States and England may have more common culture elements than New York and the Deep South.

It is not easy, from the above discussion, to form a simple definition of society. Such definitions, however, have been attempted. For example, Linton states: "A *society* is any group of people who have lived and worked together long enough to get themselves organized and to think of themselves as a social unit with defined limits." [2] To MacIver society means "a system of ordered relations." [3] To Herskovits a society is "the organized aggregate of individuals who follow a given way of life." [4] In all of these concepts, the idea of society as a social system and as a system of long-established relationships is emphasized. Society is more than just a group of people; it is a system of ordered relationships with the qualities we have pointed out above.

## THE SOURCES OF GREGARIOUSNESS

A troublesome and controversial problem is how people came to organize themselves to live and to work together. The answer to this question is a bit clouded. Anthropology and archaeology give us evidence of groupings but not the reasons for them. We must, therefore, rely upon the psychologist and the sociologist for an explanation of social groupings, and for knowledge of the integration of these groupings into larger social systems, called societies. The contribution of the social anthropologist also enhances our concept of society.

### The instinct theory

Professor Franklin Giddings made famous a theory of social grouping which he called "the consciousness of kind." By this he meant there is a tendency for people to seek out persons of their own kind and establish relatively durable

[2] Ralph Linton, *The Study of Man* (New York: Appleton-Century-Crofts, 1936), p. 91.

[3] R. M. MacIver, *The Web of Government* (New York: The Macmillan Co., 1947), p. 22.

[4] Melville J. Herskovits, *Man and His Works* (New York: Alfred A. Knopf, 1948), p. 29.

social relationships with them. This is essentially what we mean by gregariousness. *Gregariousness is the desire or tendency of people to want to be with other people, and particularly people of their own kind.*

The cultural emphasis upon gregariousness and the degree of gregariousness varies greatly from place to place and under different conditions. In simple rural communities made up of a few family lines, the gregarious tendency may be very strong, almost clanlike. On the other hand, in large cities people may cherish whatever anonymity and isolation they can get. Away from their jobs they may almost seek to avoid gregariousness.

The gregarious nature of human beings is shown by the fact that most people are fearful of solitude and are unhappy with it. They are sensitive to the attitudes and responses of members of their social systems—the group, the community, and the public at local, state, and national levels. Most children and adults are unhappy when not accepted by groups of their kind, and achieve, by devious methods, ways and means of being recognized. Isolation from one's fellows, particularly where nonvoluntary, becomes intolerable.

Gregarious behavior would be easy to explain if we knew for sure that there were a definite innate instinct or drive to be with others.

W. D. Trotter, a psychologist, took the position that there was a gregarious instinct, as did other psychologists of his time. Trotter held that there were four instincts: gregariousness, self-preservation, the desire for nutrition, and sex. In the following statement he emphasizes the importance of what he called the gregarious instinct. He says:

The only medium in which man's mind can function satisfactorily is the herd, which therefore is not only the source of his opinions, his credulities, his disbeliefs, and his weaknesses, but of his altruism, his charity, his enthusiasms, and his power.[5]

[5] W. D. Trotter, *Instincts of the Herd in Peace and War* (London: Allen and Unwin, 1919), p. 47.

Some scholars attempt to explain gregariousness by linking it with gregariousness in the animal world where the grouping tendency is strong among both animals and insects. Even here mammal pairing is common, and it is not unusual to find mammals like tigers and the higher apes living not in herds but singly and in pairs.

Studies have shown that lambs[6] and monkeys, reared in isolation and then brought together, show little tendency to form integrated groups. In commenting upon his investigation with monkeys reared in isolation and then brought together, one investigator says: "They have not been socialized, i.e., they have not learned to make fitting responses to each other as complexes of stimuli."[7]

The animal psychologists show species both with and without gregarious tendencies. The results of their work would appear to show a greater influence of learning in the development of gregarious tendencies among animals used in research than we have commonly supposed. After reviewing the works on theories of instinct, and upon the development of gregarious tendencies in research animals, Otto Klineberg comes to the following conclusion:

The second criterion, namely that of a known physiological basis for the drive, is not satisfied in the case of gregariousness. It may be that further research will someday uncover such a foundation, but that is unlikely. In the light of our present knowledge of physiology it is difficult to conceive of a neurological or endocrine pattern which would directly lead to gregarious activity. It is possible, however, that in the early experiences of the child the faces and persons of adults have a high stimulus value, partly because they actually constitute a large part of the environment and partly also because they are related to the satisfaction of fundamental needs. This might represent a very indirect physiological basis, not in the

[6] J. P. Scott, "Social Behavior, Organization, and Leadership in a Small Flock of Domestic Sheep," *Comparative Psychology Monographs,* 18:1-29, 1945.
[7] C. R. Carpenter, "Characteristics of Social Behavior in Non-human Primates," *Transactions of the New York Academy of Sciences,* 4:Series II; 248-58, 1942.

form of a visceral or tissue need, but determined by the perceptual primacy of other human beings.[8]

Another psychologist summarizes his position on the development of gregariousness as follows:

Though it is often described as an instinct, gregariousness probably is not a basically unlearned urge—it arises from a complex of needs. Sheep flock together, for example, for protection and warmth. Animals live and travel in groups because habits of group behavior are built up early in life. The need for security, sympathy, and understanding is certainly important in human gregariousness, as well as the need for the approval of the group to which one belongs.[9]

On the basis then of research to date, sociology must reject the theory that human beings have a gregarious instinct. Sociology does accept the theory that the gregarious tendency is learned and that it begins with the dependence of the young infant upon the mother. Gregariousness is no doubt made up of several drives or quasi drives, such as fear, curiosity, sex, and the wish for new experiences.[10] There is a theory that the social system we call "the family" originated out of this association.

### Other possible explanations

Within the framework of learning there would seem to be many ways in which gregariousness is developed.

As we have just stated, an important linkage in the gregarious learning pattern is the mother-child linkage. The child is born helpless, and must rely upon the mother or mother substitute for food, clothing, shelter, and attention to keep him alive. There is then built

up from birth a stimulus-response pattern from which the child derives pleasure. The child then becomes conditioned to the presence of others and the gregarious tendency becomes established. In each new generation the culture perpetuates this pattern of learning all over again.

The ill effects of family and intratribal incest, which is the prohibited mating of the close of kin, without a doubt led to the establishment of incest taboos in most societies, the Egyptians of the Cleopatra era excepted. These taboos forced people to make contacts outside their families and kin groups. Such taboos would necessarily lead to the extension of friendly contacts with other families and tribes. Culture systems would, of course, continue to enforce the interaction patterns against incest in marriage, as they do today.

Likewise, endogamous marriage patterns, requiring persons to marry within certain defined groups, such as caste, racial, religious, and occupational groupings, would tend to increase contacts and interaction in these prescribed groups. Such endogamous requirements would give a depth element to interaction patterns even though they are restrictive in discouraging a wide range of contacts or relationships.

When once people recognize the advantages of working and living together, they necessarily tend to perpetuate gregarious patterns through their culture. Malinowski believes that such patterns of cooperation, and the pleasantness of them, develop out of family bonds and the extension of these bonds.[11]

Around simple acts of satisfying basic needs we learn patterns of behavior which not only involve the physical satisfaction of hunger, sex, and other elemental needs, but also relations of pleasant companionship with others. As an illustration, when a person becomes hungry a physical tension develops in his stomach. The satisfaction of this hunger requires not only food, but also physical and

[8] Otto Klineberg, *Social Psychology* (Rev. ed.; New York: Henry Holt and Co., 1954), pp. 157-58.

[9] Henry E. Garrett, *General Psychology* (New York: American Book Co., 1955), pp. 262-63.

[10] Perhaps Luther Lee Bernard's *Instinct* (New York: Henry Holt and Co., 1924) did as much as any other work to eliminate the use of the word "instinct" among sociologists.

[11] Bronislaw Malinowski, *The Father in Primitive Psychology* (New York: W. W. Norton and Co., 1927).

*The above illustration shows how a culture complex, with some gregarious elements, becomes a part of the process of eating a meal.*

social components which make the culture complex of eating a convenient and pleasant occasion.

Specialization in our present society both discourages and encourages gregarious tendencies in people. Specialized groups, for instance botanists, chemists, physicists, or neurosurgeons, develop a "consciousness of kind" with each other and with their profession. They exchange information, correspond with each other, have annual meetings, lunch together, and read the professional journals representing their particular professions. Thus gregariousness develops in depth within a professional group. This very specialization may act as a barrier to association and understanding outside one's profession or groups. A specialist in mushrooms may have international contacts with other mushroom collectors and classifiers, but may not know intimately a single person who serves on the city council in the community where he lives.

The interdependence of one specialty upon another may require gregarious relationships outside one's own craft. Most people make their living by working for other people. This means that satisfactory working relationships must be established with other people, both their coworkers and supervisors. Relationships and "connections" with other groups are established. Many of these become friendly and intimate and represent gregariousness of people of unlike, but related, interests at their best. Excellent illustrations are found in the weekly civic clubs like Rotary, Kiwanis, Civitan, Lions, and Exchange.

## THE FORMATION OF LARGER SOCIAL GROUPINGS

One of the next problems relating to the development of society is the development of larger social units. By this we mean the development of groups of size larger than the family.

### The two universal groupings

Competent anthropologists tell us that there are two kinds of universal social groupings.[12] This means that the groupings are found in all societies. They are the family and place groupings, or locality groupings. We will deal with theories of family origin in a later chapter on the family. We have already hinted at the possibility that the dependence of the helpless child upon its mother may have been the key link in the development of the family.

Locality groupings have various names in various cultures. A local grouping of Australian aborigines may be called a *horde,* of American Indians a *band,* of Orientals a *village,* and of current Americans a *community* or *neighborhood.* At the present time, the most universal pattern of settlement is, of course, the village. India and Pakistan alone have some 700,000 villages.

Whatever the term, as Mandelbaum says:

The essential idea, no matter which particular term is used, is that of a group of people, all of whom live within a limited area and cooperate to some extent. The area may be a valley or the shores of a lake or city block, but the families within the area usually know each other, or at least recognize enough common interests so that they can act together in certain ways to meet mutual problems. This mutual action to meet common problems accomplishes more than just the attainment of some specific goals. It renews the solidarity of the people of the group, preparing them for more action together. Because in acting together they feel rewarded for so doing, they are ready and willing to work together in the future.[13]

How, then, do local groupings arise? Some, no doubt, are merely extensions of the family. Even in remote rural sections of this country we have locality groupings made up of less than a dozen family lines. In pre-Communist China it was not unusual to find villages made up of a single family name. The formation of clans in Scotland constitutes a good example of extended family groupings. In speaking of the Scottish clans, Mandelbaum says:

The Scottish clans traced descent through the father, and so were of the type called patrilineal clans. That is, all the children of the family, both boys and girls, were members of the MacDonald clan if their father was a MacDonald. If a Mac-Donald girl married a man of the clan Gordon, she still was accounted a MacDonald, although her children were Gordons and stood by the Gordons in time of clan need.[14]

In some areas, for example, parts of India, clans were matrilineal. As a rule, clan leadership and clan loyalty are the two major factors in integrating clans into effective social units.

Mandelbaum shows rather clearly the role of the clan. He says:

Just as a person's family helps him and stands by him in case of need, so does his clan support him when he needs its aid. This support may range from helping him collect the price of a bride to protecting his life should he incur the wrath of other clansmen bent on blood-vengeance. This very collective responsibility of the clan for the deeds and demeanor of its individual members makes it a strong force for social order. Since all the clansmen know that they will bear a share of the trouble if one of his clan-mates goes astray, they try to see to it that a potentially erring member is kept within socially approved limits.[15]

New local place groupings would necessarily develop out of some families' moving away from settlements in search of a better food supply, new lands, or better opportunities of

[12] David G. Mandelbaum, "Social Groupings," in *Man, Culture and Society,* ed. Harry L. Shapiro (New York: Oxford University Press, 1956), pp. 286-309.
[13] *Ibid.,* p. 288.

[14] *Ibid.,* p. 292.
[15] *Ibid.*

whatever kind. This tendency to split off from other groupings would be aggravated where the food supplies were limited because the size of local groupings would have to be limited. Goodenough found that communities depending upon hunting, food gathering, or fishing usually had populations of less than 50, whereas communities with a plant and animal agricultural economy usually had about 450 persons. Migratory bands had smaller populations, around 50.[16] After the development of irrigation agriculture, accompanied by the domestication of plants and animals, good-sized villages and cities in the Middle East developed. Later, the beginnings of commerce and industrialization launched the urbanward trend in population, and units of population grew larger.

New local groupings would naturally grow out of the factions and disputes between leaders in existing settlements. There is no reason to assume that local factions were absent in preliterate societies any more than they are today. Tribe and clan leaders had more distinct hold upon local groupings than modern community leaders have; therefore, the splintering of local groupings would be more easily achieved under tribal and clan conditions than today. Communities and neighborhoods today have many legal and property foundations which preliterate communities did not have.

The growth of new cultural interests in a population may lead to new local groupings. A good illustration of this is the growth of political and religious groupings. Pilgrim groupings in New England, Catholic communities in Louisiana and along the St. Lawrence river, Mennonite colonies in Pennsylvania and Ohio, and Mormon settlements in Utah are examples. In present-day suburban communities, Catholics may be attracted to a new community containing a parochial school or Jews to a new area containing a synagogue.

[16] W. H. Goodenough, "Basic Economy and the Community," unpublished article, quoted in George Peter Murdock, *Social Structure* (New York: The Macmillan Co., 1949), p. 81.

## The achievement of larger groupings

Historically, and even today in remote parts of the world, the tribe is an important kind of social grouping. Tribes may be made up of many families; they occupy a definite territory which they recognize and which is recognized by other tribes. However, certain hunting and fishing lands may be held in common and may be used by more than one tribe. Among the Plains Cree Indians a warrior society existed, which was made up of hunters from the various tribal bands. The society existed for the purpose of regulating the buffalo hunts which were tribal affairs.

Tribes speak the same language, which is an important factor in the unification of people. In general they follow the same way of life and are controlled by a governing mechanism, or authority, usually a tribal council. Each tribe has approved methods for socializing the young into the ways of the tribe. The socialization process involves not only the training necessary for making a good tribe member, but also inculcation of expected attitudes and relations toward other tribes.

Another illustration of the growth of larger social groupings that have some degree of unification is the confederation of tribes. Confederations are achieved for two purposes as a rule: to achieve peace and mutual aid, and to cooperate in war against another confederation or a strange tribe. A good example of confederation in this country was the League of the Iroquois in New York State. There is a possibility that the confederation might have developed into an Indian state had the white culture not interfered with its structuring and operations. On the other hand, it was threats from the whites which made the league effective.

Many modern states came into being not through confederation but through conquest. This was true of many of the city states of the Middle East and of Greece and Rome. This is explained by Mandelbaum:

When tribesmen over-run an established state,

they usually take over much of the established system of government. This happened when the Mongol tribes conquered the Chinese kingdoms and when the Vandals and other tribes defeated Rome. But in the modern world, subject peoples have a way of remembering their old independence and of overthrowing the conquerors sooner or later. Hence some nations have pretty much given up the idea of keeping other nations permanently under their rule. Defeated peoples are dealt with so that they supposedly will never be a threat to the victors again, and independent government, real or presumed, is returned to a conquered nation.[17]

This change parallels the rapid disappearance of colonialism.

Many modern states have come into existence through confederation. In the United States we have a confederation of states plus, of course, some form of fairly strong central government, or unit of control, to give unity and organization to the over-all national structure. Thus we call the United States a nation. It is also a society. Within the nation there are the 50 states with a certain amount of autonomy and with individual governing bodies. These are also societies. The national structure holds the states together in a loosely unified structure. Control is greatly aided by the fact that the people have certain patterns of life and value systems which have elements of uniformity throughout the nation. We spoke of some of these in Chapter 1.

Attempts have been made to bring about a confederation of nations. To some extent the British Empire is an example of this. So, too, was the League of Nations, and the current United Nations is an effort toward a confederation of nations for the purpose of preventing aggression and promoting cooperation toward peaceful ends and on common problems, although there is no central government. The rather recent attempt to organize the Arab states in the Middle East was to some extent a trend toward confederation, although, again, no central government. The tie of the Arabs to each other is partially one of a common racial origin and partially the unity affected by their belief in the Mohammedan religion.

### The achievement of integration in a society

The achievement of integration in a society depends upon many things. As we indicated in Chapter 1, a social system, of whatever level, must have certain ends—certain goals to be attained—and these ends must be understood and the people must work toward them. No better example of this exists than in families and communities. If the leadership and the members do not have certain goals which they, as a group, are trying to understand and attain, there is not likely to be much integration. For instance, in this country the general principle of freedom of religion must be accepted and understood if religious intolerance and bitterness are to be avoided. Every society requires certain institutions to be set up to help achieve the ends which the society seeks. As new individuals are born into the societies, the institutions indoctrinate and train them in the culture-ways of the society.

The very concept of society implies certain cultural ties. Language is one of these ties, and a common language is necessary for integration. This does not mean that the people all speak the same language—they may speak two or three—but they must be able to understand at least one and to use it for communication and as a basis for establishing agreement and reaching consensus on important issues.

Social control is necessary for integration in a society. One of the most effective mechanisms for control is government, although it is by no means the only one, and government is no test of a society. Where there exist 50 separate states in a federation, a strong, stable, central government is necessary. Societies within states develop within a framework of state and local governments. A cultural society, such as a Mormon religious society, must also have a governing group. An Indian society, such as the Navajo's, is likely to have a governing

---

[17] Mandelbaum, *op. cit.*, p. 302.

group; the very effective Navajo Tribal Council cooperates with the federal and state governments in matters of the tribe. Eskimos have practically nothing of this nature, Eskimo societies often being referred to as "individual anarchies." In many societies which civilization has not touched too strongly, leadership is rotating, temporary, and dependent largely on the immediate situation. Frequently there is nothing permanent in the line of an elders' governing council. Often there are no laws in any strict sense, just informal public opinion and norms.

Probably nothing informally accomplishes integration in a society as much as does a common core of cultural materials and physical traits. Common physical traits and culture complexes and patterns, participated in and enjoyed by most of the people, strengthen the identification of people with each other and with their society. Where there is a society of cultural haves and cultural have-nots, the restlessness of the have-nots is a perpetual threat to the solidarity of the society. In the same society the dominance of the haves is likely to force upon the have-nots ways of life which are disturbing, discriminating, and frustrating. If integration exists in outward forms, there is inward rebellion. Rebellion by any considerable number of people in a nation, a state, or a community society is hardly an index of social integration, even though rebellion exists largely in the mind and has not reached a stage of overt action.

## SUMMARY

We began this chapter by defining society. Such definitions as we accepted stress the fact that a society involves a fairly large number of people who live in a definite territory and enjoy a common culture. Societies may range in size from tribal and community societies, to cite some of the smaller ones, to states and nations, among the larger ones.

The formation of social systems, including those which we call societies, would be easier to explain if there were a definite, biologically based, gregarious instinct. After exploring the literature on instincts, we rejected the instinct theory in favor of the theory that gregariousness is learned. Perhaps it begins with the contact of the infant at birth with its parents, especially its mother, and continues as part of the socialization process. Group contacts become culturally pleasant and also are rewarding in many ways.

The explanations of social groupings are numerous. Many of them grow out of extended family relations and are enforced by taboos of one kind or another. Groupings of people develop out of new leadership, disputes, and factions. The expediency and the gain from working together in a cooperative relationship also account for groupings.

The two universal groupings in all societies are family and place groupings. The size of place groupings depends upon many factors, one of the most important being food supply. The consolidation and confederation of place groupings into larger social units paved the way for such social systems as the state and nation.

One of the problems of societies, at whatever level, is integration. Stability of a society depends upon integration. One of the important factors in bringing about integration is a recognition on the part of the people making up the society of what goals the society is trying to accomplish. These are ends. The people must not only understand ends but work toward their accomplishment. Social control, especially through stable governments, is also necessary for integration, as well as is participation in a common core of culture by the people in the society. Common cultural ties are necessary for an integrated society, and this implies dynamic participation in the society's culture.

THINGS TO DO AND TO DISCUSS

1. Look up in the references several concepts of "society" and arrive at a concept which you are willing to defend. Analyze your own community to determine if it is a society.
2. What are the major differences between human societies and animal societies?
3. How does the gregarious tendency in people develop?
4. Do you have people in your community who do not like to be with other people, or who do not want to identify themselves with other people? Who are such people and how do you explain their behavior?
5. What two social groupings appear to be universal?
6. What are some factors influencing the size of place groupings?
7. How may a national society be formed? Indicate some of the ways.
8. What is meant by "the integration of a society?" What are some of the factors influencing integration?

FOR FURTHER STUDY

GARRETT, HENRY E. *General Psychology.* New York: American Book Co., 1955. Good treatment of the physiological bases of behavior and the role of feelings and emotions.

HERSKOVITS, MELVILLE J. *Man and His Works.* New York: Alfred A. Knopf, 1948. Some good discussions of the meaning of society.

KLINEBERG, OTTO. *Social Psychology.* (Rev. ed.) New York: Henry Holt and Co., 1954. The sociopsychological basis of society is well treated.

LINDESMITH, ALFRED R., and STRAUSS, ANSELM L. *Social Psychology.* New York: Dryden Press, 1956. More than adequate discussion of subhuman societies.

LINTON, RALPH. *The Study of Man.* New York: Appleton-Century-Crofts, 1936. Much on the societies man creates and develops.

MACIVER, R. M. *The Web of Government.* New York: The Macmillan Co., 1947. The nature of government and how government develops.

MALINOWSKI, BRONISLAW. *A Scientific Theory of Culture and Other Essays.* Chapel Hill, N. C.: University of North Carolina Press, 1944. How the drives tend to develop a demand for social organization.

MURDOCK, GEORGE PETER. *Social Structure.* New York: The Macmillan Co., 1949. Good treatment of social organization.

NEWCOMB, THEODORE M. *Social Psychology.* New York: Dryden Press, 1950. Good discussion of gregariousness and the psychological bases for social organization.

PARSONS, TALCOTT. "Man in His Social Environment—As Viewed by Modern Social Science," *The Centennial Review of Arts and Science,* 1:50-70, Winter, 1957.

SHAPIRO, HARRY L. (ed.). *Man, Culture, and Society.* New York: Oxford University Press, 1956. Many topics including a good discussion of various kinds of social groupings and also how human society operates.

PART **II** THE STRUCTURE OF SOCIETY

IT IS THE PURPOSE of Part II to show the structure of society, analyzing its basic components. Throughout this discussion the student should keep in mind that one does not meet society in single components only. For instance, the family as a group belongs to a larger related unit—the family as an institution. Special interest groups may be related to peer groupings and place groupings. Analysis of individual structure units should not blind one to relationships between parts of the total structure. However, analysis of components should help the student to understand total structure. Structure, in turn, is related to function, as we shall see in Part III.

Chapter 6 is concerned with the population make-up of society.

Chapter 7 is an analysis of groups and how they influence us. This chapter lays a foundation for the next four chapters.

Chapter 8 is concerned with the family—the most universal and influential social group.

Chapter 9 treats peer groupings and reference groups.

Chapter 10 concerns itself largely with different kinds of place groupings, such as neighborhoods and communities.

Chapter 11 has to do with the characteristics of social institutions, and sets forth the major social institutions.

Chapter 12 indicates the major social needs served by social institutions and discusses, in some detail, the institutional structures designed to meet these needs.

# 6. DEMOGRAPHIC STRUCTURE

SOCIAL SYSTEMS, whether small groups or whole societies, are made up of people. The study of the size, distribution, composition, and growth of population is known as *demography*. Population specialists are referred to as *demographers*.

There is a close relation between demography and sociology. While demography has reached considerable status as a science and is taught in a number of disciplines, American sociology has "captured" the field more than has any other discipline, even though the study of population may be older than sociology as a separate discipline.[1] The close relationship between demographic and social phenomena is immediately seen in the fact that social systems and economic organization and development affect population growth. In turn population size and structure, such as age-sex distribution, set conditions to which any social system must accommodate itself.

The greatest concentration of demographers in this country is found in the U.S. Bureau of the Census, which is part of the U.S. Department of Commerce. Demographers are also employed by economic and sociology research bureaus, by life insurance companies, by population research centers, like the Scripps Foundation for Research in Population, by the United Nations Statistical Office, and by state departments of health. The Bureau of the Census is responsible for making the decennial population census of the United States. This is made every ten years as a decade begins, i.e., 1910, 1920, and so on. The drafters of the American Constitution in 1787 inserted in the document a provision that a census of the United States be made within three years of the date of the first meeting of the Congress of the United States and within every subsequent period of ten years. The first United States census was in 1790. A similar plan for a decen-

---

[1] For a brief treatment of these points, *see* Philip M. Hauser, "Demography in Relation to Sociology," *The American Journal of Sociology,* **65:**169-73, September, 1959. For a more extended discussion, *see* Philip M. Hauser and Otis Dudley Duncan (eds.), *The Study of Population: An Inventory and Appraisal* (Chicago: University of Chicago Press, 1959).

nial census had previously been made in the Constitution of the State of New York. However, the first New York State census was not made until 1795. Every five years there is a census of agriculture. At intervals there are other special censuses. The best source of population statistics on a world-wide basis is the Statistical Office of the United Nations, especially its *Demographic Yearbook,* which is now published annually.

## WORLD POPULATION

### The census enumeration of population

The idea of the population census is very old. Censuses were made in Biblical times, and perhaps earlier, for the counting of people for taxation and for determining fighting strength. Even now not all the population of the world is covered by adequate census enumerations. Better census enumerations are growing rapidly, in great measure, because the leadership of the United Nations and other groups is interested in adequate, comparative population data. In 1860 only 24 sovereign countries were taking a population census every ten years. By 1955 the number had increased to 65. Today, more than 70 countries have passed legislation to assure a census every ten years. Whereas in 1940 only about 1.3 billion of the world's population was covered by decennial census, today more than 2 billion people are covered by such enumerations. This increase in covered population results from both population increase and from fuller coverage.

The first English census was taken in 1801. France had a general enumeration in 1800. The United States is usually given the credit for introducing the first census which enumerated all the people and also gave many of their major characteristics. This was the census of 1790 of which we have spoken.

We have in this country what is called a *de jure* census count. Such an enumeration includes everybody who usually resides in an area as belonging to that area, wherever they might be at the time of the enumeration. Some 25 countries have a *de facto* census, which means that all persons present in a country, whether citizens or aliens, are counted in the area where they are physically present at the time the census is taken.

*Table 6*

#### WORLD POPULATION GROWTH: 1650 TO 1954
(in millions)

| Continent | 1650 | 1750 | 1800 | 1850 | 1900 | 1920 | 1930 | 1940 | 1950 | 1954 |
|---|---|---|---|---|---|---|---|---|---|---|
| Africa | 100 | 100 | 100 | 100 | 141 | 140 | 155 | 172 | 198 | 210 |
| America, North | 1 | 1.3 | 5.7 | 26 | 81 | 117 | 135 | 146 | 168 | 179 |
| America, Central South | 12 | 11.1 | 18.9 | 33 | 63 | 91 | 109 | 131 | 162 | 178 |
| Asia | 250 | 406 | 522 | 671 | 859 | 967[1] | 1073 | 1213 | 1368 | 1451 |
| Europe | 100 | 140 | 187 | 260 | 401 | 328[1] | 355 | 380 | 393 | 404 |
| Oceania | 2 | 2 | 2 | 2 | 6 | 8.8 | 10.4 | 11.3 | 13.0 | 14.4 |
| U.S.S.R. | — | — | — | — | — | 158 | 176 | 196 | 202 | 214 |
| Total | 465 | 660 | 836 | 1098 | 1551 | 1810 | 2013 | 2250 | 2505 | 2652 |

[1] Exclusive of U.S.S.R. from 1920 to 1954.

Sources: The data for 1650 to 1900 are from A. M. Carr-Saunders, *World Population* (Oxford: Clarendon Press, 1936), p. 30. The data for 1920 to 1954 are from the *Demographic Yearbook, 1955* (New York: Statistical Office of the United Nations, 1955), p. 115.

*U.S. Bureau of the Census*

*This is the console of one of the electronic computers used in the Bureau of the Census to speed up and better facilitate the computing and arrangement of census data. The 1960 Census was the first one to use electronic computers widely.*

The Statistical Office of the United Nations, in cooperation with many groups interested in the improvement of census enumerations, is giving leadership to the development of improved censuses, and it should not be many years before there are adequate data on all the populations of the world.

*World population growth*

Few estimates of the world's total population extend back to A.D. 1650. The population in that year has been estimated at 465 million. A hundred years later it was estimated at 660 million. By 1850 it had reached 1,098 million, and by 1950, 2,505 million (Table 6). These figures show that it took perhaps a million years to produce a world population of 1 billion, yet in the next 100 years more than a billion and a half people have been added to the population. Growth in the modern period has been particularly great.

The present population of the world is about 2.8 billion, which again is roughly twice as many people as 75 years ago. There is at present an indication that the world population may double in the next 40 years.[2]

The average rate of growth of the population of the world per decade was almost three times as great between 1950 and 1960 as it was during the period 1850-1900 (see Table 7). For

[2] Kingsley Davis, "Analysis of the Population Explosion," *New York Times Magazine*, September 22, 1957, pp. 15, 77-79.

Table 7

INCREASE IN THE WORLD'S POPULATION
PER DECADE, 1850-1960

| Period | Per Cent Increase Per Decade |
|---|---|
| 1850-1900 | 6 |
| 1900-1930 | 7 |
| 1930-1950 | 10 |
| 1950-1960 | 17 |

Source: Kingsley Davis, "Analysis of the Population Explosion," *New York Times Magazine,* September 22, 1957, pp. 15, 77-79.

instance, in the period 1850-1900 the world population grew 6 per cent for each ten-year period. From 1930-1950 the growth was 10 per cent for each ten-year period. In the decade 1950-1960 the increase was 17 per cent.

At present the world population growth is almost 47 million annually. This is about the size of the population of Italy. Even before 1970 the increase may be 75 million annually, which will be one-third greater than the population of the United Kingdom. By the year 2000, the population of the world may reach 6 billion, a figure which was predicted for 2050 about 1928.[3] By 2050, at the present rate of growth the world population may reach 13 billion, which is 2 billion more people than was predicted for the world in 2100 back in 1928.

Why this great increase in world population in the last 100 years and the even greater recent upswing? The leading cause of the increase has been a decline in the death rate. Many factors have contributed to this decline. Over the years an improved food supply and better facilities for transporting and preserving foodstuffs have made it possible to reduce famines and to reduce greatly death from malnutrition. Preventive medicine, mass inoculation, improved water supplies, sewage disposal, insect control, especially of malaria mosquitoes, and environ-mental sanitation, including garbage collection and better personal cleanliness, have been factors in the reduction of the death rate.

The use of antibiotics and other new and improved medicines, along with improvements in surgery, have also been important causes of the declining death rate. For instance, the infant and maternal death rate has been reduced materially by improved gynecological methods involving both surgery and medication. Endemic syphilis has been greatly reduced by the use of antibiotics. The wide use of biologicals for immunization has caused a decline in the prevalence of diseases like typhoid fever, smallpox, diphtheria, scarlet fever, and polio. In improving the health of the people throughout the world, the work of the World Health Organization (WHO), one of the agencies of the United Nations, has been very effective.

In countries of western Europe and in the United States the birth rate declined dangerously up to 1930, raising fears of population decline, but, with high employment and economic activity during and since World War II, the birth rate has risen in nearly every country where it was low.

Births minus deaths equal the natural increase, which may be expressed in terms of whole numbers, percentage increase, or in terms of a rate per 1,000 population. Therefore, if the birth rate declines slowly and the death rate declines rapidly, the natural increase in the population becomes greater.[4] It requires a certain amount of education, sophistication, and improvement in standard of living before people are willing to practice birth control. In many parts of the world there are very strong religious convictions against the use of contraceptive devices or methods. In the more underdeveloped countries substantial declines in death rates are taking place, while the decline in birth rates is relatively slow. Such areas are likely to have a high natural increase in population.

[3] George Knibbs, "Menace of Increasing Population," *Scientific American,* 137:338-40, 1928.

[4] *See* Lyle W. Shannon, *Underdeveloped Areas* (New York: Harper and Bros., 1957), Chap. III, "The Demographic Characteristics of Underdeveloped Areas."

## Composition of the world's population

As to racial and color composition, we do not have a clear picture of the world's population. This is because color and racial connections are rather difficult to identify in many peoples, since they may be a mixture of two or more races. Of the present population of 2.8 billion, perhaps a billion belong to the Caucasoid, or white, race, which includes the dark-skinned peoples of India, whose political and emotional sympathies are likely to be non-white; almost 200 million belong to the black race; a few million are of doubtful or very mixed racial lineage, and the yellow and brown, or Mongoloid race, without a doubt, exceeds 1.5 billion. It is also true that, taken

collectively, the birth rates are higher among the colored peoples of the world; so are the death rates. The continued efforts for better health conditions in the underdeveloped areas of the world should speedily reduce the death rates. This will mean that for the next 50 years the natural increase among the colored peoples of the world is likely to be, on the whole, greater than among the white peoples.

Data on illiteracy are variable and difficult to compare. For this reason a world-wide picture of illiteracy is difficult to construct. Data indicate that almost 50 per cent of the world's population ten years of age and older are illiterate, with illiteracy reaching more than 90 per cent in some of the underdeveloped areas and falling as low as 2 per cent in developed

*Table 8*

## PER CENT ILLITERACY IN DEVELOPED AND UNDERDEVELOPED COUNTRIES, 1950 [a]

| Geographical | All Countries | Developed Countries | Underdeveloped Countries |
|---|---|---|---|
| World | 47 | 6 | 70 |
| North America [b] | 2 | 2 | No country in this category |
| Europe | 8 | 3 | 20 |
| Oceania | 11 | 1 | 88 |
| U.S.S.R. [c] | 11 | 11 | No country in this category |
| South America | 42 | 17 | 51 |
| Middle America [d] | 48 | 20 | 52 |
| Asia | 70 | 2 | 75 |
| Africa | 88 | 55 | 91 |

Source: Hilda Hertz Golden, "Literacy and Social Change in Underdeveloped Countries," *Rural Sociology*, **20**:1-6, March, 1955. *See also* Frank C. Laubach, *The Silent Million Speak* (New York: Friendship Press, 1943). For more on the population characteristics of underdeveloped countries, *see* Lyle W. Shannon, *Underdeveloped Areas* (New York: Harper and Bros., 1957), pp. 53-95.

[a] Developed countries are those with less than 50 per cent of their economically active males in agricultural pursuits, including hunting, fishing, and forestry; underdeveloped countries are those with 50 per cent or more of their economically active males in these pursuits.

[b] U.S.A., Canada, and Alaska.

[c] The U.S.S.R. is a borderline case but has been classed here among the developed countries, since today its agricultural labor force is probably slightly below 50 per cent.

[d] The Central American Republics and the islands of the Caribbean.

areas (see Table 8). Even though illiteracy is high in underdeveloped countries, it is declining rapidly as mass education programs and other opportunities are made available. For instance, 50 years ago some 95 per cent of India's population over ten years of age was illiterate. Today the percentage is less than 75. Today's emphasis is upon literacy, and the flood of mass media is fast making it available for the peoples of the world. Indeed, literacy is becoming increasingly indispensable for the intelligent citizen.

World-wide economic comparisons are practically impossible to make. Figures on cash income are difficult to obtain in many countries. Many of the world's people receive their income in kind—food, crops, tenancy, and housing. To reduce such remuneration to a per capita or per family income basis is almost impossible.

In 1950, some 63 per cent of the world's population was in 147 political entities which were classed as underdeveloped areas. Some 48 areas were classed as developed and included the other 37 per cent of the population.[5]

## World population problems and outlook

There are two extreme points of view regarding current world population increases. There are, first of all, the alarmists. They visualize "standing room" only unless speedy programs of family limitation are imposed upon the underdeveloped areas of the world where birth rates are high.[6] The second group of extremists are those who feel that modern agricultural and industrial production facilities are adequate and may be extended to meet the needs of any predictable world population increase. The representatives of this group point to the

[5] *Ibid.*, p. 11.
[6] For authoritative works on world population and resources, *see* W. S. and E. S. Woytinsky, *World Population and Production: Trends and Outlook* (New York: Twentieth Century Fund, 1953), and Paul K. Hatt (ed.), *World Population and Future Resources* (New York: American Book Co., 1952).

necessity of control of agricultural production in this country in order to reduce food surpluses; they indicate that most of the land of the tropics is not in production, and that crop zones may be extended northward through plant breeding and greenhouse culture; they foresee fantastic futures in chemiculture and the use of the seas, which make up 70 per cent of the earth's surface, for food production. These people may rely more heavily than they admit upon Malthus' checks, such as disease, famines, disaster, and wars, as well as birth control, to take care of any dangerous population increase.

It is clear that unless the increase in population, whatever the country, is accompanied by an increase in economic opportunities, the standard of living may decline. The political effects of population pressure may also be great. We may take Japan as an example of this. Japan has developed a very intensive agriculture. It has poor prospects of expanding its fisheries under existing competition. It has a fairly intensive system of both heavy and light industries, with emphasis upon textiles. Japan's population was 70 million in 1937 and is now more than 90 million. Even during World War II its population increased. The density of Japan's population is about 600 persons per square mile as compared to a density of about 55 per square mile in this country, 538 in the United Kingdom, and 100 in France. Japan's prospect of territorial expansion is at present negligible. In the last decade Japan has greatly lowered its birth rate mostly by encouraging and legalizing abortion, in the eyes of many a questionable procedure. As far as we know, no government in history has before managed this sort of population control. Even with this the population has grown steadily. Unless Japan can find outlets for her manufactured products, the Japanese population is likely to experience a steady decline in its standard of living. Furthermore, if the democracies do not trade with Japan, she will necessarily be forced to turn her attention to increased trading with Communist China or

Russia and their satellites. Lacking trade outlets for her goods, she may be encouraged by population pressure to return to imperialistic ventures in the future, such as those she has undertaken in the past.

With the existing racial divisions in the world's population, it is apparent that unsatisfactory relationships between racial groupings in any part of the world may become a target for propaganda and incidents in other parts. Two examples are enough to indicate this: the Nationalist movement in South Africa, which has been characterized by antiwhite friction and race riots and propaganda; and the extensive efforts of communist nations to appeal to the colored peoples of the world by featuring the incidents that have followed the attempts to desegregate public schools in the United States. Since more will be said about segregation and desegregation attempts in the United States in subsequent chapters, we shall only discuss the South African Nationalist movement at this point.

The tension in the racial situation in South Africa was dramatized by the bloody race riots in Durban as early as 1949. Following these riots the International Court of Justice ruled that the Union of South Africa had to report to the United Nations on the welfare of 300,000 natives in the Territory of South West Africa administered as a League of Nations mandate.[7]

For many years prior to the formation of the Union of South Africa in 1910, the apartheid (a Dutch word for apartness or separatedness) policy had characterized race relations in South Africa. This policy dates back to the tribal wars and Dutch Calvinism of the nineteenth century, the latter holding that redemption was for the elect. Segregation of natives as a basic policy of land occupancy was developed in 1913 when some 23 million acres of land were set up in native reserves. Since 1910 a dual system of schools, hospitals, and other services, and residence segregation in cities had been officially supported. With urbanward migration of natives from the reserves set aside for them, large overcrowded segregated areas have developed in the South African cities. The theory of segregation is cogently put in the classical statement: "The lion and the elephant can live together, but they can live better apart."[8]

The composition of the population of the Union of South Africa in 1950 was as follows: 7.7 million natives, 2.3 million of European birth and lineage, 905,000 mixed peoples, and 283,000 Asiatics. To further add to the confusion of relationships, splits and disputes have frequently developed between the Dutch and English-speaking whites. Some three-fourths of the natives are engaged in agriculture, but this percentage is declining rapidly as urbanization increases.

One study of economic conditions of the people of South Africa indicated that the Europeans forming one-fifth of the population received three-fourths of the national income. The native population, making up two-thirds of the population, received one-fifth of the income. A study made in 1950 indicated that 64,000 new houses would have to be built in two major cities to replace slum shacks. As one authority has put it: "The sum of the segregation laws are an effort to prevent failure in a white man and success in a black man."[9]

Since the rise to power of the nationalist government in 1948, increased friction has risen between the colored elements and other elements of South Africa's population.[10] The new theory of racism developed by the Nationalists has attracted much attention among the leading powers of the world.

The solution to the population pressures of numerous countries must be multiple, rather

[7] "Race Problems in South Africa," *Editorial Research Reports*, 11:507-24, 1950.

[8] Eugene P. Duorin, *Racial Separation in South Africa* (Chicago: University of Chicago Press, 1952). From the frontispiece.

[9] C. W. Kiewiet, *The Anatomy of South African Misery* (London: Oxford University Press, 1955), p. 55.

[10] *See* Adamastor (pseud.), *White Man Boss* (Boston: Beacon Press, 1951).

than singular, in character. The interested student may want to explore some of these solutions in standard references listed at the end of the chapter.

One cannot help but conclude that there are grave implications for democracy in the world population trends indicated in Tables 6, 7, and 8.[11]

As indicated in Table 8, about 50 per cent of the world's population over ten years of age is illiterate. In underdeveloped countries this percentage may be 90. Food experts tell us that half the world's population is undernourished. Laboratory experiments on human hunger, and the records of prisoners of war held under semistarvation conditions, show that people who are hungry and undernourished not only lose interest, initiative, and morale, but become confused and suspicious. To expect humanitarian, democratic relationships between such people is just too much. Such people are therefore likely to follow the leaders who promise them the most in immediate creature comforts. A basic danger is that among such people regimentation and

totalitarianism will grow. Such growth has implications, not only for the expansion of democratic ideologies and institutions but also for the peace of the world. In addition, about four-fifths of the people of the world have incomes of less than ten dollars weekly. The great poverty indicated by such figures looms large as a problem for the industrial and highly productive agricultural nations trying to expand production in the face of already accumulated surpluses of goods and growing productive capacity.

Over a half century ago Thomas Malthus, an English clergyman, developed his celebrated Malthusian doctrine. This doctrine held that population tends to increase in geometrical ratio and food supply in an arithmetical ratio. In time, the population would outrun the food supply. In some of the underdeveloped countries the Malthusian doctrine has become a truth. In developed countries it has been the food supply that has assumed geometrical proportions in its growth. World-wide, the danger that Malthus depicted does not appear to be an immediate one.

### THE POPULATION OF THE UNITED STATES

In an introductory text in sociology the treatment of population of the United States has to be brief. The interested college student may want to pursue the topic further in standard books and references or in specialized courses in population.[12]

#### The demographer's statistical tools

The population expert has the use of many formulas and statistical tools. In discussing

these we will focus our attention on American demography, even though there are many attempts at standardization of population terms and methods on a world-wide basis.

Demographers have a basic concern with birth and death rate data. These data are referred to as vital statistics. In presenting birth rate data the *crude birth rate* is usually used. This is the annual number of births per 1,000 population. At times demographers use a *refined birth rate* formula. This is the number of births annually per 1,000 married women, or per 1,000 women ages 16 to 45. Such rates are "more refined" because they take into consideration age, marital status, and sex composition of the population. The *crude death rate* is the number of deaths per 1,000 population in any given year. When death rates are computed for individual diseases, this is usually

[11] For a good discussion of this problem, *see* Gerald Barnes, "Democracy and the Birth Rate," *The Antioch Review,* **10**:435-46, December, 1950.

[12] As an example: Paul H. Landis and Paul K. Hatt, *Population Problems,* (2nd ed.; New York: American Book Co., 1954); Warren S. Thompson, *Population Problems* (4th ed; New York: McGraw-Hill Book Co., 1953); Otis D. Duncan and Albert J. Reiss, Jr., *Social Characteristics of Urban and Rural Communities, 1950* (New York: John Wiley and Sons, 1956).

done on the basis of each 100,000 population. For instance, in 1956 the death rate from diseases of the heart was 360.5, from malignant tumors 147.9, accidents 56.7, and influenza and pneumonia 28.2. The *rate of natural increase* is obtained by subtracting the death rate from the birth rate. The reason that the birth and death rates are called "crude" is that they do not take into consideration the differences in the age composition of the population. When this is done, the birth and death rates are said to be "age adjusted."

Two demographic terms which are often confused in the public mind are fecundity and fertility. *Fecundity* is the potentiality or capacity to reproduce. As far as is known, women in well-advanced cultures have the same fecundity or capacity to reproduce as primitive women had. *Fertility* is fecundity expressed in performance and it is therefore measurable. Most women are capable of having a child per year; however, few women reproduce to the limit of their capacity.

A useful term in measuring population replacement is the *net reproduction rate*. It measures the degree to which women in the current generation are replacing themselves with potential mothers in the next. It is based on the age-specific fertility observed in a given year, but is modified by the mortality which prevents some girl babies from living to the age at which their mothers bore them. If the net reproduction rate is 1, the present generation of mothers would just be replaced. If the rate is 1.75, the present generation of mothers would be replaced one and three-fourths times.

The demographer is concerned with density of population. Density is some indication of the population pressure and problems a community or a nation faces. It may be an indication of land overcrowding, especially in a country that depends upon an agricultural economy. Of course, density *per se* does not mean much because soil conditions, rainfall, and temperature factors are more important than just man-land ratios, as are also land-use practices. For a productive economy four kinds

of resources are required: a people of quality, favorable natural resources, a rich organic environment of plants and animals, and technological and institutional resources.

*Population density* is expressed on the basis of the number of people per square mile in the United States and per square kilometer in countries using the metric system. International statistics on density compiled by the United Nations are expressed in terms of the number of people per square kilometer.

Another basic concern of demographers is with both the age and the sex composition of the population. Sex composition is measured by the *sex ratio*, which means the number of males in the population per 100 females. In the United States there are born 105.7 white males in the population per 100 females. This ratio has been maintained since 1850. The sex ratio of Negroes at birth is lower than for whites, there being born 103.3 Negro male babies for each 100 female babies. The infant death rate of male babies is higher, however, and so are death rates of males at all ages from birth to death. As a result there are more females than males. We shall say more about the changing sex ratios in the population later in the chapter.

## Growth of population in the United States

A country like the United States has several sources from which its population may grow. The primary source is *natural increase*. Natural increase results when the birth rate is higher than the death rate. If, in a country enjoying population growth, the birth rate should remain stable and the death rate decline, the population will grow more rapidly, unless emigration occurs. If the birth rate increases and the death rate declines, the natural increase becomes very great, as it has been in the United States since World War II.

In 1915 the crude birth rate was 25.0 per 1,000 population. In 1935, a depression year, it had dropped to 16.9. By 1945 it was up to 19.5 and by 1950 had reached 23.6. From 1950 to

1955 the birth rate averaged 24.8. A median series of projections assumes that a high birth rate may continue, with some leveling, for some years to come (Table 9).

Against this background of sustained high birth rates, the United States population over a period of decades has had a low death rate. The prospects are good that this death rate will continue to decline. In 1940 the crude death rate was 10.8 per 1,000 population. By 1950 it had declined to 9.6. Over the period 1950 to 1955 it averaged 9.5. Bureau of the Census projections assume that the crude death rate may decline to about 8.1 (Table 10).

Thus, with the high birth rates and the low death rates indicated above, the United States in the years ahead should have a very substantial natural increase in population. More about this later.

A country may grow from *immigration*. In the past, much of the growth of the United States has been by immigration. For instance, between 1820 to 1950, 40.5 million immigrants were admitted to the United States. The heaviest decade for immigration was from 1901-10 when 8.8 million immigrants were admitted. Immigration quotas allotted to various countries change with the passage of new laws. Un-

*Table 9*

CRUDE BIRTH RATES, UNITED STATES, 1950 TO 1955, AND PROJECTED TO 1980

| Period | Average Annual Rate Per 1,000 of Mid Period Population |
|--------|----------------------------|
| 1950 to 1955 | 24.8 |
| 1955 to 1960 | 24.7 |
| 1960 to 1965 | 23.9 |
| 1965 to 1970 | 24.8 |
| 1970 to 1975 | 26.2 |
| 1975 to 1980 | 26.9 |

Source: Adapted from Meyer Zitter and Jacob S. Siegel, "Illustrative Projections of the Population of the United States, by Age and Sex 1960 to 1980," *Current Population Reports, Population Estimates,* Series P-25, No. 187, November 10, 1958, p. 10.

*Table 10*

CRUDE DEATH RATES, UNITED STATES, 1950 TO 1955, AND PROJECTED TO 1980

| Period | Rate Per 1000 Population |
|--------|------------------------|
| 1950 to 1955 | 9.5 |
| 1955 to 1960 | 9.2 |
| 1960 to 1965 | 8.9 |
| 1965 to 1970 | 8.7 |
| 1970 to 1975 | 8.4 |
| 1975 to 1980 | 8.1 |

Source: Adapted from Meyer Zitter and Jacob S. Siegel, "Illustrative Projections of the Population of the United States, by Age and Sex 1960 to 1980," *Current Population Reports, Population Estimates,* Series P-25, No. 187, November 10, 1958, p. 13.

der the 1952 Immigration and Nationality Act the quotas were set at 154,657. Under special laws and provisions passed from time to time nonquota immigrants are admitted. In recent years the number of aliens admitted to the United States has varied between 635,000 and 800,000, with immigrants usually not exceeding 250,000 in number annually.[13] Each year, of course, there is some *emigration* out of the country. This usually does not exceed 30,000 annually.

The United States gains some population growth through *migration* from its possessions. Migration from the possessions is not subject to immigration quotas. Of late years the largest volume of migration has been from Puerto Rico, with destinations being chiefly the Atlantic seaboard, especially New York City, where many Puerto Ricans are employed in the garment trades. In some years the Puerto Rican migrants to New York alone have numbered in excess of 25,000. This number of people would populate a small city. Increasingly, Alaska and Hawaii are likely to be sources of migrants to the mainland.

At this point we need to stress that popula-

[13] For comprehensive data on immigration, *see* U.S. Bureau of the Census, *Statistical Abstract of the United States: 1958* (79th ed.; Washington, D. C.: U.S. Government Printing Office, 1958).

## One Person in Five Moves Each Year

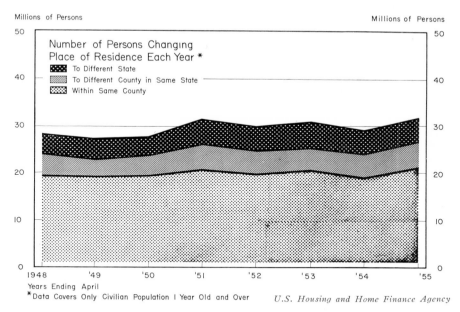

FIG. 3. POPULATION MOBILITY IN THE UNITED STATES

tion change in the United States is the result of social change. Our rapidly growing cities were magnets drawing in huge waves of immigrants, and this same urban industrial development led later to lower birth rates and contributed to the tremendous decline in mortality.

A locality, for instance Chicago, may grow in population from four sources: natural increase, immigration from other countries, migration from rural areas, and migration from other cities. While internal migration within a country does not affect the size of the country, it may deflate or inflate the size of localities.

No one knows the size of the Indian population at the time America was discovered. Estimates vary greatly. Probably a conservative estimate is that there were 1 million people north of Mexico and 3 million in Central and South America. By 1650 the non-Indian population was around 52,000, and by 1750, 1.2 million.

The first population census of the United States was in 1790 when the population was 3.9 million. A hundred years later it was 62.9 million. By January 1, 1958, the population had reached 172.2 million, and increased to 180.0 million by 1960 (Table 11; also pp. 102-3). The prospects are that population growth at fairly rapid pace will continue beyond 1960, reaching perhaps 214 million in 1970, 228 million by 1975, 260 million by 1980, and 320 million by 2000.

Table 11 indicates that about 30 million new citizens were added to the population of the United States between 1950 and 1960. The implications of this increase are tied up in the fact that at certain age levels certain activities begin. We call these *age thresholds* which change from time to time. For most children school begins about six years of age; at 14 they enter high school, and at 18 college. In most states at 21 a new crop of voters begins, and at age 18 those young people who do not go to college begin to seek new job oppor-

*Table 11*

POPULATION OF THE UNITED STATES,
1790-1960

| Census Year | Population | Increase over Preceding Census | |
|---|---|---|---|
| | | Number | Per Cent |
| 1960 | 179,323,175 | 27,997,377 | 18.5 |
| 1950 | 151,325,798 | 19,161,229 | 14.5 |
| 1940 | 131,669,275 | 8,894,229 | 7.2 |
| 1930 | 122,775,046 | 17,064,426 | 16.1 |
| 1920 | 105,710,620 | 13,738,354 | 14.9 |
| 1910 | 91,972,266 | 15,977,691 | 21.0 |
| 1900 | 75,994,575 | 13,046,861 | 20.7 |
| 1890 | 62,947,714 | 12,791,931 | 25.5 |
| 1880 | 50,155,783 | 10,337,334 | 26.0 |
| 1870 | 39,818,449 | 8,375,128 | 26.6 |
| 1860 | 31,443,321 | 8,251,445 | 35.6 |
| 1850 | 23,191,876 | 6,122,423 | 35.9 |
| 1840 | 17,069,453 | 4,203,433 | 32.7 |
| 1830 | 12,866,020 | 3,227,567 | 33.5 |
| 1820 | 9,638,453 | 2,398,572 | 33.1 |
| 1810 | 7,239,881 | 1,931,398 | 36.4 |
| 1800 | 5,308,483 | 1,379,269 | 35.1 |
| 1790 | 3,929,214 | — | — |

Source: U. S. Bureau of the Census, *Statistical Abstract of the United States: 1959* (80th ed.; Washington, D. C.: U.S. Government Printing Office, 1959), p. 5, and *1960 Census of Population, Advance Report,* Final Population Counts, PC(A1)-1, November 15, 1960. The 1960 data includes Alaska and Hawaii.

tunities. By 21 many young people are married. Retirement at 65 or 70 is the general practice in this country.

These age thresholds mean that new opportunities and facilities have to be made available as a growing population reaches each age threshold. The outlook ahead in population growth in this country will demand new school and church facilities, more jobs, more homes, more automobiles, furniture, food, and services. To a country with the production facilities that ours has, a growing population is a tremendous economic asset. On the other hand, if job opportunities are not made available, a rapid increase in population could mean a decline in the American standard of living.

## Composition and trends

Of the total population of the United States, 51.2 per cent was urban (mostly made up of people in incorporated places of 2,500 or more) in 1920; 56.2 per cent in 1930; 56.5 in 1940, and, on the basis of comparable definitions, 59.0 per cent in 1950. In 1950 a new definition of urban was used to include unincorporated as well as incorporated places of 2,500 or more. On the basis of this "new" definition, 64.0 per cent of the population was urban in 1950 and 70 per cent in 1960. While the rural population in the total population is declining, the decline is largely in the rural farm population, there being an increase in the rural nonfarm population. About 1,000,000 leave the farms for the cities each year.

Racially, about 10.5 per cent of the population of the United States is nonwhite, chiefly Negro. The nonwhite population in 1960 was in excess of 18 million. While the number of

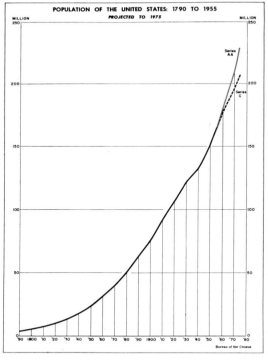

FIG. 4. POPULATION GROWTH IN THE UNITED STATES

*E. I. du Pont de Nemours & Co., Inc.*

*An increase in population means a vast increase in goods and services needed.*

nonwhites, mostly Negroes and Indians, in the population is increasing numerically, there had been a long-range decline of the percentage of nonwhites in the population up to 1940. From 1940 to 1960 the percentage of nonwhites in the total population increased.

There have been great changes in the distribution of the Negro population. In 1950, 68 per cent lived in the South; 14.8 per cent in the North Central states, with the largest concentration in Chicago, 13.5 per cent in the New England and Middle Atlantic areas, and 3.7 per cent in the West. Today 40 per cent of Negroes live outside the South as compared to 31.5 per cent in 1950, 23 per cent in 1940, 15 per cent in 1920, and 10 per cent in 1900. From 1940 to 1950, 1.6 million Negroes moved out of the ten southern states that had the largest Negro populations, 326,000 leaving Mississippi alone and 240,000 leaving Georgia.

In 1940, 278,000 Negroes lived in Chicago; today the number is almost 800,000. In 1940, New York had 458,000 Negroes; today the Negro population approaches 875,000. Los Angeles had 64,000 Negroes in 1940, but today the number is about 300,000.

The concentration of Negroes in cities gives them a unity, an identification, and a source of power which they did not have when they were dispersed over the agricultural areas of the South. Problems of housing, jobs, schools, and health have also arisen as a result of such concentration.

Another ethnic trend in the composition of the population has been a decline in the foreign-born, the percentages being 13.6 in 1900 and 6.7 per cent in 1950. Of course, originally, except for the Indians, all the population of the United States was foreign-born. As the population has become older, with the natural increase in population and the rather rigid restriction of immigration, it was expected that the percentage of foreign-born in the population would decline. In individual cities like Buffalo, Chicago, Detroit, or San Francisco, this has meant the decline of ethnic islands, such as Polish and Italian communities, of foreign-born people. The children of the foreign-born in succeeding generations tend to disperse throughout a city more than their parents do. Language factors and higher incomes are responsible in part for this, although there are other reasons why the children of the foreign-born tend to break cultural ties with their parents and grandparents.

We have already spoken about the declining ratio of men to women in the population of the United States. This is the result of a number of factors. While a greater number of boys than girls are born each year, males experience

## POPULATION OF THE UNITED STATES BY REGIONS, DIVISIONS, AND STATES, 1960 AND 1950

### (Minus sign (—) denotes decrease)

| Area | Population | | Increase, 1950 to 1960 | |
|---|---|---|---|---|
| | *1960* | *1950* | *Number* | *Per-cent* |
| United States .......... | 179,323,175 | 151,325,798 | 27,997,377 | 18.5 |
| **Regions:** | | | | |
| Northeast ............... | 44,677,819 | 39,477,986 | 5,199,833 | 13.2 |
| North Central ........... | 51,619,139 | 44,460,762 | 7,158,377 | 16.1 |
| South .................. | 54,973,113 | 47,197,088 | 7,776,025 | 16.5 |
| West .................. | 28,053,104 | 20,189,962 | 7,863,142 | 38.9 |
| **Divisions:** | | | | |
| New England ............ | 10,509,367 | 9,314,453 | 1,194,914 | 12.8 |
| Middle Atlantic .......... | 34,168,452 | 30,163,533 | 4,004,919 | 13.3 |
| East North Central ....... | 36,225,024 | 30,399,368 | 5,825,656 | 19.2 |
| West North Central ...... | 15,394,115 | 14,061,394 | 1,332,721 | 9.5 |
| South Atlantic ........... | 25,971,732 | 21,182,335 | 4,789,397 | 22.6 |
| East South Central ....... | 12,050,126 | 11,477,181 | 572,945 | 5.0 |
| West South Central ...... | 16,951,255 | 14,537,572 | 2,413,683 | 16.6 |
| Mountain ............... | 6,855,060 | 5,074,998 | 1,780,062 | 35.1 |
| Pacific ................. | 21,198,044 | 15,114,964 | 6,083,080 | 40.2 |
| **New England:** | | | | |
| Maine ................. | 969,265 | 913,774 | 55,491 | 6.1 |
| New Hampshire ......... | 606,921 | 533,242 | 73,679 | 13.8 |
| Vermont ............... | 389,881 | 377,747 | 12,134 | 3.2 |
| Massachusetts ........... | 5,148,578 | 4,690,514 | 458,064 | 9.8 |
| Rhode Island ........... | 859,488 | 791,896 | 67,592 | 8.5 |
| Connecticut ............ | 2,535,234 | 2,007,280 | 527,954 | 26.3 |
| **Middle Atlantic:** | | | | |
| New York .............. | 16,782,304 | 14,830,192 | 1,952,112 | 13.2 |
| New Jersey ............. | 6,066,782 | 4,835,329 | 1,231,453 | 25.5 |
| Pennsylvania ........... | 11,319,366 | 10,498,012 | 821,354 | 7.8 |
| **East North Central:** | | | | |
| Ohio .................. | 9,706,397 | 7,946,627 | 1,759,770 | 22.1 |
| Indiana ................ | 4,662,498 | 3,934,224 | 728,274 | 18.5 |
| Illinois ................ | 10,081,158 | 8,712,176 | 1,368,982 | 15.7 |
| Michigan .............. | 7,823,194 | 6,371,766 | 1,451,428 | 22.8 |
| Wisconsin .............. | 3,951,777 | 3,434,575 | 517,202 | 15.1 |
| **West North Central:** | | | | |
| Minnesota .............. | 3,413,864 | 2,982,483 | 431,381 | 14.5 |
| Iowa .................. | 2,757,537 | 2,621,073 | 136,464 | 5.2 |
| Missouri ............... | 4,319,813 | 3,954,653 | 365,160 | 9.2 |
| North Dakota ........... | 632,446 | 619,636 | 12,810 | 2.1 |
| South Dakota ........... | 680,514 | 652,740 | 27,774 | 4.3 |
| Nebraska .............. | 1,411,330 | 1,325,510 | 85,820 | 6.5 |
| Kansas ................ | 2,178,611 | 1,905,299 | 273,312 | 14.3 |

## POPULATION OF THE UNITED STATES BY REGIONS, DIVISIONS, AND STATES, 1960 AND 1950—*Continued*

(Minus sign (—) denotes decrease)

| AREA | POPULATION | | INCREASE, 1950 TO 1960 | |
|---|---|---|---|---|
| | *1960* | *1950* | *Number* | *Per-cent* |
| SOUTH ATLANTIC: | | | | |
| Delaware ............... | 446,292 | 318,085 | 128,207 | 40.3 |
| Maryland .............. | 3,100,689 | 2,343,001 | 757,688 | 32.3 |
| District of Columbia ....... | 763,956 | 802,178 | —38,222 | —4.8 |
| Virginia ............... | 3,966,949 | 3,318,680 | 648,269 | 19.5 |
| West Virginia ........... | 1,860,421 | 2,005,552 | —145,131 | —7.2 |
| North Carolina .......... | 4,556,155 | 4,061,929 | 494,226 | 12.2 |
| South Carolina ........... | 2,382,594 | 2,117,027 | 265,567 | 12.5 |
| Georgia ............... | 3,943,116 | 3,444,578 | 498,538 | 14.5 |
| Florida ............... | 4,951,560 | 2,771,305 | 2,180,255 | 78.7 |
| EAST SOUTH CENTRAL: | | | | |
| Kentucky ............... | 3,038,156 | 2,944,806 | 93,350 | 3.2 |
| Tennessee .............. | 3,567,089 | 3,291,718 | 275,371 | 8.4 |
| Alabama .............. | 3,266,740 | 3,061,743 | 204,997 | 6.7 |
| Mississippi ............. | 2,178,141 | 2,178,914 | —773 | (1) |
| WEST SOUTH CENTRAL: | | | | |
| Arkansas ............... | 1,786,272 | 1,909,511 | —123,239 | —6.5 |
| Louisiana .............. | 3,257,022 | 2,683,516 | 573,506 | 21.4 |
| Oklahoma .............. | 2,328,284 | 2,233,351 | 94,933 | 4.3 |
| Texas ................. | 9,579,677 | 7,711,194 | 1,868,483 | 24.2 |
| MOUNTAIN: | | | | |
| Montana ............... | 674,767 | 591,024 | 83,743 | 14.2 |
| Idaho ................. | 667,191 | 588,637 | 78,554 | 13.3 |
| Wyoming .............. | 330,066 | 290,529 | 39,537 | 13.6 |
| Colorado ............... | 1,753,947 | 1,325,089 | 428,858 | 32.4 |
| New Mexico ............. | 951,023 | 681,187 | 269,836 | 39.6 |
| Arizona ............... | 1,302,161 | 749,587 | 552,574 | 73.7 |
| Utah ................. | 890,627 | 688,862 | 201,765 | 29.3 |
| Nevada ................ | 285,278 | 160,083 | 125,195 | 78.2 |
| PACIFIC: | | | | |
| Washington ............. | 2,853,214 | 2,378,963 | 474,251 | 19.9 |
| Oregon ................ | 1,768,687 | 1,521,341 | 247,346 | 16.3 |
| California .............. | 15,717,204 | 10,586,223 | 5,130,981 | 48.5 |
| Alaska ................ | 226,167 | 128,643 | 97,524 | 75.8 |
| Hawaii ................ | 632,772 | 499,794 | 132,978 | 26.6 |

[1] Less than 0.1 percent.        *Source: U.S. Bureau of the Census.*

a higher mortality at each age, so that the male numerical superiority is gradually reduced. Males experience a higher infant, civilian, and military death rate than women do, and have a shorter life expectancy. In 1956, white males at five years of age would be expected to live 64.0 more years, whereas white females would be expected to live 70.3 more years. Negro males would be expected to live 62.4 years and Negro females 65.8 years. The death rate is higher for males than females at all age levels. We are not sure of the reasons for this during the infant and childhood years of life. From the teenage period on, males are subjected to greater work hazards, traffic accidents, and military casualties than women are. In addition, women perhaps care for their health better than men do. Also, while childbearing was once a hazard, modern health facilities and practices have so reduced the maternal mortality rate that even in the childbearing ages the mortality rates for women are lower than for males at the same age levels.

Earlier in the chapter we referred to the sex ratio of the population. One of the population trends in the United States during the first half of the twentieth century has been the increase in the proportion of the females in the total population.

In 1910 there were 943 females per 1,000 males in the population, reflecting especially the accrued results of several decades of heavy immigration with its high percentage of males. In 1950 there were 1,008 females per 1,000 males in the population. This ratio is expected to increase to 1,029 females per 1,000 males by 1970, and remain at this figure through 1980 (see Table 12). By 1975, females probably may outnumber males by as much as 3.5 million in the population of the United States.

There are two basic reasons for the changes in sex ratios in the population. The limitation of immigration and the death of foreign-born immigrants who came to this country in the latter half of the nineteenth century and early decades of the twentieth century are among the reasons for the change. The immigrants to this country had a low ratio of females. As immigration has been restricted, and as the older generations of immigrants have died off, this has had the effect of reducing the ratio of men in the population. Since World War II the sex composition of the immigrant population has changed to what it was prior to World War II. From 1945 to 1957, about 25,600 more males than females left the United States. In the same period approximately 287,800 more

*Table 12*

RATIO OF FEMALES TO MALES IN THE POPULATION OF THE UNITED STATES, 1910-1980

| Year | Number in Thousands * | | Females Per 1000 Males |
|---|---|---|---|
| | *Males* | *Females* | |
| 1910 | 47,554 | 44,853 | 943 |
| 1920 | 54,295 | 52,171 | 961 |
| 1930 | 62,297 | 60,780 | 976 |
| 1940 | 66,352 | 65,770 | 991 |
| 1950 | 75,530 | 76,153 | 1,008 |
| 1960 | 88,932 | 90,841 | 1,021 |
| 1970 | 102,592 | 105,607 | 1,029 |
| 1980 | 120,979 | 124,430 | 1,029 |

Source: U.S. Bureau of the Census, *Current Population Reports, Population Estimates,* Series P-25, Nos. 98, 114, 146, 170, and 187.
* Includes armed forces overseas beginning with 1940.

females than males came into the country, a net gain of 313,400. A large influx of war brides came during this period.

A greater number of boys than girls are born each year. Males, however, experience a greater mortality at each age, so that their numerical superiority is gradually reduced.[14] This discrepancy poses some interesting as well as critical problems which relate to marriage chances, competition in the marriage "market," dependency, widowhood, and job opportunities.[15] We shall discuss the problem of widowhood in the chapter on the family.

One of the trends in the labor force has been the greater employment of women. In 1890 there were some 4 million women in the labor force, which was one-sixth of the working population. By 1956 22 million women were employed, which was about one-third of the civilian labor force. By 1975 the female labor

[14] For a good discussion of changes in sex ratios in the population, *see* "Proportion of Women in Population Increasing," *Statistical Bulletin* (Metropolitan Life Insurance Co.), 39:6-8, November, 1958.
[15] For a layman's discussion of this problem, *see* Selig Greenberg, "Why Women Live Longer Than Men," *Harpers,* 215:70-73, October, 1957.

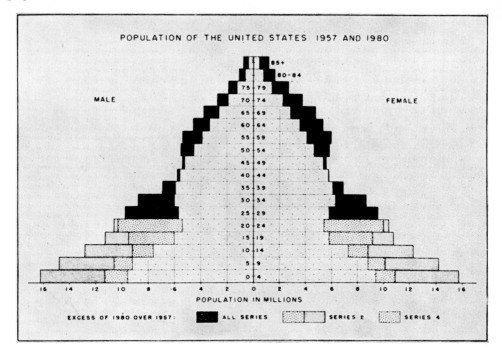

FIG. 5. POPULATION PYRAMID FOR THE U.S. FOR 1957 WITH PROJECTION TO 1980

SOURCE: Meyer Zitter and Jacob S. Siegel, "Illustrative Projections of the Population of the United States, by Age and Sex 1960 to 1980," *Current Population Reports, Population Estimates,* Series P-25, No. 187, November 10, 1958.

force may reach 34 million.[16] Currently, about 60 per cent of women over 65 who are separated, divorced, or widowed are working.

In age composition two trends are noticeable in the population—the increase in the aged, that is, those over 65 years of age, and an increase in younger age groups, following the high birth rates after 1946.

A common graphic method of showing the age composition of a population is through use of the age pyramid. In such pyramids vertical lines indicate the age of the population and horizontal lines the number or the percentage of each age element in the population (*see* Figs. 5 and 6). Figure 5 shows how the age pyramid of the United States may change from 1957 to 1980.

Another way of indicating the age of the population is by the use of data on median

[16] National Manpower Council, *Woman Power* (New York: Columbia University Press, 1957), p. 10.

*Table 13*

MEDIAN AGE OF THE POPULATION:
1900 TO 1960

| Year | Age (years) |
|------|------|
| 1960 | 29.5 |
| 1950 | 30.2 |
| 1940 | 29.0 |
| 1930 | 26.5 |
| 1920 | 25.3 |
| 1910 | 24.1 |
| 1900 | 22.9 |

Source: U.S. Bureau of the Census, "Estimates of the Population of the United States, by Age, Color, and Sex, July 1, 1955 to 1957." *Current Population Reports,* Series P-25, No. 170, December 18, 1957.

ages. As Table 13 shows, the median age of the population was 22.9 years in 1900 and 29.5 years in 1960. Because of the increase in birth rates following 1946, there was a slight decline in the median age of the population to 29.5 years when it was computed for 1960.

In 1900 the nation's population contained only 3 million people over 65 years of age; by 1940 the number had reached 6 million; by 1950 12.3 million, and by 1957 14.7 million. It is predicted that by 1975 there will be 20.7 million people in the population over 65 years of age. On the average, 386,000 males and 429,000 females reached 65 years of age annually between 1930 and 1940; between 1950 and 1957 the number of persons reaching 65 annually was 576,000 males and 677,000 females. The percentage of persons in the population over 65 years of age increased from 3.4 per cent in 1880 to 5.4 per cent in 1930; it was 8.2 per cent in 1950, 10.2 in 1960, and is likely to reach 14.4 per cent by 1980.

Because they are related to the growing number of aged persons, at this point we should mention two terms that are used widely in discussing the age composition of population. One of these is life span and the other life expectancy. *Life span* refers to the extreme length of life of the species, in our case man. This might, under ideal conditions, reach 100 years. *Life expectancy,* or *expectation of life,* refers to the average length of life a person can expect to attain.

Life expectancy in the United States has increased greatly and may be expected to increase considerably in the future. In 1900 the average length of life for males was 46.3 years and for females 48.3 years. The expectation of life at birth in 1955 was 66.7 years for all males and 72.9 years for all females. By 1975 the expectation may increase to 69.8 years for males and 76.0 years for females. A projection for 2000 is an expectation of 71.3 years for males and 77.1 years for females.[17]

In comparing the age structure of the population of the United States (Table 14), atten-

17 *See* Meyer Zitter and Jacob S. Siegel, "Illustrative Projections of the Population of the United States, by Age and Sex 1960 to 1980," *Current Population Reports,* Series P-25, No. 187, November 10, 1958.

*Table 14*

## POPULATION CHANGES BY AGE: 1950 TO 1957

| Age | Population Including Armed Forces Overseas | |
|---|---|---|
| | 1957 | 1950 |
| All ages | 171,229,000 | 151,132,000 |
| Under 5 years | 19,144,000 | 16,164,000 |
| 5 to 13 years | 30,062,000 | 22,180,000 |
| 14 to 17 years | 10,176,000 | 8,409,000 |
| 18 to 24 years | 15,327,000 | 16,081,000 |
| 25 to 44 years | 47,107,000 | 45,385,000 |
| 45 to 64 years | 34,664,000 | 30,720,000 |
| 65 years and over | 14,749,000 | 12,195,000 |

Source: U.S. Bureau of the Census, "Estimates of the Population of the United States, by Age, Color, and Sex, July 1, 1955 to 1957." *Current Population Reports,* Series P-25, No. 170, December 18, 1957.

tion should be called to the growth of dependent age groups—those under 13 years of age and those over 65 years of age. The most effective working age groups are between these two. As shown in Table 14, dependent age groups are on the increase in the population. Regarding our practice of retiring people at 65, it is interesting to note that the age for retirement in communist countries is 60 for males and 55 for females.

In 1900, 23.7 per cent of the population was under ten years of age. This percentage declined to 16.1 in 1940 and then increased to 19.5 in 1950, 21.5 in 1955, and is likely to be sustained above 20.0 per cent through 1965.

The increase in young age groups in the population has been reflected in increases in school enrollment for the past several years. In the fall of 1952, 32.5 million persons between five and 34 years of age enrolled in schools. In the fall of 1957, 41.2 million persons were enrolled. This was an increase of 8.7 million persons enrolled in schools over a five-year period. In succeeding years the increase will continue.

The last trend in population we will discuss

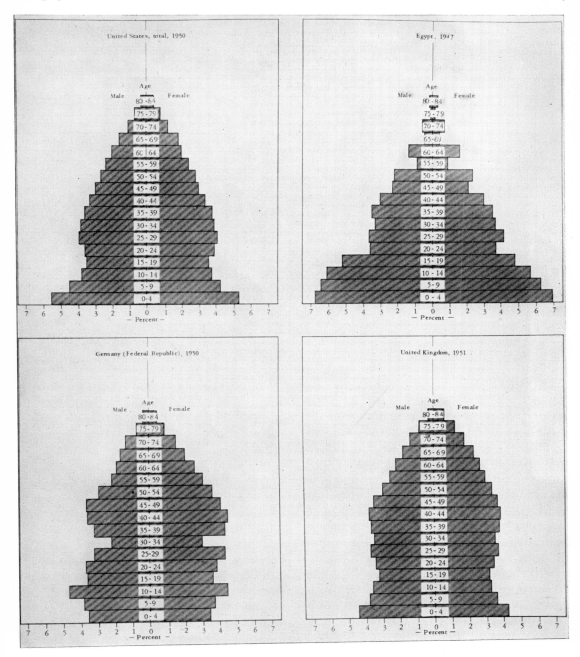

FIG. 6. AGE PYRAMID SHOWING DISTRIBUTION OF AGE AND SEX IN THE POPULATION OF THE UNITED STATES AND THREE OTHER NATIONS

Age structure, as indicated here, is the result of the past history of births and deaths in the four countries.

SOURCE: Donald J. Bogue, *Population of the United States* (Glencoe, Ill.: Free Press, 1959), p. 107.

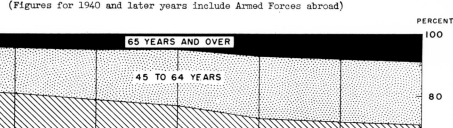

(Figures for 1940 and later years include Armed Forces abroad)

FIG. 7. PER CENT DISTRIBUTION BY AGE OF THE POPULATION OF THE UNITED STATES, 1900–1959

SOURCE: U.S. Bureau of the Census, *Current Population Reports, Population Estimates,* Series P-25, No. 212, January 26, 1960.

is the increase in educational attainment of the population. In 1940 males 25 years and older averaged 8.6 years of schooling, and females 8.7 years. By 1957 they had attained 10.3 and 10.9 years of schooling respectively. Nonwhite males and females had a lower educational attainment than whites, the figures being 7.3 years for males, 8.1 years for females in 1957.

Whereas the average educational level of the population 25 years and over was 9.3 years in 1950, the average was around 11.1 years in 1960 and may be 12.0 years in 1970, and 12.2 years in 1980 (*see* Fig. 8).

In 1950 there were 6 million persons in the United States who were college graduates. This number was expanded to 8 million by 1960, and may reach 11 million by 1970, and almost 15 million by 1980.

In recognizing the increase in schooling in the population, it is important to recognize also that every occupation has increased its educational standards or job qualifications. There is, of course, no way of telling whether qualifications have increased faster than the preparation for jobs.

A fairly new concept that has come into use, especially via the armed forces, is the concept of *functional illiteracy.* One who has not completed six or seven years of schooling is likely to be looked upon as functionally illiterate by the armed forces.

*The quality of the population*

In general the public appears to have more interest in numbers in the population than in quality. In gauging quality in the population, one of the problems is the lack of adequate bench marks against which to compare qualities at a later date. If number of years schooling completed is an index of quality, then the quality of the population is improving. Physically, because of better diets and food supplements of one kind or another, children develop faster today than they did several generations ago. Babies are no taller today than they were 50 years ago. By about 18 months height differences begin to develop. A boy of 14 today is, on the average, five inches taller and 12 pounds heavier than a 14-year-old in 1900.[18]

There are two areas of eugenics which directly relate to improving the quality of the population: positive and negative. *Positive eugenics* measures are designed to encourage better mate selection and the development of good physical, mental, and emotional characteristics in the population after birth. *Negative eugenics* policies are designed to keep the unfit from reproducing. The best illustration of the application of negative eugenics policies in the population of the United States is in the handling of feeble-minded classes. Institutionalization is widely practiced, and in some states feeble-minded persons may be sterilized, usually with their consent or with the consent of relatives, before being released from institutional care if there is evidence their feeble-mindedness was inherited. Of course, sterilization is sometimes applied to other persons, including habitual criminals in some states. Here the application of sterilization is directed toward their being bad social risks rather than to the fact that they are not always eugenically fit. Sometimes they are and sometimes they are not. "Fitness" is somewhat of a relative term, and often we do not have the scientific predictability to act as a guide in eugenic practices.

Birth control movements may have both

18 *Today's Health*, **36**:40, November, 1958.

positive and negative eugenic emphases. They may seek to develop a desire on the part of upper economic and better-educated groups to have more children. On the other hand, they may seek to develop attitudes, information, and facilities and services designed to reduce the size of families in the lower economic and lesser-educated groups. Often a eugenic argument is involved in such proposals. Ability, however, is not highly correlated with economic level.

It is, of course, more difficult to develop and apply a science of eugenics at the human level than in plant and animal breeding where controls are easier to establish and the emotional element is absent.

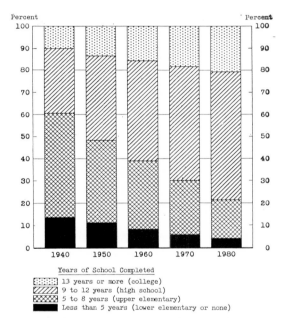

Years of School Completed
- 13 years or more (college)
- 9 to 12 years (high school)
- 5 to 8 years (upper elementary)
- Less than 5 years (lower elementary or none)

**Note:** Figures for 1970 and 1980 include Series B projections for younger adult ages (see text for explanation).

FIG. 8. YEARS OF SCHOOL COMPLETED BY THE POPULATION 1940 AND 1950 WITH PROJECTIONS FOR 1960, 1970, AND 1980

SOURCE: U.S. Bureau of the Census, "Projections of Educational Attainment in the United States, 1960 to 1980," *Current Population Reports*, Series P-20, No. 91, January 12, 1959.

## SUMMARY

The ultimate and smallest unit of population is, of course, the individual. Individual units in interaction with other individual units make up the social systems of a society from the smallest group to the largest crowd, audience, or state. The study of population is the science of demography and demographers are population specialists.

World population trends may vitally affect the welfare of the people of any given country. While the exact size of the world population is not known, improved census enumerations indicate that it may be about 2.8 billion, having increased to this figure from 1.0 billion in 1850, 1.5 billion in 1900, and 2.0 billion in 1930. The rate of growth of the world's population has been increasing, being more than twice as great in the decade 1950-60 than in the average decade between 1900 and 1930. Many factors have contributed to this increase, including improved food supplies, better health and medical practices, improved water supplies, better sewage disposal facilities, and improved environmental sanitation, including the increased cleanliness of people. As illustrative of the tools which the demographers use, we have included some common formulas and terms used by American demographers in their population research.

The population of the United States on January 1, 1958, was about 172.2 million. By 1960 it had reached 180 million. This country's population growth has, historically, been considerable because of immigration. Within the last three decades the growth has been largely from the excess of births over deaths, or what is called "natural increase." Immigration and migration from the possessions now account for a smaller part of the increase.

Trends in the population include rapid urbanization, a decline in rural farm population, a decline in the per cent of foreign-born in the population, and a long-range decline in the percentage of Negroes in the total population up to 1940 and then a slight increase to 1960. Numerically, the Negro population has increased with each census period. There has been a significant change in the distribution of the Negro population, chiefly a movement out of the South to other sections of the country and out of the rural regions of the South to the cities of the South. The Negro movement to the Pacific Coast states has been considerable.

The ratio of men to women in the population is declining. In 1950, for the first time the sex ratio fell below 100. In 1950 females outnumbered males by 1 million. With present trends, by 1975 the number of females may exceed males by 3.5 million. Associated with this trend has been a great increase in the number of women in the labor force.

Other significant trends in the population are the increase in the number of aged and the number of young people in the population, and, finally, an increase in the educational attainment of the population. There is some question as to whether or not the increase in educational attainment has kept pace with the increased standards for work in most occupations.

There are various attempts to improve the population through both positive and negative eugenic measures. The application of a science of eugenics at the human level is beset with many more difficulties than in the fields of animal and plant eugenics; however, some practical applications are being made.

THINGS TO DO AND TO DISCUSS

1. Construct a line graph showing the trends in world population from 1650 to the present.
2. What is the distinction between a *de jure* census and a *de facto* census? Which does the United States have?
3. To what do you attribute the recent increase in world population growth?
4. What is the relation between economic development and the rate of illiteracy in countries, according to data in the text?
5. Why is literacy becoming more and more indispensable for the intelligent citizen?
6. What are two extreme points of view with respect to the future outlook in world population? Evaluate each.
7. What races are likely to predominate in numbers in the world population of the future?
8. Do you or do you not see a real danger in world overpopulation? Amplify your answer.
9. From what sources has the population of the United States grown?
10. Will it ever be justifiable, for the obvious welfare of the majority, to place limits on the size of families? How might such social control be effectively and democratically achieved?
11. How do you account for the rapid population growth of the United States since 1950?
12. What outstanding trends do you notice in the growth and distribution of the Negro population in the United States?
13. Why the declining sex ratio in the population of the United States? What are some of its implications?
14. Why the increase in aged in the population of the United States?
15. What are likely to be some of the social consequences of the growing number of aged in our population?
16. Construct an age pyramid for the population of your state and county.
17. How do you account for the increase of young persons in our population?
18. In the West, should the nation's population continue to increase, without a comparable increase in jobs, what will be the implications?

FOR FURTHER STUDY

BARNES, GERALD. "Democracy and the Birth Ratio," *The Antioch Review,* **10:**436-46, December, 1950.

BOGUE, DONALD J. *The Population of the United States.* Glencoe, Ill.: Free Press, 1959. Excellent treatment of the growth, distribution, and composition of the population of the United States. Also has sections on Alaska and Hawaii. This volume faces up well to the implications of population change.

CARR-SAUNDERS, A. M. *World Population.* Oxford: Clarendon Press, 1936. An old but classic treatment of world population.

DUNCAN, OTIS D., and DUNCAN, BEVERLY. *The Negro Population of Chicago.* Chicago: University of Chicago Press, 1957. An intensive analysis of the population of one of America's principal biracial cities.

DUNCAN, OTIS D., and REISS, ALBERT J., JR. *Social Characteristics of Urban and Rural Communities, 1950.* New York: John Wiley and Sons, 1956. Much on the population differences between urban and rural communities.

GLICK, PAUL C. *American Families.* New York: John Wiley and Sons, 1957.

————. "The Life Cycle of the Family," *Marriage and Family Living,* **17**:3-9, February, 1955. What happens to the family at various stages in its life cycle.

HATT, PAUL K. (ed.). *World Population and Future Resources.* New York: American Book Co., 1952. Good appraisal of the productive capacity of the world to support its potential population.

HAUSER, PHILIP M. "Demography in Relation to Sociology," *The American Journal of Sociology,* **65**:169-73, September, 1959. An excellent discussion of the relationship between sociology and demography.

HERTZLER, J. O. *The Crisis in World Population.* Lincoln, Neb.: University of Nebraska Press, 1956. An analysis of the critical aspects of world population increase.

HUXLEY, ALDOUS. *Brave New World Revisited.* New York: Harper and Bros., 1959. What the future may hold in population control.

KRADER, LAWRENCE, and AIRD, JOHN S. "Sources of Demographic Data on Mainland China," *American Sociological Review,* **24**:623-29, October, 1959. Sources of data, as well as considerable factual material on China's population.

LANDIS, PAUL H., and HATT, PAUL K. *Population Problems.* 2nd ed. New York: American Book Co., 1954. One of the better standard texts on population.

NATIONAL MANPOWER COUNCIL. *Womanpower.* New York: Columbia University Press, 1957. An analysis of womanpower in the labor force, with projections.

PHELPS, HAROLD A., and HENDERSON, DAVID. *Population in Its Human Aspects.* New York: Appleton-Century-Crofts, 1958. The socioeconomic aspects of population analysis.

PIDDINGTON, ROBERT ALFRED. *The Limits of Mankind.* Bristol, Eng.: J. Wright, 1956. The optimum ceiling in world population explored.

PYKE, MARGARET. "Population Planning in Great Britain," *Eugenic Quarterly,* **3**:148-51, September, 1956. Toward a British population policy.

ROBERTS, GEORGE W. *The Population of Jamaica.* New York: Cambridge University Press, 1957. An intensive analysis of Jamaica's population.

SHANNON, LYLE W. *Underdeveloped Areas.* New York: Harper and Bros., 1957. One of the better treatments of the problems and characteristics of underdeveloped areas.

SMITH, T. LYNN. *Fundamentals of Population Study.* Chicago: J. B. Lippincott Co., 1960. Scope, methods, and materials involved in the study of population.

TAEUBER, CONRAD, and TAEUBER, IRENE B. *The Changing Population of the United States.* New York: John Wiley and Sons, 1958. One of the better analyses of changes taking place in the population of the United States.

TAEUBER, IRENE B. "Population Policies in Communist China," *Population Index,* 22:261-74, October, 1956. What the Communists have developed in the way of the problems and characteristics of underdeveloped areas.

THOMPSON, WARREN S. *Population Problems.* 4th ed. New York: McGraw-Hill Book Co., 1953. An excellent standard text on population.

———. *Population and Progress in the Far East.* Chicago: University of Chicago Press, 1959. Develops the theme that population is growing faster than agricultural and industrial development.

U. S. BUREAU OF THE CENSUS. *Historical Statistics of the United States: Colonial Times to 1957.* Washington: Superintendent of Documents, U. S. Government Printing Office, 1961.

WOYTINSKY, W. S., and WOYTINSKY, E. S. *World Population and Production: Trends and Outlook.* New York: Twentieth Century Fund, 1953. Probably the most extensive treatment on world population and production.

WRONG, DENNIS H. *Population.* New York: Random House, 1956. Some interesting observations on population phenomena.

# 7. THE BASIC SOCIAL UNIT— THE GROUP

IN CHAPTER 5 we discussed the development of society. Here we considered the gregarious nature of human beings and the origin of social groupings. In this discussion of gregariousness in human behavior we have discarded the theory of a gregarious instinct. We have taken the position that the behavioral tendency of people to want to be with other people is learned. The opening pages of Chapter 5 should then be considered as basic to the treatment of groups in this and the following chapter.

## THE GROUP DEFINED

The individual alone is not a social unit. It takes at least two people, a dyad, to make up a social unit. Two persons standing on the street corner are not a group. *A group is a unit of interacting personalities with an interdependence of role and status existing between the members.* An *aggregate,* as we have said, is composed of individuals who are physically contiguous and who have temporary or slight contact and interdependence with each other. A group, on the other hand, is made up of a number of people in definable interaction and directed toward achieving common goals through agreed upon means. Nothing is implied regarding size, permanence, form, or purpose.

Sherif carries the concept of the group a little further than the above definition, as follows:

A group is a social unit (1) which consists of a number of individuals who, at a given time, stand in more or less definite interdependent status and role relationships with one another and (2) which explicitly or implicitly possesses a set of values or norms regulating the behavior of individual members, at least in matters of consequence to the group. Thus, shared attitudes, sentiments, aspirations, and goals are related to and implicit in the common values or norms of the group.[1]

[1] Muzafer Sherif, "Superordinate Goals in the Reduction of Intergroup Conflict," *The American Journal of Sociology,* **63**:349-56, January, 1958.

Groups are smaller than crowds and audiences and the degree of interaction between group members is usually greater, although there is interaction in crowds and audiences. Groups are determined by relationships between people, but not necessarily subjective ones. Group stimuli may come from person-to-person contact, whereas crowd or audience stimulation is likely to come from a movie, an accident, a sports event, a minister, or some other kind of leader. In groups, especially primary groups, leaders are recognized as persons rather than as individuals. By this we mean that persons are individuals with recognized names, statuses, and, often, roles.

In groups the persons interact. They stimulate each other and behave toward other group members. The dynamics of this stimulus-response mechanism we described in Chapter 1. The smallest group is the dyad, or two-person group, and the next largest size the triad, or three-person group. There is no size limit to groups, but it would seem reasonable to assume that it would be difficult to maintain the characteristics of a group, as defined by us, in a population unit of large size. Much would depend upon the leader, the emotional ties between members, the group structure, the value systems, and the ends the group is trying to achieve. James found that informal groups ranged in size from two to seven persons, with a mean size of 2.41 persons. Work groups ranged in size from two to six persons, with a mean size of 2.35 persons. Action groups were smaller than nonaction groups. James' research was done in Portland, Oregon.[2]

## KINDS OF GROUPS

Sociologists have long recognized differences in groups and have used these differences as a basis for a wide variety of group classifications. The most often used classifications of groups which we shall discuss in this chapter are: (1) primary groups, (2) secondary groups, (3) in, or we, groups, (4) out, or they, groups, (5) functional groups, and (6) vertical and horizontal groups. In Chapter 9 peer groups and reference groups are fully discussed. As we consider the following classification of groups, the student should keep in mind that there is overlapping of categories and that one is not mutually exclusive of the other.

### Primary groups

In 1887 a German sociologist, Ferdinand Tonnies, divided group relationships into two classes. Close, familial, communal relationships he called *Gemeinschaft,* and more remote, impersonal group relationships he classed as *Gesellschaft.*[3] On the basis of his classification, Tonnies would characterize rural societies as showing a preponderance of *Gemeinschaft* characteristics and urban societies as predominating in *Gesellschaft* relationships.

In 1909, one of the great pioneers in American sociology, Charles H. Cooley, developed a theory of primary groups similar to that of Tonnies' *Gemeinschaft* characterization.

Cooley characterized primary groups as follows:

By primary groups I mean those characterized by intimate face to face association and cooperation. They are primary in several senses, but chiefly in that they are fundamental in forming the social nature and ideals of the individual. The result of intimate association psychologically is a certain fusion of individualities in a common whole, so that one's very self, for many purposes at least, is the common life and purpose of the group. Perhaps the simplest way of describing this wholeness is by

[2] John James, "A Preliminary Study of the Size Determinant in Small Group Interaction," *American Sociological Review,* **16**:474-77, August, 1951.

[3] For the original work, *see* Ferdinand Tonnies, *Gemeinschaft and Gesellschaft* (Leipzig: Fues's Verlag, 1887). For an English translation, *see* Charles P. Loomis, *Fundamental Concepts of Sociology* (New York: American Book Co., 1940).

saying it as a "we"; it involves the sort of sympathy and mutual identification for which "we" is the natural expression.[4]

Examples of primary groups, according to Cooley, would be families, play groups, neighboring groups, and association groups like cliques, gangs, or courtship groups. Cooley speaks of such groups as "face-to-face groups," in which the relationships are characterized by "sympathy and mutual identification."

Davis says that primary groups have certain physical conditions and a quality of relations which characterize them. These characteristics are as follows:

1. *The physical conditions of primary groups:*
   a. physical proximity or close contact
   b. smallness of the group
   c. duration of relationship, intimacy being a matter of frequency and duration as well as intensity of contact

2. *The character of primary relations:*
   a. identity of ends, in which two or more persons recognize certain common ends and strive to attain them
   b. the relationship is an end within itself
   c. the relationship is personal, in which each person's interest is centered in others as persons
   d. the relationship is inclusive, in that primary groups serve inclusive needs of the group members
   e. the relationship is spontaneous, and is not dictated by protocol or necessarily by planning [5]

Where primary groups of one type are absent, such as family, neighborhood, or courtship groups, primary groups of other kinds are substituted for them. Examples are found in the armed forces, where comradeship relations between men may in some respect serve as compensation for the family or courtship groups.

Primary groups reflect a high degree of cohesiveness. Sociologists and psychologists have not done enough research on group cohesiveness to isolate all the factors contributing to cohesive primary groups. Homogeneity is not always a factor in cohesiveness; however, group thinking and feeling together often are. Respect for the group and happiness within it contributes to its primariness and its cohesiveness. Long acquaintance between members prior to group membership contributes to the cohesive quality of groups, according to some research.[6]

Occasionally a group, or even an entire community, may maintain its primary qualities in a hostile social and cultural environment. A case in point are the Amish, with their survivals of old-world values and social institutions. Since 1693, when they split with their parent Swiss Mennonites, the Amish have been able to establish communities reflecting a high degree of primariness. To develop and maintain this primariness in community subcultures the Amish have developed hostility toward change. They have developed a strong "we" feeling in their followers and tend to isolate themselves from intimate association with the non-Amish community through the practice of *Meidung,* or the shunning of nonorthodox persons. A nonconforming Amish child is encouraged to marry outside the Amish adherents, thus further insulating the Amish community against contamination. The perpetuation of the original conflict of the Amish with the Swiss Mennonites helps to develop cohesiveness and primariness in the Amish community.[7]

Obviously, primary groups serve to satisfy certain elemental human needs, such as affection, love, intimate contacts, security, and a

[4] Charles H. Cooley, *Social Organization* (New York: Charles Scribner's Sons, 1909), copyrighted in 1937 by Elsie Jones Cooley, p. 23.

[5] Adapted from Kingsley Davis, *Human Society* (New York: The Macmillan Co., 1949), pp. 290-98.

[6] T. C. Keedy, Jr., "Factors in the Cohesiveness of Small Groups," *Sociology and Social Research,* **40:**329-32, May-June, 1956. *See also* Eric F. Gardner and George G. Thompson, *Social Relations and Morale in Small Groups* (New York: Appleton-Century-Crofts, 1956).

[7] John A. Hostetler, "Old World Extinction and New World Survival of the Amish: A Study of Group Maintenance and Dissolution," *Rural Sociology,* **20:**213-19, September-December, 1955.

sense of belonging.[8] Later in the chapter we shall have more to say about the primariness of groups in relation to size.

## Secondary groups

Cooley confined himself to primary groups and did not make a second classification called "secondary groups." Secondary groups are loosely defined. The interaction is not on a face-to-face basis but is rather indirect, impersonal, and relatively less influential. Unlike primary groups they are as a rule larger, less intimate, more contractual, and more temporary in nature. The two pairs of groups, primary and secondary, may be thought of as occupying opposite ends of a continuum. A school club, a fraternity, or a sorority would likely be secondary groups, although there might be smaller primary subgroups, for example cliques, within each. Luncheon clubs are likely to be secondary rather than primary, as are also church circles, classes in school, or welfare and service clubs. Davis gives a good characterization of secondary groups. He says:

The nature of secondary contacts is obvious. They may be face to face, but if so they are of the touch-and-go variety. The contact with the street car motorman, with the grocery clerk, or with the bank cashier is a perfect illustration. Many contacts are entirely indirect, being handled through long-distance communication, the two persons never seeing each other. Thus an insurance salesman may call a prospective client by telephone and handle the entire transaction by wire, mail and check; or a scholar thousands of miles away may write for a reprint of a scientific paper which he has seen referred to. Actually a great part of the essential business of the modern world is handled through impersonal contacts, whether of the face-to-face or the indirect variety. Such contacts do not necessarily imply any identity of ends as between the parties concerned, any interest in the other party as an end in himself, any conception of the rela-

tionship as an end in itself, or any sentiment whatever attaching to the contact. They do not require that the parties know each other in an inclusive sense but only in a very special context, and when this context changes the relationship has no significance. One party may be substituted for another without affecting the relationship. The contact is viewed purely as a means to an end and is dropped as soon as the end changes. It, along with the other party, is treated in a rational context. In other words the secondary contact is entered into in the spirit of rational calculation—in the spirit of technological, economic, and political manipulation.[9]

## In-groups

Groups to which we belong, to which we owe allegiance, and in which we participate, are called in-groups. We identify ourselves with in-groups. We usually assume that they have superior qualities of some kind. These superior qualities may be of material nature, like the "best" fraternity house on the campus, or they may be intangible, as a system of values, or a system of beliefs, as in a religion. The members of a family may feel that they are superior in religion, morals, and manners to the neighbors next door. This is usually a subjective in-group attitude.

One person's in-group may be another person's out-group. Opposing youth cliques and gangs are a bad example of this. Toward our in-groups we are likely to attribute positive qualities of which we approve. Toward our out-groups we are likely to associate qualities of which we do not approve.

## Out-groups

Out-groups in the main are groups to which we do not have allegiance and in which we do not participate. Out-group feelings may range from a somewhat neutral attitude toward a group to a violent antagonism. One may seek to avoid contact with out-groups rather than show antagonism toward them. When once antagonism is built up in a gen-

[8] *See* Edward Gross, "Primary Functions of the Small Group," *The American Journal of Sociology*, **60**:24-29, July, 1954; *also* G. C. Homans, *The Human Group* (New York: Harcourt, Brace and Co., 1950).

[9] Davis, *op. cit.*, pp. 302-3.

© *New York Daily News from United Press*

*Conflict is often the source of developing strong in-group, out-group attitudes.*

eration toward an out-group, the antagonism may continue to exist over a period of generations.[10] This is clearly noticeable in race relations.

In-group feelings are usually more stable and constant than are out-group feelings. While out-group feelings tend to persist, the emotional intensity of them rises and falls. A good example of this is found in labor relations. Labor and management may look upon each other as out-groups in some situations, but without any noticeable antagonism. However, let a strike arise and the out-group feelings are likely to intensify.[11] One boys' gang may ap-propriate a block and look upon another gang in another block as an out-group. Let one gang try to invade another gang's territory, however, and the fight is on.

### Functional or special interest groups

As a society becomes more complex many groupings arise which center around special functions or objectives. Often these groups represent a special occupational category, like the realtors, or they may be seeking some reform, as temperance groups, or they may be dedicated to opposing change, like groups which oppose the fluoride treatment of water.

While special interest groups may have units in local communities, top leadership may come from outside the community and local

[10] Emory S. Bogardus, "Changes in Racial Distances," *International Journal of Opinion and Attitude Research,* **I**:55-62, 1947.

[11] *See* E. T. Hiller, *The Strike* (Chicago: University of Chicago Press, 1928).

response may be determined by direction from out-of-community leadership. The individual units of such groups are often held together by cheap, fast, and abundant communication.

While we have referred to pressure groups in various places of the text, we should say more about them at this point. Of all social institutions, perhaps education and government receive most pressure from special interest groups who seek to use the schools to advance their causes. Legislatures have often frozen special interest group ideas into laws. One state requires schools to teach nonacademic subjects in safety, fire prevention, conservation, morals, and dangers of alcohol. Special holidays are often set aside in response to the demands of pressure groups. One school estimates that a single community festival required 2,000 student hours of released time. This situation is pointed out not as criticism, because such activities and experiences are of some educational and citizenship value, but merely as examples of special interest pressure group activities. Of course, there are many special interest groups which are more or less self-contained and do not try to project their ideas and programs upon other groups.

*Horizontal and vertical groups*

Groups composed of people who belong to the same social hierarchy, occupational level, or income class are often referred to as horizontal groups. Craft unions would be an example. Although there may be considerable variation in skill and wage levels within a carpenters' union, in general it may be called a horizontal group.

A group made up of people of diverse education, skills, occupations, incomes, and social position is called a vertical group. This means that the group cuts across positional layers and that there is more opportunity for mobility up and down the layers than in a horizontal group. A company union, a Rotary club, or a country club membership would be an example. In American society, with its emphasis upon democracy and social mobility, the opportunity to participate in vertical groups is immensely significant.

## HOW GROUPS INFLUENCE US

What are some of the functions of groups and how do they influence us? Later in the chapter we shall relate some of the findings of group research as they apply to the interaction of group members.

1. *Groups are culture bearers.* Groups are carriers of the culture. This means that they play important roles in the socialization process or learning of the culture. While groups may bear their own distinctive culture traits and patterns and teach these to their members, especially the young, they are also culture bearers of many phases of the general mass culture. The socialization process in the family is an illustration. A family may transmit its own distinctive value system and culture traits and patterns to its young, but it is likely to transmit much of the general culture in the socialization process. For example, most American families make an effort to teach the young to use English, civic knowledge, or simple mathematics as a part of the common culture.

The socialization process in normal family situations begins to develop out of mother-child and father-child relationships, with perhaps older children participating in the training of the young. Under the influence of its role as culture bearer, the family has certain characteristics which may make it very influential. As we shall see in the next chapter, children come into the family at birth, or at an early age in most foster homes. They are, therefore, plastic and unconditioned. The time spent in the home is important in culture transmission. There is much repetition of attitudes, values, and behavior patterns in families. The prestige of parents and appeal to the mother and father principle in child training is tremendous. Parents may compel their children to conform to their wishes. Finally, the family caters to many needs of the child so that its impact touches the development of the child at many points. The child may be influenced physically, socially, mentally, and spiritually, in action as well as in ideals.

The group's function as culture bearer begins soon after the birth of the child. Before the child can speak it recognizes gestures which are a part of the culture, and makes responses to these gestures. After verbalization begins, socialization takes place at an accelerated rate. The child may acquire the religious and political ideologies of its parents. As the child matures, other groups leave the imprint of their roles as culture bearers. Among these are play groups, the clique, the courtship group, the gang, and other association and special interest groups, such as Boy and Girl Scouts, and religious and recreational groups.

2. *Group contacts stimulate us.* This point needs little discussion. The presence of two persons together in interaction is a stimulus to each other, although perhaps in unequal ratios. A stimulus may evoke a favorable or unfavorable response, depending upon the principals involved.

There was a time in sociology and psychology when certain leaders believed that the bringing together of two or more persons in a group, or a larger number of persons in a crowd or mob, was a kind of creative synthesis in which the end product—in this case behavior—was greater than the behavior potential of the parts, or the individuals, taken separately. In explaining this behavior the chemical formula for water was sometimes used. For instance, both hydrogen and oxygen are gases, but where combined in proper proportions the result is a liquid, $H_2O$. In other words, the end product, a liquid, was very different from the parts which are gases. The process was called creative synthesis. Much has been written along this line.[12]

12 For a classical treatment, *see* Gustave LeBon, *The Crowd* (London: Allen and Unwin, 1899).

The theory of creative synthesis in groups has pretty well been discarded. The explanations used now are those of stimulation and response. One person stimulates another, who responds. His response is, in turn, a feedback stimulus to the initial stimulation.

In the socialization process the various groups of which the individual is a member may exert competitive stimuli. The family may face the competitive stimulus of an association clique. Church groups may face the competitive stimulus (we call it competition) of recreation groups. One in-group may be in competition with another in-group for the time and loyalty of individuals. This often leads to much competition between in-groups for the loyalty of their members.

3. *Groups control us.* Group pressure upon members is one of the strongest methods of social control, which is essentially control of the individual by groups, or the mass society, in contrast to self-control.

The whole process of learning a culture, which we have referred to as enculturation, is a controlled process as carried on by social systems, especially educational institutions. Elements of group and mass culture in the form of value systems, culture concepts, behavior patterns, and knowledge of material objects are transmitted in the process of socialization to become part of the individual culture equipment.

A good illustration of the controlled transmission of the group and mass culture takes place in the elementary and high schools. Here the basic language, approved attitudes, approved historical knowledge, and behavior patterns are taught. The society may in a course in world history put its own stamp upon certain events and personalities so that what a Canadian, an American, or a Russian child learns about the same events may be different. The same is true of political behavior. The Russian child and the Canadian child may be taught codes of citizen conduct greatly different from each other. In the high school and college there is more provision for individual

*This man carries the culture of his tribal group.*

learning, but even here the social control of the learning process is still prominent.

Groups, whether family, clique, gang, or courtship, have a tendency to classify behavior as approved or disapproved or, more often, "good" or "bad." In developing and enforcing group control "good" behavior is reinforced through approval and rewards, whereas "bad" behavior is disapproved or punished. Emotional reinforcement may be involved in both. In giving approval to behavior, the emotions employed may be affection or appeal to status and approval, whereas in punishment the emotions may be anger, loss of status, and disapproval.

The effectiveness of the group as a controlling force in human behavior is well summarized by Skinner. He says:

> The power of the group is, of course, great. Even the political tyrant, the despotic father, the bully in the street gang, or any other exceptionally strong individual usually yields eventually to the group as a whole.[13]

4. *Groups insulate us.* Groups may insulate their members from interaction with other groups. Parents who are anti-Semitic in attitudes and prejudice will try to discourage their children from association with Jewish children. In a community where there is racial strife, families may encourage their children to associate and identify themselves with members of their own race almost exclusively. One of the problems in breaking up juvenile gangs is that they insulate their members from contact with nongang members. The gang culture becomes a kind of subculture cocoon around the members of the gang. One gang member in discussing this said that he didn't know the kids of his neighborhood were such nice fellows until his gang was broken up by an appeal of a Boys Club Program in his section of the city. Class-conscious families will perhaps try to limit their associations and contacts,

[13] B. F. Skinner, *Science and Human Behavior* (New York: The Macmillan Co., 1953), p. 327.

except for purposes of service, to people of their own class or strata. One country club "set" may be almost completely insulated from another country club "set."

5. *Groups may have therapeutic value.* Group interaction may be one means of bringing an individual into the range of approved behavior or conduct. Let us use as an illustration a "very shy child." Because of his shyness, the behavior of the child may not fall within range of approved behavior or approved personality type. A few days or weeks of group contact may result in the child's losing his shyness and becoming a "normal" child with normal roles and attitudes. In this case a deviation has been overcome as a result of group contacts. As we shall see in the next chapter, the sociogram is often used as a means of determining acceptance and rejection in groups, especially school-age groups.

Group psychotherapy is now used in mental hospitals as well as in the private practice of psychiatry and clinical psychology. Normal interaction may be greatly modified by mental illness, the particular nature of the modification being determined by the kind and degree of illness. Psychotherapy may restore normal interaction. Group psychotherapy has also been used in the treatment of other illnesses, especially tuberculosis and alcoholism, where the patients had a sense of isolation and shame which grew out of their illness or their addiction.

Group psychotherapy involves the development of small groups of patients, usually not more than eight, and more often five or six persons. The groups meet together under the supervision of a psychiatrist or clinical psychologist to plan their treatment procedures and discuss their mutual problems. There are several ways in which these group methods may be attributed to the improvement of the individual. They may raise the interaction level of the individual to somewhere near the level expected in normal group interaction. Group contacts may provide parental, sibling, or other affection substitutes of the nature pro-

*An individual's race may insulate him from contact with other races.*

vided in normal group relationships, which may be important in mental therapy. Group psychotherapy is also a method for utilizing the resources which patients have to help each other, and is used, of course, under the supervision of a therapist.[14] Group therapy may also be used to relieve tensions, anxieties, insecurities between the members of a group, or relieve anxieties over one's particular problems. Individual expression is often freed and confidence restored by the participating members of a group under treatment by group therapy methods.[15]

If group methods are successful in therapy, then it would seem obvious that wholesome and satisfactory group relations are important in the prevention of mental illnesses and other forms of deviation, such as delinquency or addiction.

6. *Group membership gives us prestige and status.* Group belonging may satisfy a desire for prestige and status. In many groups, for example youth groups where attendance and participation are not compulsory, one may leave the group unless it gives him some element of prestige, recognition, or status.

Groups such as sororities and fraternities, which develop in-group feelings in their membership and have distinctive dress, jewelry, and other symbols, serve as status and prestige groups for their members. Luncheon clubs, country clubs, and larger association groups of secondary nature also have a prestige and status value to their membership.

7. *Groups make for effective effort and accomplishment.* One of the things that Hunter found in Regional City (Atlanta) was that very few power leaders worked alone.[16] They

[14] *See* Marvin K. Opler, "Group Psychotherapy: Individual and Cultural Dynamics in a Group Process," *The American Journal of Psychiatry,* 5:433-38, November, 1957.

[15] *See* S. R. Slavson, *Analytic Group Therapy* (New York: Columbia University Press, 1951), and G. R. Bach, *Intensive Group Therapy* (New York: Ronald Press, 1954).

[16] Floyd Hunter, *Community Power Structure* (Chapel Hill, N.C.: University of North Carolina Press, 1955).

usually worked in cooperation with other power structure leaders. Group effort shows up at its best in cooperation, which is essentially a synthesis of thought and effort toward the accomplishment of a mutual end or objective being sought.

More and more small-group research is testing ways of organizing and managing groups to determine which kinds of organization and management are most effective in terms of production, group solidarity, and happiness of group members.[17]

## MAJOR TRENDS IN GROUP LIFE

One of the important trends in group life is the mutiplication of group contacts. This has been brought about by the increased mobility of people, and by an increase in the number of groups, especially special interest groups. People settle close together in cities or in suburbs where opportunities for group contact increase, for instance the opportunity for participating in play groups and for visitation. In economic and social pursuits, people move swiftly from one group contact to another. Specialization and increased culture complexity add each year a large number of new, special interest groups.

While group contacts have increased, the length of contacts has lessened. The competition for time, under pressure of increased contacts, necessarily limits the length of group contacts. The doctor, for example, who used to sit and visit with his patients, now moves them into a hospital where he conducts an assembly-line visitation, going from one to the other before his office day starts or during the lunch hour.

Most writers say that there has been a decline in primary groups and a corresponding decline in secondary group contacts. Primary influences of family groups tend to be dissipated as children, upon maturity, move away from home. Mobility breaks up kinship groups. Good highways and automobiles and school consolidation have caused primary neighborhoods to be replaced by larger, more impersonal, community areas. Recently, through neighborhood planning, some attempts have been made to provide a physical layout arrangement in housing and urban development which will encourage neighboring between families.

It is wrong, of course, to assume that cities completely discourage primary group contacts. Rather, the studies show a considerable variety of primary group contacts repeated frequently in cities.[18]

## SOME FINDINGS FROM GROUP RESEARCH

The amount of research on the structure and dynamics of small groups is considerable and, on the whole, the significant findings of this research are well reported.[19] Probably the most productive areas of group research have had to do with (1) group size in relation to function, (2) the process of communication between group members, and (3) the person-

alities of group members and their influence upon group interaction patterns.

There is much evidence that as size of groups increase, intimacy and contacts decrease.[20] Cliques, as a rule, are made up of

[17] *See* Paul Hare, Edgar F. Borgatta, and Robert F. Bales, *Small Groups* (New York: Alfred A. Knopf, 1955).
[18] Floyd Dotson, "Patterns of Voluntary Association among Urban Working Class Families," *American Sociological Review*, **16**:687-93, October, 1951.

[19] In such sources as Hare, Borgatta, and Bales, *op. cit.*, and a chapter by the same authors, "Structure and Dynamics of Small Groups: A Review of Four Variables," in *Review of Sociology: Analysis of A Decade*, ed., Joseph B. Gittler (New York: John Wiley and Sons, 1957), pp. 391-422.
[20] P. H. Fischer, "An Analysis of the Primary Group," *Sociometry*, **16**:272-76, 1953.

three or four persons.[21] James concludes that there is a tendency for work groups of college students to gravitate in the direction of two-person groups. Function appears smoothest when the mean size is close to 2.4 persons.[22]

As numbers of a group increase, the more difficult it is for the group members to relate to each other as persons, hence intimacy is likely to decline as the size of the group increases. The larger the group, the greater the number of pairs and other subgroups possible within the larger units. Such subgroups may weaken the structure of the parent group. Some research indicates that group leadership difficulties may develop where group size is larger than six persons. This may relate to the fact that most group leaders can only give maximum individual attention to a fairly small number of persons as they interact with each other in group situations.[23] Other investigators note the emergence of leadership with increasing group size. Obviously, the techniques of group leadership vary with the size of the group.[24] Perhaps we might conclude that optimum size of groups depends upon the tasks to be done. It may take six men to move a piano but only two to carry a sofa. There are also many factors that influence the interaction process of group members in addition to size and leadership.

The patterns and channels of communication between members of a group have been the subject of considerable research. Much attention has been given to the spatial arrangement of group members in relation to each other so as to get the maximum production from the group commensurate also with the greatest satisfaction. As an illustration, in a modern college of education building the student desk arrangement is usually circular or in the form of a rectangle where the professor sits at the head of the rectangle. The interaction of the students appears to be better where they are seated in a circular arrangement, with everyone feeling that he has an equal chance for class participation, than when they sit in a series of rows where the persons seated within the rows are more central in the communication process than the persons at the ends of the rows. The interaction between the professor and the front row students is likely to be greater than that between back- and middle-row students and the professor.

Centrality in communication is important.[25]

The man in the position of hub of a five-man wheel pattern, the man at the juncture of a Y formation, and the middle man of a linear chain, are central in decreasing degrees, while in a fourth pattern, the circle, no person is central. In general, task efficiency increases with centralization. The wheel allows the fastest trial. The central person tends to receive and send more messages than other members, is regarded as leader by them, and shows higher and increasing satisfaction. But the highest average satisfaction is found in the circle pattern, where members have more independence of action.[26]

It has been found that members of a group tend to address more communications to people sitting across the table from them than to persons sitting next to them.[27] Eye contact is important in communication. In communication feedback response from receiver to sender apparently increases the accuracy with which information is transmitted, as well as

[21] A. B. Hollingshead, *Elmtown's Youth* (New York: John Wiley and Sons, 1949).

[22] John James, "A Preliminary Study of the Size Determinant in Small Group Interaction," *American Sociological Review*, 16:474-77, 1951.

[23] For some interesting research on this point, *see* Bernard M. Bass and Fay-Tyler M. Norton, "Group Size and Leaderless Discussions," *Journal of Applied Psychology*, 35:397-400, 1951.

[24] *See* J. K. Hemphill, "Relations between the Size of the Group and the Behavior of 'Superior' Leaders," *Journal of Social Psychology*, 32:11-22, 1950.

[25] A. Bavelas, "A Mathematical Model for Group Structures," *Applied Anthropology*, 7:16-30, 1948.

[26] Robert F. Bales, Paul Hare, and Edgar F. Borgatta, "Structure and Dynamics of Small Groups: A Review of Four Variables," in *Review of Sociology: Analysis of A Decade*, ed. Joseph B. Gittler (New York: John Wiley and Sons, 1957), p. 404.

[27] B. Steinzar, "The Spatial Factor in Face to Face Discussion Groups," *Journal of Abnormal and Social Psychology*, 45:552-55, 1950.

increasing the confidence of both sender and receiver in the communication task accomplished.

Group decision-making, compared to leader or management decision-making, has been a subject of considerable research. Bavelas' work at Massachusetts Institute of Technology showed that the production rate of sewing machine operators increased when they had liberal opportunity to use group decisions in setting working goals and in determining the conditions under which they were to work. Such arrangements contrasted to controlled group situations in which management set the production goals and defined the working conditions.[28] Much work has also been done on the influence of supervisory and authoritarian leadership versus participatory leadership in group situations. Much of the evidence favors participatory leadership, but the results are in no way conclusive. The interested student may well check the individual studies.[29]

## SUMMARY

The tendency to want to be with other persons is learned. Human interaction is perhaps at its best in groups, which are essentially small units of interpersonal interaction.

Primary groups are the intimate, face-to-face groups, such as the family, play groups, cliques and gangs, which are first in shaping the attitudes and behavior of persons. Lesser influential groups are called secondary groups. In-groups are the groups to which we belong and to which we have allegiance. Out-groups are groups to which we have no allegiance, in fact we may have antagonism toward them.

Groups influence us in many ways. They are carriers of the culture. They stimulate and control us. They give us status and enable us to achieve goals that we cannot achieve individually.

One of the trends in group life is the multiplication and shortening of group contacts. Another trend is the decline of group contacts of primary type and the increase of secondary groups. While the growth of cities creates conditions unfavorable to primary group contacts, such contacts are by no means absent in urban environments.

THINGS TO DO AND TO DISCUSS

1. After some investigation from sociological sources, arrive at what is a suitable concept of a group.
2. Differentiate between primary and secondary groups.
3. What are some important characteristics of a primary group?
4. Clearly distinguish between in-groups and out-groups. Make a listing of out- and in-groups in your community.
5. What are horizontal and vertical groups?
6. What are some of the special interest groups in your community in the pressure group class?
7. How do groups influence us, generally speaking? From your own experiences or observations indicate some of the major ways in which groups influence people.

[28] *See* N. R. F. Maier, *Psychology in Industry* (Boston: Houghton Mifflin Co., 1946); John B. Knox, *Human Relations in Industry* (New York: Random House, 1955); and E. Paul Torrence, "Group Decision Making and Disagreement," *Social Forces*, **35**:314-18, May, 1957.

[29] Such as those cited in Paul Hare, Edgar F. Borgatta, and Robert F. Bales, *Small Groups* (New York: Alfred A. Knopf, 1955), Chap. 10.

8. What are some major group trends in the United States?
9. What influence does size of a group have upon group interaction?
10. Experiment with the physical placement of the members of a group to show how placement of group members influences communication and interaction between members.

FOR FURTHER STUDY

COOLEY, CHARLES H. *Social Organization*. New York: Charles Scribner's Sons, 1909. Contains his noted treatment of primary groups.

DAVIS, KINGSLEY. *Human Society*. New York: The Macmillan Co., 1949. One of the better discussions of primary groups.

GARDNER, ERIC F., and THOMPSON, GEORGE G. *Social Relations and Morale in Small Groups*. New York: Appleton-Century-Crofts, 1956. Small group interaction and morale.

GITTLER, JOSEPH B. (ed). *Review of Sociology: Analysis of a Decade*. New York: John Wiley and Sons, 1957. Good review of the group concept and supporting literature.

HARE, PAUL; BORGATTA, EDGAR F.; and BALES, ROBERT F. *Small Groups*. New York: Alfred A. Knopf, 1955. A wealth of research data on small groups.

HOMANS, G. C. *The Human Group*. New York: Harcourt, Brace and Co., 1950. A study of group organization and behavior plus a theoretical structure for the analysis of groups.

HOSTETLER, JOHN A. "Old World Extinction and New World Survival of the Amish: A Study of Group Maintenance and Dissolution," *Rural Sociology*, **20**:213-19, September-December, 1955. How old world traits of the Amish survive in a new social environment.

JAMES, JOHN. "A Preliminary Study of the Size Determinant in Small Group Interaction," *American Sociological Review*, **16**:474-77, August, 1951. Size of groups in relation to interaction.

KEEDY, T. C., JR. "Factors in the Cohesiveness of Small Groups," *Sociology and Social Research*, **40**:329-32, May-June, 1956. Factors maintaining group cohesiveness.

LOOMIS, CHARLES P. *Fundamental Concepts of Sociology*. New York: American Book Co., 1940. Translation of Tonnies *Gemeinshaft* and *Gesellschaft* concepts.

SHERIF, MUZAFER. "Superordinate Goals in the Reduction of Intergroup Conflict," *The American Journal of Sociology*, **63**:349-56, January, 1958. How intergroup conflict and tension may be reduced.

SKINNER, B. F. *Science and Human Behavior*. New York: The Macmillan Co., 1953. Some scientific findings related to group behavior.

THIBALT, JOHN W., and KELLEY, HAROLD H. *The Social Psychology of Groups*. New York: John Wiley and Sons, 1959. One of the better works on small group behavior.

# 8. THE FAMILY— NURSERY OF HUMAN NATURE

So far in this section on the structure of society we have been concerned with kinds of groups and their structure, and with the role of specific groups in the lives of individuals. We shall now study in some detail the most universal and most influential of all groups—the family. Emphasis is placed upon structure, functions, and trends.

## THE FAMILY AND SOCIALIZATION

We have indicated that socialization is the process of learning a culture. Of all the groups that serve as media of socialization, none is more influential than the family. There are many reasons why this is so. In the first place, the family is a *universal group,* present in one form or another in nearly all societies, past and present. Second, when we observe families of today we find characteristics which make the family an effective learning and socializing medium. Some of these characteristics are:

1. The largely unconditioned state of the child at birth.

2. The large amount of time the child spends in the home, especially until the time that he enters school.

3. The repetition of attitudes and behavior patterns in the family. Repetition, when added to plasticity and duration, create in the family a powerful learning situation.

4. The prestige of parents which is a powerful factor in learning, especially in learning by example and imitation.

5. Parental authority, backed in modern societies by legal authority.

6. The intimacy of the family, which

touches the child at many points in its growth and contributes to its physical, mental, social, and spiritual development.

7. The emotional reinforcement of the family group, with emphasis upon affection, concern, and fidelity.

The socialization role of families obviously varies greatly from family to family. One family may produce one or more antisocial personalities. In other families the personalities are highly competent and normal, receiving the full stamp of approval of the culture in which the family lives.

## THE SEARCH FOR FAMILY ORIGINS

The origins of the family are lost in antiquity. In the main there are three theories of how the family originated. One is that animals pair, and that in the process of biological development the strong attraction of male for female led to a pairing arrangement between the human sexes. Some of the higher apes pair but others are clearly polyandrous or polygynous, living with more than one mate.

Another theory of family origin is that the original family was a patriarchal family dominated by a powerful male head who had more than one wife. The situation was roughly equivalent to what one finds in a herd of elk, where an old elk is lord and master of the flock which may contain several cows and younger males.[1] This theory is conjectural and there is little reason to accept it as fact.

A more convincing theory is that the family originated out of strong ties between the mother and the dependent, helpless child. This theory stresses the mother-child bonds as the stable bonds in family origin. The role of the father was much less important than the mother role. However, since both mother and child were to some extent dependent upon the father, and perhaps to some extent the father had an emotional tie to his young, the father role was not an unimportant one. As knowledge of the relation between the father and the reproduction process increased, as cultures changed and became more complex, and as sex ratios between men and women became more equalized in societies, the relationship of the father to the mother and the child became more important and the family as a unit became more stabilized. Of all the theories of family origin this one appears to be most plausible.[2]

Although we have mentioned the universality of the family, it is wrong to say that there have not been societies in which the family was not a recognized unit. In speaking of such societies, Levi-Strauss says:

These extreme positions, however, suffer equally from over-simplification. It is well known that, in very rare cases, family bonds cannot be claimed to exist. A telling case comes from the Nyar, a very large group living on the Malabar coast of India. In former times, the warlike type of life of the Nyar men did not allow them to found a family. Marriage was a purely symbolical ceremony which did not result in a permanent tie between a man and a woman. As a matter of fact, married women were permitted to have as many lovers as they wished. Children belonged exclusively to the mother line, and familial as well as land authority was exercised, not by the ephemeral husband but by the wife's brothers. Since land was cultivated by an inferior caste, subservient to the Nyar, a woman's brothers were as completely free as their sister's temporary husband or lovers to devote themselves to military activities.[3]

[1] *See* Edward Westermarck, *The History of Human Marriage* (3 vols.; New York: Allerton Book Co., 1922).

[2] *See* Robert Briffault, *The Mothers* (3 vols.; New York: The Macmillan Co., 1927).

[3] Claude Levi-Strauss, "The Family," in *Man, Culture and Society,* ed. Harry L. Shapiro (New York: Oxford University Press, 1956), pp. 261-85. *See also* E. Adamson Hoebel, *Man in the Primitive World* (New York: McGraw-Hill Book Co., 1958), pp. 281-368.

## SOME IMPORTANT MARRIAGE AND FAMILY VARIATIONS

Among the interesting phases of the history and sociology of the family are the variations one finds in marriage and family patterns. The causes of these variations are themselves variable. The physical environment, with limitations upon the food supply, may be a factor in the size and location of family groupings. Danger may also be a factor. The culture of a people may, in time, influence the sex composition of the population. For instance, tribes long at war are likely to have more females than males in the population unless, of course, the females had been stolen by the victors. Where people migrate long distances, males are likely to migrate in larger numbers than women.

Infanticide, a fairly common practice among preliterate people, may lead to a disparity in sex ratios; its practice is especially likely to lead to more males in the population than females.

The practice of infanticide is more apt to involve the sacrifice of newborn female children, although during periods of acute famines older children are likely to be killed. Female children are more likely to be selected for sacrifice than male children. The reasons for this are variable. Where women are deemed essential to the gathering of the food supply and the preparation of food, no sex discrimination in infanticide may be made. Since inadequate food supply, brought on by temporary shortage of food sources, or by the prolonged build-up of population pressure to a saturation point, is the major cause of infanticide, males are looked upon as being more able to survive during such periods. Some people also believed that ancestral cults and other qualities were transmitted through male lines and therefore favored the survival of males. In some societies, notably in early Rome, Greece, India, and China, where women were often pampered and became an economic burden, female children were selected in infanti-

cide to reduce this burden. Thus changes in ratios of males to females is brought about by infanticide to change marriage patterns. More about this later.

### Variations in family size and relationships

Zimmerman identifies three major types of families: the *trustee* family, the *domestic* family, and the *atomistic* family.[4]

The term "trustee family" is used by Zimmerman to describe clanlike family structures made up of several individual families, bearing perhaps the same family name, living close together in somewhat isolated communities. Within such families the relationships and allegiances may be so strong that its members may act to protect its name and honor. The trustee family tends to place close kin, bearing a common name, under common allegiance and leadership. When a member of the family is harmed by someone outside the family, other members may seek to avenge the family's honor, thus resulting in feuds between families. Where a member of the family does harm to another family or a member of his own family, the family may punish the offender or it may feel honorbound to deliver him to the proper authorities for punishment. Zimmerman points out that the very strong position of the head of the early Roman family lay in the role of acting as trustee for the family and in carrying out public responsibilities for the family.

The head of the Chinese Great Family acted for the family as a trustee. Perhaps the best examples of trustee families today in the United States are found in remote areas of the Appalachians and the Ozarks, where many families of the close of kin live in the same general area, and where the heads of family units feel a trustee obligation to the family line and act

[4] Carle C. Zimmerman, *Family and Civilization* (New York: Harper and Bros., 1947), pp. 1-10.

accordingly. Trustee families are larger than domestic and atomistic families, and the whole complex of individual families holds a trustee relationship to the family name.

The most common type of family, according to Zimmerman, is the *domestic* family. This type family represents something of a compromise between attachment to family bonds, such as is found in the trustee family, and great individual freedom, as found in the atomistic family. To some extent the domestic family is an extended family. It is essentially one man's family but may have relatives, especially parents, living in the household. The parents of a domestic family may have close contact with the families of their children who live in the same town or community. In decision-making the parents are frequently consulted and may be visited often. The relationship ties here are more limited in their obligation than in the trustee family, yet they are stronger than in the atomistic family.

The *atomistic* family is, as a rule, smaller than the domestic family. Its kin contacts and relationships are also more limited. The goals which are sought are less family goals than those of the primary family, as found in the trustee and domestic family, but are more the goals of the individual members. The marriage relationship is viewed more often as a private civil relationship than as a religious one, and the affectional element is typically stressed.

Zimmerman contrasts the trustee and atomistic families in the following language:

If the trustee family represents the great family, measuring greatness in terms of legal and social power and responsibilities given the family, the atomistic family represents the great individual, measuring individualism in terms of legal and social power and responsibility given the individual. In trustee times, the family was held responsible for the individual and the individual was held accountable to the family. In atomistic times the individual is held responsible for himself and he alone is accountable to the state, or through the state to other persons.[5]

[5] *Ibid.*, p. 134.

Zimmerman continues:

Thus the atomistic family is essentially the one found in societies where law and custom bring the individual, as far as possible, out from under the *covert,* the *manus,* the *potestas* of the family, and make him the agent of the government, the one responsible directly to the law, and bound least to family obligations.[6]

It would seem, from the above statement, that dictator countries, where a special attempt is made to centralize family control in the state, would favor an atomistic type of family pattern. Democratic countries, in their best traditions, would seem to favor the trustee and domestic types; however, feminism goes often with democracy and the atomistic family.

*Variations in the selection of marriage mates*

In this country the selection of mates is largely by *mutual consent.* On the other hand, a young Korean graduate student relates that when he returns to his country he will marry a girl selected for him by his parents. This practice is known as *parental selection.* In some cultures such arrangements may be made at birth of a child.

The sources from which mates may be selected are defined by cultures. Almost universally the *incest taboo* is rigidly enforced. This means that one is prohibited from marrying the close of kin. In our culture we usually disapprove of first cousins marrying. Marriages between those more closely related are also prohibited.

Where one is required to marry within defined classes, as in his own race, as is true in the South and parts of the West, we call the requirement *endogamy.* Some religions favor endogamous marriages, that is, they try to prevent their members from marrying outside their religious faith. The requirement that one marry outside certain defined classes is called *exogamy.* Kinship exogamy is the most common form. In primitive cultures tribal ex-

[6] *Ibid.*, p. 137.

ogamy is often required. Two explanations are given for tribal exogamy. One is that it tends to prevent the close of kin from marrying, and, second, it is often a means of strengthening political alliances with other tribes.

### Variation in the number of marriage spouses

*Monogamy,* the requirement that the number of spouses be limited to one person at a time, is the current and almost universal practice.

*Polygyny,* permitting a male to marry more than one wife, has been a common practice in preliterate societies. Where the practice has been common it is usually permissive rather than an absolute requirement. That is, usually a small minority, those with the desire, status, and resources to have more than one wife, are permitted to practice polygyny. *Polygamy* is the practice of marrying more than one mate, whether a husband or wife.

At the end of World War I, when war casualties had resulted in the death of millions of young German males, there were many more young women available for marriage than males. One of the recommendations made in the postwar period was that Germany legalize polygyny to offset the disparity in sex ratios in the population of marriageable age. This, of course, was not done.

After World War II, even as late as 1950, in the Federal Republic of Germany in the age group 25 to 29 years there were only 750 males per 1,000 females. In the age group 30 to 34 years the number was 738.[7] Such figures mean, of course, that under a system of absolute monogamy many females of marriageable age found it impossible to marry German men of any age.

As we have said, over the years the trend is definitely toward monogamy and away from other forms. Compelling arguments for mo-

nogamy are that the sex ratios are reasonably in balance unless cultural factors, including war, interfere with them. Monogamy reflects the psychological theory of possessiveness of mates so common in the Western world, and it meets the requirements of the idealism of a large number of the world's religious bodies.

*Polyandry* is the simultaneous marriage of more than one male to one female. The practice is rare in contrast to the prevalence of monogamy and polygyny. Murdock calls the polyandrous family an ethnological curiosity. Of 250 societies studied by him, 43 were monogamous, 193 polygynous, and two polyandrous. For 12 there were no data regarding marriage forms.[8]

A principal form of polyandry is fraternal polyandry, where the culture prescribes that a widow marry preferentially the brother of her deceased husband; thus the brother becomes a secondary spouse. This form of marriage regulation is known as the levirate. Where the culture rules favor a widower marrying the sister of his deceased wife, the marriage form is called the *sororate.* When plural marriages, rather than successive marriages, are involved, sororal polygyny results.[9]

More males than females in a population, resulting from female infanticide, the heavy migration of males into an area, or the application of the rules of the levirate, create conditions which may favor polyandry.

### The selection of residence

Some cultures require that a young married couple establish their new home or take up residence in the home of the bride's parents. This practice is called *matrilocal residence.* In other cultures residence is established in the groom's home, which is known as *patrilocal residence.* The terms come from the Latin words *mater* (mother) and *pater* (father). In our own American culture we have patri-

[7] Paul F. Myers and W. Parker Mauldin, *Population of the Federal Republic of Germany and West Berlin,* U.S. Bureau of the Census, *Statistics Report, International Population,* Series P-20, No. 1 (Washington, D.C., 1952).

[8] George Peter Murdock, *Social Structure* (New York: The Macmillan Co., 1949).
[9] *Ibid.,* p. 28.

local residence in that the decision in choosing the place of residence is, legally at least, a matter for the groom to decide. Failure to accompany the groom to the new residence satisfies a ground for divorce (desertion) and could, under some circumstances, constitute a legal cause for marriage annulment.

## Variation in tracing descent

In societies where descent is traced through the mother, the society is said to be *matrilineal,* or has what is called a *matronymic* name system. Where descent is traced through the father, the society is *patrilineal,* or has a *patronymic* name system. Our own society is patrilineal but not absolutely so, there being many instances where descent may be traced through the mother line. Some women continue to retain their maiden family name after marriage. Also after divorce, where the mother is custodian of the children, or children have

not been born, and the mother's name is restored by the courts, her children may assume her name.

## Variation in the location of authority

Families which are dominated by a husband or a father or an elderly male, as in the Chinese Great Family, are said to be *patriarchal.* Mother-dominated families are *matriarchal.* Early New England Puritan families were strongly patriarchal. Perhaps the best examples of patriarchal native American families today are found in Appalachian and Ozark mountain families.

In the past, Negro families have been strongly matriarchal in the United States. Slavery contributed to this. Husbands were often sold, while mothers and young children remained together. Even in 1940 women were the heads of more than a fifth of the Negro families of the South.[10]

### BASIC FAMILY FUNCTIONS

Any consideration of family functions must admit of exceptions in the instance of specific families. Therefore, the functions we are about to consider are generalized functions. Bierstedt, recognizing two areas of family functions, one societal and the other individual, states them as follows: [11]

| For Society | For the Individual |
|---|---|
| Replacement of the species | Life and survival |
| Sexual control | Sexual opportunity |
| Maintenance | Protection and support |
| Culture transmission | Socialization |
| Status ascription | Societal identification |

In at least two instances we have already discussed the culture-bearing functions of groups

[10] *See* E. Franklin Frazier, *The Negro in the United States* (Rev. ed.; New York: The Macmillan Co., 1957), pp. 316-21.

[11] Robert Bierstedt, *The Social Order* (New York: McGraw-Hill Book Co., 1957), p. 363. *See also* William F. Ogburn and Meyer F. Nimkoff, *Technology and the Changing Family* (Boston: Houghton Mifflin Co., 1955).

and some of the specific reasons why the family is so influential in the socialization process. We shall, therefore, not discuss these functions further except briefly under education.

## Biological functions

As an institution for bringing children into the world and rearing them through the period of biological dependency, the family has no equal. With the long-range decline in the size of households, the reproductive function has declined, but it is still a basic one. A major concern of society is that the human species be perpetuated or else in time it would become extinct. Fortunately this is no problem except for individual families who may be in process of biological liquidation.

Within the family pattern, sex relations are legalized and regulated. Also related to affection are the nonprocreative functions of sex which, in the Western world, are deemed im-

*"Gregory hasn't actually proposed in so many words, but he did give me an electric blanket with dual controls."*

SOURCE: *Saturday Evening Post,* May 8, 1948. Reproduced by permission of the artist.

portant. The family is a medium for sex expression and for the regulation of this expression.

### Affectional functions

The major reasons why couples marry in the United States are for companionship and for purposes of obtaining a source of affectionate expression and response. Society requires, of course, that certain forms of this expression and response be regulated. Thus the family serves as a medium of this expression and regulation.

As other functions of the family have weakened, for example, the educational and economic functions, the affectional function in marriage looms large as a major factor in keeping the family happy and intact. The increase in marriage, as we shall see later, in the face of some trends which would normally discourage marriage, is perhaps one indication of the growth of the affectional function. In fact some people place the blame for family disorganization on the overemphasis on romanticism in American courtship and marriage.

The emphasis upon the affectional function in the modern American family favors the development of situations within which acute jealousies may arise, some of which may result in family disorganization.

As Davis points out, jealousy has a direct connection with the sociology of intimacy.[12] Even though affection is deeply present in the family, jealousy of mates may result from attention paid to persons outside the family. Spouses may become jealous of in-laws or even children. The emphasis placed upon affection in the family creates a desire for intimate response, and for this desire to be complete and limited to one's marriage mate. There are basic fears of losing this response, if achieved. Davis points to the constructive and destructive role of jealousy in a marriage relationship:

But after ownership has been attained, jealousy is a fear and rage reaction fitted to protect, maintain, and prolong the intimate association of love. It shelters the personal relationship from outside intrusion. This is not to say that it never defeats its own purpose by overshooting the mark. So deeply emotional is jealousy that its appearance in the midst of modern social relationships (which are most profitably manipulated by self-composed shrewdness) is like a bull in a china shop. Nonetheless its intention is protective. It is a denial of the harmony of intimacy only in so far as its presence admits a breach; and is destructive of it only in so far as it muddles its own purpose.[13]

### Learning and educational functions

Although the family has declined as a formal education medium, with children in some families now starting nursery school at the age of three, the family, as we have already indicated, is perhaps the most effective group found in a society for the transmission of the culture, a process we have referred to as enculturation and socialization. Early language training is found in the home. The child is

[12] Kingsley Davis, *Human Society* (New York: The Macmillan Co., 1949), pp. 183-84.
[13] *Ibid.,* p. 183.

trained in personal habits, in roles, and in value systems. The family teaches much about the social organization of the society and its prohibitions and expectations.

In education, as in religion, the modern family has surrendered more than it has acquired. However, new educational roles for the family have developed by way of cooperative relationships with schools, with individual teachers in schools, and with the peer groups of children in school-related and nonschool-related groups. New fields, such as child psychology, nutrition, child care, and interpersonal relations, open up new knowledge areas in which parents may be expected to know something.

In its learning and educational roles the family has an important influence upon the religious and ethical idealism of its members, especially the young. It is well known that the correlations between the moral idealism and attitudes of parents and their children is high. Attitudes toward church and religious teachings and participation of young people in church and church-related activities is influenced greatly by parental attitudes.

## Protective functions

As we have indicated the young child is physically dependent upon its parents, either real or substitute. The family not only is a unit of physical protection, but is also a unit of moral protection. The family likewise is an economic unit, with economic resources, which means that it furnishes economic protection to its members. This is true of families with even moderate resources.

## Economic functions

In our society most children are economically dependent until they are 16 or 18 years of age, when they may be released from compulsory education. In some occupations chil-dren are accepted at 16 years of age, and in the more dangerous trades at 18. In many families where the children go to college and are supported by the family they may not become self-supporting until the early twenties.

As earners of wealth, as holders of wealth, as exchangers of wealth, and as consumption units, families constitute perhaps the most basic economic unit found in all societies, and especially in our own society.

## Recreational functions

The modern family, in general, has surrendered recreational functions. Of course, the play life and recreational life of the young child is largely home-oriented. After the child starts school recreation becomes school-oriented and increasingly associated with peer groups outside school and home, as well as with commercial recreational outlets.

The family is important, not only for the role it performs in providing recreation, but also in providing counsel in the choice of recreational activities. In providing funds for the recreational activities of its members, the family performs an important function. A case in point may be the cost of providing one or more family cars which are largely used for recreational purposes.

There are other functions of the family. As Bierstedt indicates in the previous listing of functions, it provides status and identification for its members. "That Jones kid," for instance, is a specific identification; so is "the John Jones family." Functions are not constant in time. At one period in history, or at one time in a culture, one function may be accentuated more than at another. For instance, since 1946 the birth rate in the United States has been high and the American family has been doing a better job in biological reproduction than it did for ten years prior to 1946.

## SOME SIGNIFICANT TRENDS IN THE AMERICAN FAMILY

In some areas of family trends there are inadequate supporting data to form objective bases for charting trends. In other areas enough objective data are available to support trend lines.

### The trend toward earlier marriage

One of the striking differences between marriage in many European countries and in this country is the earlier age of marriage in America. As much as anything else this is a reflection of the abundance of the American economy, veterans' allotments, installment buying and working wives, war and threat of war. Schools now do not frown upon married students as was the case in the past. High school and college are completed at an earlier age than formerly. There is also a possibility that biological maturity of females comes at a little earlier age now than it did 50 years ago. The compelling reasons for earlier marriage are economic ones.

*Table 15*

#### MEDIAN AGE AT FIRST MARRIAGE FOR THE UNITED STATES, 1890-1959

| YEAR | MEDIAN AGE AT FIRST MARRIAGE | |
|---|---|---|
| | *Male* | *Female* |
| 1959 | 22.3 | 20.2 |
| 1958 | 22.4 | 20.2 |
| 1957 | 22.5 | 20.3 |
| 1956 | 22.3 | 20.1 |
| 1955 | 22.5 | 20.2 |
| 1950 | 22.8 | 20.3 |
| 1940 | 24.3 | 21.5 |
| 1930 | 24.3 | 21.3 |
| 1920 | 24.6 | 21.2 |
| 1910 | 25.1 | 21.6 |
| 1900 | 25.9 | 21.9 |
| 1890 | 26.1 | 22.0 |

Source: *Current Population Reports, Population Characteristics,* Series P-20, No. 96, November 23, 1959, p. 1.

As the data will show (Table 15) the median age at first marriage in the United States was 26.1 years for males and 22.0 years for females in 1890. This compares to 22.3 years for males and 20.2 years for females at first marriage in 1959. Of course, there is a decline in marriage in the very young ages, in general the ages under 18. The trend in marriage age is toward marriage in the late teens for women and the early adult years for men.

### The increase in marriage

Along with the trend toward earlier marriage there is also an increase in the percentage of the population that is married. For instance, in 1890 the percentage of male population (14 years of age and over) that was married was 52.1 per cent and the female population 54.8 per cent. By 1958 the percentage of the married population had increased to 69.8 and 66.0 per cent for males and females respectively (Table 16). Without a doubt, the same factors operating to lower the median age for marriage have also been effective in increasing the frequency of marriage in the population. Probably there is also an increased tendency for divorced people to remarry. We do not have any reliable trend data on the percentage

*Table 16*

#### MARITAL STATUS OF THE POPULATION 14 YEARS OF AGE AND OVER, INTERVALS, 1890 TO 1958

| YEAR | PER CENT MARRIED | |
|---|---|---|
| | *Male* | *Female* |
| 1958 | 69.8 | 66.0 |
| 1950 | 68.0 | 66.1 |
| 1940 | 59.7 | 59.5 |
| 1890 | 52.1 | 54.8 |

Source: U.S. Bureau of the Census, *Statistical Abstract of the United States: 1959* (80th ed.; Washington, D.C.: U.S. Government Printing Office, 1959), p. 38.

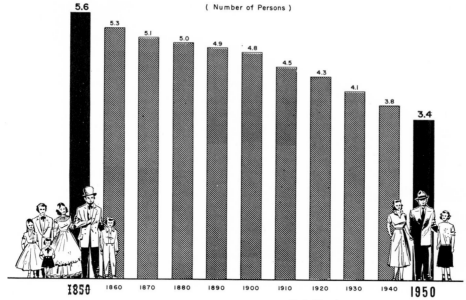

( Number of Persons )

*U.S. Housing and Home Finance Agency*

FIG. 9. THE DECLINING TREND IN THE SIZE OF AMERICAN HOUSEHOLDS

of widowed persons who remarry. We rather suspect that a smaller percentage of widowed females remarry today than formerly because there are more females than males in the population, and that, over the years, this numerical superiority of females has been increasing. Also, it is easier for women to have a job or even a career outside marriage than was formerly true.

The increase in marriage, the increase in the total population, and the growing tendency for young married couples to establish a home of their own rather than to move in with their parents, has led to a great increase in the number of households. For instance, in 1930 there were 29,905,000 households in the United States. In 1940 there were 34,949,000, and in 1950 43,554,000 households. In 1960 the number of households is likely to reach 52 million. By 1970 the number should increase to 62 million, and reach 75 million by 1980.

The increase in households during the past decades, and the projected increase for the years ahead, has many implications. Such growth is a tremendous boost to the economy, especially to the building trades, the appliance, furniture, and clothing fields, and to the food industries. All institutions, especially schools, also feel the impact of the growth.[14]

### The decline in family size

Another trend has been the decline in the size of the American family. For our purpose we shall use size of household data to indicate this trend. The Bureau of the Census defines "household" as "all persons who occupy a dwelling unit," whereas a family refers to "a group of two or more persons related by blood, marriage, or adoption and residing together."

In 1890, American households had 4.93 persons per household. By 1958 the size had declined to 3.35 persons (Table 17). Because of

[14] For more on this topic, *see* U.S. Bureau of the Census, "Illustrative Projections of the Number of Households and Families: 1960 to 1980," *Current Population Reports, Population Characteristics*, Series P-20, No. 90, December 29, 1958.

the sustained high birth rate during the 1950's, it is estimated that the median size of households will be about the same in 1960 as in 1958.

In 1958, the average population of white households was 3.29 persons and nonwhite households 3.90 members. Households in the Northeast states average 3.30 members, and in the West 3.16 members. In the South white households averaged 3.38 members, while nonwhite families averaged 4.09 members.[15]

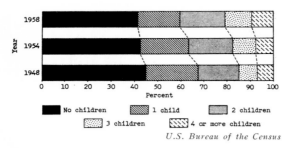

*U.S. Bureau of the Census*

FIG. 10. PER CENT DISTRIBUTION OF HUSBAND-WIFE FAMILIES BY NUMBER OF OWN CHILDREN UNDER 18 YEARS OLD IN THE HOME, FOR THE UNITED STATES: 1958, 1954, AND 1948

Changes in the number of children in families of the United States are indicated in Figures 9 and 10. As Figure 10 shows, the percentage of families having no children declined during the decade 1948 to 1958. The proportion of families with two or more children of their own in the home increased from 32 per cent in 1948 to 41 per cent in 1958. The percentage of families with three children appears to have grown in recent years, while families with four or more children also show an increase.

The population per family is a little larger than the population per household. For instance, in 1950 the population per family was 3.54 members as compared to the population per household of 3.37 persons. In 1958 the

15 U.S. Bureau of the Census, "Household and Family Characteristics: March 1958," *Current Population Reports, Population Characteristics,* Series P-20, No. 88, November 17, 1958.

average population per household was 3.35 members, whereas the average population per family was 3.65 members.

There is some question as to how significant the data on household and family size are and what the declining trends indicated in Table 17 really mean. Related to the decline in size of households is the decline in the number of domestic and hired help. Related to the de-

*Table 17*

POPULATION PER HOUSEHOLD, 1890 TO 1958

| Year | Number Persons |
|------|----------------|
| 1958 | 3.35 |
| 1950 | 3.37 |
| 1940 | 3.67 |
| 1930 | 4.11 |
| 1920 | 4.34 |
| 1910 | 4.54 |
| 1900 | 4.76 |
| 1890 | 4.93 |

Source: U.S. Bureau of the Census, *Statistical Abstract of the United States, 1955* (Washington, D.C., 1955), p. 49. Also *Current Population Reports,* Series P-20, No. 81, March 19, 1958, and Series P-20, No. 88, November 17, 1958.

cline in the size of families is the tendency of single adults in our culture to leave the family roof and for parents of married children to live apart from the children.

Of late years there has been a tendency for single men and women to purchase houses and occupy unit apartments rather than live in single rooms in rooming houses or in houses with relatives. This would have some tendency to reduce the size of households. However, the main reason for the decline indicated in Table 17 was the decline in the birth rate prior to the World War II period.

*The loss of traditional functions*

As we indicated in the discussion of family functions, there has been a decline in some family functions, an increase in others, and a change of emphasis in others. These changes we need not discuss again except perhaps to emphasize one or more.

For emphasis we might use the protective health function of families. At one time the family looked after the purity of its food supply and its water supply. Today this is pretty much a public responsibility, except in rural areas. Even in rural communities public water districts and cooperative water supplies are very common. The prevention of disease 50 years ago was heavily an individual and family responsibility. Today the state and community supplies and enforces many health measures which give protection to family members.

We have already made the point that the family is very important in the teaching of ethical attitudes and conduct and in the developing of value systems. On the other hand, family prayer and family Bible reading, once fairly common in families, is comparatively rare. This would appear to mean that the formal religious functions of the family have declined, as we have pointed out earlier in the chapter.

### More disruption

One of the ways of showing disruption or breakup of the American family is to look at the marital status of the population at any given period (Table 18).

In 1958, of the population 14 years and older who were married, the mate was absent in 4 million instances. Over 2 million persons were separated from their mates; how many were temporarily absent we do not know. More than 10 million were widowed, and 2.5 million were divorced (Table 18).

Death is the most common cause of marriage disruption. Widowhood is an especially acute problem with females because males tend to marry females younger than they, and because females have a longer expectation of life than males do. Males, when they remarry, tend to marry women younger than they, thus creating marriage difficulties for widowed females. Partially because of this and partially because of the excess of females in the population, widowed men have a much better chance of remarriage than women do.

In March, 1958, there were 8,047,000 widowed females in the United States, an increase of over 1 million since 1950, and nearly three times the total in 1900 (Table 18). Among women over 14 years of age, 12.6 per cent were widowed in 1956 as compared to 10.9 per cent

*Table 18*

### MARITAL STATUS OF THE POPULATION 14 YEARS OLD AND OVER, 1958

| MARITAL STATUS | THOUSANDS | |
|---|---|---|
| | *Male* | *Female* |
| Total population 14 years of age and over | 58,462 | 62,784 |
| Single | 14,331 | 11,822 |
| Married | 40,831 | 41,457 |
|   Mate present | 39,182 | 39,182 |
|   Mate absent | 1,649 | 2,275 |
|     Separated | 865 | 1,342 |
|     Other | 784 | 701 |
|     Husband in armed forces | — | 232 |
| Widowed | 2,272 | 8,047 |
| Divorced | 1,028 | 1,458 |

Source: U.S. Bureau of the Census, "Marital Status and Family Status: March, 1958," *Current Population Reports, Population Characteristics*, Series P-20, No. 87, November 14, 1958.

in 1900. A rather alarming fact is that 25 per cent of women in the age group 55 to 64 are widowed. This figure increases to 55 per cent for the age group 65 and over (Table 19). In 1958, over 100,000 children were orphaned by the death of fathers who died before they reached 45. An additional 87,000 survived fathers who died at ages 45 to 54.

In commenting upon the mounting problem of widowhood, one of the major insurance companies remarks:

Paradoxically, while remarkable progress has been made in reducing mortality, the chances that a wife will outlive her husband have increased, and the duration of widowhood has lengthened for

## Table 19

### WIDOWS IN THE UNITED STATES, 1956 AND 1900

| Age Period (Years) | 1956 | | 1900 | |
|---|---|---|---|---|
| | Per Cent of All Widows | Per Cent of All Women | Per Cent of All Widows | Per Cent of All Women |
| 14 and over | 100.0 | 12.6 | 100.0 | 10.9 |
| 14-34 | 1.7 | 0.5 | 10.2 | 2.0 |
| 35-44 | 6.2 | 4.1 | 13.8 | 8.6 |
| 45-54 | 12.4 | 9.9 | 19.5 | 17.6 |
| 55-64 | 24.5 | 25.1 | 23.1 | 32.3 |
| 65 and over | 55.2 | 55.1 | 33.4 | 59.5 |
| 65-74 | 29.3 | 44.9 | — | — |
| 75 and over | 25.9 | 74.0 | — | — |

Source: *Statistical Bulletin* (Metropolitan Life Insurance Co.), 39:1-3, November, 1958.

women at every period of life. Widowhood very often brings with it many problems, whatever the age of the woman. Young widows frequently must seek gainful employment even though they have young children in their care. Many of the women who lose their husbands later in life still have dependent children, and, in addition, are handicapped by lack of specific qualifications for employment. The benefits provided by Social Security provide only for minimum needs.[16]

In 1867 there were less than 10,000 divorces in the United States. This was a rate of 0.30 divorces per 1,000 population. An all-time high divorce rate was reached in 1946. In that year 610,000 people were granted divorces in the United States, giving a rate of 4.3 divorces per 1,000 population (Table 20).

Expressed in terms of ratio of divorces to marriages, just prior to the Civil War there were 1.2 divorces annually per 1,000 existing marriages. The divorce rate increased to four in 1900, and to 18.2 divorces per 1,000 existing marriages in 1946 when the divorce rate peaked. The rate then declined to 9.3 by 1956. These trends exemplify the significant fact that the divorce rate currently is about eight times as high as it was in 1860.[17]

## Table 20

### MARRIAGES AND DIVORCES; 1867-1956

| Year | Number of Marriages | Number of Divorces | Per 1,000 of Estimated Population | |
|---|---|---|---|---|
| | | | Marriages | Divorces |
| 1956 | 1,569,000 | 377,000 | 9.4 | 2.3 |
| 1955 | 1,531,000 | 377,000 | 9.3 | 2.2 |
| 1954 | 1,490,000 | 379,000 | 9.2 | 2.4 |
| 1953 | 1,546,000 | 390,000 | 9.8 | 2.5 |
| 1952 | 1,562,579 | 388,000 | 10.0 | 2.5 |
| 1951 | 1,621,159 | 381,000 | 10.6 | 2.5 |
| 1950 | 1,669,934 | 385,000 | 11.0 | 2.5 |
| 1949 | 1,579,798 | 397,000 | 10.6 | 2.7 |
| 1948 | 1,811,155 | 408,000 | 12.4 | 2.8 |
| 1947 | 1,991,878 | 483,000 | 13.9 | 3.4 |
| 1946 | 2,291,045 | 610,000 | 16.4 | 4.3 |
| 1945 | 1,618,331 | 502,000 | 12.26 | 3.59 |
| 1944 | 1,452,394 | 400,000 | 10.96 | 2.90 |
| 1943 | 1,577,050 | 359,000 | 11.77 | 2.63 |
| 1942 | 1,772,132 | 321,000 | 13.25 | 2.38 |
| 1941 | 1,695,999 | 293,000 | 12.75 | 2.20 |
| 1940 | 1,595,879 | 264,000 | 12.09 | 2.00 |
| 1939 | 1,403,633 | 251,000 | 10.72 | 1.92 |
| 1938 | 1,330,780 | 244,000 | 10.25 | 1.88 |
| 1937* | 1,426,000 | 250,000 | 11.03 | 1.93 |
| 1936* | 1,369,000 | 236,000 | 10.66 | 1.84 |
| 1935* | 1,327,000 | 218,000 | 10.41 | 1.71 |
| 1934* | 1,302,000 | 204,000 | 10.28 | 1.61 |
| 1933* | 1,098,000 | 165,000 | 8.74 | 1.31 |
| 1932 | 981,903 | 160,338 | 7.87 | 1.28 |
| 1931 | 1,060,914 | 183,664 | 8.55 | 1.48 |
| 1930 | 1,126,856 | 191,591 | 9.15 | 1.56 |
| 1900 | 709,000 | 55,751 | 9.30 | 0.70 |
| 1867 | — | 9,937 | — | 0.30 |

* Estimates taken from an article "Recent Increases in Marriage and Divorce," by Samuel A. Stouffer and Lyle M. Spencer, *American Journal of Sociology,* January, 1939, pp. 551-54.

The remainder of the data are from U.S. Bureau of the Census, *Statistical Abstract of the United States* (Washington, D.C., 1952, 1953, 1956, and 1958).

[16] *Statistical Bulletin* (Metropolitan Life Insurance Co.) 39:1-3, November, 1958. *See also Statistical Bulletin,* 40:1-3, August, 1959.

[17] Paul H. Jacobson, *American Marriage and Divorce* (New York: Rinehart and Co., 1959), pp. 90-91.

Divorces fluctuate with varied conditions of the economic situation, the marriage rate, postwar conditions, and the like. As the data show, during the depression years 1932-33 divorce rates were exceedingly low. In the post-World War II period high rates were reached.

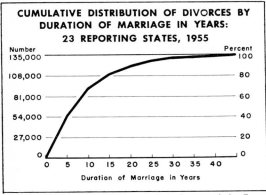

FIG. 11.  DIVORCES GRANTED IN RELATION TO DURATION OF MARRIAGE, 1955

The median duration of marriages broken by divorce and annulment in 1955 was 6.5 years.[18] As the accompanying graph (Fig. 11) shows, one-fourth of all divorces occurred within the first three years of marriage, and three-fourths within the first 12 years.[19]

On the average, about one child is involved in every divorce or marriage annulment. For instance, in 1955 there were 377,000 divorces and annulments in which 347,000 children were reported.

In 22 states for which data are available, no children were reported in 51.9 per cent of divorces and annulments; one child was reported in 22.8 per cent; two children in 14.5 per cent; three in 6.8 per cent, and four or more in 3.6 per cent. The longer the duration of marriage broken by divorce, the more children are involved.

[18] U.S. Department of Health, Education and Welfare, National Office of Vital Statistics, *Divorces and Annulments: Detailed Statistics for Reporting Areas, 1955*, Vol. 46, No. 4, April 9, 1957.

[19] *Ibid.*, p. 93.

Data for six states indicate that the median age of first married husbands at time of divorce was 30.3 years and for wives 26.8 years.

Leading grounds serving as a basis on which divorces were granted in 25 states in a single year are indicated in Table 21. Roughly, more

*Table 21*

LEGAL GROUNDS FOR GRANTING DIVORCE DECREES AND ANNULMENTS, 25 STATES, 1955

| Legal Grounds for Decree | Number |
|---|---|
| Cruelty | 77,604 |
| Desertion | 25,697 |
| Drunkenness | 2,800 |
| Adultery | 2,412 |
| Non-support | 2,308 |
| Conviction of fraud | 738 |
| Fraud | 591 |
| Bigamy | 533 |
| Under-age | 133 |
| Insanity | 128 |
| Other | 38,225* |

\* Includes gross neglect, abandonment, and indignities to the person.

Source: U.S. Department of Health, Education and Welfare, National Office of Vital Statistics, *Divorces and Annulments: Detailed Statistics for Reporting Areas, 1955*, Vol. 46, No. 4, April 9, 1957.

than 50 per cent of divorces are granted on grounds of cruelty, another 20 per cent on grounds of desertion, 5 per cent for adultery, and 3 per cent for neglect to provide. Combinations of grounds enter into some decrees. The grounds on which divorces are granted often show little or nothing of the real causes.

Some 75 per cent of divorce decrees are granted to wives. For instance, out of 147,270 divorces and annulments granted in 1955, 103,134 were granted to the wife and 39,466 to the husband. In the case of annulments it is not unusual for annulment decrees to be granted to parents or guardians, especially where one or more of the principals involved is under age.

## SUMMARY

No other group fulfills so nearly the qualities of a primary group, which we enumerated in Chapter 7, as well as the family does. It is a key group in the socialization of the young, and serves many functions to all age groups and to society itself. The origin of the family is not known but there are one or more plausible theories of its origin, perhaps the best one being the relationship created by the need of the helpless child for care by its mother.

In historical and current cultures, although the family is usual it shows many variations. These relate to size, to the relationship of members, to methods of selecting mates, to tracing descent, and to other features.

Like other groups and institutions the family performs basic functions which may change from time to time in their detail but not in their mass. Some of these functions are biological and affectional, while others relate to learning and education, protection, and economic and recreational functions.

A social trend is change in the direction of a central tendency in a group, institution, or some other aspect of society. Current family trends are the trend toward earlier marriage, the increase in the percentage of people over 14 who are married, decline in family size, the loss of traditional functions, and disruption of the family by death, desertion, and divorce.

In spite of the above trends, which indicate considerable pathology in family life, there are other trends and data which indicate a large amount of social health in marriage and the family. A large percentage of married people indicate they are happily married. The increase in property has been accompanied by an increase in marriage, a decline in childless families, and an increase in home ownership. The lowering of mortality rates has greatly favored the survival of children and the lessened chances of widowhood and orphanhood while children are dependent. Thus children are more assured today of the advantages of full family life than in past decades.

### THINGS TO DO AND TO DISCUSS

1. Why is the family so influential as a social group?
2. What do you consider the most plausible theory of family origin?
3. What conditions would favor monogamy, polygyny, and polyandry as a marriage form?
4. Give illustrations of endogamy and exogamy. What are the arguments for societies enforcing each of the practices?
5. What are the basic functions performed by marriage and the family? Give illustrations from your community. Which functions are increasing and which ones are declining?
6. Why is jealousy likely to be an important problem in the American family, where so much emphasis is placed on affection?
7. What positive and negative functions are served by jealousy?
8. Ivan Bloch, in his *Sexual Life of Our Time* (New York: Allied Books, 1926), says that it is possible for a person to love two people sincerely and passionately at the same time. Do you agree or disagree? Why?
9. What are the most significant trends in the American family at present?
10. Why is widowhood a mounting family problem?
11. When are divorce rates lowest? Highest?

12. What are the leading grounds for granting divorces?
13. Summarize the relation of size of family to the likelihood of divorce.

FOR FURTHER STUDY

AMES, DAVID O. "The Economic Base of Wolof Polygyny," *Southwestern Journal of Anthropology*, 11:391-403, 1955. A good discussion of polygyny.

BELL, NORMAN W., and VOGEL, EZRA F. *The Family*. Glencoe, Ill.: Free Press, 1960. A reader-text with emphasis on the sociological analysis of the family, the family's relationship to society, and the family's contribution to personality.

BERNARD, JESSIE. *Remarriage: A Study of Marriage*. New York: Dryden Press, 1956. Probably the best book on remarriage.

CAVAN, RUTH SHONLE. *Marriage and Family in the Modern World*. New York: Thomas Y. Crowell Co., 1960. A text covering the period from adolescent dating through early family formation.

EHRMANN, WINSTON. "A Review of Family Research in 1955," *Marriage and Family Living*, 18:168-76, May, 1956. A good review of research on the family for a single year.

ELKIN, FREDERICK. *The Child and Society*. New York: Random House, 1960. A very useful paperback on the process of socialization as it takes place in various social systems.

FRAZIER, E. FRANKLIN. *The Negro in the United States*. New York: The Macmillan Co., 1957. Excellent treatment of the structure and functions of the Negro family.

GOODE, WILLIAM J. *After Divorce*. Glencoe, Ill.: Free Press, 1956.

KIRKPATRICK, CLIFFORD. *The Family as Process and Institution*. New York: Ronald Press Co., 1955. One of the better basic texts on the family.

MURDOCK, GEORGE PETER. *Social Structure*. New York: The Macmillan Co., 1949. Excellent treatment of comparative family and marriage patterns.

NATIONAL MANPOWER COUNCIL. *Womanpower*. New York: Columbia University Press, 1957. One of the better treatments on women in the labor market.

OGBURN, WILLIAM F., and NIMKOFF, MEYER F. *Technology and the Changing Family*. Boston: Houghton Mifflin Co., 1955. The impact of technology upon the family.

SHELDON, HENRY D. *The Older Population of the United States*. New York: John Wiley and Sons, 1958. Problems of the aging population and some ways of meeting them.

SIMPSON, GEORGE. *People in Families*. New York: Thomas Y. Crowell Co., 1960.

WINCH, ROBERT. *The Modern Family*. New York: Henry Holt and Co., 1952. Good basic college text on the family today.

ZIMMERMAN, CARLE C. *Family and Civilization*. New York: Harper and Bros., 1947. Good treatment of the trustee, social, and atomistic type families.

# 9. PEER GROUPS AND REFERENCE GROUPS

IN ADDITION to the family, which we have referred to as "the nursery of human nature," we should discuss two other categories of groups which greatly influence the socialization and behavior of the individual: peer groups and reference groups.

Peer groups are present in primitive cultures as well as in current societies. They occur in their most highly developed form in African cultures, where there are a number of grades of males in some tribes.[1]

## PEER GROUPS

### A definition of peer groups

Groups in which the members are approximately equal in age and social status are called *peer groups*. One of the most common peer groups are age-mate groups. Some of these begin in childhood and continue even into the adult period.[2] As the child grows older, what Havighurst and Neugarten refer to as the "life space" of the child expands.[3] As these authors

show, the child lives in two worlds—the world of adults and the world of peers. Before birth the life space of the child is confined to the uterine environment. After birth the social life space of the child begins to expand but is confined, for the most part, in the early years of life to the family. The next circle of contacts is likely to be that of peer group influence. This expanding group influence is shown by the accompanying diagram.

[1] *See* E. Adamson Hoebel, *Man in the Primitive World* (New York: McGraw-Hill Book Co., 1958), pp. 410-13.

[2] For an example of such as groups, *see* Murray B. Seidler and Mel Jerome Ravitz, "A Jewish Peer Group," *The American Journal of Sociology*, **61**:11-15, July, 1955.

[3] Robert J. Havighurst and Bernice L. Neugarten, *Society and Education* (Boston: Allyn and Bacon, 1957), Chap. 7, "The Life Space of the Child." *See also* Chap. 5, "The Peer Group."

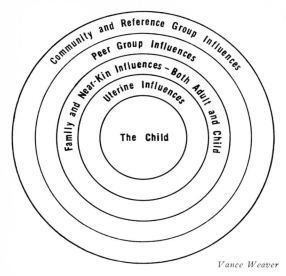

*Vance Weaver*

*The Developing Life Space of the Growing Child*

### Some kinds of peer groups

Our concern in this chapter is with peer group influences which affect the socialization of the child and youth, rather than with adult peer groups. It is enough to know that, at any age level, peer groups are formed and occupy important roles in the lives of people.

Peer groups of children and youth may be either informal or formal. Play groups, cliques, and gangs are for the most part informal, although gangs of boys may develop considerable formality. Many child and youth service organizations are formal. This is true of Boy and Girl Scout troops, some rural club groups, such as 4-H clubs, high school social clubs, and, later, sororities and fraternities. Formality is marked by organization, including officers, and often a set of standards and procedures for admission to the group and certain standardized procedures which are followed in meetings and as a member progresses from one step to another in the group. Scouting is a good example of organized progression, beginning with Cub Scouts and ending with Eagle Scouts. Even within formalized peer groups, say a fraternity, there may be a number of

informal peer groups such as cliques or other kinds of association groups or special interest groups.

1. *The play group.* The play group is a common type of peer group. Undirected play groups are characterized by informality and spontaneity, most often without adult supervision. Much play activity develops out of the fact that children live near each other in relatively compact areas.

In play groups up to the age of about eight there is little differentiation by sex. After the age of eight differentiation increases and continues into the teenage period when boy-girl pairs begin to characterize association and courtship groups. Spontaneous play usually has no important end beyond its own activity.

2. *The gang.* Gangs are important peer groups, especially in the lives of boys. Boys gang more than do girls. Gangs are better structured and have a more defined leadership than do play groups and cliques. Activity in gangs is better planned and less spontaneous. It may have a more definite culture of its own and thrives on conflict, which gives it cohesiveness. Conflict may exist between the gang and police, between two groups, or between a gang and certain adults in the neighborhood who may be soundly disliked by the gang.

The Gluecks apply a more rigid formula to the definition of a gang than is ordinarily applied. The formula they use pretty well defines the gang as a formal rather than an informal grouping. According to their concept a gang must have: (1) a recognized leader; (2) pass words and rules governing behavior; (3) a definite habitat or arrangements for meeting at stated places; and (4) planned activities of antisocial type.[4]

Of the 1,000 delinquents studied by the Gluecks, 7 per cent were members of strictly organized groups as defined above, and 19 per cent were members of more loosely organized street gangs without definite rules or leader-

---

4 *See* Sheldon and Eleanor T. Glueck, *One Thousand Juvenile Delinquents* (Cambridge, Mass.: Harvard University Press, 1934).

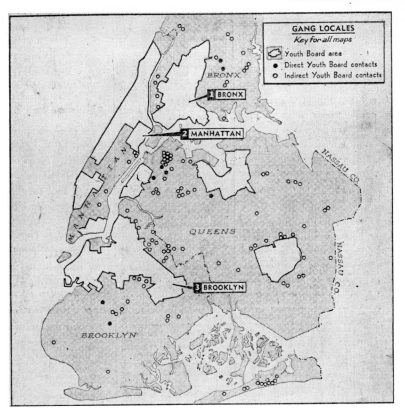

FIG. 12. GANG LOCALES IN NEW YORK CITY

SOURCE: *New York Times*, March 24, 1958, Sec. C, p. 17.

ship. Thirty per cent of the juveniles committed their offenses alone, 28 per cent with one companion, 22 per cent with two companions, and 20 per cent with three or more companions.[5]

Shaw and McKay reported on 8,484 juvenile delinquents in Chicago. Of these, 12 per cent worked alone at their offenses, whereas 88 per cent had one or more companions.[6]

Peer groups, known as gangs of the type we are discussing, are those without the discipline of family and community control. The leadership of the gang is usually based on personal achievement or some other unusual quality. Activities include fighting, loafing, drinking, gambling, listening to music, dancing if there are girl companions, smoking, playing pool, and stealing as a means of getting food and money. Behavior, therefore, is often either delinquent or predelinquent.[7]

Gangs are often defensive, discounting what other groups have to offer. They have a culture all their own which may insulate the members from contact with outsiders. Whether gangs are primary in characteristic, and to what degree, depends upon the amount of integration and solidarity within them.

Let us now look at the development and

[5] *Ibid.*, pp. 94, 100.
[6] Clifford R. Shaw and Henry D. McKay, *Social Factors in Juvenile Delinquency*, National Commission on Law Observance and Enforcement 2, No. 13 (Washington, D.C., 1931), pp. 194, 199.

[7] For a pioneering study of gangs, *see* Frederic M. Thrasher, *The Gang* (Chicago: University of Chicago Press, 1936).

characteristics of a gang as it unfolds. We shall use as this example an old, but classic, illustration.

### Rocco and His Gang

Rocco was born in this country of Italian parentage. His father came as an adult immigrant 32 years ago and has worked steadily on railroad section gangs. Five of the seven children in the family had a grade-school education or better and are now regularly employed and law-abiding. One brother, Tony, has been "signed with crime," but to no great extent. The "42" gang had its origins in a typical neighborhood group of small boys. For ten years it frequented Chicago's West Side. Though now in virtual eclipse, it has passed on heritage so that "children are growing up into a criminal life." Rocco tells his story in a matter-of-fact way and with an unusual memory for details.

*Beginning in Truancy.* My schooling at Dante was regular, and I attended to my work while there. I always, from a very small child, wanted to be an altar boy, and one day when one of the altar boys came and told me that I was chosen, I was very happy. I went to church every morning, arose at 6 and served the 7 to 8 o'clock Mass. The altar boys were my playmates. There was a little clublike room in the basement where we played games. In the wintertime we went to Hull House and spent some time in the playroom. Sometimes I went on hikes. I was never truant from school.

After we moved to Taylor and Sibly, I had to transfer to the Rees school. I arrived from Dante in the fifth grade and with a good record. I first met Peter and Louie in this room. At Dante I had never bummed. At Rees I didn't like the school because I didn't know anybody. Once in a while we would bum and run back to the old neighborhood. It was always in the afternoon so I could wait for my friends. We got so we would go to school only once in a while.

*Conflict with the Family.* I began to have trouble in school, and it was reported to my father. He talked to me and punished me. It was time, too, for my lessons for confirmation, and my father transferred me to Pompeii school. Here I behaved a little better. The principal gave me a talking to right at the beginning. Later I began to find my old friends again. I was kicked out of Pompeii and went back to Rees, where I quit in the seventh grade. By this time we were bumming and stealing.

My parents used to be notified by mail that I bummed yesterday. My mother at first tried talking and pleading with me, sometimes with tears in her eyes. "What's got in your head, Rocky? Why don't you go to school?" "I don't like that school," I said. But she never gave these notices to my father. One day the teacher brought the letter herself. She gave the letter to Albert and asked him to give it to father. He did that night. From then on my father arranged to be notified by the teacher about my absences.

After a few beatings at different times, he got disgusted and let me go. There was nothing said between us; he would just frown at me. At the table I would sit as far away from him as I could. One day he said, "You are not going to school. You are just bumming around. Why don't you go to work?" Then I got my work certificate. From then on I bummed all day every day and at home told them I had a job.

Every morning I was out at 7:30 and returned at 5:30. On Saturday I brought home ten dollars as "pay." When one of them asked me, I told them I was working downtown at the Board of Trade.

How my mother found out that I wasn't working, I don't know. When she did, she began to ask me how I got my money. I tried to lie out of it (stealing). "If your father finds out, he'll kill you. Where did you get your money?" I told her. She cried and said, "Don't do that, Rocky, you'll go to jail and never come out again." It always hurt me to see her cry, but I couldn't change. I met those fellows (the gang) every morning, and when I said I was going to look for a job, they'd laugh at me. Albert's warning has always been "You'll wind up in the gutter." He always had another set of friends.

*First Rackets.* We first started stealing from clotheslines while bumming from school. The first day we went out west, near Oak Park. We took the street car with a little sack under our arms, filled it, and came home. We "picked" silk shirts and would sell them for only a dollar or two apiece. We would shoot craps on the sidewalk, buy delicatessen, go to shows, and worry the girls.

Our next racket was robbing pennies. One of us would take a sledge hammer and with a partner start down Roosevelt Road looking for penny machines. One smash and the pennies would come rolling out. We would get four or five machines in an evening. If we were chased, we knew the

*This gang insulates its members against outsiders and thrives on conflict.*

streets like a book and would run through alleys like lightning, or over a fence into an open lot. We used to study getaways day and night, and we were never caught.

A little later we began to steal bicycles. We would go into the Oak Park district on the street-car, take the bikes, and ride them home. We were partners and would use the same basement store-room. We would sell these bikes, some worth $55 or $65 for $4, $10, or $15. We always had a half dozen bikes in the basement. One day a man came around and said he would give us $9 for a 29 x 4 tire. He told us it was easy. He explained that we could get a bar clip at a hardware store, which we did, and with it take the spare tire off the car. We delivered the tire, and he gave us the $9. Through him another customer heard of us, and these passed us on to still others. We soon got a list of phone numbers of tire customers, leaving

orders for sizes in advance. Many of our customers were legitimate working people. We stole tires all over the city. I soon owned a little Ford coupe and we cruised around until we found what we wanted.

In the delicatessen store (gang hangout), we "stoshed" some of our money. I suppose the four of us in good weeks made as high as $200. Our biggest expense then was shooting craps, and we wanted to go with girls like older fellows. We picked up two, one a German and the other Polish. They lived in a hotel. When it got hot for us, we would go over there and stay. We were suckers for those girls, bought them clothes and gave them money.

*Trouble with the Police.* We got into our first jam when I was about sixteen, and we had been a few months in the tire business. We had our basement fixed up with shelves and marked tire

*Gang activity has plagued certain sections of New York City during recent years. This is a scene from the Leonard Bernstein-Jerome Robbins musical,* West Side Story.

sizes. When a customer wanted a tire, we would take him down, switch on the light, and pull out the right size. Getting into a jam was not new to us, as we had heard a lot from older fellows about fixing the police, springing writs, and getting bail.

We were picked up around the Empire Theater by the old Marmon squad with a gong on each side of the wagon. They took us down to the Desplaines Street station. They thought the Ford I was driving was stolen, and they had us under suspicion for stealing tires. They gave us some beatings, and we didn't know anything. We were booked for disorderly, and the court discharged the case.

After that we began to be watched, and the coppers began to pick us up. I learned that when you are picked up and have money in your pocket, you can fix the cop. Twenty-five dollars will fix it on the spot.

*Code of the "42" Gang.* When Figlio opened his poolroom, we started hanging out there. The poolroom drew more fellows around the neighborhood who were in little mobs of two and four and eight, and the mobs got close, got acquainted, that way. It was there that the name "42" sprang up. The bunch were all acquainted; I could approach any fellow and ask him to go on a job. There was an elderly man there we all trusted. We left our guns, left our money to bank, and would drop him a fin or a sawbuck. You could eat there, sleep there; you could get your phone calls and call up the mouthpiece.

If you were "in," the mouthpiece knew that the mob boys were good. He'd spring a writ for you or do anything, and collect afterwards because he knew where to find you and that you'd pay if you belonged to the gang. If you didn't have it (money), the boys would take up a collection.

One time I was pinched seven Sundays in a row.

We never talked, no confessions. In some cases. they'd take us down, question us, beat us, and bring us up every two or three hours. One time a young copper came down, first talked rough, then slapped me in the face, but could get nothing on us. He came down later in a kinder mood and told me that he was an ex-hood himself. He did some favors for me, and I met him later when I was out and took him to a good Italian dinner.

*Alliance with Politicians.* On election day, Vito, Frankie, Bozzi, and Chiochio were busy at the precinct polls. All the others came around. I was an election judge, and Frankie was a worker with a badge. They told me that in the ward it was agreed that votes were to come out 50-50. There would be no trouble that day.

*Truck and Auto Rackets.* The last six months in the tire business we would go out after 1 P.M. We averaged about $75 a week—all sweet [clear], nobody to pay off. But I thought, "If I went out with the big fellows, I'd be a big shot too." Then we started getting in with the older clique. They hijacked us into their gang, but we wanted to be with them. They were 20 or 21 years of age. They were in the big money, after butter-and-egg trucks, dry goods, and shoes in loads. They were driving Chryslers and having bigger and better times— cabarets, shows, beer joints. We didn't know how to dress, and we felt that they were smarter. They taught me how to match ties and suits, what color shoes and hats to wear.

We were down in the basement at Figlio's. Vito asked me if I wanted to try a pistol, showing me how to aim. Pointing at the target, he showed how a pistol must be aimed lower than the object to always allow for the jump. Later he sold me a .36 Colt's. The older fellows were in the pistol racket (holdups) even then. They went into the pistol racket just as the butter-and-egg business was waning.

I don't remember the first time I went out after a truck, but I can give you an instance. We met one morning at Edgmont and Loomis at the appointed time. We got into Salvi's Ford and cruised around. This cruising around sometimes took an hour before we met up with anything. At Kedzie and Flournoy there stood a truck, butter and eggs. The driver was in the store. I jumped in the truck and drove east, Salvi and the Ford behind me. His work was to cut off anybody following me in a machine by crowding him to the curb. . . .

We had our garage in the neighborhood. Once there, we would unload the stuff and take the truck out of the district. We knew the places where we could dispose of the stuff, and we knew the prices. The two big "fences" would buy anything. You could get money from them any time you brought in the stuff. This racket lasted about a year when I was 19 years old. . . .

We took Gene (a newcomer) for a sucker, but he was a good head for auto work. He took us out to a saloon hangout, and we started taking orders for cars. By this time we knew how to take the ignition switch off, make connections, break the steering lock, and drive away. We would take orders for machines from the saloonkeeper. Bootleggers wanted the numbers changed, and we would have to hold cars until we got numbers from New York. We would write the make, model, and year, and the man would watch for cars of the same description. Then he would send us their license numbers.

*Sentenced, Paroled, and a Job.* In this one (and only) conviction, I got an 18-month sentence at St. Charles (boys' reformatory). First I was downhearted and lonesome. I didn't like the fellows around me. They were punks, wanting to be tough. I attended to work and kept quiet. I was moved to C cottage where I met some kids from my neighborhood. One day I separated a pair of kids who were fighting, and Colonel Whip heard about this. He called me to the office and made me a sergeant. I received no punishment in the time I was at St. Charles.

For six months after my release, I reported to a probation officer. That's the guy that got me a job as errand boy. When I went out to an employer, I tried my best not to get the job. Finally, after about four months of stalling, he took me himself. He took me to four places altogether; he pleaded with employers. I never heard anyone lie so much in one day. I worked for two months as errand boy at $15 a week. Of course I did some stealing, just enough to average around $40 a week. I quit the job after my probation period was over.

*The Gang in Dissolution.* On returning to the mob, I found that it was scattered and broken up. Babe Ruth had been killed by a cop and Jit Pargoni and one of his brothers. The rackets had changed. The trucks had two guys on them. The police had found a way to bring out original numbers on automobiles by using acid. Other numbers hard to find (body numbers) were being put on cars by manufacturers. The police could find them through charts furnished by the company. The chain stores and later the tire war made tires so cheap you could buy legit tires for less than we sold stolen ones. I nosed around among the fellows, but they were all going out with the pistol.

We did our first stick-up in a cigar store. We stayed there a full twenty minutes . . . and we got $700 in money and merchandise. In 1928-1929, I used to go out regularly with the same two fellows. This was on no tips at all, all blind joints. Working on tips is more lousy (dangerous), unless they are the right kind. The tipster may be a stool, leak, or trap. Tipsters and bad luck come together.

We're not gangsters any more. We're just hoodlums. I'm a hoodlum and a small one at that. It would be a good thing if we had a gang and somebody with money to organize us.[8]

3. *The Clique.* Cliques are relatively durable groups, made up of persons of about the same social status. On the whole they are somewhat smaller in size than gangs, are less predatory in nature, and are held together less by conflicts with outside groups than are gangs.

One of the best discussions of cliques which we have is that given by Hollingshead. He says:

A clique comes into existence when two or more persons are related one to another in an intimate fellowship that involves "going places and doing things" together, a mutual exchange of ideas, and the acceptance of each personality by the others. Perhaps the most characteristic thing about the clique is the way its members *plan* to be together, to do things together, go places together. Within the clique, personal relations with one another involve the clique mates in emotional and sentimental situations of great moment to the participants. Confidences are exchanged between some or all members; often those very personal, wholly private, experiences that occur in the family which

involve only one member may be exchanged with a best friend in the group. Relations with the opposite sex, with adults, and with young people outside the clique are discussed and decisions reached on the action to be taken by the clique, or by a particular member involved in a situation.

Membership is voluntary and informal; members are admitted gradually to a pre-existing clique and dropped by the mutual consent of its participants. Although there are no explicit rules for membership, the clique has a more or less common set of values which determines who will be admitted, what it does, how it will censure some member who does not abide by its values.

As the clique comes to be accepted by other cliques as a definite unit in the adolescent society, it develops an awareness of self, a "we feeling," sentiments, and traditions which impel its members to act and think alike. Its members frequently identify their interests with the group in contrast to the interests of the family, other cliques, the school, and society. Generally, clique interests come before those of the individual member or any outside group or interest. This attitude often results in conflicts between the clique and the family, between the clique and the school, or between the clique and the neighborhood. If this conflict element becomes the *raison d'être* of the group, the clique develops into the gang.[9]

Like gangs, cliques develop unfavorable reputations with teachers and parents and group leaders. There is some evidence that three-person cliques are difficult to maintain as a balanced relationship. What happens often is that the interaction patterns between two persons of the triad will be strong, whereas interaction bonds toward the third member may be weaker. To put it another way, a triadic group relationship is difficult to maintain on an equal basis.[10] Usually, however, adequate interactional bonds are strong enough to hold

[8] Quoted by permission from John Landesco, "The Life History of a Member of the '42' Gang," *Journal of Criminal Law and Criminology,* March-April, 1943. The arrangement of the material is briefed from that of L. A. Cook and Elaine Forsythe Cook in *A Sociological Approach to Education* (New York: McGraw-Hill Book Co., 1950), pp. 358-63. Used by permission.

[9] A. B. Hollingshead, *Elmtown's Youth* (New York: John Wiley and Sons, 1949), pp. 205-6.
[10] The whole subject of triadic group relationships is worth exploring. *See* Theodore Caplow, "A Theory of Coalitions in the Triad," *American Sociological Review,* 21:489-93, August, 1956, and W. E. Vinacke and A. Arkoff, "An Experimental Study of Coalitions in the Triad," *American Sociological Review,* 22:406-14, August, 1957.

the triad together. Perhaps the most important factor leading to the breakup of cliques is the dating complex.

### Functions of peer groups

In this discussion we shall continue our emphasis upon childhood and youth groups.

In Chapter 7 we discussed the general influence of groups; therefore, here our concern is with some of the more distinctive functions of peer groups. Of course, such functions are highly variable.[11]

1. Childhood and youth peer groups are important in gradually freeing the young person from domination by his elders. Such freedom from adult dominance is a necessary part of growing up in our culture, and peer group membership helps to achieve it. Emotional, social, and physical maturation is speeded up as a result of peer group contacts. Some authorities claim that this release from parental restraint is too complete in our culture, and takes place at too early an age. Perhaps this is so because adults often take the viewpoint that freedom and control are incompatible, whereas they are not necessarily so.

2. Peer groups are important in the learning and development of social roles. Leadership-follower roles are examples. Peer group membership offers opportunities for some group members to develop roles as leaders and others to assume roles as followers. Both roles are important in a democracy.

A couple within a courtship group learns roles as courtship mates which will be valuable later in life. While courtship groups are important in the selection of mates for marriage, they are also important in aiding the young person to help determine whom he or she should, or should not, marry.

A child, accustomed to a dominating role in his family, may have to accept a subordinate role in a peer group. This is a useful experi-

ence as well as that in which a youth, accustomed to a subordinate role in the family, finds himself in a position of dominant leadership in a peer group. Thus, in each instance a new social role is learned.

3. Peer groups are important in providing status feelings and relationships for their members. They develop in members a sense of belonging and of being a part of the peer group. It is possible that one may not feel that he has status which he thinks he should be accorded at home or in his classes at school; however, he may develop the status relationship he is seeking in his peer group relationships.

4. Peer groups may provide opportunities for social mobility. It is not unusual to find youths having membership in peer groups, especially those in schools, which are above their families in status. Within groups one may also have opportunity for social mobility as one moves from mere acceptance to a position of high status within the group. In the process of achieving mobility within the group the person may learn many lessons as to how, or how not, to achieve social mobility.

In naming their best friends in peer groups children frequently name children who are above them in social status. The process of imitation must be considerable and an important enough factor in social mobility to bear considerable attention. It is, of course, true that membership in school groups, especially in public schools, is more apt to cross class lines than the membership in out-of-school groups.

5. Peer groups are bearers of group subcultures. Peer groups have distinctive subcultures in addition to mirroring aspects of the mass culture. In the example of Rocco and his gang we saw the influences of the gang. Let us use another illustration, that of sex knowledge. Many families hesitate to teach their children sex knowledge. Schools neglect the subject. Thus, young people have to depend upon their peer group subcultures for "enlightenment" on the question of sex, as crude and wrong as this enlightenment may be.

[11] For a good discussion of the function of peer groups, *see* Robert J. Havighurst and Bernice L. Neugarten, *op. cit.,* pp. 106-28.

A "gentleman's grade" as defined by school peer groups is ofttimes a C or a B. Such definition frequently influences many male students in their academic strivings. Some subgroup cultures in schools define one type of code, or conduct, or even wearing apparel, whereas the school's administrative culture adheres to other concepts. Some experimental data indicate that only about 25 per cent of teenagers are able to resist majority group pressure in expressed opinion.

6. Peer group subcultures generate friction with other subcultures. First of all, as we indicated, the subculture of one peer group may be in conflict with the subculture of another peer group. Youth peer groups with different values, attitudes, and behaviors than adult subcultures may come in conflict with them. Friction between parents and their children may develop because the children are reflecting the values and behavior of their peer groups. Out-of-school peer groups frequently conflict with the subculture of the school and the parents of school children. Many instances of this are found in the initiation ceremonies which high school social clubs use. Such ceremonies are acceptable to the subcultures of the social clubs but are unacceptable to parents, teachers, and school administrators.

## Peer group relationships

Peer group relationships are growing in importance. Urbanization of population brings people together in large numbers and under conditions which may release youth from adult supervision for long periods of time. Also, there is growing attention to the servicing of youth through the provision of recreation and other youth service organizations. Age-grouping for various purposes is a common practice in churches, schools, and youth-serving organizations.

The tendency in American society not to accept youth into the adult culture releases youth for liberal participation in youth subcultures. For instance, youth is not usually acceptable into employment until after the age of 18. They may serve in the armed forces at an earlier age than they may vote. Youth members of a family may be rather neglected by both parents while the parents are busy "making a living." The total result is release from contact with adult cultures and from adult supervision.

Social class factors play an important part in peer group relationships. Hollingshead found that three out of five adolescent clique relationships in Elmtown were within the same social class. Only one in twenty-five crossed more than one class line. Patterns of dating consistently followed class lines.[12]

Stendler, in his study of Brasstown children, found that children crossed class lines in selecting their school friends and associates, but invariably chose their out-of-school associates from the same social class to which they belonged.[13]

## Studying peer group relationships

One of the methods of studying groups, especially at the child and youth level, for purposes of grouping arrangements, is the *sociogram* and the *sociometric test*. The procedure may be used in many ways to determine choices and rejections among group members. Let us assume that a class in high school sociology was being divided into small groups to work on projects. The procedure would be to ask each member of the class whom they would like to work with, and to indicate this in terms of first, second, and third choices. The choices would then be charted and an arrangement made on the basis of the choices. Sociograms or sociometric tests do not give reasons for acceptances and rejections, which may be necessary in developing better interpersonal relationships in a group. Where there are cleavages within a group the teacher or director of the

[12] Hollingshead, *op. cit.*, pp. 212-13.
[13] Celia B. Stendler, *Children of Brasstown* (Urbana, Ill.: Bureau of Research and Service of the College of Education, University of Illinois, 1949).

group may want to determine the causes of the cleavages, quietly and judiciously, make an interpretation of them, and set about to correct them.

The accompanying sociogram of an eighth-grade literature class shows the kinds of relationships which may be revealed in the use of sociograms.[14]

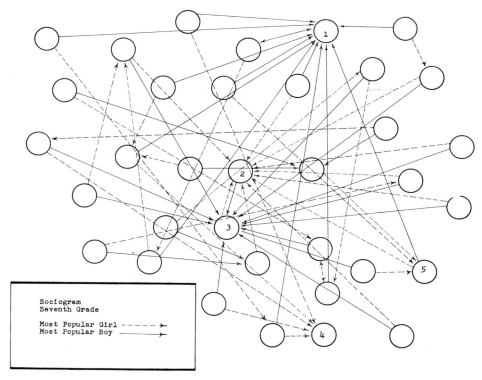

Sociogram
Seventh Grade

Most Popular Girl  - - - - ▶
Most Popular Boy  ————▶

*Sociogram of a Seventh-Grade Class*

## REFERENCE GROUPS

Some years ago H. H. Hyman, a psychologist, coined the term "reference groups."[15] Since that time a considerable amount of literature has developed on the subject.

[14] The following sources are good for the student interested in sociometric methods: Helen Hall Jennings, *Sociometry in Group Relations* (Washington, D.C.: The American Council on Education, 1948); Mary L. Northway, *A Primer of Sociometry* (Toronto, Can.: University of Toronto Press, 1952); Walter T. Smith, *Manual of Sociometry for Teachers* (Ann Arbor, Mich.: Child Development Laboratories, University of Michigan, 1951).

[15] H. H. Hyman, "The Psychology of Status," *Archives of Psychology*, **38:**15, 1942; Muzafer Sherif and M. O. Wilson (eds.), *Group Relations at the Crossroads* (New York: Harper and Bros., 1953).

A *reference group* is any group of which we are a part, and to which we relate our decisions and actions. Reference groups denote those groups to which a person aspires to belong or to join, as well as those to which he does belong. For instance, a fraternity or sorority, a city club or country club, are reference groups for the persons who aspire to belong to them as well as the persons who actually do belong to them.

A gang, clique, or family may be a reference group. Both for the arrivist and the arrived, nowhere is the influence of reference groups stronger than in high school and college. Col-

*Wide World Photos*

*The United States Chamber of Commerce in Session. This is an important reference group for many business leaders.*

*The labor union is one of the important reference groups of the worker. Here Walter Reuther speaks to a local of the UAW.*

*UAW*

leges always have their stereotype of the "lady" and the "gentleman," after which college groups tend to pattern aspects of dress, deportment, and conduct. A recent arrival on college campuses is a new group referred to as "beatniks." When a student accepts, currently, one of these groups as a reference group he may immediately adopt some of the characteristics and symbols of the beatniks. For instance, the male student may grow a beard, wear sandals, write poetry, pose an interest in music and art, and assume a bohemian attitude toward accepted moral values and approved behavior practices. Similar offbeat dress and behavior patterns are assumed by girls.

Reference groups in labor and management organizations are common. An individualist in the conduct of his business, a member of the American Manufacturers Association or the United States Chamber of Commerce may go "right down the line" in accepting the views of these two organizations and reflect this in voting behavior which involves a choice of opinion between his individual views and those of the above organizations.

Aspiration to business reference groups has been the theme of many stage and motion picture productions. William H. Whyte, in the *Organization Man*,[16] shows how the young executive is caught in a web of aspiration centering around reference groups and patterns his behavior accordingly.

Reference groups, then, are particularly im-portant because they condition our decisions and actions. We frequently revert to them when we face new situations and decisions.[17] For instance, one of the problems in dealing with a delinquent is that he may have lost the perspective of reference groups like the family, the church, nondelinquent peer groups, and the school. When the delinquent has to make a decision and take action, his decisions and behavior are influenced by reference groups, such as his gangs and cliques, the street corner society, the poolroom and the tavern. Conflicts between reference groups are, of course, common.

A practicing physician may have as his reference groups the local academy of medicine and the American Medical Association. He may abide by the codes and decisions of these groups, although his ideas of medical practice may, in some ways, be at variance with them.

A manufacturer may write letters to his congressman for or against a certain piece of legislation, depending upon the position which his reference groups have taken. Some people vote party tickets, irrespective of the candidates, because to them the party is their reference group rather than any particular candidate or group of candidates.[18]

What dictators have frequently tried to do is to outlaw or destroy the previously developed reference groups of a people, and to substitute a new set of reference groups which are sympathetic with the dictator's policies.

## SUMMARY

In addition to the family, which has a primary influence upon the individual because of birth into it and for other reasons which we discussed in the last chapters, in the circle of socialization as it develops one is influenced greatly by peer groups. These groups are essentially groups in which the members have the same age and social status.

Peer groups may be formal or informal. Al-though some gangs may be formal in organization, for the most part they are informal, as are also play groups, cliques, and other kinds of association groups.

[16] (New York: Simon and Schuster, 1956)

[17] *See* Tamotsu Shibutani, "Reference Groups as Perspectives," *The American Journal of Sociology*, **60:**562-69, May, 1955.

[18] For a study of factors in the acceptance of new reference groups, *see* Ruth E. Hartley, *The Acceptance of New Reference Groups,* Office of Naval Research, Report No. 2 (New York: College of the City of New York, 1956). Mimeographed.

Peer groups perform many functions in the lives of individuals. Each has its own subgroup culture and is a bearer or carrier of this culture. Such groups offer status to their members and provide opportunities for many new roles, including leadership and follower roles. Finally, such groups may stimulate conflict with peer groups and with other kinds of groups.

In addition to peer groups there are other kinds of reference groups to which we relate our decisions and our behavior. While many reference groups are primary in type, for example our families, many of them are secondary in nature. Among these are church groups, school groups, trade associations, status groups to which people aspire, and political parties. By destroying or reshaping one's reference groups, one's behavior and attitudes may be reshaped accordingly. Such attempts are frequently made by dictators.

THINGS TO DO AND TO DISCUSS

1. What is a peer group? Give examples of peer groups to which you belong or to which you have belonged.
2. Distinguish between a clique and a gang. How do the Gluecks characterize a gang? Do you or do you not agree with their characterization?
3. What are some functions served by peer groups? If possible, give concrete examples of the influences of peer groups.
4. How do social classes influence the structuring of peer groups? The behavior of reference groups?
5. Construct a sociogram from a group situation with which you are acquainted.
6. What are reference groups? Why are they important?
7. Make a study of reference groups in your community and try to list those for the doctor, the business man, the farmer, and the social climber.
8. Analyze Whyte's *The Organization Man* for reference group pressures.

FOR FURTHER STUDY

GORDON, C. WAYNE, and NICHOLAS, BABCHUK, "A Typology of Voluntary Associations," *American Sociological Review,* 1:22-29, February, 1959. A good attempt at classifying voluntary associations.

HAVIGHURST, ROBERT J., and NEUGARTEN, BERNICE L. *Society and Education.* Boston: Allyn and Bacon, 1957. Some good materials on peer groups.

HOLLINGSHEAD, A. B. *Elmtown's Youth.* New York: John Wiley and Sons, 1949. How youth reference groups influence behavior.

JENNINGS, HELEN HALL. *Sociometry in Group Relations.* Washington, D.C.: American Council on Education, 1948. How to study group relations in peer groups.

RAVITZ, JEROME. "A Jewish Peer Group," *The American Journal of Sociology,* 61:11-15, July, 1955. A good case study of a peer group.

ROBBINS, FLORENCE GREENHOE. *Educational Sociology.* New York: Henry Holt and Co., 1953. Good discussion of childhood and play groups.

SHIBUTANI, TAMOTSU. "Reference Groups as Perspectives," *The American Journal of Sociology,* 60:562-69, May, 1955. Excellent general treatment of reference groups.

STENDLER, CELIA. *Children of Brasstown.* Urbana, Ill.: Bureau of Research and Service of the College of Education, University of Illinois, 1949. How peer and reference groups influence the behavior of children.

THRASHER, FREDERIC M. *The Gang.* Chicago: University of Chicago Press, 1936. The classic and perhaps still the best treatment of the gang.

WHYTE, WILLIAM H. *The Organization Man.* New York: Simon and Schuster, 1956. How business groups, as reference groups, influence the behavior of young executives especially.

# 10. PLACE GROUPINGS

THE STUDY of place groupings has a triple significance. The student of society cannot understand social structure without knowledge of the structure and function of place groupings. Their study is important in throwing light upon the development of social systems, including societies. Also place groupings, especially the city and metropolitan area, the community and the region, are units of important action and development programs throughout the world.

We have indicated in previous chapters that two forms of social grouping are universal in all cultures—one is the family and the other some form of local place grouping. Almost without exception people are in some way associated with families. They also belong to some place which they recognize as their locality and territory which they are usually willing to defend, if necessary.

Place groupings are often referred to as "locality groupings." While all groupings require space on which to stand, worship, work, play, or sleep, place groupings, as we refer to them, are systems or units of people involving several or many families occupying a definite territory which they recognize as their own and to which they have a sense of belonging.

The frequency of interaction between persons depends partially upon the nature of the place grouping. For instance, contact and interaction between people in a neighborhood would be greater than it would be in a region. One might have contact with more individuals in a large city than in a small city; however, the interaction process would likely be more intimate and personal in a small city. Always there is some communal feeling and sense of belonging, as well as varying systems and degrees of interaction, in place groupings.

*159*

## SOME SIGNIFICANT PLACE GROUPINGS

### *The band and clan*

The *band* is a local grouping of families occupying a definite territory, or at least using a definite territory, with a stable place of settlement somewhere in or near the territory. Bands may vary greatly in structure and territory. A common form of band is the hunting band, made up largely of males. Such bands may range over a large territory to hunt, while the women and children remain in a fairly permanent location or camp, awaiting the return of the hunters.

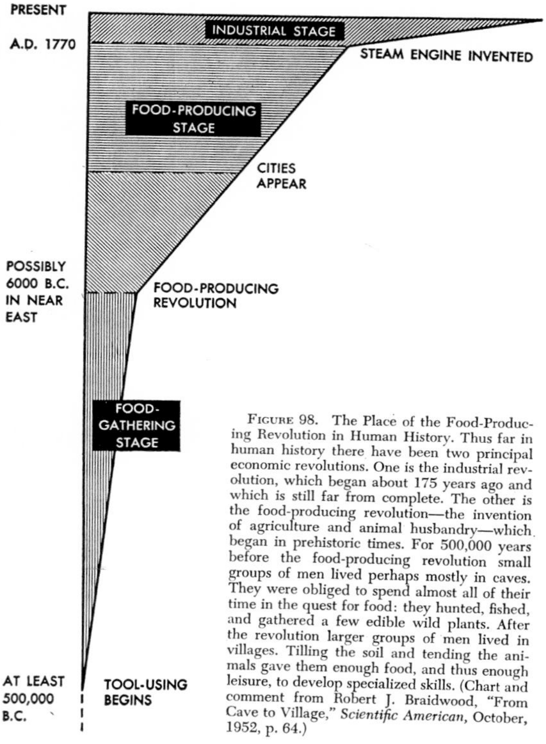
PRESENT
A.D. 1770
INDUSTRIAL STAGE
STEAM ENGINE INVENTED
FOOD-PRODUCING STAGE
CITIES APPEAR
POSSIBLY 6000 B.C. IN NEAR EAST
FOOD-PRODUCING REVOLUTION
FOOD-GATHERING STAGE
AT LEAST 500,000 B.C.
TOOL-USING BEGINS
FIGURE 98. The Place of the Food-Producing Revolution in Human History. Thus far in human history there have been two principal economic revolutions. One is the industrial revolution, which began about 175 years ago and which is still far from complete. The other is the food-producing revolution—the invention of agriculture and animal husbandry—which began in prehistoric times. For 500,000 years before the food-producing revolution small groups of men lived perhaps mostly in caves. They were obliged to spend almost all of their time in the quest for food: they hunted, fished, and gathered a few edible wild plants. After the revolution larger groups of men lived in villages. Tilling the soil and tending the animals gave them enough food, and thus enough leisure, to develop specialized skills. (Chart and comment from Robert J. Braidwood, "From Cave to Village," *Scientific American*, October, 1952, p. 64.)

FIG. 13. GRAPH SHOWING INCREASE IN THE SUPPORTING BASE FOR PLACE GROUPINGS OF LARGER POPULATIONS CAUSED BY THE REVOLUTION IN AGRICULTURE AND THE INDUSTRIAL REVOLUTION

SOURCE: Robert J. Braidwood, "From Cave to Village," *Scientific American*, 187 (October, 1952), 63-66. Reprinted with permission of Scientific American, Inc., October, 1952, Vol. 187, No. 4.

Another form of band may be one made up of complete families which move with migratory animals. The Caribou Indians in the northern part of North America did just this. As the herds moved to better grazing, the Indians would follow. This is true also of the Persian herdsmen, who may leave their villages, along with other members of their families, to go with a band of herdsmen to follow the herds into the mountains, going to higher elevations as the grazing seasons lengthen, and establishing temporary settlements while the herds graze out an area. In Australia what we call a band is referred to as a *horde*.

Among the Indians one band might have a definite territory which it hunted and was willing to protect against poachers from other bands. On the other hand, it was not unusual for different bands of Indians to hunt the same territory. This was true in Middle Tennessee where more than one Indian band would hunt the Barrens, which were lush pasture areas. No Indian tribe occupied the Barrens continuously.

The size of bands is determined largely by the food supply, that is, the number of people who can be supported by food gatherers and hunters working out of a central camp. Linton doubts that human bands exceeded 200 to 300 individuals. He feels that food-gathering bands, without domesticated animals, rarely exceeded 50 to 60 persons.[1] As the accompanying diagram shows, following the domestication of plants and animals a supporting base was laid for much larger place groupings (Fig. 13).

In describing the relation of food supply to the formation of bands, Linton indicates

[1] Ralph Linton, *The Tree of Culture* (New York: Alfred A. Knopf, 1955), p. 22. *See* Kwang-Chih Chang, "Study of the Neolithic Social Grouping: Examples from the New World," *American Anthropologist*, **60**:298-334, 1958, for the kind of New Stone Age settlements in New World Neolithic societies.

that populations spread by a sort of budding process, and that when the size of a band becomes too large for existing local resources it splits and a new band is formed. He says also that under normal conditions bands are not free-wandering units.

Each band normally occupies a definite territory within which it makes regular annual circuits, coming back to the same camp site year after year at the same seasons to exploit the local food resources. Several bands usually form a larger unit, a tribe, whose members have a vague feeling of unity based upon common language and customs, but in the absence of formal patterns of government such tribal units cannot grow to any great size. In general, trespassing on another band's territory is resented and punished. However, it is a significant fact that none of the really primitive food gathering groups indulge in anything which can be called systematic warfare. Rather than one group attempting to drive another out of its territory to provide for increasing numbers, the pattern seems to be for the population to stabilize in relation to its food supply. Although there may be considerable fluctuation from time to time in accordance with good or bad years, the general population levels remain very much the same. It is highly probable that this was also the situation with early man.[2]

The *clan* is another example of place grouping. A clan is a number of families or households, often closely knit, the heads of which claim descent from a common ancestor. Kinship bonds are the unifying element in a clan, and the members of a clan are supposed to treat each other as if they are blood relatives.

Not all clans are locality groups in the sense that the members live in one place. However, a single clan may dominate a given locality, as in Scotland. Even here, after the Scottish clans were defeated by the English in 1746, there was wide dispersal of clan members.[3] Today, the descendants of the MacDonald clan, which at one time worked and fought together,

may be found in many countries and may still retain, and on occasion wear, their distinctive tartan plaids and pipe their clan tunes.

Mandelbaum reported an unusual clan arrangement among the Kotas of southern India. Each tribal village was arranged with three rows of houses or "streets." The residents of a single street were men of a single patrilineal clan, there being three major clans in the village. As the girls of a clan grew up they married into the clan of another village or a clan of a different street.[4]

Clans may have their own sacred equipment in the form of altars, rituals, insignia, and distinctive dress. Clan totemism is common, as among the Australian tribes and the Indians of the Northwest. The animal or object which becomes the totem symbol of the clan is usually one from which the clan has benefited sometime in its existence, and which they look upon as sacred. Such nonkinship devices are important factors in clan solidarity.

Clans serve many functions. They facilitate exogamous marriage, as we have just pointed out. Clans facilitate the division of labor. Among the Hopis one clan provides the tribal leader, another the town crier, another has custody of the temple, and other clans have responsibility for various economic activities. Clans are integrative mechanisms for the members of clans and the tribes composed of clans. They provide a system of mutual aid to clan members. Clans serve a security function by offering an opposition which may appear as a united front to another clan; thus a clan may present to opposing clans a formidable organization. Clan members, usually being required to marry outside their clan, reduce aggression between clans and broaden the base of cooperation between clan members.

Clan organizations are systems of social control. They may even banish their own troublemakers or otherwise punish them. Clans may also perform government functions. For instance, among the Aztecs 20 clan heads, called

[2] *Ibid.*, pp. 22-23.
[3] *See* David G. Mandelbaum, "Social Groupings," in *Man, Culture, and Society,* ed. Harry L. Shapiro (New York: Oxford University Press, 1956), pp. 286-93.

[4] *Ibid.*

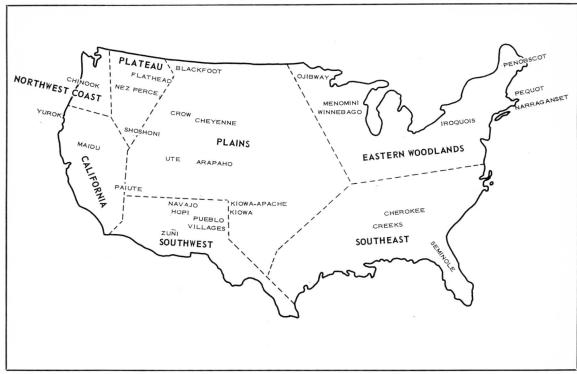

*Vance Weaver*

*The major Indian tribes of the United States can
be blocked off in fairly well defined culture areas.*

speakers, make up the Aztec tribal council and speak for the people.[5]

Clans may control and own property. They may also serve religious and ritual functions.

### The tribe

Mandelbaum gives an excellent concept of the tribe in the following description:

The families of a local community, both in societies that have clans and those that do not, almost

always have a sense of belonging to a social unit larger than the local group, one that includes a number of different communities. Among most primitive people, this larger unit of society is a tribe.[6]

Tribes are made up of people who occupy the same general territory, as a rule speak the same language, and in general have a similar culture. The accompanying map shows the important Indian tribes of the United States.

Mandelbaum describes the tribal grouping of the Plains Cree Indians of western Canada. The tribe was made up of eight bands which hunted the buffalo on the Canadian prairies.

[5] *See* George Peter Murdock, *Social Structure* (New York: The Macmillan Co., 1949), pp. 65-78. For more on the functions of clans, *see* E. Adamson Hoebel, *Man in the Primitive World* (New York: McGraw-Hill Book Co., 1958), pp. 347-51; *also* Leslie A. White, *The Evolution of Culture* (New York: McGraw-Hill Book Co., 1959), pp. 142-204.

[6] Mandelbaum, *op. cit.*, p. 295.

The tribe ranged over a Canadian territory 600 miles long. The greatest ceremonial dance of the year was the Sun Dance, in which several bands would participate. There was no tribal council with representatives from all the bands, and the members of all bands never met together on a single occasion. As the young men of one band matured to the point where they wanted to roam, they frequently went to visit another band, seeking out their relatives as they visited the bands. In the host bands they would be treated with great hospitality, an indication of tribal belonging. Often the young males would return to the encampments of their parents with brides selected from other bands, although parents preferred that their sons marry girls from their own community. When visitors from other tribes visited the Crees they were given food and shelter, but they were not treated with the same hospitality as the visitors from the bands making up the Cree tribe.[7] It was war more than anything else that welded the tribes together in a cohesive social unit. The unification of tribes was frequently the beginning of the state. A good example in this country was the League of the Iroquois in New York State, which might have developed into a state had it not been for the white man's interference.

## The village

Nowhere on earth do people live in isolated families. In a sample of 241 historical and contemporary societies studied by Murdock, 39 are organized into bands, 13 into neighborhoods without prominent nuclei, and 189 into villages or towns.[8] Goodenough, in an unpublished study, found that the mean size of historical and contemporary migratory bands was 50 people, neighborhood organizations 250, while settled villages had a mean population of 300. Agricultural villages with both animal and plant husbandry supported a mean population of around 450 people.[9]

The development of settled agriculture with domesticated crops and animals, and with irrigation, if rainfall is scarce, tends to favor permanent settlement of peoples. Fishing tends also to favor permanent settlements if the fish do not migrate, as does also a hunting economy if the animals do not migrate.

Settled residence patterns may take on the structure of a compact village, where the houses are close together and where the surrounding territory is cropped, hunted, or fished, or it may take on the form of a pattern of dispersed homesteads, as in American farming communities. Villages may comprise the nucleus of many communities made up of dispersed homesteads. In France, the Netherlands, Germany, Canada, and Louisiana, line villages are found, adapted usually to peculiar topographical features of the landscape.

In the settlement of the United States many cooperative village communities were established, in all more than 250. Usually these provided for the land resources and their operation to be vested in a group representing the community. The Hutterite communities of the United States and Canada, the Shaker communities of the United States, and the Dukhobor communities of Canada are examples of cooperative communities.

In New England the village historically was the prevailing pattern of early settlement. Possibly the best examples of agricultural villages in America are the Mormon villages in Utah and the Spanish villages of the Southwest. South of the Rio Grande the village type of community prevails in Mexico, Guatemala, Ecuador, Peru, and Bolivia. It is not unusual in these countries for the land to be communally owned. "Furthermore, over much Latin American territory the large sugar and coffee

---

[7] *Ibid.*, pp. 296-99.
[8] Murdock, *op. cit.*, p. 80

[9] W. H. Goodenough, "Basic Economy and the Community," unpublished article, quoted in George Peter Murdock, *Social Structure* (New York: The Macmillan Co., 1949), p. 81.

plantations, which generally employ the village pattern of settlement for their workers, actually are genuine village communities in and of themselves." [10]

The agricultural village was not transplanted to this country to any great extent from either Europe or the Orient. There were perhaps two reasons for this: the large amount of land available for settlement in ratio to population, and the land settlement laws which required that one live on the land he homesteaded. In most parts of the world even today it is the village and not the great city that is most important as a locality grouping. In India alone there are some 700,000 villages. The significance of the village in the lives of the Indians is well indicated by Hart:

The roots of the Indian village go deep . . . in the family of his ancestors, his caste, and his hereditary occupation. All his ties have their manifestation in the village; in the quarter and meeting place and well reserved for his kind, in the hut or courtyard of his family, in the tools or fields of his ancestral work. On the whole geography of his character and career the immemorial village temple looks down.[11]

The village and small town are still very important locality groupings in the United States. Fry reported 7,240 incorporated villages in 1900 and 10,239 in 1920.[12] In 1950, 41 per cent of the population of the United States lived in places of less than 2,500 population, and another 17.2 per cent lived in places of 2,500 to 25,000 population. In 1950, 25 states did not have a city of 250,000 population, and 13 states had no city with more than 100,000 population. However, the trend is toward a larger and larger percentage of the population living in the bigger cities and their suburbs. In fact, most of the 3 million a year population increase is in cities or their suburbs.

A study of growth of villages of 1,000 to 2,500 population in the United States shows that 47 per cent gained 10 per cent or more in population between 1940 and 1950, 6 per cent lost 10 per cent or more population, and 47 per cent neither lost nor gained population. From 1940 to 1950, 382 villages changed from village to urban status (2,500 or more population), and 554 small villages changed to medium or large village status (from 1,000 to 2,499 population).[13]

There are many reasons for village growth: (1) the rather substantial increase in population between 1940 and the present; (2) the increased accessibility of small towns and villages; (3) the increase in services and conveniences offered by small towns and villages; (4) the increase in governmental services and governmental personnel at the parish and county levels; (5) the increase in retirement of farmers, delayed by World War II; (6) suburban and fringe growth in population and industry; (7) the sale of "mill" villages making them more desirable places to live; and (8) the general desire of people to escape urban congestion. All of these contribute in one way or another to the growth of the village or the suburb.

While a few villages in this country are mining and manufacturing centers, most of them are service centers for trade, school, church, routine repairs like those for automobiles, medical services, grocery shopping, and for the services of a beautician. Some county seats are large villages, in which government services should be added to the above list. Larger places may be sought for shopping for certain items, such as furniture or highly specialized medical services. Villages serve frequently as nuclei for communities. This is especially true of farm communities. A considerable number of villages are found in urban, suburban, and fringe areas, in which case they serve as residential areas for people who may work in near-by, larger places. They

[10] T. Lynn Smith, "The Rural Community with Special Reference to Latin America," *Rural Sociology*, **23**:52-67, March, 1958.

[11] Henry C. Hart, *New India's Rivers* (Bombay: Orient Longmans, 1956), pp. 188-89.

[12] C. Luther Fry, *American Villages* (New York: Institute of Social and Religious Research, 1926).

[13] Edmund deS. Brunner, "Village Growth 1940 to 1950," *Rural Sociology*, **16**:112-18, June, 1951.

also serve as service centers for the people who live there. There is no technical definition of a village in this country. Places of less than 2,500 population are usually classed as small towns and villages, but unofficially so.

### The neighborhood

A neighborhood is nothing more than several families living close together and who neighbor with each other. Families are on a friendly, usually face to face, basis in a neighborhood. Various acts of mutual helpfulness may characterize neighboring activities. Neighborhoods differ from communities in that they are not so large, as a rule, and also that they do not provide so many services as may be found in a community. In a single community there may be several neighborhoods.

### The community

For our discussion we may say that a community has the following characteristics:

1. A definite geographical area set apart from other areas by boundary lines, sometimes hypothetical, recognized by the people living there;
2. An area to which the people have a sense of belonging;
3. Where the people enjoy a common culture;
4. And work together for certain common ends;
5. And are able to satisfy major routine needs in the area.

Other authorities characterize a community somewhat differently. For instance, Blaine E. Mercer characterizes the community as follows:

. . . An aggregate of people exhibiting the following characteristics:

1. A geographical area, whether only wholly contiguous or not.
2. An existence in time.
3. A culture more or less commonly known and shared.
4. A social system and a social structure.
5. Functional interdependence.

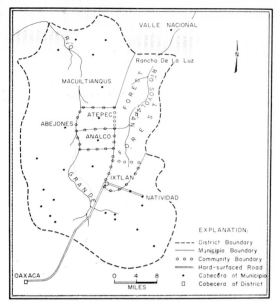

*Benjamin H. Luebke*

FIG. 14.   COMMUNITIES OF ATEPEC, ANALCO, AND
IXTLAN, STATE OF OAXACA, MEXICO

6. An awareness by the people that they have enough in common to set them off from other aggregates.[14]

Probably the community which best illustrates the above characteristics is the rural community which has a village center, and around which live families who use the village as a center for worship, education, recreation, trade, and services. Smith points out that such communities are natural areas and also areas of social interaction; that the limits are obvious to almost everyone; that they provide the basic institutions and services needed by the people such as a job, education, religion, and recreation.[15]

14 Blaine E. Mercer, *The Study of Society* (New York: Harcourt, Brace and Co., 1958), pp. 182-83. For a number of concepts of community by distinguished scholars, *see* Ernest B. Harper and Arthur Dunham, *Community Organization in Action* (New York: Association Press, 1959), pp. 23-27.

15 Smith, *op. cit.*, pp. 57-58. *See also* Selz C. Mayo, "An Approach to the Understanding of Rural Community Development," *Social Forces*, 37:95-102, December, 1958.

Another example of community, which may be somewhat less complete in function than the one we have just described, is the open country community. Frequently, the nucleus of such communities is the consolidated or centralized school, although at times it may have no other nucleus than a crossroads church and store around which the community life revolves. Small towns may have the qualities of a community, whereas a large city may have many neighborhoods and communities, although the city as a whole may be a community as far as sense of belonging, definite territory, and completeness of services is concerned. The people may not work together for certain common ends as the people in smaller communities may do. Mobility is undermining the community—at least in its older concept.

The growth of fringe and suburban communities constitutes one of the great changes taking place in the population of the United States during the last quarter century. Of the 150 million people in the United States in 1950, 90 million lived in urban communities and 20 million in fringe and suburban areas.

Suburban communities may take on specialized characteristics, although they are predominately residential. Some communities have manufacturing as an economic base, whereas others have retail trade. Other fringe and suburban communities are predominately institutional, especially educational centers. We shall say more about the suburban trend in the chapter on urbanization and suburbanization.[16]

A great deal is being said presently about community development. We shall say something about the significance of this later in the chapter.

## The city

There is no technical definition in the United States of the place grouping known as the city. What is defined are *urban* places

[16] *See also* William Dobriner (ed.), *The Suburban Community* (New York: G. P. Putnam's Sons, 1958).

which may be incorporated or unincorporated, but which must have more than 2,500 population. The densely settled fringes of cities of over 50,000 population or more are also classed as urban.

In 1930, 56.2 per cent of the population lived in urban places. In 1940 the figure was 56.5, and, in 1950, 59 per cent on the basis of previous definitions of urban (mostly incorporated places). However, in 1950 the definition of "urban" was changed to include unincorporated places of 2,500. Other changes in definition were also made, so that the new concept of urban added 5 per cent more people to the urban category than did the old definition. Thus the percentage of the population which was urban was 64 per cent.

Within large cities there may be many subcommunities, some of them very closely knit. In one study of Los Angeles 123 different communities were mapped. Four of these communities had populations of over 100,000, whereas nine had populations of less than 5,000.

While cities are place groupings, they should best be thought of as environments for people —where they are born, where they grow up, go to school, work, love, marry, worship, and die. Cities are discussed in more detail in Chapter 16 on urbanization.

## The metropolitan area

Cities are old, but the great new place groupings of the modern age are the metropolitan areas. These are urban places having a central city of 50,000 or more, with the contiguous counties economically integrated around the city. Schematically, a metropolitan area is indicated in the accompanying diagram.

Metropolitan areas range in size from the metropolitan area of Greater New York, with a population of about 14 millions, down to metropolitan areas not greatly exceeding the 50,000 population minimum. A particular characteristic of metropolitan areas is the extent to which the central cities within them dominate the communications, the economic life, and the social life of the people living within metropolitan areas. Significantly, a great many metropolitan areas in the United States are located in coastal areas and on river and lake shores. This indicates the important role of water transportation in the development of urban place groupings, especially larger cities. Within metropolitan areas there may be many cities and communities and many more neighborhoods and culture clusters or islands of one kind or another. It is not unusual to find that a large city and the area surrounding it is called a metropolitan region. The use of such a term does not do violence to it, since the test of a region when used in this sense is one of economic integration and the whole metropolitan region is in reality an economic one.

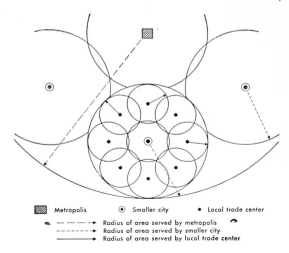

Metropolis    ⊙ Smaller city    • Local trade center

— — — → Radius of area served by metropolis
– – – → Radius of area served by smaller city
———→ Radius of area served by local trade center

FIG. 15.    A DIAGRAMMATIC SKETCH OF A METRO-POLITAN AREA

SOURCE: James A. Quinn, *Urban Sociology* (New York: American Book Co., 1955), p. 55.

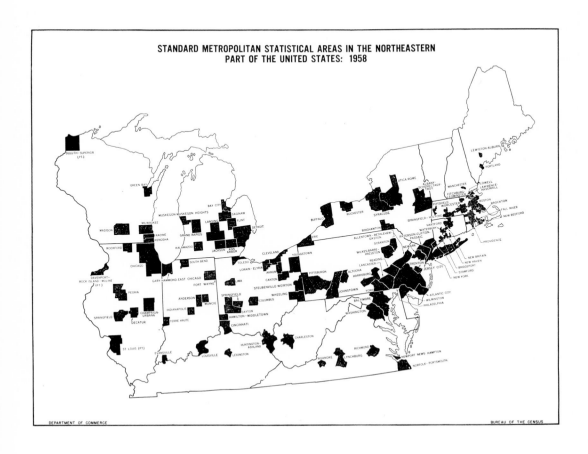

STANDARD METROPOLITAN STATISTICAL AREAS IN THE NORTHEASTERN PART OF THE UNITED STATES: 1958

DEPARTMENT OF COMMERCE                                                        BUREAU OF THE CENSUS

## The region

One of the largest place groupings is the region. Regions are areas larger than communities which have some unifying factor. The unifying factor may be a physical one, as is the case of the Tennessee Valley which is simply a watershed. Here the unifying factor is the Tennessee River and its tributaries (see Fig. 16).

The unifying factor of an agricultural region may be the species of crop grown. For instance, we have the Corn Belt, the Wheat Belt, the grasslands of the West, the Cotton Belt of the South, and other agricultural regions. As we have indicated, we may also have areas of economic integration around great cities. We frequently hear references to the industrial North or the industrial East, both of which are vaguely defined. The most adequately defined regions in the United States are the river watersheds.

## COMMUNITY DEVELOPMENT

The terms "community improvement" and "community development" are old terms in American rural sociology. Since the development of the United Nations and interest of the United States in the economic development of countries abroad, the term "community development" has become a term made popular by the International Cooperation Administration in its work with underdeveloped countries. As described by I.C.A.:

*Community development* is the term used to describe the technique many governments have adopted to reach their village people and to make more effective use of local initiative and energy for increased production and better living standards. Community development is a process of social action in which the people of a community organize themselves for planning and action; define their common and individual needs and problems; execute these plans with a maximum of reliance upon community resources; and supplement these resources when necessary with services and material from government and nongovernmental agencies outside the community.[17]

The use of the term "community development" is not uniform in all countries. In India, where the village is the important rural place grouping, the terms "village improvement" and "village development" are used. As participated in by the United States, community development in underdeveloped countries has an important role in political development as well as economic and social development.

## THE PROSPECT OF WORLD COMMUNITY

Just as there has been an evolution in the development of larger place groupings, as we have seen, there is likewise a prospect of sufficient unity in the world to constitute a prospect of world community in the not too distant future. There is already contact between the major nations of the world, as well as interdependence between nations. These are two hallmarks of a community structure. Between the more industrialized and developed nations, and the underdeveloped nations, a considerable amount of cooperation has been achieved,

another hallmark of community. It is perhaps in the institutions—political, economic, and religious—that the widest gaps exist hindering further world-wide cooperation and integration. It is here that the greatest handicaps to world-wide community of effort in the current century lie.

[17] International Cooperation Administration, "The Community Development Guidelines of the International Cooperation Administration," *Community Development Review,* No. 3, December, 1959 (Washington, D.C.), pp. 3-6.

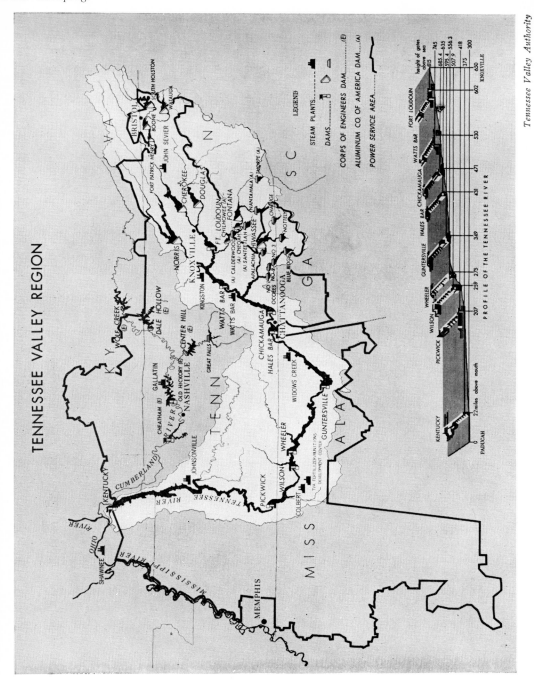

FIG. 16. THE TENNESSEE VALLEY, A WATERSHED REGION, WITH MAJOR POWER AND FLOOD-CONTROL INSTALLATIONS

## SUMMARY

The family and some form of place grouping are universal in all societies.

In simple societies, place groupings usually take the form of bands, clans, tribes, neighborhoods, or some form of fairly simple community structure. As societies grow in complexity, and especially as they develop industries, trade, commerce, and supporting services, larger place groupings in the form of cities, suburban communities, metropolitan areas, and economic regions tend to develop. Be-

tween these strong webs of interdependence develop.

Community development, a term long used by American rural sociologists, has taken on an international significance in the work which the more developed nations are carrying on with the more underdeveloped countries. While these efforts are strongly economic and social, they also have strong political implications.

### THINGS TO DO AND TO DISCUSS

1. Select a place grouping for study. Determine what kind of a place grouping it is, giving your reasons for designating it as you do.
2. What is the distinction between a band, a tribe, and a clan?
3. How does a neighborhood differ from a community? Give examples from local situations.
4. How does a city differ from a metropolitan area?
5. What are the essential characteristics of a region? What are some leading examples of regions?
6. What are some of the important changes taking place in place groupings in your state?
7. What is meant by community development? Why is it internationally significant?
8. Debate the pros and cons of the prospect for world community.

### FOR FURTHER STUDY

BROWNELL, BAKER. *The Human Community*. New York: Harper and Bros., 1950. Good comprehensive volume on the human community.

COLE, WILLIAM E. *Urban Society*. Boston: Houghton Mifflin Co., 1958. Adequate discussion of suburban communities and metropolitan areas.

DOBRINER, WILLIAM (ed.). *The Suburban Community*. New York: G. P. Putnam's Sons, 1958. Good discussion of the suburban community, its growth and role.

HART, HENRY C. *New India's Rivers*. Bombay: Orient Longmans, 1956. Some good things on the Indian village and regional development.

HATT, PAUL K., and REISS, ALBERT J., JR. (eds.). *Cities and Society*. Glencoe, Ill: Free Press, 1957. Valuable source book on cities.

HARPER, ERNEST B., and DUNHAM, ARTHUR. *Community Organization in Action*. New York: Association Press, 1959. One of the better studies on organizing community welfare services.

HAYES, WAYLAND J. *The Small Community Looks Ahead*. New York: Harcourt, Brace and Co., 1947. One of the better textbooks on the small community.

KOLB, JOHN. *Emerging Rural Communities*. Madison, Wis.: University of Wisconsin Press, 1959. Good picture of changing rural communities.

KYLE, JOHN H. *The Building of TVA*. Baton Rouge: Louisiana State University Press, 1958. Mostly on TVA structures.

MARTINDALE, DON. *American Social Structure*. New York: Appleton-Century-Crofts, 1960. Several good chapters on community structure.

MERCER, BLAINE E. *The Study of Society*. New York: Harcourt, Brace and Co., 1958. Good general treatment of community.

MURDOCK, GEORGE PETER. *Social Structure*. New York: The Macmillan Co., 1949. Excellent treatment of place groupings in simple societies.

NELSON, LOWRY; RAMSEY, CHARLES E.; and VERNER, COOLIE. *Community Structure and Change*. New York: The Macmillan Co., 1960. Sets a theoretical framework for community analysis and development.

PARK, ROBERT E.; BURGESS, ERNEST W; and McKENZIE, RODERICK D. *The City*. Chicago: University of Chicago Press, 1925. A classical study of urban structure.

SANDERS, IRWIN T. *The Community: An Introduction to a Social System*. New York, Ronald Press Co., 1958. Good general textbook on the small community.

SMITH, T. LYNN. "The Rural Community with Special Reference to Latin America," *Rural Sociology*, **23**:52-67, March, 1958. The South American rural community, its importance and its characteristics.

SUSSMAN, MARVIN B. *Community Structure and Analysis*. New York: Thomas Y. Crowell Co., 1959. Good text and supplement for courses in community.

# 11. SOCIAL INSTITUTIONS AS SOCIAL SYSTEMS

IN THE LAST SEVERAL CHAPTERS we have been concerned with the structure of social systems. Among the most important social systems in societies today are the institutional structures. Of course, the structure of institutions is secondary to their functioning. In the opening chapter of the book we referred to social institutions as social systems. All social institutions then are social systems, but not all social systems are social institutions. Some are groups, classes, and place groupings.

As we indicated in Chapter 1, social systems are made up of people. There is behavior in all social systems. Each prescribes for its members certain roles. There are norms of conduct influencing these roles. Patterns of status relationship exist between members. Certain social system personnel are clothed with authority to see that conduct norms are adhered to or that prescribed roles are carried out. This element is especially strong in social institutions. Each social system has its cultural instruments of utility as well as its symbols. Each has a habitat or locale in which it exists and functions.

Social institutions are peculiar types of social systems or clusters of culture and people oriented around major human needs. Davis gives a good formal definition of an institution in the following language:

> An institution can be defined as a *set* of interwoven folkways, mores and laws built around one or more functions. It is a part of the social structure, set off by the closeness of its organization and by the distinctiveness of its functions.[1]

The process of institutionalization usually takes place rather slowly. It is marked by a gradual shift from informal to formal controls and from a loose configuration or structure to a definite and identifiable one. We might use the institutionalization of organized labor as an illustration. At first there was no organization or unionization. Craft unions developed as one grouping and company unions as another. Later the crafts and industries organized separately. Later they merged, bringing to fruition a well-developed institutional structure.

[1] Kingsley Davis, *Human Society* (New York: The Macmillan Co., 1949), p. 71.

## THE PECULIAR CHARACTERISTICS OF SOCIAL INSTITUTIONS

Wherein, then, do social institutions differ from other social systems? They are likely to differ in complexity. A state or national government or an institution is more complex than a community, which is a place grouping. Marriage, which is an institution, and used in the sense of incorporating all marriages, is more complex than a single marriage. Education, as an institution, is more complex than a class in mathematics, which is a form of association or secondary group. From these illustrations we see that within each institutional system there may be many social systems and subsystems. For example, as part of the educational administration matrix there are many types of schools and educational programs.

We have already implied other characteristics of social institutions. They are oriented around major areas of human needs like reproduction, making a living, seeking recreation, or religious worship. Of course, all social systems have either some symbolic, sentimental, or utilitarian value, or else they would not continue in existence. The area of human need served by social institutions is likely to be broader, the services they perform are likely to be looked upon as more fundamental to the society supporting the institution, and the period of service longer than that given by most of the other social systems.

As an illustration, a basic function of marriage is procreation, or the reproduction of the race. This is fundamental in any society. The control of conditions and relations in a state requires a form of control covering the area of the state as well as major forms of human activity. A basic requirement of human beings appears to be some form of ethics or religion or some philosophical substitute; hence we have religion serving another major area of need. Thus we have another cultural cluster—organized religion—developing and institutionalized around another area of need.

Another characteristic of social institutions is longevity. Longevity is relative. There are other social systems that no doubt are older than some social institutions. For instance, a boys' gang is a form of social system. Ganging of boys must certainly be older than organized labor, an institutionalized pattern. However, by and large institutions have longevity beyond that of other social systems. Marriage as an institution continues generation after generation. Government continues while neighborhoods and communities grow and decline. Churches rise and decline, and denominations increase and decline, but organized religion as an institution continues. Scientists and scientific laboratories are developed and abandoned, but science as an institution continues.

Institutions integrate activities. The role of institutions in integrating activity is noted by MacIver and Page [2] and is developed in a statement by Robert Bierstedt, who draws a distinction between associations and institutions.

An association, as we have said, is an organized group, whether large or small. Because of its organization, it has some structure and some continuity. It has, in addition, an identity and a name. An institution, on the other hand, is not a group at all, organized or unorganized. An institution is an organized *way of doing something.* An institution is a formal, recognized, established, and stabilized way of pursuing some activity in society. As MacIver has defined it, it is an established form or condition of procedure characteristic of group activity. In succinct terms, then, an association is an organized group; an institution in an organized procedure. [3]

Bierstedt's comments indicate emphasis upon the role of social institutions in integrating their various parts into a normative social system. Each institution is a constellation of norms, cultural items, and folkways built

[2] *See* Robert M. MacIver and Charles H. Page, *Society: An Introductory Analysis* (New York: Rinehart and Co., 1949), pp. 11-18.

[3] Robert Bierstedt, *The Social Order* (New York: McGraw-Hill Book Co., 1957), p. 299.

around some major social need or major aspect of human activity. Davis explains this characteristic of social institutions as follows:

An institution can be defined as a set of interwoven folkways, mores, and laws built around one or more functions. It is part of the social structure, set off by the closeness of its organization and by the distinctiveness of its functions. It is therefore inclusive rather than exclusive of the concepts previously defined; for without folkways and mores there could be no institutions. Marriage, for example, embraces the complex of folkways surrounding the approved mating of men and women, including in our culture engagement and wedding rings, rice throwing, the honeymoon, lifting the bride over the threshold, showers, etc. It also embraces certain mores—premarital chastity, postmarital fidelity, taking of the vows, obligation to support, etc. Finally, it embraces certain laws—

license, record, right of divorce for cause, protection against fraud, proper age, absence of prohibitive kinship bonds, etc. All of these norms taken together form a definite structure—an institution of marriage—which has meaning as a whole and which, when operative in behavior, results in the performance of certain social and individual functions such as reproduction and child rearing, on the social side, sexual gratification and affection on the individual side. Similarly it can be said that economic, political, religious, and recreational institutions each represent a distinguishable set of interrelated folkways, mores and laws coherently organized and capable of performing distinct functions.[4]

The integrative role of social institutions is indicated in the above paragraph, as it has been in other writings by American sociologists.[5]

## THE ORIGIN OF INSTITUTIONS

Herskovits indicates how—

all cultures are made up of *institutions* that represent formalized and sanctioned responses to the demands of living. The institutionalized ways of behavior in which these responses are manifest, appertain to the various aspects of culture. These are like great blocks of experience which the student carves out of a functioning body of custom in order the better to achieve a workable description of it. Aspects are, so to speak, a kind of table of contents of culture; the framework about which, however unrealized, a people organize their life.[6]

Aside from some of the newer institutions, two of which we will soon discuss in the next chapter, there seems to be no point at which it can be said institutions began. Marriage and family grouping, in some form or other, have existed as long as we have had anthropological studies of groups of people. Egypt had government under its priest-kings, the Pharaohs, as early as 5000 B.C. The Greek state form of government antedated Plato, who lived from 427 B.C. to 347 B.C. The original form of trade was apparently barter, the swapping of one article for another, but when or where it started no one knows. Probably the original

ownership of private property was in the form of movable items—spears, hand axes, beads, cattle, women, shells, and bows and arrows—but when such ownership began we do not know. Other forms of private property came later. Organized religion loses itself as it is traced back in religious practices bordering on magic. The early Egyptians worshiped Ra, the God of Light, and Osiris, the God of agriculture and the Nile. They also worshiped the falcon. They had other nature gods 4,000 years before the birth of Christ.

How religious development began we do not know. There are theories that religion grew out of fear, curiosity, and speculation about echoes, birth, death, the stars, and the recurring seasons, including the death and desolation of winter and the rebirth of spring. At a later date, individual religious heroes and saints were responsible for the development of much religious thought. More about this in the chapter on religion.

[4] Kingsley Davis, *op. cit.*, pp. 71-72.
[5] For example, Talcott Parsons, *The Social System* (Glencoe, Ill.: Free Press, 1951), pp. 301-6.
[6] Melville J. Herskovits, *Man and His Works* (New York: Alfred A. Knopf, 1948), p. 229.

LaPiere speculates as to the origin of institutions in the following words:

Sociologically and in terms of consequences, a social institution might be described as originating in collective need for a long-run plan of action. A social group cannot maintain itself on the basis of day-by-day trial-and-error adjustment. The activities of today must be planned in terms of their effects upon tomorrow. Consequently, a social plan must be devised. Such a plan serves to reduce human dependence upon trial and error and to make individual behavior a contribution to collective long-run welfare. In time the plan becomes an established institution, handed down more or less intact from generation to generation. Sociologically, therefore, the institution is to be considered as a behavior-controlling mechanism for the satisfaction of one or a number of group needs—economic, educational, religious, and the like.[7]

In the simpler societies two or more institutionalized functions may be combined. For instance, government and religion, religion and medicine, or religion and economic activity, may be institutionalized together. As a society develops the two functions may separate into two institutional complexes. As an illustration, in many societies in the past, separation of church and state was thought of as untenable and impractical, yet in the United States we have adhered to the principle enunciated by Elihu Root that, if nowhere else, in matters between church and state good fences make good neighbors. We legally prohibit certain forms of religious education in public education because of institutional separation of church and state. On the other hand, the separation is not as definite as Root's statement would indicate. Religious instruction takes place in public schools. Public school busses often haul children to parochial schools. Catholics and Protestants run for public office and receive a united front in the voting.

Whatever the social institution it must be supported by other social systems. Sometimes this support comes from another institution as well as other social systems. As an illustration, organized religion in the United States supports many theories and practices of our economic institutions, such as capitalism and private property. The church justifies and upholds the institution of marriage and the family. The government lends its support to the family through many laws and various types of financial assistance.

Marriage, as an institution, is made up of millions of individual marriages. Organized religion is made up of dozens of theologies, thousands of churches, synagogues, and cathedrals representing Christianity, Judaism, and other religious faiths. The economy, just the production phase of it, is made up of thousands of production units. Some of these are associations, such as corporations, and many are enterprises operated entirely by individual families. To keep the production units functioning, millions of consumption units must exist as part of the economy.

## THE FUNCTIONS OF SOCIAL INSTITUTIONS

### Institutions are carriers of the culture

In discussing the definition and characteristics of social institutions, we have already implied some functions. In the chapters on groups we indicated some of the functions served by groups. These functions are also shared by social institutions. Groups are carriers of the culture and so are institutions. Both pass the cultural heritage on to individuals, groups, and associations making up institutional complexes. The family, school, and church have especially strong roles as carriers of the culture.[8] Government in turn gives protection to these institutions.

[7] Richard T. LaPiere, *Collective Behavior* (New York: McGraw-Hill Book Co., 1938), p. 65.

[8] For more on this point, *see* Francis E. Merrill and H. Wentworth Eldredge, *Society and Culture* (Englewood Cliffs, N.J.: Prentice-Hall, 1957), pp. 345-67.

## Institutions serve survival needs

Survival needs are served, for example, by marriage. The child is born helpless to a married couple, which begins a family unit. His needs must be attended to. Food must be provided and attention must be given. The mother-father relationship is peculiarly suited to this task. Food, clothing, shelter, and security are survival needs, as is also protection from disease. Contributing in some way to the supplying of these survival needs are most of the institutions.

## Institutions serve social control functions

The way in which social institutions develop, and the fact that they are clusters of people, folkways, mores, and instruments of utility and symbol, make them especially strong sources of social control. As Parsons says: "Institutions . . . are *normative* patterns which define what are felt to be, in the given society, proper, legitimate, or expected modes of action or of social relationships." [9] Out of the experience of the human race certain phases of the racial experience are selected and become part of each institutional cluster. The institution stands for these clustered experiences, believes that they are important, and proceeds to pass them on to each new generation. The mores, the folkways, and the value systems, serving as controls, are inculcated in the members of a society. As a result, much self-control results. Self-control, however, is not adequate, so laws are set up by government, the strongest institution of formal social control. For other institutions rules and regulations are important. Institutional pressures are exerted for "right" conduct in the home, the church, and the school. Systems of ethics are developed which reflect the institutions' stand. The result is a varied but effective system of informal and formal social controls, emanating from social institutions. These influence other social systems and the

[9] Talcott Parsons, *Essays in Sociological Theory Pure and Applied* (Glencoe, Ill.: Free Press, 1949), p. 203.

conduct and behavior of the people making them up.

## Institutions integrate

We have already indicated the integrative functions served by institutions. The nature of institutions assures their serving this function. This is seen in the church. Out of the religious experience of peoples from the ancient Hebrew, before the birth of Christ, to the present, there has come down to us Judaism and Christianity as systems of integrated religious beliefs and practices. We must hasten to add that the institutionalization of religious thinking, which divides religious followers into different religious bodies, is also a divisive force in societies. The institution of marriage integrates a cluster of beliefs, attitudes, people, and behavior practices ranging from affection to the everyday task of making a living. Government integrates the activity of a nation and sometimes an empire.

## Institutions socialize

The fact that institutions are carriers of the culture and are normative social systems means that they socialize. The learning of a culture takes place through enculturation and socialization. Although the most effective units of either are the social systems making up the institutional matrix, the nature of the institution conditions the products sought in the enculturation and socialization process. Status relationships are also influenced by the nature of the institutions. Roles are defined accordingly. The type of personality which is developed conforms to the type prescribed as desirable by the institutional complexes. Western institutions, on the whole, tolerate and support an aggressive type of personality, while some of the cultures of India support a more reserved, quieter one. Korean culture develops a concern for parents in children to a degree that does not hold true of the socialized process in most American communities. Thus it is that social systems in the socializing process are greatly influenced by the institutional complexes. Personality development becomes a major end of the socializing function of social systems, including institutions.

## THE MASTER SOCIAL INSTITUTIONS

Figure 17 in the following chapter shows the institutional complexes found in most societies, and also some of the large areas of need served by the institutions. As between different societies, institutions vary more in make-up, function, and structure than they do in kind. As an example, in all societies there is the institution of marriage. However, marriage patterns vary from society to society. Religion is institutionalized in all societies, more so in complex than in the simple societies. Particular complexes of religious beliefs and practices vary greatly from one society to another.

As we will see in the following chapter, the major institutions are marriage and the family structures growing out of marriage, government, religion, science, recreation, the economic institutions, and education.

## THE INTERRELATION OF SOCIAL INSTITUTIONS

Social behavior is related to all the institutional complexes. For instance the motivation of an individual or a group may be shaped more or less simultaneously by religious, economic, recreational, and governmental institutional complexes. Marriage trends and the formation of new families, causing an upswing in population, may be a major factor in the prosperity of the economic institutions, and in the demand for new educational facilities and programs. The inability of the economic institutions to control production or to increase or restrict it may bring into being governmental regulation. On the other hand, the kind of tax structure a people may have may impede or encourage economic development. The religion of a people may provide a supporting base for strong economic activity, or it may impede economic effort. Thus it is that the institutional complexes are interrelated and intertwined with each other. Some authors liken the interrelationships between institutions to a wheel, with marriage and the family as the hub and the spokes providing the institutionalized functions of government, religion, education, and the economy. The rim of the wheel becomes the community in which the institutions function.

## SOME PROBLEMS PECULIAR TO SOCIAL INSTITUTIONS

Social institutions may contribute to social stagnation and cultural lag. Cultural lag appears as a problem peculiar to social institutions. This is the tendency of one or more aspects of an institution to lag behind some other aspect of it. For instance, a government may grow in size but not in quality. An entire institutional complex may lag behind another institution. The reason for cultural lag in institutions is that the process of institutionalization tends to bring about conformity and rigidity in the institution itself. Traditions, practices, and services may be continued long after they have served their usefulness. Government may lag behind science or the economic system. The church may lag behind all three institutions in its program and in its adaptation to new needs and conditions. For example, in the family there has developed a terrific problem of care of the aged. Yet in the provision of care, work, adequate retirement, and recreation for the aged, most institutions have lagged.

How is it then that social institutions con-

*How many institutionalized functions are reflected in this street scene? What are they?*

tribute to social stagnation and cutural lag? The very process of institutionalization involves a solidification of a social system. Institutionalization takes time, and when a cultural and behavior system becomes institutionalized it takes time for the complex to be changed. Thus a government suited to a horse and buggy age does not change rapidly enough to keep pace with the changes of a space age. For example, modern cities need governmental structures with functions and boundaries to serve the people of a metropolitan area. What has happened is that old institutionalized forms exist by the dozens in metropolitan areas. Halos surround constitutions, thus handicapping changes in them. The "cult of the an-

cestors" may handicap governmental change.

Education furnishes many examples of cultural lag and educational stagnation. When once a curriculum for the B.A. degree is formalized in a college or university, departmental and personal interests and narrowness of viewpoint may impede changes in the curriculum for two generations. Even the charters of educational institutions may impede change in the programs.

Vested interests are factors in institutional stagnation and culture lag. An obsolete government, as an obsolete educational system or a church, will have its followers with vested interests, some intellectual, some financial, and all emotional. They lay upon institutional change the cold hand of *status quo* and change has to await a new set of leaders, sometimes a new generation.

Another problem of social institutions is bigness and complexity. This is true also of institutional subsystems, such as units of government, churches, universities, industry, and business. This trend toward bigness and complexity is often referred to as bureaucracy, and it is a characteristic not only of government but also of many other large institutions.

In addition to bigness and complexity, bureaucracy in an institution, or its subsystems, is often characterized by rigidity and tradition, an elaboration of offices and officials, and a complicated system of statuses and roles. It was precisely this concept of bureaucracy which was developed by the German sociologist Max Weber. The literature on the subject is so extensive and interesting that the student of introductory sociology may want to pursue it further.[10] The greatest disadvantage of bureaucracy in an institution of government is that it absorbs so much of the energy of the institution in keeping the structure going that adequate functioning may be reduced accordingly.[11]

## SUMMARY

Institutions are cultural clusters built around the serving of major human needs. These clusters tend to become rigid so that they reflect considerable uniformities and norms in human thought and action.

While social institutions are made up of the same elements as other social systems, as a rule they are more complex than most other systems; they are more oriented to the serving of critical human needs, have greater longevity, and are integrative in function.

In most societies eight to ten major phases of human activity are institutionalized, but the number of institutions and the nature of the institutionalized cultural configuration varies from society to society. Of all institutions the family seems common to most societies. Science and labor are much more institutionalized in the United States and Europe than in other parts of the world. They are among the latest institutions to emerge, as we shall see in the next chapter.

The origin of some institutions is lost in antiquity; others have developed rather recently. Most of them have developed through gradual processes of cultural selection, accumulation, and survival.

Social institutions share with other social systems many functions which peculiarly are carriers of the culture, and serve survival needs and contribute to the informal and formal social control of their members. In their functioning each institution is closely interrelated, as we have illustrated.

Major problems of social institutions are the tendency for cultural lags to develop in institutions, the tendency for them to become big and rigid, and for much of their energy and many of their resources to be utilized in keeping the institutional structure going.

THINGS TO DO AND TO DISCUSS

1. What are the hallmarks of a social institution? How does an institution differ from a group or association?

2. What social institutions are found in your community? Are any conspicuously absent?

[10] Max Weber, *The Theory of Social and Economic Organization*, trans. A. M. Henderson and Talcott Parsons (New York: Oxford University Press, 1947), pp. 329-40.

[11] Robert K. Merton, "Bureaucratic Structure and Personality," *Social Forces*, **18**:560-68, May, 1940. *See also* Robert K. Merton, *et al.*, *Reader in Bureaucracy* (Glencoe, Ill.: Free Press, 1952).

3. What are the peculiar characteristics of social institutions?
4. How does the process of institutionalization take place?
5. What generalized functions do institutions serve?
6. Show how institutions are interested in function.
7. What are the peculiar problems of social institutions?
8. Give illustrations of institutional stagnation and cultural lag to which institutions have contributed in your community.

FOR FURTHER STUDY

BARNES, HARRY ELMER. *Social Institutions*. New York: Prentice-Hall, 1946. An older but readable text on social institutions.

CHAPIN, F. STUART. *Contemporary Social Institutions*. New York: Harper and Bros., 1935. Good discussion of institutions and the process of institutionalization.

———. "The Growth of Bureaucracy—An Hypothesis," *American Sociological Review,* 16:835-36, 1951. Hypothesis of how bigness and bureaucracy in institutions develop.

DAVIS, KINGSLEY. *American Society*. New York: The Macmillan Co., 1949. Has an excellent chapter on institutionalized social forms.

FIEBLEMAN, JAMES K. *The Institutions of Society*. New York: The Macmillan Co., 1957. Comprehensive picture of society's institutions.

HERTZLER, J. O. *Social Institutions*. Lincoln, Neb.: University of Nebraska Press, 1946. Good general treatment of social institutions.

HOULT, THOMAS F. *The Sociology of Religion*. New York: Dryden Press, 1958. Good treatment of religion as an institution.

LOOMIS, CHARLES P. *Social Systems: Essays on Their Persistence and Change*. Princeton, N. J.: D. Van Nostrand Co., 1960. Some good discussion of social institutions as social systems.

MERRILL, FRANCIS E., and ELDREDGE, H. WENTWORTH. *Society and Culture*. Englewood Cliffs, N. J.: Prentice-Hall, 1957. Contains a good brief treatment of social institutions.

MERTON, ROBERT K. *Social Theory and Social Structure*. New York: Columbia University Press, 1954. The nature of the institutional structure is clearly stated.

PARSONS, TALCOTT. *The Social System*. Glencoe, Ill.: Free Press, 1954. A classic treatment of social systems, with much on institutions.

# 12. THE MAJOR SOCIAL INSTITUTIONS

IN CHAPTER 11 brief reference was made to the major or master social institutions. In this chapter we shall discuss rather briefly each of the important institutional complexes, laying emphasis largely upon those which are strongly sociological in character. This will leave those that are strongly economic or political in character to other courses in the social sciences for more detailed consideration.

Figure 17 shows the basic cultural needs served by institutions, and also the corresponding institutions which have been developed in societies to meet these needs. The thing that Figure 17 does not show is the interrelationship between institutions, which was discussed in Chapter 11. The arrangement shown in Figure 17 is schematic and is designed primarily to give a rough picture of the major institutions and the major areas of need which they serve. As we have indicated, social institutions are cultural complexes of people, concepts, behavior patterns, and cultural traits and patterns that have developed around great human needs.

## MARRIAGE AND THE FAMILY

In Chapter 10 we indicated that there were two basic social systems present in all societies. One is some form of marriage and some form of family organization, and the other is some form of place grouping. Since Chapter 8 is devoted to the family, and inasmuch as various phases of the institutions of marriage were discussed in this chapter, we will not give more attention to it at this time. In other chapters we have referred to the role of the family in the development of status and role relationships.

There is considerable belief that the original institution to be developed in societies was marriage and the family, and that all of the other institutions, which we have indicated

THE MASTER SOCIAL INSTITUTIONS

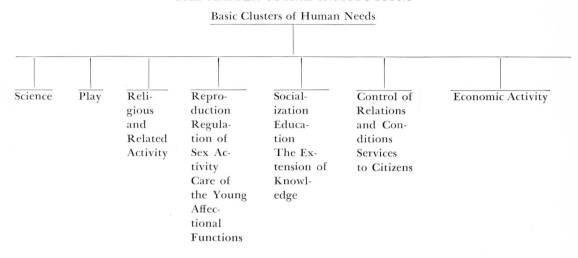

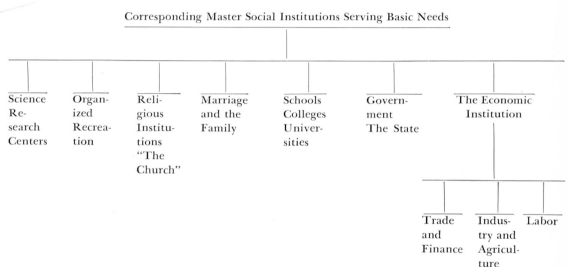

FIG. 17. SCHEMATIC ARRANGEMENT SHOWING SOME OF THE MAJOR SOCIAL
INSTITUTIONS AND MAJOR CULTURAL NEEDS FROM WHICH THEY
HAVE DEVELOPED AND WHICH THEY CURRENTLY SERVE

in Figure 17, grew out of marriage and the family institutional complex. This belief, of course, is based largely on anthropological and archaeological evidence, such as burial remains, cave drawings, and other evidence left by early man indicating the presence of some form of family pattern. Literature on the subject of marriage and family origins is extensive, and the student of sociology may want to explore it.

## GOVERNMENT

Wherever people are thrown together in any considerable number, problems of relations and problems of conditions of people arise. In simple societies the heads of families individually, and collectively, usually handle such problems. Thus they, in a real sense of the word, serve as governing heads of the group. However, as settlements or units of people become larger, forms of control become more necessary and more formal forms of government develop. As societies develop above the level where family controls are adequate, the power to control relations and conditions, and to make decisions which influence the society as a whole, may lie with a tribal chief, a council of elders, or some other form of governing mechanism. In the beginnings of government in the simple societies lie the origin of the state with its varied and lesser units of government. For instance, in the development of the governments of ancient Athens and ancient Rome they, in a real sense of the word, were originally made up of a confederation of governments of many smaller units, some of them tribal in character.

The national state and the smaller state divisions of government are the keystones of political and governmental structures of the United States. Within the individual states are the local units of government with control over county and parish divisions, and incorporated places, ranging from small incorporated villages to central cities of large metropolitan areas. The state has institutionalized power as well as institutionalized political structure. It serves major institutionalized functions over the people within the state.

In addition to regulatory and control functions, modern states perform many services, such as welfare functions, educational and health functions, and the promotion of industrial development.

The state has an important function in settling disputes and in adjudicating conflicts. Whereas other groups and institutions make wide use of informal controls, a key to government-controlled functions is law, court decisions, public opinion, and the decisions and activities of enforcing the laws.

The national state may have to defend itself against another state. Most national states have some form of armed forces which can be pressed into service when necessary. In the United States, of course, the state divisions of the republic support national guards. These may be pressed into service when the national state is endangered, or when its security or stability is threatened by riots, violence, or some other emergency.

Government in the Unted States is structured to divide its functions into executive, legislative, and judicial areas or branches. Stress is placed on the use of the secret ballot in voting.

Two political parties usually are active and compete in elections. At times minor parties develop and show some strength, but are likely to die out after unsuccessful efforts at the polls. One of the most interesting characteristics of the two major political parties in the United States is class selectivity in membership and fellowship. This selectivity is shown in Table 22. This table, from a survey made by one of the Chicago newspapers, indicates that 62 per cent of business and professional men had a preference for the Republican party, and only 21 per cent for the Democratic party. Farmers, on the other hand, showed a different selectivity—23 per cent selected the Republican party and 57 per cent the Democratic party. Among the skilled workers, 18 per cent selected the Republican party and 58 per cent the Democratic party, and 11 per cent of the unskilled workers chose the Republican party and 65 per cent the Democratic party. The percentage of people in each of these various groups expressing no choice or opinion, which indicated that they possibly were willing to vote for an individual irrespective of party, according to the circumstances of the case.

ranged from 17 to 24 per cent. Table 22 is only indicative. Selectivity of political party by classes would possibly vary greatly with the conditions of economy and with the emotional situations and climate that develop as election campaigns get under way.

*Table 22*

## OCCUPATIONAL STATUS AND CHOICE OF POLITICAL PARTY

| Occupation of Family Head | Per Cent Choosing Republican | Per Cent Choosing Democrat | No Choice or Opinion |
|---|---|---|---|
| Business and professional | 62 | 21 | 17 |
| White collar workers | 51 | 32 | 17 |
| Farmers | 23 | 57 | 20 |
| Skilled workers | 18 | 58 | 24 |
| Unskilled workers | 11 | 65 | 24 |

Source: Chicago *Sun-Times*, February 28, 1955, p. 21.

The United States, of course, has a republican form of government in which elected representatives represent the people. Within this republican form of government, and within the democratic ideology to which it adheres,

there are two important governmental trends worth indicating. One is the greater autonomy of governmental units, especially local governments. There has been a great clamoring, for instance, for more local control among urban governments, and as a result the states have gradually given local urban governments more power so that they now have a greater degree of self-government than they have had in the past. Another trend has been the increase in the size and power of governments generally. This trend is sometimes spoken of as a bureaucratic trend. This trend is not confined to government and we have discussed it to some extent in Chapter 11. Bureaucracy is an emphasis on government by bureaus, as well as the development of governmental agencies employing large numbers of employees.

It is also worth mentioning that one of the trends which is noticeable throughout the world as far as national government is concerned is the increase in self-government of peoples and an accomanying decline in colonialism. This trend has taken place largely because of the self-development that has gone on in individual nations, allowing them to govern themselves, rather than depend upon empire states for government. We can say truthfully that colonialism is on its way out as a pattern of government.

## RELIGION

### The concept of religion

A definition or concept of religion is rather elusive and difficult to formalize. Part of this difficulty arises out of the fact that the differences between religious thinking and behavior and nonreligious thinking and behavior are of degree rather than of kind. A religious experience may also be associated with other experiences. The same is true of the elements of religion. For instance, Professor Richard Dewey points out that the element of awe, explanation of the unknown, supernaturalism, the quest for a feeling of security, often given

as unique elements of religion, are also associated with other phenomena and experiences, such as the viewing of a sunset, a great fire, or an atomic explosion.[1]

The simplest religions of nature people are often naturalistic, drawing upon objects from the existential world. In activities which man can control, he has a tendency to stress the use of naturalistic elements which he knows in his religious behavior. In activities which he recognizes as beyond his control, he tends to resort to supernatural thinking and be-

[1] Richard Dewey, *Introductory Sociology* (Urbana, Ill.: University of Illinois Press, 1955), p. X-1.

havior. It does not follow that all religions of simple cultures are naturalistic. Complicated ethical religions and philosophies and economic-cultural-political systems like communism, fascism, or nazism are strongly naturalistic, emphasizing man's control over nature and his release from supernatural forces.

In some advanced religions supernatural elements are not strong. This is especially true in Buddhism and Confucianism. The ways of life expressed by Gautama Siddhartha (563-483 B.C.), later called Buddha, and by Confucius (551-478 B.C.), essentially stressed behavior patterns and attitudes which were more ethical than supernatural. Buddha stressed right belief, right speech, right conduct, right subsistence, right effort, right reflection and self-discipline,[2] while filial piety was the primary virtue stressed by Confucius. Confucianism is more of a natural religion than Christianity, which has strong elements of supernaturalism. Both, of course, are designed as ways of life, but Christianity has a Supreme God and belief in supernatural objects to a degree not true of Confucianism or Buddhism. Some religions have never developed the concept of spiritual beings called gods. Some, like Christianity, are monotheistic, believing in a single Supreme God. Others are polytheistic, believing in more than one god.[3] Some religions have a messiah, as does Christianity. Prophets are not uncommon, as in Judaism. The system of beliefs and philosophies in some modern religions is very finely developed and is extensive. Such systems are referred to as theologies, and such religions are called theological religions.

In general, religions have some common elements. In the main, these are a system of beliefs and teachings, sacred objects and sacred places, a following, a system of ritual and worship, symbols, a belief in some supernatural force, being, or religious hero, a habitat or place in which ceremonies are held, and a specialized group of functionaries, shamans, priests, rabbis, or ministers, whose function it is to be the custodians, the purveyors, and teachers of the religion. Put these together and an institutionalized social system exists. Dewey, in defining religion, says:

> Religion is a groupway which results from strong emotional identification with an object (or objects), and acceptance of the object or objects as being sacro-sanct, inviolable, and beyond criticism. The object may be physical, a person, a belief, or a groupway; it may be a belief in an impersonal force (animatism) or it may involve supernatural beings (animism).[4]

## Cult, sect, denomination, and church

The terms "cult," "sect," "denomination," and "church" are in common use and should be differentiated from each other. A *cult* or *sect* is usually thought of as a small number of religious believers developing from, or growing up within, or without, a church or a religious denomination, and holding to beliefs that are not new or at least not conventional to the society in which they are found. Dewey points out that cults and sects prize their exclusiveness, and that the cult and sect leaders often exploit the group for personal gain.[5] A *denomination* is a body of people holding to a definite set of religious beliefs and having an affiliation with the same religious name grouping. They may have developed from sects but have usually made an adjustment to, and gained acceptance in, a secular world.

Young and Mack give a good concept of a *church*. "In a broad sense a church is (1) a body of devotees, (2) organized for a religious purpose and developing as an agency for this with (3) a hierarchy of officials and leaders and (4) a body of doctrine and philosophy which ties the whole together into a more or less

---

[2] George Foot Moore, *History of Religions* (New York: Charles Scribner's Sons, 1949), p. 295.
[3] For a good discussion of the development of institutionalized religion, *see* E. Adamson Hoebel, *Man in the Primitive World* (New York: American Book Co., 1959), p. 393.

[4] Dewey, *op. cit.*, pp. X-6, X-19.
[5] *Ibid.*, p. X-13.

systematic unit." [6] In a limited sense the term "church" is often used as synonymous with "congregation."

## The major world religions

Since the world's population is incompletely covered by censuses, and especially by religious censuses, the size of the major religious bodies of the world is not exactly known.

From the data presented in Table 23 and Figure 18, we see that the Christian religions number something more than 800 million, of which some 210 million are Protestant and 496 million Roman Catholic. Around 420 million persons are Moslems, 320 million Hindus, 300 million Confucianists. Some 12 million persons are of the Jewish faith, while the followers of various primitive faiths number 120 millions. Table 23 shows the distribution of the major world religions by continents.

[6] Kimball Young and Raymond W. Mack, *Sociology and Social Life* (New York: American Book Co., 1959), p. 393.

## Religious bodies in the United States

The U.S. Bureau of the Census has not made a detailed census enumeration of the religious composition of the population of the United States since 1936. The best current source of the size of religious bodies is *The Yearbook of American Churches,* published annually by the National Council of Churches of Christ in the United States of America. The number of religious bodies reporting their membership varies from time to time; however, the number is usually from 250 to 270. Some data on religious bodies are reported from time to time by the Bureau of the Census.

Of 119 million persons over 14 years of age who reported their religious following in a recent year, 79 million reported they were Protestant, 31 million that they were Catholic, 4 million that they were Jewish, 1.5 million reported other religions, and 3 million reported no religion (Table 24 and Fig. 19).

Although Protestant denominations make up a population more than twice the size of the Catholic body in the United States, the

*Table 23*

### PRINCIPAL RELIGIONS OF THE WORLD

| Religion | North America | South America | Europe | Asia | Africa | Oceania * | Total |
|---|---|---|---|---|---|---|---|
| Christian—Total | 160,760,567 | 117,397,913 | 456,357,814 | 47,175,262 | 30,879,417 | 10,828,482 | 820,399,455 |
| Roman Catholic | 90,582,000** | 111,922,000 | 230,338,000x | 30,144,000 | 18,608,000 | 2,483,000 | 484,077,000 |
| Eastern Orthodox | 2,386,000 | .......... | 112,447,669 | 8,106,071 | 5,868,089 | .......... | 128,807,829 |
| Protestant | 67,792,567 | 2,475,913 | 113,572,145 | 8,925,191 | 6,403,328 | 8,345,482 | 207,514,626 |
| Jewish xx | 5,430,000 | 632,362 | 3,442,627 | 1,684,454 | 660,750 | 58,250 | 11,908,443 |
| Moslem | 33,000 | 342,615 | 12,425,300 | 318,341,515 | 85,325,598 | 102,000 | 416,570,028 |
| Zoroastrian | .......... | .......... | .......... | 140,000 | .......... | .......... | 140,000 |
| Shinto | .......... | .......... | .......... | 30,000,000 | .......... | .......... | 30,000,000 |
| Taoist | 15,000 | 17,000 | 12,000 | 50,000,000 | 1,200 | 8,000 | 50,053,200 |
| Confucian | 86,000 | 95,000 | 50,000 | 300,000,000 | 7,500 | 52,000 | 300,290,500 |
| Buddhist | 165,000 | 135,000 | 10,000 | 150,000,000 | .......... | .......... | 150,310,000 |
| Hindu | 10,000 | 275,000 | .......... | 318,467,610 | 300,000 | 100,000 | 319,152,610 |
| Primitive | 50,000 | 1,000,000 | .......... | 45,000,000 | 75,000,000 | 100,000 | 121,150,000 |
| Others or none | 67,422,433 | 872,110 | 86,807,259 | 229,790,159 | 17,739,535 | 3,308,268 | 405,939,764 |
| Grand Total | 233,972,000 | 117,767,000 | 559,105,000 | 1,490,599,000 | 209,914,000 | 14,557,000 | 2,625,914,000 |

* Includes Australia New Zealand, and Oceania. ** Includes Catholics in Central America and the West Indies. x Includes Communist-controlled Eurasia. xx Includes Jewish population whether or not related to the synagogue.

Source: Kimball Young and Raymond W. Mack, *Sociology and Social Life* (New York: American Book Co., 1959), p. 397.

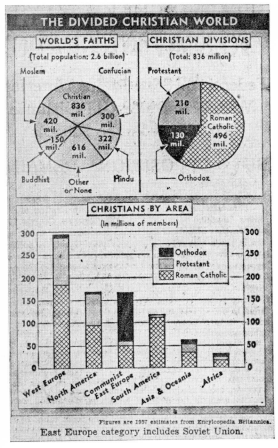

FIG. 18. WORLD'S FAITHS AND CHRISTIAN DIVI-
SIONS

SOURCE: *New York Times*, February 1, 1959,
Sec. E, p. 4.

### Table 24

RELIGION REPORTED BY THE CIVILIAN
POPULATION OF THE UNITED STATES,
14 YEARS OF AGE AND OVER, 1957

| Religion | Number (Millions) |
|---|---|
| Total | 119.3 |
| Protestant | 79.0 |
| Baptist | 23.5 |
| Lutheran | 8.4 |
| Methodist | 16.7 |
| Presbyterian | 6.7 |
| Other Protestant | 23.7 |
| Roman Catholic | 30.7 |
| Jewish | 3.9 |
| Other religion | 1.5 |
| No religion | 3.1 |
| Religion not reported | 1.1 |

Source: U.S. Bureau of the Census, *Statistical Abstract
of The United States: 1958* (79th ed.; Washington, D.C.,
U.S. Government Printing Office, 1958), p. 50.

### Some trends in church membership

Available data indicate two trends in church
membership worth mentioning at this time;
one is the increase in the percentage of the
population indicating church membership,
and the other is the trend toward larger
churches. In 1926, 47 per cent of the population of the United States indicated that they
were church members. The figures rose to 49
per cent in 1940, 57 per cent in 1950, 61 per
cent in 1955, and 61 per cent in 1957. The
average number of members per church increased from 235 in 1926 to 265 in 1940, 304
in 1950, 328 in 1955, 334 in 1956, and 339 in
1957.[7]

Much has been written about the increase
in the percentage of the population showing
church membership. Perhaps two wars, the
uncertainty of living in an atomic age under
cold-war conditions, the quest for new values,
the increase in church membership among

[7] U.S. Bureau of the Census, *Statistical Abstract of the
United States: 1959* (80th ed.; Washington, D.C., U.S.
Government Printing Office, 1959), p. 48.

former is somewhat weakened because of its
denominational divisions. Within the Protestant categories the Baptists have a following
of over 23 million, the Methodists more than
16 million, the Lutherans 8 million, and the
Presbyterians more than 6 million (Table 24).
Other Protestant bodies number 24 million.

One of the things that has encouraged the
growth of denominationalism in the United
States has been the guarantee of freedom of
worship set forth in the founding documents
of the republic. The size and diversity of the
country, the large volume of immigration, historically, into the United States encouraged
denominationalism.

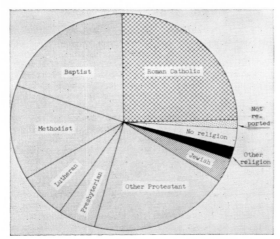

*U.S. Bureau of the Census*

FIG. 19. RELIGION REPORTED BY PERSONS 14 YEARS OLD AND OVER: CIVILIAN POPULATION, MARCH, 1957

children, and the greater accessibility and availability of churches has had something to do with the increase.

### Some social functions of religion

Institutionalized religion serves some of the general functions of social institutions set forth in the last chapter. These functions we need not repeat at this time.

While large mass groups may respond to religious revivals and to waves of religious enthusiasm, religious experiences are often highly individualistic. Often it is even somewhat difficult for the religious follower to relate a religious experience. Thousands or millions of individual religious experiences are difficult to summarize, and it is even more difficult to make generalizations from such summaries.

The emotional attachment to religious belief and behavior is an important factor in personal as well as societal stability and integration. In speaking of this Dewey says:

. . . one might infer that religion (being many things to many people, frequently unrelated to any objective ethic, and at times based upon private, subjective views of life) is expendable in any rationally

organized society. This does not appear to be the actual case. In all of human life there is inevitable emotional attachment to objects, be they material or non-material. If these commitments are private, diverse, and heterogeneous, there can be no order, and if the diversity of emotional attitudes become exaggerated, there can be no society. Further, if the emotional commitments are weak, if they do not motivate the individual to support the custom, institution, etc., even under adverse circumstances, the order and continuity of society are threatened. Societies persist only because their members are willing to pay prices, often extreme prices, for the basic values in which they believe. We speak of these strong emotional attachments to values in such terms as devotion, patriotism, dedication, loyalty, love, and (more specifically) as emotional identification. Whatever we call them, these relationships among mankind account for his willingness to work long and hard at earning a living for his family, at solving problems in the laboratory, at strengthening his group against all out-groups, and account for his or her willingness to die a martyr's death for a way of believing and acting which he accepts as basic and indispensable, as correct and necessary.[8]

Thus the emphasis that order is essential to life and to society.

Dewey emphasizes that a religion is not to be judged sociologically by its antiquity, the size of its following, the devotion of its membership, or by its organization.

It is judged sociologically by the objects of its devotion, and by the results of this attachment. If the religious object is a groupway which makes for rational relationships among men, is based upon knowledge of man's nature, if it reduces strife and bigotry and augments other institutions which enable men to relate themselves to each other and to the environment rationally, thus it is a good religion. If, on the other hand, it is subjective and divides men into ethnocentric groups, enhances prejudice and separation, encourages subjective and incomplete views of mankind's nature, if it does not permit men to connect meaningfully and peacefully with other men and with the non-human environment, then it is deficient and wrong. If its teachings conflict with established knowledge about

[8] Dewey, *op. cit.*, p. X-12.

*University News Bureau, Cornell University*

*This interfaith chapel on the campus of Cornell University is so appointed that its sanctuary may be easily arranged for Jewish, Roman Catholic, or Protestant services.*

all manner of things, if its own success and continuation depends upon censorship of investigation and learning, if it does not support a social order which makes men free, then it is not good. If, on the other hand, it modifies its teachings to keep step with new knowledge, if it encourages the expansion of freedom through rational order, if it enables man to fulfill his fullest endowment as a human being, then it is a good institution. Most emphatically, this does not mean that the good religion is one which yields easily to the latest whims or fashions in thought and action, which is afflicted with neo-philia, which derides established groupways merely because they are of ancient origin. Irresponsible iconoclasm is no more to be prized than is the embalming of the groupways of the past.[9]

Religion has traditionally been of use in explaining many of the mysteries of life. Religious beliefs also provide satisfying explanations of life beyond the grave and no doubt play a major role in sustaining people in this life. Religion motivates people to belief and to action. Religious ideology and practices control the behavior of individuals and groups. A substantial amount of welfare services were at one time administered by religious bodies, although these services are declining as public agencies increasingly assume responsibility for welfare activity.

Many church bodies have been leaders in education and today support systems of schools or individual schools and colleges. An ethical

9 Dewey, *op. cit.*, pp. X-12, X-13. *See also* Georg Simmel, *The Sociology of Religion*, trans. Curt Rosenthal (New York: The Philosophical Library, 1959). Simmel's

three components of religion: man's reaction to exterior nature, his response to his fate, and his relation to his environment.

basis of economic and political activity may be provided for by religion. For instance, it was not just an accident that capitalism, individualism, democracy, and Protestantism developed together in this country and in Europe. The four are related to each other and, to some degree, at least, sustain each other.[10]

Such traits as asceticism and unworldliness in the beliefs and practices of people are sustained by their religions. Examples of this may be seen in the religion of the Jesuits and the Trappist monks.

On the negative side, organized religions divide populations. Historically and currently they have increased intolerance and hate.

## THE ECONOMIC INSTITUTIONS

The economy, the "economic system," or the economic institutions, as the economic culture complex is referred to, is peculiarly concerned with the satisfaction of human wants. Human wants are basically those associated with the meeting of physical needs, and the meeting of such needs is a basic function of the economy. Over and above these basic wants are a complicated maze of other wants such as Figure 20 indicates.

A want is something needed or desired. If we desire something, we are likely to feel that we need it. If we need it, we are likely to desire it.

Sources of want are many. As indicated above, some originate as biogenic needs—air, food, shelter, water—and these are primary. Other wants are associated with the maturation and aging processes. From the culture there develops an endless list of wants associated with communication, marriage and family patterns, religious and moral practices, artistic and recreational interests. Many wants in modern societies are associated with the imitation of classes. In general, people imitate the classes above them rather than those below them. In no small way, the purpose of the economic institutions is the satisfaction of human wants.

In the satisfaction of these wants, various kinds of utility are involved. One is form utility. A tree may not be of value until it is converted into lumber for furniture. Place utility is also important. Furniture made in Grand Rapids must be delivered to Dallas to be of use to a Dallas family. Time utility is important. Furniture to a Dallas family may not be as important before their house is built as after it is completed. A fur coat is "out of season" in July. Ownership utility is important. Furniture would not likely satisfy the Dallas family unless they owned it or were in the process of owning it. A Cadillac owned by someone else may not satisfy one's wants unless he has driving privileges. In the field of the services, service utility is important. A good illustration is one's need for a psychiatrist. He contributes to his patient a service and not a commodity.

Around each of these forms of utility revolve many economic services and institutional subsystems such as those of production, transportation, finance, and the like. As indicated in Figure 17, the institutionalized economic complexes or clusters are related to production, trade, finance, and labor.

At one time most economic functions were tied closely to the home. Finally, the cottage system of industries gave way to the factory system. This was accompanied by institutionalized trade, commerce, and finance. The family-owned factory has been largely replaced by the corporation.

Labor is the latest of the economic functions to be institutionalized in the United States.

---

[10] For a good discussion of this point, *see* Max Weber, *The Protestant Ethic and the Spirit of Capitalism,* trans. Talcott Parsons (New York: Charles Scribner's Sons, 1930), and R. H. Tawney, *Religion and the Rise of Capitalism* (New York: Harcourt, Brace and Co., 1926). *See also* Raymond W. Mack and Raymond J. Murphy, "The Protestant Ethic, Level of Aspiration and Social Mobility," *American Sociological Review,* **21**:295-300, 1956.

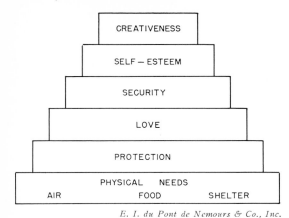

CREATIVENESS

SELF — ESTEEM

SECURITY

LOVE

PROTECTION

PHYSICAL NEEDS
AIR         FOOD          SHELTER

*E. I. du Pont de Nemours & Co., Inc.*

FIG. 20. THE PYRAMID OF HUMAN WANTS

This process of institutionalization has continued as the American Federation of Labor and the Congress of Industrial Organizations grew. Further institutionalization was achieved with the merger of the two labor organizations.

Although there are socialistic trends in the American economy, such as the presence of economic controls, and public ownership of some means of production, as in the case of atomic energy materials, and some public power generation facilities, and in distribution, as in the case of public distribution of electric power or water for irrigation, the capitalistic economic culture has at its center private ownership of property. In this capitalistic culture the striving for property, and the ownership and operation of property, appears as a central feature of the economy. Private ownership is in contrast to various forms of communal or public ownership. The inheritance of property is another feature of the system of individual ownership of property.

It is not alone the mere ownership of property that is important in the American economy; it is the meaning of property that is important. In simple societies there may be only slight differences between the status or the human condition of the man who has property and the person who does not. All may enjoy substantially the same level of food and comfort. Even the tribal chief or king may not really belong to a leisure class. This is not so in contemporary advanced societies. Property may mean class differentiation, leisure, luxury, comfort, power over people and resources, and the ability to buy and control. In the current economy there are those who stress the disabilities of ownership, those who would rather work for a wage or salary than go through what they call the "painful process" of managing property. Should this attitude become general, it could mean a major fracture in the future strength of the American economy.

The profit motive is a major feature of the American economy. The theory of profit rests on two major folkways and folk beliefs of the capitalistic system. One is that if one renders a service he should be paid a profit for this service and, second, that there are risks in economic undertakings and one should be paid for assuming these risks. While profits are necessary for continuity of business, profits are not the only rewards. The element of creativeness, of competing in a chain of economic activities, and of maintaining a going economic enterprise from which people derive incomes, from which they can satisfy other wants, are also motivating elements in the economy.

A system of free markets is also another hallmark of the current American economy. In a laissez-faire economy the free market regulates production. While the theory of the free market still persists, there are many exceptions to it and variations of it. Minimum wages and labor unions may be important factors in the marketing of one's labor. Price supports and crop controls limit the operation of the free market in agriculture. Many items are fair traded. Collusion in so-called competitive bidding on contracts is rather common. Emergencies, such as wars and depressions, may limit severely the system of free markets, the theory of which is that the free market should continue to exist with a minimum of noneconomic interference.

The elaborate use of money and credit, including installment purchasing, is another characteristic of the American economy which hardly needs elaboration, as all consuming citizens are aware of this characteristic.

One of the important trends in the economy of the United States, which amounts almost to a social movement, is the trend toward a mixed economy. This represents a departure from the past and is looked upon by some as a liberal alternative to the capitalism of the past and to socialism and dictatorship.

## EDUCATION

### *The basic task in education*

Each generation is born with substantially the same mental ability as the previous one. The period of change in the time span of a generation may bring about major changes in the complexity of the culture of a society and the relationship of people to people.

Every people, then, is faced with the problem of transmitting its cultural heritage to each new generation and of bringing the original nature of developing infants and children into conformity with the group ways and group expectations of the social systems of each society. We have spoken of this process as enculturation and socialization in previous chapters. Through undirected and directed learning, or education, the culture heritage is transmitted to each new generation. To take care of the formal process of this transmission, societies have institutionalized education or, in common parlance, established schools and developed educational programs.

If the anthropologists are correct, then the functions of education are vastly different in primitive and modern societies. Education in primitive societies is concerned with the perpetuation of the current mode of life, whereas in modern societies it is concerned with changing the current mode of life, and particularly changing the desires of learners. Margaret Mead phrases these differences in function of education in the following language:

Primitive education was a process by which continuity was maintained between parents and children.... Modern education includes a heavy emphasis upon the function of education to create discontinuity—to turn the child of the peasant into a clerk, the farmer into a lawyer, or the Italian immigrant into an American, of the illiterate into a literate.[11]

The practice of supporting an elementary school system of compulsory nature is based strongly on a theory of the need for a compulsory school system for purposes of social integration. This theory holds that at the elementary level a major function of the school is the transmission of the cultural heritage—the perpetuation of selected phases of the past and present culture—and the production of these changes believed to be desirable for all people. The development of new knowledge belongs at the other end of the educational continuum, the graduate school in the university or college. As Mead indicates, modern education, at all levels, stresses the development of new desires, improved practices, new interpersonal relationships, new communities, bigger and better technologies, and better social systems, especially institutions.

Education at the elementary level stresses enculturation, socialization, integration, and mastery of the fundamental or "tool" subjects. At the secondary level, the school tries to serve, through differentiated curricula, electives and special activities, group and individual differences. At the college level, through differentiated colleges, curricula within colleges, electives, and so on, more attention is given to individual and group needs. A major purpose also of institutions of higher learning

[11] Margaret Mead, "Our Education Emphases in Primitive Perspective," *American Journal of Sociology,* **48**:633-39, May, 1943. *See also* Robert Redfield, *The Primitive World and Its Transformations* (Ithaca, N.Y.: Cornell University Press. 1953), pp. 111-38.

is research and the development and extension of new knowledge. All schools, at whatever level, are concerned with contributing to the integration of the society supporting the school system.

## Some problems of educational institutions

In many parts of the world the primary educational task is the reduction of illiteracy. In the world's population of around 2.5 billion in 1950, of the adults 15 years and older, from 690 to 720 million were illiterate. This represents from 43 to 45 per cent of adults.[12] While in parts of Europe and America illiteracy rates are from 1 to 9 per cent of adults, in parts of Asia they may reach 85 per cent. In some parts of the world female illiteracy exceeds 90 per cent of adults. Illiteracy rates in the United States amount to about 2.5 per cent of adults. Rural illiteracy is twice as high and rates for nonwhite four times greater. The armed forces frequently reject 18 to 20 per cent of Selective Service registrants because of functional illiteracy.

The problem of making education accessible and adequate is a fundamental American one. The school population in the age bracket five to 17 years, which reached 31.5 million in 1950, grew beyond 44.2 million in 1960. During the same interval, school enrollments increased from 28.6 million to 43.6 million (see Fig. 21), and will grow four million more by 1965. One in five schools are obsolete. The need for new teachers is currently around 100,000 annually, while 60,000 are available. Obsolescence in

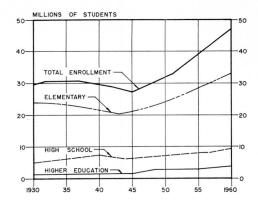

FIG. 21.  TRENDS IN SCHOOL ENROLLMENT, 1930 TO 1960

SOURCE: Adapted from the *New York Times*, September 6, 1959, Sec. E, p. 9.

curricula offerings in the face of great social and cultural change is a major problem in education as is also the pressure of new offerings.

The above problems are only a few which the interested student of institutionalized education may want to pursue. Others are the integration of public schools in the South; the mounting cost of education, especially college, university, and professional schooling to both students and administrative agencies; wasted brain power in the educational system; the battle of philosophies of education; the problem of religious education in public schools, and the provision of refresher education to many kinds of groups. These are some of the basic problems confronting institutionalized education.

## RECREATION

Play is universal among primitive people. Leisure is not alone an attribute of civilization but its emphasis, magnification, and exploitation belong to present-day urbanized and industrialized cultures. To contribute to this

emphasis recreation has become institutionalized both in terms of private, commercial, and public recreation. Our concern here is largely with the American scene.

Around 4 per cent of the national income and 5 per cent of the consumption expenditures of people in the United States is spent for recreation. Federal and state revenues from

12 United Nations Educational, Scientific, and Cultural Organization, *Basic Facts and Figures, 1958* (Paris: UNESCO, 1958), pp. 11-14.

recreational pursuits equal 1 billion dollars annually. A restricted inventory of recreation industries shows expenditures of around 15 billion dollars annually. More than 200 million acres of land are in parks and national forests. Visitors to national parks amount to 50 million annually, whereas automobile registrations exceed this figure. Mass media—television, radio, and motion pictures—keep people in touch with the best of entertainment. Hobby industries thrive and are a key element in the rising economy. Attendance at spectator sports runs into hundreds of millions. All of this is simply evidence of the mass leisure and the attempts of Americans to use it. Because the material trappings of the culture change more slowly than the behavior and habits of men, conflicts in the use of leisure rise, as well as conflict between leisure and recreation commitments and commitments to church, family, and job.

Why mass leisure? Some answers may be found in the continued existence of leisure classes, which have enlarged greatly with the growth of cities. Other factors are the shorter workday, the shorter work week—normally five days; the long week end; vacation provisions for union and nonunion workers; the increased mobility of people, and a rapid increase in their earning power. Mass advertis-

ing, helping to create new recreation desires, and the decline of segregation in the use of public recreation facilities, have contributed to the mass leisure.

The growing need for more and better use of leisure time and recreation is reflected in a series of evolving needs. First of all, there has been a decline in human energy in the labor output of people. There has been, lately, a rapid increase in the stress diseases and an increase in competition and high-level performance in white-collar jobs. Instead of providing its own recreational facilities and program, a commercial or industrial establishment now looks to public programs to provide recreational facilities and programs. The emphasis upon year-round recreation programs and facilities and upon recreational opportunities for all ages and classes places great pressure upon existing public recreational programs and facilities, and creates new demands. In the suburbs around our great cities are found many recreational "deserts," both as to facilities and programs. Finally, the use of recreation in both the prevention of individual and group deviation and for individual and group therapy emphasizes a most significant depth element in recreation not measured in terms of attendance or mass participation statistics.

## *SCIENCE*

As Hartung points out, science is often defined in terms of knowledge, method, and attitude.[13] One who uses and is dedicated to the scientific method is a scientist. The scientific institutions are among the latest to develop. Science is much more institutionalized now than formerly. It was the impact of World War II and the rapid gains in technology and the contributions of research to this technology that brought about the institutionalization of

science. This institutionalization is reflected in great laboratories and research institutes set up in association with industries, universities, and hospitals. Examples are found in the atomic energy research centers such as Oak Ridge, Los Alamos, or Hanford. The General Motors Research Center or the development laboratories of the Radio Corporation of America are examples of industrial research centers. Such centers are definitely institutional complexes. They are clusters of scientists and technicians, tools, instruments, folkways, and mores of science. These fulfill all the hallmarks of an institution.

[13] Frank E. Hartung, "Science as an Institution," *Philosophy of Science*, **18**:35-54, January, 1951. This article also has a good bibliography on science as an institution which the interested student will want to use.

*The great scientific research and production center is evidence of one of the latest social institutions to emerge.*

Science is also becoming an international institution. There is almost a world fraternity of scientists. The world-wide character of science as an institution is shown in the recent geophysical year; in the educational, health, economic, and food organizations of the United Nations; and in the meeting of scientists of all nations to discuss fallout and bomb-test inspection.

As scientific research becomes more and more a need of people, and fulfills contributing needs to the economic institutions, to governments, to the family, and perhaps to religion itself, all the more will science be institutionalized. However, like the state, much of its efforts will be contributory to the culture complexes of other institutionalized social structures.

## SUMMARY

In Chapter 11 the nature, origin, general development, functions, and persistent problems of institutions was discussed. This chapter is devoted to some discussion of major social institutions, with emphasis upon those that are strongly sociological in nature. The institution of marriage is treated only briefly due to more detailed treatment in another chapter.

The basic cultural needs served by each of the institutional complexes is indicated in Figure 17. Around these needs the basic insti-

tutions of marriage and the family, government, religion, the economic institutions, education, recreation, and science have developed. Of all the complexes perhaps institutionalized labor and science are the latest to develop.

### THINGS TO DO AND TO DISCUSS

1. Analyze the functions of government as administered in your community. Differentiate the major services and functions by levels of government.
2. Analyze voting in your community and determine if the major political parties are class selective.
3. How do you define religion?
4. What is the difference between an ethical and a supernatural religion?
5. What would you say are the functions served by institutionalized religion in your community?
6. Do you or do you not agree that organized labor qualifies as a social institution?
7. What are the basic functions performed by institutionalized education?
8. As you see education in your state and community, what are the most persistent problems?
9. What major recreational problems now face recreational institutions?
10. Do you agree that science is an institution? Why, or why not?
11. What are some of the major problems faced by institutionalized science?

### FOR FURTHER STUDY

ARGYLE, MICHAEL. *Religious Behavior*. London: Routledge and Kegan Paul, 1959. A rich amount of empirical evidence on religious beliefs and practices in England and in America.

BARNES, HARRY ELMER. *Social Institutions*. New York: Prentice-Hall, 1946. Comprehensive, basic work on social institutions.

CHAPIN, F. STUART. *Contemporary Social Institutions*. New York: Harper and Bros., 1935. Standard work on social institutions.

COGLEY, JOHN (ed.). *Religion in America: Original Essays on Religion in A Free Society*. New York: Meridian Books, 1958. Eleven essays delivered in a seminar on religion in a free society.

DAVIS, KINGSLEY. *Human Society*. New York: The Macmillan Co., 1950. Good general treatment on a number of major social institutions.

FIEBLEMAN, JAMES K. *The Institutions of Society*. New York: The Macmillan Co., 1957. The development, nature, and function of social institutions.

HERTZLER, JOYCE O. *American Social Institutions: A Sociological Analysis*. Boston: Allyn and Bacon, 1961. A good analysis of the structure and functioning of American social institutions.

————. *Social Institutions*. Lincoln, Neb.: University of Nebraska Press, 1946. Good general treatment of social institutions.

HARTUNG, FRANK E. "Science as an Institution," *Philosophy of Science,* **18**:35-
54, January, 1951. One of the better articles on this subject.

HOULT, THOMAS F. *The Sociology of Religion.* New York: Dryden Press,
1958. About all aspects of religion as an institution in which the student
is interested.

McLAUGHLIN, WILLIAM G., JR. *Modern Revivalism: Charles Grandison Fin-
ney to Billy Graham.* New York: Ronald Press Co., 1959. A good ana-
lytical and historical document on revivalism in America.

ROSE, ARNOLD M. (ed.). *The Institutions of Advanced Societies.* (Text ed.).
Minneapolis: University of Minnesota Press, 1959. A comparative study
of institutions in selected areas of the world.

SCHNEIDER, LOUIS, and DORNBUSCH, SANFORD M. *Popular Religions: Inspirational Books in America.* Chicago: University of Chicago Press, 1958. An
analysis of wide-selling inspirational books, many religious in nature,
published in America between 1875 and 1955.

WARNER, W. LLOYD, and MARTIN, NORMAN H. (eds.). *Industrial Man.* New
York: Harper and Bros., 1959. One of the better compilations on the
major economic institutions.

WHYTE, WILLIAM H., JR. *The Organization Man.* New York: Simon and
Schuster, 1956. The condition of men under the influence of the economic
institutions.

YINGER, MILTON J. *Religion, Society, and the Individual: An Introduction to
the Sociology of Religion.* New York: The Macmillan Co., 1956. One of
the better basic texts in sociology of religion.

**III** # THE FUNCTIONING OF SOCIETY

U P TO THIS POINT we have been concerned with the development and structure of society. The present division of the text deals with the functioning of society, or what goes on in our sociey. Following this section attention will be turned to the products of our society.

Chapter 13 is in the nature of an introduction to the remainder of Part III. It opens with a discussion of social interaction, the master social processes, and includes a brief discussion of the major social processes.

In every society the process of developing systems of statuses and roles is continuous (Chap. 14). In this process definite layers of social strata are developed. These strata operate in a very functional manner to influence people and their behavior. The nature and influence of stratification is discussed in Chapter 15.

In societies people have a tendency to arrange themselves and their activities into patterns and clusters which the sociologist calls ecological areas. These patterns are the result of systems of rather clearly differentiated ecological processes. The process of clustering and its causes is discussed in Chapter 16.

One of the most significant ecological processes in American societies is centralization of population. The culmination of this tendency is seen in the urbanization of the population. Along with urbanization, there has been a counter movement toward the suburbs. Both urbanization and suburbanization are discussed in Chapter 17.

Basic to the development and functioning of societies is communication. Since urban communities dominate the mass media of communication, such as newspapers, the radio, and television, we have discussed the communication process and its impact in Chapter 18, following the discussion of urbanization.

Out of the functioning of society, from time to time there develop certain persistent trends toward reform and change which are called social movements. It is not universal for these movements to result in very marked changes in the structure and organization of a society. The nature and causes of social movements are the subject of Chapter 19.

All societies undergo basic deviations from the past, not only in social structure and social processes, but in all phases of culture. The phenomenon of cultural and social change and some of its major causes is treated in Chapter 20.

Finally, a part of society is the development of control techniques, collectively called social control, whereby attempts are made to control the relations of people and the conditions under which they live (Chap. 21). Social control is necessary for an orderly society, even though the society may be a simple one. In modern complex societies the problem of control becomes more complex.

# 13. THE BASIC SOCIAL PROCESSES

## THE MEANING OF SOCIAL PROCESS

SOCIAL PROCESSES are consistent patterns of social behavior or interaction which can be identified in a society. For example, cooperation in a family or between management and labor in an industry may show up as a consistent pattern. In another family or industry conflict may be just as consistent.

The social processes fall into two general categories—those making for consensus, cooperation, and unity in society, and those making for opposition, disunity, and disorganization. Hertzler classifies two social processes into categories—those making for normalization, equilibrium, and control, and those making for destructuralization and defunctionalization.[1] The latter terms are used to denote the breakup or decline in both the structure and functioning of social systems, such as groups, associations, place groupings, institutions, or societies.

## THE BASIC SOCIAL PROCESSES

### Interaction as a basic social process

In several places in the text we have already indicated that the basic social process in social systems is interaction. By this we mean that all social processes are forms of interaction.

As we have seen in previous chapters, especially Chapter 1, interaction is basically the way in which members of a social system influ-

ence and relate themselves to each other. Through contact and stimulus with one another, the behavior of each person is influenced and stimulated. In this case the social system, whether group or community or crowd, is an interaction pattern. Each individual is an entity within a social system. Each individual may be an entity of different strength. In the system reaction or stimulus of one individual causes reaction by another individual.

The initiating stage in interaction is con-

[1] Joyce O. Hertzler, *Society in Action* (New York: Dryden Press, 1954), pp. 247-389.

tact; the next stage is communication, which is the transmission of meanings by the use of symbols. Symbols may be words, physical objects, gestures, dress, sounds, writing, or a combination of these. Communication is fundamental to social life and may take place at various levels of emotional intensity. A loving word spoken into the ear of a courtship mate is likely to be met with more emotional response than the same words written into a letter. "Community of experience," as Hertzler calls it, is an important factor in communication.[2] Language sounds or symbols do not mean much to the individuals of a social system unless there is a community of experience. The wolf whistle or the thumbed nose would have little meaning in communication if they were outside the experience realm of the receiver or listener. If such symbols of communication are used it is assumed that they would have some relation to the sender's experience. We will treat communication in some detail in another chapter.

We have already spoken of interaction in primary and secondary groups. Interaction in primary groups is likely to be more effective and influential than in secondary groups. This is because they are smaller and more intimate. In secondary groupings, like businesses, associations, civic clubs, or college or university classes, people have difficulty in relating them-

[2] *Ibid.*

selves intimately to each other unless it is done in small cliques or other subsystems within the secondary groupings.

*Order and fluidity in the social processes*

The problem of arranging the social processes in logical order is a troublesome one. Sutherland, Woodward, and Maxwell show how, out of the processes of interaction, social processes of cooperation or unity may develop as accommodation and assimilation. In the same manner, processes of opposition or disunity, as competition and conflict, may develop (see Fig. 22). This illustration is also valuable in that it is a good, graphic representation of the basic process of interaction, which may be looked upon as a kind of master process.

Lundberg places the social processes along what he calls a "tension continuum" and arranges them as follows: conflict—competition—accommodation—cooperation.[3] Some psychologists might list "identification" along with cooperation or they might even list it as a separate process. People who cooperate often identify themselves with each other. Gandhi identified himself with the people of India.

There is fluidity and constant interaction

[3] George A. Lundberg, Clarence C. Shrag, and Otto N. Larsen, *Sociology* (Rev. ed.; New York: Harper and Bros., 1958), pp. 242-70.

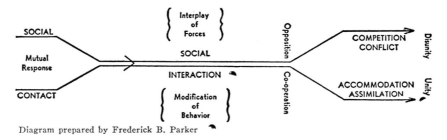

Diagram prepared by Frederick B. Parker

FIG. 22. GRAPHIC REPRESENTATION OF THE MASTER PROCESS OF SOCIAL INTERACTION SHOWING THE DEVELOPMENT OF OTHER SOCIAL PROCESSES FROM IT

SOURCE: Robert L. Sutherland, Julian L. Woodward, and Milton A. Maxwell, *Introductory Sociology* (4th ed.; Philadelphia: J. B. Lippincott Co., 1948), p. 228.

*Philip Gendreau, N.Y.*

*The process of assimilation takes place rapidly in this citizenship class for aliens who wish to become American citizens.*

among the social processes. Except for a no-holds-barred battle in no man's land, or other exceptional situations, there is competition in all cooperation, and vice versa. Also, in life, the social processes come in mixed form, and one social process is constantly slipping over into another and, often, back again. Conflict with an out-group can cause unprecedented in-group cooperation. We may advance in one direction along the continuum indicated above, skip a step here, slip back a couple of steps there, until some sort of temporary equilibrium is achieved. This fluid quality of the social processes should be kept in mind as they are studied.

## Assimilation

*Assimilation is the process by which individuals, groups, or other social systems are merged into homogeneous units.* In the process of stimulus-response, as it takes place in systems of interaction, social assimilation continues. One absorbs, or "assimilates," the cues for behavior set in motion by others. Peoples from different cultures come together in various situations and in different types of social systems, sharing and assimilating each other's attitudes, behavior patterns, and other cultural traits, to a point where cultural differences are at a minimum. The people become

*The Negro in America. The guard, left, is of three racial stocks—Negroid, Causcasian, and American Indian—in contrast to the worker, right, who is of pure Negroid stock.*

more or less socially homogeneous. This means that they communicate with each other, like the same things, and follow, in general, the same patterns of behavior.

The culture of a larger population group may absorb or assimilate the very different culture of a smaller group. An example might be the removal of a number of non-English-speaking families into a Midwest farming community. Eventually the families learn the English language, attend and develop allegiance to American institutions, and otherwise become assimilated into the culture of the American Midwest. Through the process of assimilation the stranger in a culture absorbs the culture and loses his strangeness. The Americanization of immigrants is a good example of cultural assimilation. Immigrants come into the nation from diverse racial, religious, nationality, and cultural backgrounds. The foreign-born may hold some of their distinctive cultural traits

for a while, but these almost surely will be lost in the first- and second-generation immigrants when the assimilation process is complete.

Other instances of assimilation take place in courtship groups and in marriage where the desires, wishes, and behavior patterns of two people may be merged into a homogeneous companionship relationship.

## Amalgamation

Closely related to assimilation is amalgamation, although, in a real sense of the word, amalgamation is a biological process which has social significance, especially demographic significance. *The fusion of racial stocks is called amalgamation.* In the fusion process each racial stock loses its identity in the amalgamation. As an illustration of this we may cite the American Negro. The current-day Negro represents the amalgamation of the three racial

*Arbitration is an accommodation procedure whereby management and labor agree to abide by the decision of the arbitrator.*

stocks—white, Negro, and American Indian. Today, the Negro in America has racial features very different from either of the principal stocks. He is lighter in skin color, taller and heavier than most Negroid stocks, and has other distinctive physical features.

As a rule racial amalgamation speeds up cultural assimilation. This is so because points around which social distance and culture separation develop are often distinct physical differences. As these differences decline, assimilation becomes easier.

## Accommodation

In interaction patterns complete assimilation does not usually take place. Groups and individuals may hold to many attitudes, behavior patterns, and other cultural practices which are different from those held by other individuals and groups. To avoid conflict be-

cause of these unlikenesses, in every society human beings have to learn to accommodate themselves to differences. *Accommodation is adjustment and change in situations, relationships, or conditions which are not completely satisfactory.* The purpose of accommodation is to avoid, reduce, or eliminate conflict, and to promote reciprocal adjustment. As an example, one does not give up his college roommate just because the roommate snores; one tries to accommodate himself to the situation. One does not quit his job, usually, just because the boss is domineering, but tries to work out a system of relationships which permit the working relationship to continue. One does not raise an argument on the subway because a seat is not available. He seeks to accommodate himself to the situation.

Individuals may accommodate themselves to each other and to groups. A group may accommodate itself to another group. Two families living next door to each other may suffer some strains and estrangements with each other but they usually accommodate themselves to the situation and no conflict develops.

A minority element in a biracial culture may endure snobbery and discrimination and a lower-class position without conflict with the majority element. In such situations accommodation becomes the chief process by which adjustment is made by the minority group to the majority group.

There are many kinds of accommodating subprocesses and procedures. One is *compromise. Compromise is simply a mutual concession, shared in by two or more persons or two or more groups, which serves as a basis for a satisfactory working relationship, although perhaps not completely satisfactory to either party.*

In compromise, the parties concerned are willing to give up something for some other kind of compensating gain. Sometimes this gain is harmony or peace. When the interests of a group are interdependent with the interests of another group, compromise may be more easily effected than if the two groups are completely independent. Management and labor furnish many examples of compromise effected, in part, by interdependence, the need for jobs, and the need for labor.

In the development of ways and means of effecting compromise between labor and management, formalized procedures for reaching agreement have been developed. These usually involve the role of a third party. Where a third party—a disinterested party—brings the two contending parties together and stays with them until they reach a compromise agreement, the process is called *mediation*. Where the two competing parties agree to commit their dispute to the decision of a third party after both parties have been heard, this process is called *arbitration*. The third party makes the decision in arbitration, but not in mediation, where he simply refuses or guides the two parties as they work together to reach an agreement through mediation.

*Toleration* is another accommodating subprocess. In this process contending or opposing persons or groups who feel that they cannot make concessions to each other, as in compromise, go their respective ways and bear with each other, perhaps hoping that conditions will take a turn for the better. Toleration is often shown where two contending persons or groups are of about equal strength. In a heterogeneous culture like our own, toleration becomes a fine adjustive process, as well as fine evidence of social maturity. It is expressed in such statements as: "I do not agree with what you say, but you surely have every right to say it."

### Consensus

The development of consensus in a society, while a result, is also a process. *Consensus is general agreement among the members of a society as to allegiances, goals to be pursued, and procedures for pursuing such goals.* As such it is closely related to cooperation. It is perhaps true, however, that there could be an automatic kind of cooperation between people without consensus—that is, agreement upon goals, ends, or means of reaching the ends.

Where there is consensus in a social system or in a society, there is likely to be solidarity and stability. Where there is no agreement upon values, goals, or means of achieving the goals, there is likely to be social instability or instability of the particular social system involved. Consensus shows up in public opinion as experienced in voting, public opinion polls, and in social movements and other forms of social action.

### Cooperation and identification

Cooperation is one of the great social processes making for unity in societies as well as in social systems. *Cooperation is the form of interaction in which persons or groups combine their activities for the promotion of common ends or objectives.* The ends may be sales,

*The United Nations is a symbol of international cooperation. Here, the delegates stand in silent tribute to the memory of the late Secretary-General Dag Hammarskjold, September 19, 1961.*

profits, work output, personal improvement, or the obtainment of articles or services of worth. Cooperation at its best involves: (1) the understanding of goals and their values—sometimes called thought synthesis; and (2) working together to achieve such goals—or synthesis of effort. A cooperative effort may become a desirable goal in itself with no particular thought of either immediate or long-range gain. However, for cooperation to succeed the cooperators must either believe in the cooperative process or else hope that they will profit in some way by it. Cooperation, of course, may be organized or spontaneous. Much spontaneous cooperation is in the form of informal mutual aid.

## Competition

By the time the student reaches college he is well aware of the competitive process and how it works. In elementary and high school he competed for honors which were perhaps represented by symbols, such as gold stars, medals, and special lists of pupils who had achieved certain grades or accomplished certain tasks. In high school the competitive process was accelerated and perhaps became more specialized. Competition in athletics became a fact both to competing athletes, competing teams, and student supporters. Offices in extraclass activities were competed for, sometimes through wide-open lists and sometimes from "lists" of eligibles from which nominees were made and elections held to select from nominees. Membership in social clubs was competitive. Beauty contests were perhaps held in which competitive spirit ran high. Grade lists reflected the competition in studies. Finally, the high school annual listed many of those who had competed for and achieved various honors, ranging from captain of the football team to "the one most likely to succeed."

Now, in college, the student may have had to compete for college entrance, perhaps taking College Board Examinations. Once in college, he has to compete in order to stay in college. Fraternities compete for members and then for honors in intramural activities.

*Competition is the process of competing for scarce goods, goals, and values.* It therefore represents a form of struggle, and would not arise if there were not scarcities. In competition, unlike conflict, the attention of the competitors is not upon each other so much as upon the goods, the goals, the status, and the recognition that the competitors are seeking. In conflict, the competitors are likely to be interested in each other as well as in the goals sought. The competitor is likely to be more conscious of the goals sought than in the intricacies of the competitive process.

The way goals are sought in competition and in cooperation may be stated as follows:

Competition or cooperation is behavior directed toward the same social end by at least two individuals. In competition, moreover, the end sought can be achieved in equal amounts by some, but not by all, of the individuals thus behaving; whereas in cooperation it can be achieved by all, or almost all, of the individuals concerned.[4]

Competition is not limited to human societies. The element of competition in social interaction may vary greatly from culture to culture. In American culture, the competitive element is very strong in spite of the many rewards available to competitors. Even at an

early age, in school, rewards of one kind or another are given for those who surpass fellow pupils in the classroom. We have already spoken of this. The anthropologists have pointed to the highly competitive culture of the Northwest Coast Indians and to the equally well-developed cooperative culture of the Zuni Indians of the Southwest.

The tendency to recognize the competitively successful in American culture indicates the prevalent folk belief that competition is required to bring out the best performance in those seeking the same ends. This tends to institutionalize the competitive process in a wide range of human activities.

Occasionally, in the competitive process, we see those driven out of business or down the economic scale by those who go up. A good illustration of this is found in the grocery business where the small independent grocer has been practically driven out of the competitive market by the large grocery chains. Some minorities, for instance the American Indian, find it difficult to compete economically or politically with the nonminorities. As educational qualifications for jobs increase, the functional illiterate, defined usually as a person with less than a sixth-grade education, has difficulty in getting jobs which pay a living wage.

There is no basic data to support the thesis that people innately are more competitive than they are cooperative. The culture sets the stage to determine whether the society and its subgroupings are competitive, cooperative, or constantly embroiled in conflict. The socially recognized norms also shape the rules of the game of the competitive process, and influence greatly the quality of it. More about this at the end of the chapter.

### Conflict

*Conflict is a highly personalized form of struggle in which the competing parties try to reach the goals sought by injuring or destroying each other.* As an illustration, in war, vic-

---

[4] *Competition and Cooperation,* Social Science Research Council, Bulletin No. 25, p. 3.

*Conflict, both individual and collective, is rife in the world today. This is a scene from Leopoldville in the Congo.*

tory is sought by the elimination of competitors. Of course, outmaneuvering an enemy is part of this process.

Conflict may develop somewhat slowly and naturally out of a situation, or it may be induced or invoked. A shot fired, a gesture made, a new law passed, a person assaulted, a sign painted, or a policy changed are often enough to induce conflict into a tense situation. The most violent form of conflict is revolution, in which leaders of the losing side may be killed or executed, much property may be destroyed, peaceful citizens may be harangued and abused, the streets or the countryside may become a battleground, while neither life nor property has any sanctity. Many revolutions are short in duration and are often developed as means of putting politicians in and out of office.

The alternatives in a conflict situation, say industrial conflict, are indicated by Kerr. He says:

Faced by conflict, each party to it has three broad alternatives: it may withdraw; it may seek to destroy or to dominate the other party; or it may accept the adversary more or less permanently, adjust itself to the fact of conflict, and adapt itself to live with it.[5]

Kerr also indicates the contributions that tactical mediation may make to the adjustment of industrial disputes and conflict. These are as follows: [6]

1. The reduction of irrationality
2. The removal of non-rationality
3. The exploration of solutions
4. Assistance in the graceful retreat
5. Raising the cost of conflict

The strike is one of the most important evidences of industrial conflict, although some

[5] Clark Kerr, "Industrial Conflict and Its Mediation," *The American Journal of Sociology,* **60:**230-45, November, 1954.
[6] *Ibid.,* pp. 236-39.

strikes are induced just to bring the competitive process to a head. For instance:

A strike is not an isolated event, a solitary episode. It occurs within a given social context, a surrounding economic and political environment. The major variations in the incidence of such conflict relate not to the efficacy of the direct ministrations to the conflict, such as tactical mediation, but to the total milieu within which it arises. Fewer strikes are experienced in Sweden than in the United States, and fewer in the garment industry than in coal mining, not because tactical mediation is more skilled in Sweden than it is in the United States, nor is it more skilled in one industry than in another, but rather because of the differing surrounding environments. Aggressive industrial conflict varies greatly from nation to nation, industry to industry, firm to firm, and time to time.[7]

The nature of conflict varies from culture to culture and from class to class. People living under frontier conditions may seek to settle conflicts by direct physical means, especially fighting, whereas people who live in more stable, urban cultures will seek settlement through legal means, arbitration, or mediation. The role of government in settling conflict may be greater in urban-industrial cultures than in simpler cultures. Lower economic and social classes are more likely to engage in physical conflict than are higher, more sophisticated economic and social classes.

Conflict within the person is sociologically significant. Such conflict may or may not relate to the systems of interpersonal relations in which one finds himself. Let us illustrate what we mean. One may have an inner conflict over a moral problem which may involve one or more additional persons. One may have a conflict between two ideologies, say as to whether or not he believes there is a heaven or hell, which may cause him real concern. In this no second person may be involved. One may have a schizophrenic personality with mental conflicts which may very well influence the rationality of his conduct and the state of his interpersonal relationships with others. A wife may have a conflict of roles as she seeks to fulfill the role of wife and the role of career woman at the same time. In this case others as well as herself may be involved to make the conflict situation more difficult.

The results of conflict are not always bad. Conflict may promote solution to problems and the development of cooperation. It may reduce tension, providing it terminates or is not repeated too often. Conflict, or its threat, may help to keep a balance of power between conflicting or competing groups. Finally, as in industrial conflict, it may benefit the worker more than if either labor or management dominated a labor market. Where there are goals which are highly appealing to members of two or more groups, the desirability of such goals may be a factor in reducing conflict and in encouraging cooperation.[8]

## Quality in the social processes

Now that the major social processes have been studied and their differences set forth, it is important to point out that quality in the social processes is important. Cooperation under pressure and duress is not good cooperation. Assimilation may be very undemocratic, equal to a boa constrictor assimilating a rabbit, or it may be intelligent, sympathetic, a two-way process of acculturation. Old-style imperialism and Americanization lean toward the first type; so does communist imperialism, despite its screams about Western imperialism. In contrast are the Point Four plans of economic cooperation now being carried out as part of the economic development of underdeveloped countries. These plans reflect a high-quality form of democratic cooperation and assimilation in which both leaders and followers learn from each other, with programs being modified accordingly. Much of the work of the United Nations is at this high level of quality.

[7] *Ibid.,* pp. 242-43.

[8] Muzafer Sherif, "Superordinate Goals in the Reduction of Intergroup Conflict," *The American Journal of Sociology,* **63**:349-56, January, 1958. *See also* Muzafer and Carolyn W. Sherif, *Groups in Harmony and Tension* (New York: Harper and Bros., 1953).

## SUMMARY

Patterns of behavior functioning in a society which have a central tendency or characteristic so that they may be labeled or named are known as social processes. In general, social processes fall into two general groups: (1) those making for social unity, and (2) those making for disunity or disorganization in society. Between each there is much fluidity.

Interaction is the basic social process, and other social processes are forms of interaction. While social processes take on a variety of forms or subtypes, the most important ones are: assimilation, amalgamation, accommodation, consensus, cooperation and identification, competition, and conflict. Quality is important in the social processes, and this quality determines much of the satisfaction or dissatisfaction arising out of the processes.

THINGS TO DO AND TO DISCUSS

1. What is meant by a social process?
2. When we say that interaction is a master process, what do we mean?
3. What are the major social processes? Why is there fluidity between them?
4. Why may amalgamation hasten assimilation, and vice versa?
5. What is accommodation and what are some of its important major subtypes?
6. Why is consensus important in a society and why is it necessary for cooperation?
7. Distinguish between competition and conflict.
8. Why is competition so highly regarded in American society? Evaluate the emphasis upon it.
9. What are some positive results that may arise out of conflict?
10. How may conflict be channelized and avoided?
11. Why is quality important in the social processes? Illustrate what is meant by quality.

FOR FURTHER STUDY

BALES, R. H. *Interaction Process Analysis.* Boston: Addison-Wesley Press, 1950. How the process of interaction may be studied.

BERRY, BREWTON. *Race and Ethnic Relations.* Boston: Houghton Mifflin Co., 1958. Good treatment of the social processes involved in adjustment in a biracial society.

BERNARD, JESSIE. "The Theory of Games of Strategy as A Modern Sociology of Conflict," *The American Journal of Sociology,* **59**:411-24, March, 1954. How the games theory may be applied in study of conflict.

BLAU, PETER M. "Cooperation and Competition in A Democracy," *The American Journal of Sociology,* **59**:530-35, May, 1954. The role of these two processes in a democracy.

COLEMAN, JAMES S. *Community Conflict.* Glencoe, Ill.: Free Press, 1957. An analysis of community conflict.

DAVIS, KINGSLEY. *Human Society.* New York: The Macmillan Co., 1949. Good text treatment on the social processes.

HERTZLER, JOYCE O. *Society in Action.* New York: Dryden Press, 1954. A text with emphasis upon social processes.

KERR, CLARK. "Industrial Conflict and Its Mediation," *The American Journal of Sociology,* **60**:230-45, November, 1954. The nature of industrial conflict and its solution.

KLINEBERG, OTTO. *Social Psychology.* New York: Henry Holt and Co., 1954. Psychologist's treatment of social processes.

KNOWLES, K. G. J. C. *Strikes—A Study in Industrial Conflict.* Oxford: Basil Blackwell, 1952. Use of the strike in labor-management conflict.

SHERIF, MUZAFER. "Superordinate Goals in the Reduction of Intergroup Conflict," *The American Journal of Sociology,* **63**:349-56, January, 1958. One method of reduction of conflict analyzed.

SHERIF, MUZAFER, and SHERIF, CAROLYN W. *Groups in Harmony and Tension.* New York: Harper and Bros., 1953. An analysis of tension and harmony in group conflict.

SIMMEL, GEORG. *Conflict and the Web of Group Relations.* Translated by KURT H. WOLFF and REINHARD BENDIX. Glencoe, Ill.: Free Press, 1955. Translation of a classic treatment of group conflict.

STAGNER, ROSS. *The Psychology of Industrial Conflict.* New York: John Wiley and Sons, 1956. Analysis of and how to deal with industrial conflict.

THRASHER, FREDERICK M. *The Gang.* Chicago: University of Chicago Press, 1927. Good discussion of gang conflict with other gangs, with the law, and so on.

WEY, HERBERT, and COREY, JOHN. *Action Patterns in School Segregation.* Bloomington, Ind.: Phi Delta Kappa Inc., 1959. Behavior in segregated school situations.

WIRTH, LOUIS. "Social Interaction: The Probem of the Individual and the Group," *American Journal of Sociology,* **44**:965-78, 1939. A good discussion of interaction and basic social process.

WOOD, MARGARET MARY. *Paths of Loneliness.* New York: Columbia University Press, 1953. How some classes withdraw and adjust in a competitive society.

# 14. THE DEVELOPMENT OF STATUSES AND ROLES

IN EVERY SOCIETY people occupy varying degrees of status.[1] In addition, there is considerable differentiation in what people do and how they do it. Status and role relationships are not fixed. They undergo modification from time to time, in some societies changing much more rapidly than in others.

## THE CONCEPT OF STATUS

*Status* refers to the class position or the position in social space one occupies in a social system such as a group or an institution.

The status position which one occupies is defined by himself and by others in terms of expectations. Expectations are made possible by norms of behavior in the culture. One may have an occupation which carries with it a status position ascribed as high or low or middle by the society of which he is a part. Likewise, in the group to which one belongs, one may have a position which is different from that occupied by other members of the group.[2]

A person has a *generalized status* which is the sum total of all his statuses. In addition, one may have a series of *specific statuses* in the various social systems of which he is a member. For instance, a husband's and father's status in his family may be different from his status in a luncheon club or church. A college student's status in a class in sociology may be different from his generalized status in the university or his specific status in his fraternity.

[1] For a discussion of status and roles in primitive cultures, *see* E. Adamson Hoebel, *Man in the Primitive World* (New York: McGraw-Hill Book Co., 1958), pp. 384-400.

[2] For a good discussion of the concepts of status and role, *see* Gottfried Lang, "The Concepts of Status and Role in Anthropology: Their Definition and Use," *American Catholic Sociological Review,* **17**:206-18, October, 1956.

## CONCEPT OF ROLE

A social *role* is the pattern of behavior expected of a person in a certain status. This means that one may have many roles. This is so because one has many statuses, and each role is related to a status. For example, a male member of a family may fulfill the role of husband, father, son-in-law, and several other specific roles as well as a generalized role of citizen.

Turner defines role as follows:

By *role* we mean a collection of patterns of behavior which are thought to constitute a meaningful unit and deemed appropriate to a person occupying a particular status in society (e.g., doctor or father), occupying an informally defined position in interpersonal relations (e.g., leader or compromiser), or identified with a particular value in society (e.g., honest man or patriot).[3]

## THE KINDS OF STATUSES AND ROLES

In general there are two kinds of statuses and roles, *ascribed* and *achieved*. Ascribed statuses and roles are those more or less set or assigned by a culture. Let us first indicate some examples of ascribed statuses. Universally, women are responsible for the rearing of children. They have the ascribed status of mother, and their role of being responsible for the care of young children is also generally ascribed. Of course, this function is shared by other members of the family. The status of cook, and the role of cook, is one usually ascribed to women in most cultures. There are, of course, exceptions to this. The bearing of arms in battle is usually a function ascribed to males; hence, the status and role of soldier is usually limited to men.

Statuses may also be assigned to certain offices, although the individual holding the office may increase or detract from the status of the office. For example, the office of President of the United States and a judgeship on the bench of the Supreme Court have a high ascribed status. This means that any persons occupying these offices would be ascribed a high status, irrespective of their personal characteristics. However, the status of either office

would be modified by the personality of the man occupying it. The mayor's position in a city may not pay a salary but may be sought by many people because it carries with it a high ascribed status in the community.

Statuses may also be *achieved*. The status of a good baseball player or a good surgeon is largely one of achievement, although baseball as a sport, or the occupation of surgeon, may have a high ascribed status in a culture. Here again there are vast differences. A surgeon in Korea has a much lower status than a surgeon in the United States. On the other hand, a government job in Korea has more status than that of a surgeon.

A movie star gains his or her status position largely through achievement, as does also a good artist or singer. All of these positions have in general high statuses. On the other hand, a man may be an exceptional garbage collector—clean and useful—but it is doubtful if his achievement would give him a high generalized status, although he might have a high achieved status within his own firm which might be a small social subsystem of garbage collectors. Exceptional achievement opens the way to achieved status.

## THE DEVELOPMENT OF STATUSES AND ROLES

Statuses and roles are learned. They are part of early socialization. For instance, societies have certain status positions which are ascribed to children. Certain role expectations go with these statuses and the child is taught

what his status and role expectations are. By the time the child enters the teenage period

[3] Ralph H. Turner, "Role-taking, Role Standpoint, and Reference Group Behavior," *The American Journal of Sociology,* **61**:316-39, January, 1956.

he has some knowledge of what his status is and the roles that are expected of him. He learns much, also, about the statuses and roles of other persons in his family—his brothers or sisters or other relatives.

The learning of status and role relationships is much more complicated in a society like our own than in a simple society. In a simple society, even the occupations which the child may follow when he grows up are pretty well known. Their requirements are also known. Conduct norms are pretty clearly defined in simple societies, but much less clearly defined in complex societies. Conduct norms are much less related to statuses than to roles, but status is frequently judged on the basis of such norms.

Institutions play important roles in socialization. Not only are they social systems in which individuals learn statuses and roles, but they serve to enforce status and role systems. A church may release a minister who violates the expected statuses and roles of his office. The state courts may commit to prison a person who develops a role of law violator. Each state has an elaborate system of statutes or codes in which certain forms of conduct against the state are prohibited and for which offenders may be punished.

Each social system may influence status and role development. One of the best examples of this has been in the caste systems of India where endogamous marriage within castes was the historic role requirement. Also, occupations tended to have a strong caste orientation as did education.[4] (See Chap. 15.)

Another example of conditioning of statuses and roles in a social system is found in peer groups. A clique of girls or a boys' gang may define a different status and role relationship from that of the family, and proceed to furnish an environment in which this relationship will develop. The family may stress the status of daughter, son, and "good child." The peer group may stress the status of companion, "good egg," coworker in delinquency, or co-participant in activities which the family may frown upon. As a result of the conditioning influence of the two subsystems, role conflicts may develop within the child and between the parents and the child.

As a result also of culture accretion, as we indicated in the discussion of ascribed statuses and roles, a hierarchy of statuses tends to develop in a culture. Likewise, a complex of role relationships tends to develop. The social systems tend to reflect these and condition the young accordingly, so that their perpetuation, with some deviation, tends to take place. The status and role relationship of the Negro in the Deep South is a good example of this, as is the status hierarchy of jobs in the occupational structure. Despite cultural differences between nations, the prestige of comparable occupations in major industrialized countries shows a remarkably high correlation.[5]

All roles include privileges or rights and responsibilities or obligations. The more mature and intelligent a role, the better the balance between the two. Also, the privileges of one role are the responsibilities of the reciprocal role, and vice versa. The student is well aware of the privileges and responsibilities involved in role. He encounters these in the classroom and in other academic requirements, as well as in his fraternity and home life. Citizen roles also furnish good illustrations of role and status responsibilities and obligations.

## MARGINAL ROLES

There are many marginal roles in a society. Part of this situation comes about as a result of people occupying a single role which is marginal, or occupying two or more roles and

---

[4] *See* Noel P. Gist, "Caste Differentials in South India," *American Sociological Review,* **19**:126-37, April, 1954.

[5] *See* Alex Inkeles and Peter H. Rossi, "National Comparisons of Occupational Prestige," *The American Journal of Sociology,* **61**:329-39, January, 1956.

Like the actor, the individual may have several social roles. Here are some of the roles of Queen Elizabeth II.

*Princess Elizabeth in the W.A.S.C.* During World War II, Princess Elizabeth served as a driver in the Women's Auxiliary Service Corps (equivalent to the WAC's). Here she is shown changing a wheel.

*Princess Elizabeth at a party.* During the Royal Tour of Canada in 1951 Princess Elizabeth and the Duke of Edinburgh enjoyed a Canadian square dance at a private party given in Government House, Ottawa, by the Governor General, Viscount Alexander.

*Princess Elizabeth as a mother. The baby whom the Princess is holding is Prince Charles, now the Prince of Wales.*

*Her Majesty Queen Elizabeth II. This formal portrait photograph was taken after the coronation in June, 1953.*

217

perhaps not succeeding very well in either. An example of the latter-type role may be a mother who tries to combine child rearing and a career and may be unable to succeed except marginally in one or more of the roles.

Cottrell has pointed out three things which seem to be necessary in satisfactory role adjustment: [6]

1. The clarity with which a role is defined
2. The compatability of alternate role behaviors required of a person in a given status position.
3. The satisfactory attainment of the goals which are highly valued in the social systems and the subcultural groups to which one belongs

Deficiencies in one or more aspects of role performance indicated above would produce strain in social roles which in turn produce anxiety, frustration, or tension. The nature of some roles will produce what Parsons has called "socially structured strain." [7] By such strain Parsons means situations in which the goals defined as appropriate for a role cannot be attained.

Wardwell speaks of the marginal role of the chiropractor compared to the well-established, institutionalized role of the medical doctor.[8] Chiropractors practice their healing arts much the same as any other doctor, but they are not accepted by the American Medical Association and the local medical academies and societies. Furthermore, in some states the state medical societies have made vigorous attempts to legislate against chiropractors. Wardwell says:

The chiropractor's role is marginal to that of the physician in at least the following five respects: (1) amount of technical competence; (2) breadth of scope of practice; (3) legal status; (4) income; and (5) prestige. The role's marginality derives from the fact that chiropractors claim to be doctors of a special kind and are so regarded by many

people but that society at large does not accord them this status.[9]

The element of strain in the chiropractor's role is the result of several things related to the above factors. In the first place the role of chiropractor is more ambiguous than that of most medical practitioners. Although he practices the healing arts, he is not an accepted member of the medical profession. Chiropractors have been the subject of litigation and legislation. Not being accepted by the medical profession, they tend to go their own individualistic ways rather than the ways of doctors whose practices are closely related to their professional groups, which also afford the doctors considerable social security in their roles. Chiropractors are normally not permitted the use of hospitals and clinics as other physicians are. Another strain-producing element is the fact that the income of chiropractors is lower than the income of medical doctors.

Wardwell shows that chiropractors tend to develop certain strain-reducing patterns in response to their marginal roles.[10] Physical withdrawal from contact with the medical profession and rationalization of their behavior and their profession are examples of strain-reducing adjustments. Wardwell shows also that many chiropractors have developed an ideology of an oppressed minority, frequently going to some length to explain their position to their patients. This often takes the form of verbal aggression.

In states that do not have a licensing law against the practice of chiropractic, other patterns of behavior are developed. These are:

(1) uniting for mutual aid, both informally and in associations which provide insurance protection and experienced defense counsel; (2) practicing under the guise of physiotherapists or masseurs; (3) restricting practice to "safe" illnesses and

---

[6] Leonard Cottrell, "The Adjustment of the Individual to His Age and Sex Roles," *American Sociological Review,* 7:617-20, 1942.

[7] Talcott Parsons, *The Social System.* (Glencoe, Ill.: Free Press, 1951), pp. 70 ff.

[8] Walter I. Wardwell, "The Reduction of Strain in a Marginal Social Role," *The American Journal of Sociology,* **61**:16-25, July, 1955.

[9] *Ibid.,* p. 17. *See also* Walter I. Wardwell, "A Marginal Professional Role; The Chiropractor," *Social Forces,* **30**:339-48, 1952.

[10] Wardwell, "The Reduction of Strain in a Marginal Social Role," p. 19.

trusted patients; (4) participation in civic and fraternal activities in order to gain community acceptance; and (5) attempting to obtain a favorable licensing law by engaging in campaigns to educate the public, organizing patients into laymen's units for the purpose of exerting pressure on legislators and forming friendships with politically important people.[11]

The chiropractor is likely to look upon the organized medical fraternity as his chief source of opposition and frustration. Sometimes he may criticize the lack of unity in his own craft and the lack of public understanding and appreciation of the role and work of the chiropractor.

In relation to the medical profession, the clinical psychologist may find himself in a somewhat marginal position which the psychiatrist does not have. The psychiatrist has an M.D. degree, may prescribe drugs in his practice—which the clinical psychologist cannot do, and is accepted in official medical organizations, whereas the clinical psychologist is not. In some states the organized medical societies have attempted to legislate against the practices of the clinical psychologist. Often he finds the best solution to his problem by teaming up with a psychiatrist. Such partnerships are frequently complementary to each other. Another thing that clinical psychologists and also psychiatrists find frustrating is that the courts of law in some states will accept any medical doctor's testimony as an expert in testimony involving the mental condition of a person.

It has been pointed out that pharmacy is somewhat of a marginal occupation—marginal between a business and a profession,[12] and that the role of the pharmacist is somewhat marginal. The well-trained pharmacist, in smaller drugstores, often finds it frustrating to act as clerk, have to oversee fountain service, and occasionally lend a hand at shooting-a-coke.

11 *Ibid.*, p. 19.
12 Thelma Herman McCormack, "The Druggist's Dilemma: Problems of a Marginal Occupation," *The American Journal of Sociology*, **61**:308-15, January, 1956.

In describing the marginal aspects of pharmacy as an occupation, McCormack says:

The young pharmacist today is trained as a professional; his interests and ability for scientific research are carefully developed, preparing him for the laboratory work required by hospitals, schools, and pharmaceutical companies. Yet few pharmacists see themselves in this position. Most expect to become proprietors, with the status of independent professionals, thus fusing the two systems and avoiding a final choice. In this process the entrepreneurial drive is modified by criticism of big business and by retreat from highly competitive circumstances; the professional drive is blunted by subordinating a social service goal to individual achievement for its own sake.[13]

The above examples of professional marginal roles are only illustrative of marginal roles that develop in the specialties and professions of a highly organized nature. A second-generation foreigner may have to adjust to marginal roles. His foreign-born parents may have role expectations which they feel he should fulfill which are entirely different from the second-generation foreign-born groups with which he associates. Interfaith marriages often involve marginal roles, even though one of the mates is converted to the religion of the other spouse. Where the separate religions are kept, the children may be caught in a marginal religious role situation.

The above illustrations are adequate to show what is meant by marginal roles. One may be caught in a situation where the role one performs is marginal. Society may define a role as marginal or one or more persons in the role situation may recognize its marginality. Because of one's race, age, or religion, a person may be marginal in a job situation. He may be the first to go when business enterprises slump and the last to be taken on when business picks up. Years ago Stonequist wrote of the role of the marginal man—the person who was borderline between two races or cultures—the mulatto or the Eurasian. In a world

13 *Ibid.*, p. 315.

much more cosmopolitan than formerly, the so-called marginal man that Stonequist defined and described has lost some of his marginality.[14]

Modern communication has enlarged the whole prestige and status area of people and has given wide knowledge of how people who have achieved high-status positions live and think. Perhaps not nearly as much is known about how the people of low-class status live because they are not in the communication limelight.

C. Wright Mills shows the impact of communication upon disseminating information about high-status groups. He says:

> The rich of previous eras could not so readily be known by the public, the way they lived being known only by heresay and glimpses through curtained windows. But by the 1920's in America a democracy of status vision had come about; the area of prestige was truly rational; now the bottom could see the top—at least the version of it that was put on display. It did not matter if this top was sometimes contrived and often a cloak. It did not matter if the real top was even more secluded and unseen than before. For those on the bottom, the top presented was real and it was dazzling.[15]

## ROLE CONFLICT

In the study of marginal roles we have indicated some of the causes of role conflict. In the adjustment to marginal role situations we have also indicated some of the ways in which adjustments may be made to role conflict.

Role conflict may be largely intrapersonal, although it is perhaps difficult, if not impossible, to eliminate interpersonal relationship factors from intrapersonal relations. One may have a role conflict of intrapersonal nature where problems of honesty or performance of work are involved. The bank teller who handles money all the time, but receives little of it, may have conflict over whether to be honest or try to take some of the money he handles and "fix" his accounts. As another example, religious conflicts may arise within the person's religious convictions.

Role conflict is usually of interpersonal nature. A father may define the role of son and daughter for his children. The high school club may define conflicting roles for the same children. The role of good student may conflict with the role of good Joe in the fraternity.

By role conflict we mean situations in which actors are required to fill roles simultaneously which will be in conflict with each other.

Getzels and Guba describe such situations as follows:

> In certain situations role conflicts occur. That is, the situations are so ordered that an actor is required to fill simultaneously two or more roles that present inconsistent, contradictory, or even mutually exclusive expectations. The actor cannot realistically conform to these expectations. He is then forced to choose one of several alternatives: he may abandon one role and cling to the other, he may attempt some compromise between the roles, or he may withdraw either physically or psychologically from the roles altogether. In any event, over any long-term period he cannot fully meet the expectations of all roles, and to the extent that he fails to meet the expectations, he is judged *ineffective* in the management of one or another of the roles by the defining groups.[16]

There are many factors and situations which make for role conflict. Some of these are:

1. The attempt of the actor to fill an incompatible role or a marginal role situation
2. Lack of clarity in the definition of a role
3. Change in role expectation or role definition

[14] Everett V. Stonequist, *The Marginal Man* (New York: Charles Scribner's Sons, 1937).

[15] C. Wright Mills, *White Collar* (New York: Oxford University Press, 1956), pp. 253-54.

[16] J. W. Getzels and E. G. Guba, "Role, Role Conflict and Effectiveness: An Empirical Study," *American Sociological Review*, **19**:164-75, April, 1954.

without consulting with the actor or actors involved

4. Pressure placed upon the actor to fulfill two roles or to accept a single role against his wishes, and the actor's definition of role expectations

5. Role expectations which are beyond the capability or adequacy of the actor or actors to accept or achieve

In every society conflicting social norms may be conducive to conflicts in roles. Actually, perhaps most people accept the conflict in norms and roles and make fairly good adjustment to them. It is the exceptional deviate who impresses us most in conflicting role situations.

## SOCIAL DISTANCE IN STATUS-ROLE RELATIONS

Constraints in interaction patterns, due to cultural differences, or to class-status differentiations or feelings, are, collectively, referred to as social distance.

There is a tendency to identify ourselves with our own class-conscious groups, and to avoid association with groups we feel superior or inferior to. Where we do make contacts with such groups, the interaction patterns may be modified by our consciousness of existing class and status differentiation. The ideologies and patterns of interaction involved in social distance are learned, much attitude formation taking place in the family, community, church, and school. Unhappy experiences with the representatives of class and status groups may increase the feeling of distance toward them.

Social distance, ideologically conceived, is often different from an interaction pattern one may follow or accept when faced with a life situation. For instance, as part of a classroom situation, an American student may express willingness to accept an attractive Eurasian girl into her sorority, only to vote against the girl should her name be presented. Perhaps the same girl would have no objection to working with the same young lady on a class committee.

Circumstances and situations influence social distance variables. During World War II, Germans and Japanese nationals were pretty soundly hated by many Americans. In the cold war which followed, social distance attitudes relaxed and more favorable attitudes toward German and Japanese nationals developed rapidly.

Even within the same families, social distances vary, as between family members. Where the distances are slight, relationships may be warm and affectionate. Where the distances are marked, the relationships may be constrained, reserved, cold, and mechanical. Even in the case of stereotyped roles, the quality of the role relationships is modified by distance factors. Contacts and stereotyped roles may be carried out despite the feelings that often enter into such roles.

Social distance may be measured both by attitude scales and by an analysis of interaction patterns. Again we wish to stress that a person's performance or rating on a social distance scale is no real indication of the behavior the same individual will follow in a life situation.[17] In an intellectual exercise the response may be different from that in real life.

## SUMMARY

Status and role relationships are closely related. One's position in social space is his status, and the behavior expected in a status position is one's role. One may have a number of specific statuses and a generalized status which is the sum total of all of one's statuses.

Statuses may be ascribed by the culture in which one lives or they may be achieved by

17 *See* Emory S. Bogardus, "Measuring Social Distance," *Journal of Applied Psychology*, 9:299-308, 1925, for one of the earlier works on measuring social distance. From this original work many scales have been patterned.

the person in a status system. An achieved status may or may not have a high ascribed status. One may have a high achieved status, as a pickpocket in a subculture of pickpockets would have, but would hardly have a high ascribed status.

Statuses and roles are learned. Some are biologically based. For example, the role of childbearer is dictated by biology, although who shall care for children after they are born is not as clearly defined biologically as it is culturally determined. Institutions are key points in which social roles and statuses are learned. Ascribed statuses develop in cultures gradually and may remain fairly stable over long periods

of time. Empirical studies of the prestige of comparable occupations show surprising uniformity in prestige positions in widely different cultures.

Because of the nature of their occupational or other roles, some people are forced to assume marginal roles. Empirical studies are throwing some light upon marginal roles and the kinds of adjustments made to them. Such studies are also throwing considerable light upon the causes of role conflict and the kinds of accommodations made to conflicting situations. Useful also is the concept of social distance which influences the amount of reserve or constraint present in interaction patterns.

THINGS TO DO AND TO DISCUSS

1. Evaluate various concepts of status and role.
2. How does one develop a status? Illustrate generalized and specific status.
3. How does one develop a role?
4. Show how roles include obligations as well as privileges.
5. What is a marginal role, and how does it develop? Give illustrations of marginal roles from your own community.
6. What are some of the important conditions which make for satisfactory role performance and adjustment in roles?
7. What is role conflict and what are some of the major causes of it?
8. What kinds of adjustments may one make to role conflict situations?
9. What is meant by social distance? How does it influence the probability and quality of interaction patterns? Illustrate.

FOR FURTHER STUDY

BARBER, BERNARD. *Social Stratification: A Comparative Analysis of Structure and Process.* New York: Harcourt, Brace and Co., 1957. Comprehensive treatment of stratification.

COTTRELL, LEONARD. "The Adjustment of the Individual to His Age and Sex Roles," *American Sociological Review,* 7:617-20, 1942. How adjustment is made to age and sex roles.

GETZELS, J. W., and GUBA, E. G. "Role, Role Conflict, and Effectiveness: An Empirical Study," *American Sociological Review,* 19:164-75, April, 1954. One of the better objective studies of role conflict.

GIST, NOEL P. "Caste Differentials in South India," *American Sociological Review,* 19:126-37, April, 1954. Some of the major bases for Indian caste differentials.

GOLDSCHMIDT, WALTER. "Social Class and the Dynamics of Status in America," *American Anthropologist,* 57:1209-17, December, 1955. An anthropologist's analysis of class dynamics.

HAVIGHURST, ROBERT J., and FEIGENBAUM, KENNETH. "Leisure and Life-Style," *The American Journal of Sociology,* **64**:394-404, January, 1959. How leisure and life style is status and class related.

INKELES, ALEX, and ROSSI, PETER H. "National Comparisons of Occupational Prestige," *The American Journal of Sociology,* **61**:329-39, January, 1956. Differences in the prestige of occupations in the United States, Great Britain, U.S.S.R., Japan, and New Zealand.

KAHL, JOSEPH A. *The American Class Structure.* New York: Rinehart and Co., 1957. Good comprehensive analysis of American class structure and its functioning.

LUNDBERG, GEORGE A.; SCHRAG, CLARENCE C.; and LARSEN, OTTO N. *Sociology.* Rev. ed. New York: Harper and Bros., 1958. Comprehensive text treatment of class.

McCORMACK, THELMA HERMAN. "The Druggist's Dilemma: Problems of a Marginal Occupation," *The American Journal of Sociology,* **61**:308-15, January, 1956. The marginal role and status of the druggist.

PACKARD, VANCE. *The Status Seekers.* New York: David McKay Co., 1959. Popular account of class striving in America.

PARSONS, TALCOTT. *The Social System.* Glencoe, Ill.: Free Press, 1951. Class as a social system is treated along with other systems.

STONEQUIST, EVERETT V. *The Marginal Man.* New York: Charles Scribner's Sons, 1937. An old but classic treatment of different kinds of marginality.

TURNER, RALPH H. "Role-taking, Role Standpoint, and Reference Group Behavior," *The American Journal of Sociology,* **61**:316-39, January, 1956. The relation of reference groups to roles.

WARDWELL, WALTER I. "A Marginal Professional Role: The Chiropractor," *Social Forces,* **30**:339-48, 1952. Chiropractory as a marginal profession.

———. "The Reduction of Strain in a Marginal Social Role," *The American Journal of Sociology,* **61**:16-25, July, 1955. How strain may be reduced in a marginal social role.

# 15. SOCIAL STRATI-FICATION AND ITS FUNCTIONING

By this time the student of sociology is aware of the relationship between the structure-function aspects of society. Structure is related to function and function to structure. It is because of the dynamics of class and the fact that social strata are in process of forming and reforming in America that we treat the subject in Part III of the text, The Functioning of Society, rather than in Part II, The Structure of Society.

## OPEN-CLASS IDEOLOGY

We have in the United States what is called an open-class ideology. By this is meant that the social chances are, theoretically, equal in respect to raising or lowering one's self up and down the hierarchy of social classes, limited only by one's ability and other personal characteristics not associated with race, religion, or politics. The theory of the open-class society is set forth in the Declaration of Independence which declares that all people have the right to life, liberty, and the pursuit of happiness under the Constitution of the United States. In a more practical sense the status groups in a society are "open" when there is fairly easy movement toward either higher- or lower-status positions.

Open-class ideology is an ideological concept. This country has perhaps gone further toward accomplishing the ideal of an open-class society than any other country. This accomplishment has not been easy, especially in our biracial society with slavery as a background. A closed-class society is one in which the class strata are rigidly maintained and in which it is difficult to rise from one class level to another. English class structure is not as open as is American class structure. In England at the top there is a class layer of the aristocracy which we do not have in this country. The closest approach to a closed-class system would be a caste system in which one is born into a class and cannot rise above the class position that has been ascribed him because of birth. Some say that we have a closed-class system between the Negro and white class structure in many biracial communities in this country. They say that in many biracial communities there is a white class structure and a Negro class structure, but that between the two there is a strong class or mild caste barrier, and that the Negro is assigned his position on account of his race irrespective of what personal qualities he may have.

The particular class structure we have in this country with respect to open and closed systems is pretty much open to debate. The purpose of the foregoing discussion is not to settle this debate but merely to open it.

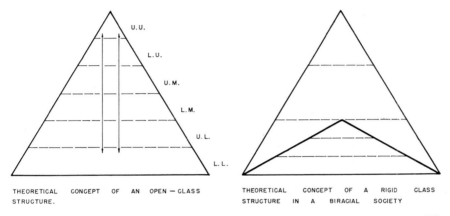

THEORETICAL  CONCEPT  OF  AN  OPEN—CLASS
STRUCTURE.

THEORETICAL  CONCEPT  OF  A  RIGID  CLASS
STRUCTURE  IN  A  BIRACIAL  SOCIETY

FIG. 23.  OPEN-CLASS THEORETICAL CONCEPT COMPARED WITH A SOUTHERN
WHITE PERSON'S CONCEPT OF THE CLASS STRUCTURE OF A BIRACIAL
SOCIETY

## SOME BASIC CONCEPTS

In our earlier discussion of status and role, certain terms were used which also have significance in this chapter. Some of these will be repeated. Social classes are social systems. *A social class is a status grouping,* and class is used, singularly, to denote all persons within the same status grouping, or all persons occupying the same social station in a society. A caste position, on the other hand, is one fixed by birth and from which it is difficult to move upward from one caste to another. India is our best example of a closed-class system made possible through a system of castes. A class society is "one in which the hierarchy of prestige and status is divisible into groups each with its own economic, attitudinal, and cultural characteristics, and each having differ-

ential degrees of power in community decisions." [1]

The original inhabitants of India were a very dark-skinned people known as Dravidians, who were invaded by light-skinned people known as Aryans. The Aryans were well established by 1500 B.C. The antiquity of the caste system makes it difficult to determine how it developed. One theory is that the caste system arose out of the accommodation, adjustment, and wars between nomadic tribes when these races were first settled, and when the defeated Dravidians were required to do me-

[1] Walter Goldschmidt, "Social Class in America—A Critical Review," *American Anthropologist,* **52**:492, October-December, 1952. *See also* Leonard Reissman, *Class in American Society* (Glencoe, Ill.: Free Press, 1959).

nial jobs while the victors were elevated to upper-class positions. Many upper-class Hindus feel that their castes were of divine origin. More will be said about the accommodation adjustments arising out of the caste structure later.

There are five main castes in Hindu India. These are as follows:

1. The Brahmans—the priests and religious leaders

2. The Ksatriyas—the warriors and the military nobles

3. The Vaisyas—the merchants, artisans, farmers, and clerical workers

4. The Sudras—domestic servants and farm laborers predominantly, but not exclusively

5. The Untouchables—below all castes. Cleaners of the latrines, sweepers, scavengers. These people are often referred to as Harijans, apparently a Ghandian euphemism, used by many Indians for pariahs or outcasts, particularly of the more untouchable varieties.

The names of local castes in India vary from one part of the country to another, although they belong to the previous five groupings. In northern India the largest cultivating caste, numbering about 9 million people, is known as the Jats. This caste is outstanding for the skill of its farmers. Immediately above them are the Rajputs.

In the village of Rampur, also in northern India, six castes are found. The type of service which each performs is designated, as is also the remuneration given for these services (Table 25):

Detailed studies of caste systems in Indian villages indicate that the economic functioning of castes and the economic interaction pattern between castes have been neglected by sociologists.[2]

Lewis shows that under the system of exchange of labor in an Indian village—

each caste group within the village is expected to give certain standardized services to the families of other castes. A khati (carpenter) repairs tools, for example, a nai (barber) cuts hair; but they do not necessarily perform these services for everyone. Each man works for a particular family or group of families with which he has hereditary ties. His father worked for the same families before him, and his son will continue to work for them, the occupation or service being determined by caste. The family, or family head served by an individual is known as his *Jajman*, while the man who performs service is known as the *Jajman's Kamin* or *Kam Karm-Wala* (literally, worker).[3]

These are terms used in northeastern India. Other terms may be used in other parts of the country.

As the Jajmani system functions, it assures a stable labor supply for the dominating agricultural caste, by limiting the upward mobility of the lower castes who assist the agricultural caste. If a Kamin leaves a village he is expected to get someone, usually a member of his family, to take his place. Because they have rights and privileges, they hesitate to move from one family to another or one village to another. The system, as it originally functioned, brought a degree of peace and contentment to villagers.

In commenting upon the division of labor between castes, and the interaction between castes in the performance of this labor, Opler and Singh say:

Not only does everyone have some place within the Hindu system, but it is significant that every group, from the Brahman to the Charmar caste, has been somehow integrated into the social and ceremonial round of the community and has been given some opportunity to feel indispensable and proud.[4]

[2] Such as Oscar Lewis, *Village Life in Northern India* (Urbana, Ill.: University of Illinois Press, 1958). For a classic study of the Hindu Jajmani system, *see also* William H. Wiser, *The Hindu Jajmani System* (Lucknow, India: Lucknow Publishing House, 1936).

[3] Lewis, *op. cit.*, p. 56.
[4] Morris E. Opler and Rudra Datt Singh, "The Division of Labor in an Indian Village," in *A Reader in General Anthropology*, ed. C. S. Coon (New York: Henry Holt and Co., 1948), p. 496.

*Table 25*

CASTES, RULES OF SERVICE, AND RIGHTS AND REMUNERATION
EARNED, VILLAGE OF RAMPUR

| Caste | Type of Service | Rights Earned through Service |
|---|---|---|
| Khati (carpenter) | To repair agricultural tools | One maund of grain per year along with ori rights (2½ sirs of grain twice a year at each sowing season) * |
| Lohar (blacksmith) | As above | As above |
| Kumhar (potter) | To supply earthenware vessels and to render services of light nature at weddings | Grain to the value of the vessels. Additional grain at the son's or daughter's marriage, according to status and capacity |
| Hajjam or Nai (barber) | To shave and cut hair; to attend to guests on their arrival and to render other services of light nature at weddings | At each harvest as much grain as the man can lift by himself. Additional grain at the son's or daughter's marriage, according to status and capacity |
| Khakrul or Bhangi (sweeper) | To prepare cow-dung cakes; to gather sweepings, to remove dead mules and donkeys; to collect cots for extraordinary needs, and to render services at weddings | Meals and rabri twice a day; at each harvest as much grain as the man can lift by himself and also at the son's or daughter's marriage, according to status and capacity |
| Camar (leatherworker) | If a man, assists in agriculture and gives all kinds of light services. If he does begar (compulsory labor) renders ordinary service, and removes dead cattle | He gets one-twentieth of the produce<br>He gets one-fourth of the produce and the skins of dead cattle |

* Maund: a unit of weight containing 40 sirs, or about 80 pounds.
Source: Oscar Lewis, *Village Life in Northern India* (Urbana, Ill.: University of Illinois Press, 1958), p. 61.

Increasingly, as education and nationalism have developed in India, the accommodation to caste is much less in evidence now than formerly, and increasingly tension within and between castes is indicated.[5] More about this in succeeding paragraphs.

[5] *See* Radhakamal Mukerji, *Inter-Caste Tensions* (Lucknow, India: University of Lucknow, 1951). Mimeographed. *See also* J. H. Hutton, *Caste in India* (New York: Oxford University Press, 1951).

It was Mohandas Gandhi who gave the name Harijan to the Untouchables. The term means "children of god." Out of a population of 400 million, India's Untouchables number 55 million. While the Constitution of 1946 did much to modify the legal basis of the caste systems, socially they are still strong. The New Delhi parliament reserves 76 of its 500 seats for Untouchables. Of all government jobs 12.5 per cent are reserved for Untouchables. In the larger cities the Untouchables eat in the restaurants and attend the movies. Scholarships are available for them so that they may attend colleges. Some of the national leaders are Untouchables. The Untouchables work with others in government positions. The chances are, however, that when the day's work is done or the school is out, people will revert to some of the customs of class. A Sudra may work as a servant in a Brahman's home but the family may not allow an Untouchable to enter the home except to clean the latrine, which may be entered by a door other than through the home. Whereas a Sudra may cook the Brahman family's food, the Untouchable may not.[6]

According to the teachings of the castes, the Untouchables could not read the sacred literature of the Hindus. If they should, by accident, gain access to the books of Hinduism like the *Riga-Veda* and the *Upanishads* to read them would be useless, if they could read, because they were beyond salvation anyway.

*Prestige* is the value or importance attached to a status or class layer, whereas *esteem* is more of a personal quality which others attach to a person irrespective of his social status.

## THE HALLMARKS OF CLASS

Social class systems tend to thrive in the larger and more complex societies. Wherever they arise, they divide the society into a number of status groups.

The determination of who belongs in a social class is not easily accomplished. The simplest method of ranking people by classes is to ask them to determine their own class status through a system of *self-rating*. Richard Centers of Princeton, using the facilities of the National Opinion Research Center, asked a national sample of adults to indicate whether they identified themselves with the "upper class," "middle class," "working class," or "lower class." [7] Most of them chose the "middle" and "working" classes.

The preference of Americans for middle-class identification results from many factors. First of all, the middle class in America includes a large percentage of the population. Current values make it "snobby" to designate one's self as "upper," even when one rates one's self that way. On the other hand, emulation and wishful thinking (partly unconscious) makes one call one's self "middle," when in strict honesty one knows he is "lower." This is a good example of the "banana peels" that litter the interviewer or the polling expert studying class as he tries to draw scientific conclusions from his data.

Warner, in his study of Yankee City, has developed an evaluated participation technique of measuring social status and has combined this with an *index of status characteristics*. In evaluated participation a person is assigned to a class by a rater or raters on the basis of his status reputation, his memberships in institutions and associations, comparison with others who hold class positions, and on the basis of other characteristics and information about the person which an informant may reveal.[8]

In his index of status characteristics, which Warner used in his Jonesville study, another method of placing people in social classes is exemplified. The procedure is roughly as follows. After becoming acquainted with the community the investigator is studying, he divides residential areas into prestige types according to the views held by local residents. The investigator then looks at the exterior of each house he is studying and rates it accord-

[6] *See* Alie Abel, "India's Untouchables—Still the 'Black Sin,' " *The New York Times Magazine,* March 1, 1959, pp. 21, 38, 41-42, 44.

[7] Richard Centers, *The Psychology of Social Classes* (Princeton, N.J.: Princeton University Press, 1949).

[8] W. Lloyd Warner, *et al., Social Class in America: A Manual of Procedure for the Measurement of Social Status* (Chicago: Science Research Associates, 1949).

*E. I. du Pont de Nemours & Co., Inc.*

*Among the most influential groupings in American society is the suburban family.*

ing to its prestige value. The subject then is rated according to occupation and major source of income. The composite rating is then made on the basis of the following characteristics.[9]

1. Dwelling area
2. House type
3. Occupation:
   a. Professionals and proprietors of large businesses
   b. Semiprofessionals and smaller officials of large businesses
   c. Clerks and kindred workers
   d. Skilled workers
   e. Proprietors of small businesses
   f. Semiskilled workers
   g. Unskilled workers

4. Primary source of income:
   a. Inherited wealth
   b. Earned wealth
   c. Profits and fees
   d. Salary and sales commissions
   e. Wages
   f. Private relief
   g. Public relief and nonrespectable income

Another and rather unusual method of gauging the class status of a family was developed by Chapin. This was a method of measuring the prestige value of living-room furnishings which Chapin holds symbolizes the class value of a family. In addition to living-room items which are checked, the interviewer gives his own estimate of the taste and appropriateness of the room.[10]

[9] W. Lloyd Warner, *et al.*, *Democracy in Jonesville* (New York: Harper and Bros., 1949).

[10] *See* F. Stuart Chapin, *Contemporary American Institutions* (New York: Harper and Bros., 1935), pp. 373-97.

## *THE SOCIAL DIMENSIONS OF CLASS*

The methods of measuring class indicate some of the characteristics of class which students of class feel are important. After an intensive study of existing class studies and their measurement, Kahl arrives at the following characteristics, variables, or dimensions of class in America: [11]

1. Personal prestige
2. Occupations
3. Possessions
4. Interaction or behavior
5. Class consciousness
6. Value orientation

In commenting upon the above "variables" of class, which he prefers to call them, Kahl indicates that, while either variable might stratify a population, all are mutually dependent in that they influence each other.[12]

Not all of the above variables need much discussion. Prestige is a sentiment and may be attached to an individual or a class. Personal prestige may hold a person in high position even though his occupation may not necessarily be one of high prestige. A Jewish owner of a laundry might have high status in the upper Gentile social classes because of the tremendous personal esteem for the man.

There are various marks of the status of an occupation. These may be different within an organization and without it. Dubin indicates some of the marks of occupational status within an industry or a corporation. The more important ones are: title, kind of work done, seniority, privileges, insignia and dress, the number of people supervised, work location, the amount of authority one has, and office appointments. The importance of work done and the exclusiveness of work done is a mark of occupational status whether within or outside an organization.[13] Blue-collar jobs and white-collar jobs fall in different classes. Manual labor jobs receive different class ratings than do nonmanual labor jobs.

North and Hatt, by using polls conducted by the National Opinion Research Center, obtained the ratings on occupations of a national sample of 2,920 persons. In this study Supreme Court justices ranked first, physicians second, mayors sixth, college professors seventh, and bankers tenth in prestige of occupation. At the lower end of the continuum were found waiters with a rank of 79, night watchmen 81, janitors 85, and shoeshiners 90.[14]

Although there is a solid core of culture enjoyed by all classes, there are many class variables in possessions, even though possessions as symbols of class and status change. Certain makes of automobiles, when purchased new especially, mark class lines. While an office secretary may have a mink coat, this would tend to be the exception, and expensive furs normally mark wealthier class lines and positions. On the other hand, all classes are likely to have well-styled clothes, yet casual dress may be an upper-class symbol. Expensive boats or houses are class symbols, yet suburbanization has caused an increase in good housing among the middle classes. Stocks and bonds, at one time a symbol of high status, are now owned by too many people in the population to be reliable class symbols. Travel has become such a mass activity that it does not follow the class lines it once did.

With whom one interacts, that is, within what class limits one interacts, is also a mark of class. Also, how one behaves may separate one class position from another. In what circles one moves has definite class connotations. Many examples of this may be seen from your own communities.

The greater the identification a member of a class has with the class, the greater is likely

[11] *See* Joseph A. Kahl, *The American Class Structure* (New York: Rinehart and Co., 1957), pp. 8-9.

[12] *Ibid.*, p. 11.

[13] *See* Robert Dubin, *The World of Work* (Englewood Cliffs, N.J.: Prentice-Hall, 1958), pp. 37-39.

[14] *See* National Opinion Research Center, "Jobs and Occupations: A Popular Evaluation," *Opinion News,* **9:**3-13, September 1, 1947.

*Among the "New Men" of status and power in Western society is the scientist.*

to be the class consciousness of the members of the class. Should the position of the class be challenged in any way, identification and class consciousness would tend to be strengthened by the challenge. The greater the difference between classes, the more marked is likely to be the consciousness of one or more of the classes. In open-class structures, the consciousness of class may not be as great as in class systems where change from one class to another is difficult and the exception rather than the rule.

Kahl identifies five major social classes and the value orientation of each of these classes as follows: [15]

| Class | Value Orientation |
|---|---|
| Upper class | Graceful living |
| Upper middle | Career |
| Lower middle | Respectability |
| Working class | Getting by |
| Lower class | Apathy |

In identifying the major values around which the above classes are oriented, Kahl also identifies the five major classes which he thinks exist in the United States. Some students of class do not like the distinction "working" class and consider it a hazy differentiation.

[15] *See* Joseph A. Kahl, *op. cit.,* pp. 184-220, for an excellent discussion of the value systems around which each social class is organized.

## CLASS PROFILES IN AMERICA

Warner, in Yankee City, identified six social classes.[16] Each may be briefly characterized as follows:

1. *The upper-upper class,* making up 1.4 per cent of the total population. This class was made up of the oldest New England families, though not always the wealthiest ones. Their wealth nevertheless had been in the family for more than one generation. There was a feeling of family lineage, and its importance in this class and the value orientation of the family often revolved around this lineage. This class favored the private preparatory schools and the private colleges over the public ones for the schooling of their children. The Episcopal and Unitarian churches were firm choices for church membership. These people lived in big houses in the best residential areas.

2. *The lower-upper class* made up 1.6 per cent of the population. On the average, this group was wealthier than the upper-uppers but the wealth was newer and less of it had been inherited. About half of this class was native to Yankee City and only 1 per cent had been born outside the United States. About 80 per cent of the employment from this group was in professional and proprietory occupations. Wholesale and retail managers were represented in this class, as was also manufacturing, especially shoe and silverware manufacturing. This class lived in large and medium-sized houses in the areas where the upper-upper class lived. In manners this class was not so polished and sophisticated as the upper-uppers. Their feeling of family lineage was also less pronounced. Like the upper-uppers, they sent their children to private preparatory schools and private colleges. Only four students from this class were in the public high schools.

3. *The upper-middle class,* comprising 10.0 per cent of the population. Family lineage for the most part was unimportant to this class, although 83 per cent were Yankees, and 58 per cent had been born in Yankee City. Men who had been only moderately successful in business and a few highly skilled workers were found in this class. Wholesale and retail businesses were well represented in the class. Houses were of medium size and value and were located outside the areas where the two upper classes lived. The favored church denominations were the Baptist, Congregationalist, and Christian Science. Most children attended the public high schools.

4. *The lower-middle class,* constituting 28.4 per cent of the population. This class was made up chiefly of minor business men, school teachers, foremen in industry, clerks in retail establishments, and skilled and semiskilled workers. Many ethnics were found in this class, among them Irish, French Canadians, and Jews. Sixty-seven per cent were Yankees by birth and tradition. The Congregational and Episcopal churches were favored, and many were fundamentalists in viewpoint. They were ardent churchgoers, joiners of fraternal lodges, and strong participants in patriotic organizations.

5. *The upper-lower class,* making up 33.0 per cent of the population. This class contained the smallest percentage of Yankees of any class: 38 per cent. Of the ethnic groups "about one half of the Irish and Armenians, between 40 and 50 per cent of the Jews, French Canadians, and Italians, about one-third of the Greeks, one-fourth of the Russians, and one-tenth of the Poles are in this class."[17] The employment from this class was largely in shoe manufacturing, retail trade, transportation, and the building trades. This class made up a solid respectable laboring class in Yankee City. More than half of this class lived in small houses, and 42 per cent of the houses were in poor physical condition. The Roman Catholic population in Yankee City was drawn largely

[16] The descriptions are based on W. Lloyd Warner and Paul S. Lunt, *The Social Life of a Modern Community* (New Haven: Yale University Press, 1941), pp. 422-50.

[17] *Ibid.,* p. 444.

from this class. Protestant representation was low except for Methodists.

6. *The lower-lower class* made up 25.6 per cent of the population. This class had the highest percentage of children of any of the social classes and married earlier than in any other social classes. It contained all the Negroes, nine-tenths of the Poles, and seven-tenths of the Russians in Yankee City. Seventy per cent of this class were born in the United States, and 45 per cent in or near Yankee City. The semiskilled and unskilled workers and those on public relief comprised the bulk of this category. Only 6 per cent owned their homes, and a substantial number worked at part-time jobs. More children from this class went to work before they were sixteen than from any other class. On the whole, the Episcopal, Unitarian, and Congregational churches were avoided in favor of Presbyterian, Congregational, Methodist, and Catholic faiths.

In his Yankee City studies, Warner found a fairly clear distinction between all classes except the lower-middle and the upper-lower classes, where the distinctions were somewhat blurred.

In a later interpretation of the Yankee City class hierarchy (Fig. 24), Warner indicates that the three upper classes represent the class levels above the common man, the lower-middle and the upper-lower classes represent

the common man, whereas the lower-lower class is below the level of the common man.

In general, we have indicated the dimensions of class, such as occupation, style of life, value orientation, style of house, and place of residence. Some additional factors in the

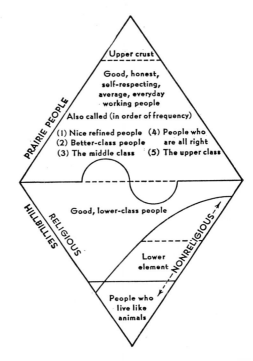

FIG. 25. THE CLASS STRUCTURE OF PLAINVILLE, AN OZARK COMMUNITY

SOURCE: James West, *Plainville, U.S.A.* (New York: Columbia University Press, 1945). p. 117.

structuring of a class profile are indicated in Figure 25. Place of residence, style of life, and religion versus nonreligion were important in the class structure of Plainville.[18]

We have already indicated earlier in the text some of the ways in which the class structure of a biracial community may be depicted. Figure 26 shows the resulting class profile when the same index of status characteristics

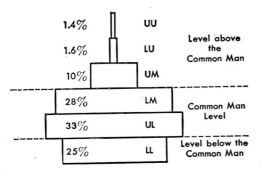

FIG. 24. THE SOCIAL CLASS HIERARCHY OF YANKEE CITY

SOURCE: W. Lloyd Warner, *American Life: Dream and Reality* (Chicago: University of Chicago Press, 1953). Reproduced by permission of the University of Chicago Press.

[18] James West, *Plainville U.S.A.* (New York: Columbia University Press, 1945). *See also* John Useem, Pierre Tangent, and Ruth Useem, "Stratification in a Prairie Town," *American Sociological Review,* 7:331-92, 1942.

is applied to the Negro and white populations of a Southern town. The index includes occupation, source of income, house type, dwelling area, and education. One observes from Figure 26 that the white race distributes itself pretty well along a curve of normal economic distribution, whereas the Negro part of the curve skews toward the lower economic groups.

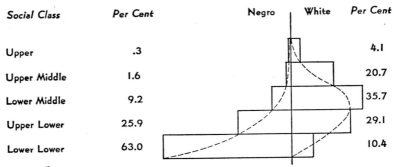

| Social Class | Per Cent | | | Per Cent |
|---|---|---|---|---|
| | | Negro | White | |
| Upper | .3 | | | 4.1 |
| Upper Middle | 1.6 | | | 20.7 |
| Lower Middle | 9.2 | | | 35.7 |
| Upper Lower | 25.9 | | | 29.1 |
| Lower Lower | 63.0 | | | 10.4 |

FIG. 26. CLASS PROFILE OF GEORGIA TOWN
Here the same index of status characteristics is applied to two racial elements in a biracial community.

SOURCE: Mozell C. Hill and Bevode C. McCall, "Social Stratification in Georgia Town," *American Sociological Review,* 15 (December, 1950), 721-29.

### THE FUNCTIONING OF CLASSES

If social classes did not influence people, then there would be no great need to study them other than as intellectual exercises. The facts are, though, that they are social systems, made up of smaller subsystems, especially groups which influence people materially. One inherits a social class just the same as he inherits a family. This class reflects certain attitudes and value systems.

1. *Social classes influence one's life chances.* The chances of being born and living through the first year of life are influenced by class. Birth rates and the mortality and morbidity rates are higher among the lower classes than among the upper classes. Expectation of life at birth is greater for whites than nonwhites and greater for higher economic than lower economic classes.[19] Education is a life chance, yet dropouts are highest among the lower classes. The hope of going to college may not be in the life plans of any considerable proportion of the lower classes, but it is part of the normal expectation of upper social classes.

2. *Social classes influence our early socialization.* The learning of a culture is influenced by social class. The early feeding and training procedures employed by families are related to class. Middle-class parents are more exacting in feeding, cleanliness, and personal hygiene training than lower-class parents are. Lower-class mothers are more apt to breastfeed their infants than middle- and upper-class mothers. Feeding schedules are less likely to be rigidly adhered to by lower-class mothers. Child-training responsibilities in upper-class families are likely to be left to servants. Play is much more likely to be supervised, and hours of sleep, rest, and play are more likely to be regulated among middle- and upper-class families.[20] How these different routines affect personality development later in life, we do not know.

3. *Social classes influence the organization*

[19] *See* Reinhard Bendix and Seymour Martin Lipset, *Class, Status and Power* (Glencoe, Ill.: Free Press, 1953), pp. 281-92.

[20] *See* Allison Davis, *Social-Class Influences upon Learning* (Cambridge, Mass.: Harvard University Press, 1951). *See also* Martha C. Ericson, "Child Rearing and Social Status," *American Journal of Sociology,* 52:190-92, 1946-47.

*of society.* The class system defines somewhat vaguely the various status grades or layers in a society, thus dividing the population into several classes, each one more or less recognizable.

Within the framework of the class structure the class system defines in a general way the relationship of the members of one class to the members of another class. A good example of this is found in the South where a pretty well-defined system of etiquette of Negrowhite relations is reflected by the class system. Historically, this system was based upon slavery and segregation. Even as late as 1896 the Supreme Court upheld the "separate but equal" principle. The particular case (*Plessy* v. *Ferguson*, May 18, 1896, 163 U.S. 537 [1896]) involved the use of interstate transportation facilities, but the "separate but equal" principle was generally applied to education, medical and health services, and recreation facilities.[21] Part of the system of race relations developed in the biracial culture of the South involves not only differentials and segregation in the provision and use of facilities, but also the white race's use of symbols of inferiority, such as hat tipping of Negroes to whites, or the requirement that Negroes use the back door when reporting to the homes of whites. Covenants, deed restrictions, and sometimes zoning restrictions, as well as social pressures, were used to keep Negroes in segregated areas. Along with the Negro, who had a more defined lower-class position than the whites, were the poor whites of the South, who, in the class status, were just above the Negroes but whose opportunities were frequently not so good as those of the Negro. Especially was this true in plantation farming, where Negroes were preferred as laborers over the poor whites.[22]

After World War II the legal ax of the Supreme Court began to fall pretty hard and pretty steadily upon segregation in race relations and its attendant discriminations. Racial restrictions in zoning were declared unconstitutional. Segregation in interstate bus and railway transportation was declared unconstitutional for some time before it disappeared. The use of public funds to provide segregated facilities for recreation—like parks and swimming pools—was held to be unconstitutional. The Supreme Court's declaration that a "separate but equal" facility for the education of Negroes at the college level, in this case a segregated college of law, shook the halls of higher learning in the South, but it was the decision of the court that segregation in the public schools was unconstitutional that brought the critical issue of caste and class to the attention of the American people. The Supreme Court's decisions in *Brown* v. *Board of Education,* 347 U.S. 483 (1954), 349 U.S. 294 (1955) and *Bolling* v. *Sharpe,* 347 U.S. 497 (1954) invalidated century-old state and federal statutes providing for racially segregated schools. The decisions also set aside the "separate but equal" doctrine deemed settled for 60 years by the case of *Plessy* v. *Ferguson,* 163 U.S. 537 (1896). Decisions of the Supreme Court have now been tempered to some degree to permit schools of the South to begin desegregation on a gradual basis.[23]

It is apparent that in the system of social organization established by the class system in the United States there are majority and minority elements as well as a complex of majority and minority relations. Whites constitute the majority racial element and the American Negro and American Indian the largest racial minority elements. Of course, each minority element, like the majority element, has its own subclasses.

[21] *See* Rayford W. Logan, *The Negro in the United States* (New York: D. Van Nostrand Co., 1957), and C. Vann Woodward, *The Strange Career of Jim Crow* (New York: Oxford University Press, 1955).

[22] *See* Shields McIlwaine, *The Southern Poor White: From Lubberland to Tobacco Road* (Norman, Okla.: University of Oklahoma Press, 1939).

[23] Since the problem of segregation in education belongs to the area of social problems rather than to an introductory course, we will not treat the problem in more detail at this point. The interested student should explore sources like the following: "Segregation in the Public Schools," *Journal of Public Law* (Emory University Law School), Vol. 3, Spring, 1953.

The majority-minority class system specifies and defines the kinds of relationships that are permitted with minority groups. Often the circumstances under which such relationships are permitted are defined. For instance, minority and majority class members may stand together in an audience in some communities but may not sit together in the same audience in other communities. They may go to the same park but may not be permitted to swim together. Back of the majority-minority systems are also a complex set of reasons as to why one element is superior to another, that is, why one element has a majority status and another a minority status. Class lines become a basis for prejudice and discrimination.[24]

The illustrations we have drawn of how class influences the organization of society are American examples. Other societies may show a different set of influences.

4. *Social classes influence role expectations and role projections.* The expectation that one's daughter or son will complete high school and go on to college is "much more in the cards" for the middle- and upper-class families. In the lower class the expectation is more that one will get married and go to work,

or at least go to work when one leaves high school, if one even manages to complete high school. In general, role development and fulfillment are more equally supervised and guided in middle- and upper-class families than in lower-class families. We would expect parental role projections to be stronger in the upper classes. The expectation placed upon chastity, especially of females, seems to be a stronger upper- and middle-class characteristic than a lower-class one. There is a relation between sex behavior and social class, both among youth and adults.

5. *Social classes influence social mobility.* The chances of one's moving out of a class stratum in America are very good, but there are class limitations. If one is a Negro and moves from a low-class tenant farm class into a skilled labor position in a tool machinery factory in Ohio, there still may be limits to his class mobility because he is Negro.

Kahl indicates that some 67 per cent of the labor force was mobile in 1950 with respect to their fathers.[25] The total movement upward in occupational mobility, as calculated in 1950, was much greater than the movement down, as indicated in Table 26.

As Table 26 shows, three-fourths of the professional group had moved up above their

24 *See* Pierre L. Van Den Berghe, "The Dynamics of Racial Prejudice: An Ideal Type Dichotomy," *Social Forces*, 37:138-41, December, 1958.

25 Kahl, *op. cit.*, p. 261.

*Table 26*

UPWARD AND DOWNWARD MOBILITY IN OCCUPATIONS, 1950

| Socio-Economic Group | Per Cent Who Have: | | | |
|---|---|---|---|---|
| | *Moved Up* | *Moved Down* | *Remained* | *Total* |
| Professional persons | 77 | — | 23 | 100 |
| Proprietors, managers and officials, non-farm | 65 | 4 | 31 | 100 |
| Clerks, salespeople, and kindred | 53 | 32 | 15 | 100 |
| Skilled workers and foremen | 56 | 14 | 30 | 100 |
| Semiskilled workers | 43 | 38 | 19 | 100 |
| Farmers and farm laborers | 3 | 13 | 84 | 100 |
| Unskilled workers, nonfarm | — | 73 | 27 | 100 |

Source: Joseph A. Kahl, *The American Class Structure* (New York: Rinehart and Co., 1957), p. 261.

fathers in occupational mobility. Few had fallen in comparison, whereas 23 per cent remained in the occupational class of their fathers. In the managerial and proprietorial classes, 65 per cent had moved up above the occupational levels of their fathers, only 4 per cent had moved down, and 31 per cent remained. Of the farmers and farm laborers, only 3 per cent had moved up above their fathers, 13 per cent had moved down, and 84 per cent had remained. Among the nonskilled most had moved down from the occupational classes of their fathers or had remained at their father's occupational level. The relationship here between the occupational class to which one's father belongs and occupational mobility is clear.

One of the greatest factors in social mobility is education. For example, a cotton farmer mortgages his farm to send his son to medical school, an actual case. The son becomes a leading physician in a Texas city, almost immediately lifting himself from the low-class hierarchy of his parents into an upper-middle-class hierarchy.[26]

6. *Value orientation is influenced by class.* In the previous discussion we have had some indication of the way in which social class attitudes and value systems influence behavior. Value systems among lower economic classes are more related to meeting the necessities of life than the value systems of upper classes are. If upper classes have money, and the chances are good that they will have, the necessities of life are not a problem and time can be spent in pursuing values of nonsubsistence nature.

Centers found more political conservation among middle classes than among working classes. His findings are shown in Table 27.

On the whole, the lower social classes favor more government control of business and more participation by the government in welfare activities than the upper classes do. Religious fundamentalism and traditionalism are stronger among the lower classes. Because of

[26] On education and mobility, *see* Kahl, *op. cit.*, pp. 276-98.

*Table 27*

POLITICAL CONSERVATISM AND RADICALISM AMONG SOCIAL CLASSES

| Ideology | Middle Class (per cent) | Working Class (per cent) |
|---|---|---|
| Ultra-conservative | 35 | 12 |
| Conservative | 33 | 23 |
| Intermediate | 21 | 33 |
| Radical | 7 | 19 |
| Ultra-radical | 4 | 13 |

Source: Adapted from Richard Centers, *The Psychology of Social Classes* (Princeton, N.J.: Princeton University Press, 1949), p. 120.

the more limited education of lower classes, their perspective is more restricted to their immediate environment and affairs. Upper classes may be better read, better traveled, and more cosmopolitan in interests. In biracial cultures lower classes are more apt to be rabid on race relations and to be participants in race violence than are the middle and upper classes. Consistency in attitudes, however, does not always follow class lines.[27]

7. *Social class influences social pathology.* Most social pathology rates are related to class lines. For instance, juvenile and adult delinquency rates are higher among the lower social classes.[28] This does not mean that delinquency is limited to such classes, but simply that higher rates persist. Dependency rates of course follow class lines. There is a relationship between mental illness and psychiatric disorders and class. The lower the class, the greater the proportion of mental patients in the population. The kind of mental disease varies also with social class.[29]

[27] For more on this topic, *see* Arthur Kornhauser, "Public Opinion and Social Class," *America:1 Journal of Sociology,* 55:333-35, January, 1950.

[28] F. Ivan Nye, James F. Short, Jr., and Virgil J. Olson, "Socioeconomic Status and Delinquent Behavior," *The American Journal of Sociology,* 63:381-89, January, 1958.

[29] For an excellent study of the relation of social class to mental disorders, *see* August B. Hollingshead and Frederick G. Redlich, *Social Class and Mental Illness* (New York: John Wiley and Sons, 1958).

## *TRENDS TOWARD GREATER CLASS FLEXIBILITY AND STABILITY*

There are those who feel that social class as a social system is declining in importance. Illustrative of this trend of thinking is one author who feels that social class as a substantive, tangible, functional, recognizable relationship is declining in importance.[30] The same author points out the decline of the political unity of class, the decline of class-limited education, and the decline of the conception and prevalence of the "gentleman" characteristic of the upper class of England and parts of the United States. He feels that status seeking has supplanted class mobility and that we live in a society governed by status and not by class values and lines. He says:

The very forces which dissolved the class lines of pre-industrial society acted, in the long run, to prevent any new classes from becoming fixed. National democracy, economic and social pluralism, ethical individualism, and an ever-widening educational front joined to create new patterns of social power and status and make class obsolete in constantly widening sectors of Western society.[31]

We must point out that much status seeking is class related, in that the person seeking status often attempts to emulate or be accepted in the social strata above the one in which he belongs.

There is no doubt but that in American society there are changes contributing to class flexibility. Some of these are:

1. The growth of cities with their diverse economic opportunities, and the loss of class-related kindred groups.

2. The growing accessibility and adequacy of education, especially at the elementary and secondary levels.

3. The great growth in the professional, skilled, and semiskilled labor categories, nominally middle class.

4. The decline of symbols of caste and low-class positions in our society, such as segregation, discrimination, and rules of etiquette which were related to these positions.

5. An increase in communication between classes, giving each more knowledge of the other's conditions of life.

These trends at least account for some of the remarkable amount of class flexibility present in our society.

There are also trends toward class stability in our culture. The attempts to change patterns of segregation and discrimination have met a wave of legal and social resistance in many American communities. In spite of the availability of elementary and high school education, college, and especially professional education, is class selective even though there is a great growth in the number of fellowships and scholarships available and the fact that graduate training is heavily subsidized. The increase in specialization and division of labor make for mobility from one social class layer to another. The same may be true in growing complex bureaucratic organizations employing white-collar workers. It has been shown that more than 40 per cent of the sons of unskilled workers follow in their fathers' footsteps, that is, they accept unskilled jobs. The growth of large corporations and combines, while opening many jobs in these corporations, makes individual ownership extremely difficult. The grocery business is a good illustration. The chances of the small independent grocer competing with the large chains is remote in most communities. The frontier in land and other natural resources, which once existed, favored social mobility. For the most part these frontiers no longer exist. Even commercialization of agriculture makes it difficult for the family-sized farm to exist and compete. Inflation of the 1950's may have been a factor in stabilizing classes. While earnings reached unprecedented peaks for most labor and professional groups, increased costs of living and of operating busi-

[30] Robert A. Nisbet, "The Decline and Fall of Social Class," *The Pacific Sociological Review,* 2:11-17, Spring, 1959.

[31] *Ibid.,* p. 14.

nesses and farms and professional offices reduced much of the flexibility and social mobility that might have developed from the increased earnings and the unprecedented economic activity and cultural diffusion of the 1950's.

## SUMMARY

Social classes are status groupings which exist in all societies, although they are more highly developed in the more complex cultures. Societies in which the social chances are made equal, and in which there is ease of mobility from one social class to another, are called open-class societies. Societies in which social mobility is very difficult are often called closed-class societies. The best examples of closed-class systems are found in societies in which there are caste systems. Caste systems make for rigid class structures.

There are basically two methods of determining classes: self-rating and rating by others. An attempt toward objectivity in rating is partially achieved by the preparation of indices of status characteristics. These are based upon the use of such standards as dwelling area, house type, occupation, income, and source of income.

While the characteristics of class or the dimensions of class vary from community to community, classes are usually delineated from one another on the basis of prestige, occupation, possessions, behavior, class consciousness, and value orientation. In one community a single dimension may be stronger than in another. For instance, class consciousness is conspicuously absent in some communities and conspicuously present in others.

When people are asked to rate themselves, they are likely to place themselves strongly in middle-class groupings. Class profile studies in communities usually reveal three, five, and sometimes six classes. The profiles will vary greatly from community to community in composition and shape. The most complicated profiles to show are those of biracial communities where there are strong "caste" or class line relationships between the two races.

Social classes are social systems. Being social systems they are dynamic in the way that they influence us. They influence our life chances, our early socialization, the organization of society, and the system of majority-minority relations, role expectations and role projections, social mobility, and the value systems of individuals.

There are a number of trends toward greater class flexibility in American society. These relate to the growth of cities with their many opportunities, the growing accessibility of education, the great increase in professional and skilled occupations, and the decline of the symbols of caste and low-class positions in our society. Counter to these trends are those toward greater class stability. Among these are the decline of the American frontier, the increase in occupational skills and specializations, the growth of large corporations, and increases in the cost of college and professional education, making it class selective.

THINGS TO DO AND TO DISCUSS

1. To what extent is open-class ideology achieved in your community?
2. What do you understand to be the main distinctions between open-class structure and rigid class structure?
3. How may social classes be delineated in a community?
4. On what bases would you differentiate the social classes in your community?
5. In terms of the social classes in your own community, evaluate Kahl's dimensions of class. Which ones are pertinent and which ones are not?

6.  Develop a scale for measurement of occupational prestige. Give it to a sample of students and report the results.
7.  What are class profiles? How many classes were found in Yankee City? Characterize the class extremes in Yankee City.
8.  How do social classes influence social organization?
9.  What are some of the more direct personal influences of class?
10. What are the important trends toward stability of social classes in the United States? What are major trends toward class flexibility? In the trend race which group is winning?

FOR FURTHER STUDY

BARBER, BERNARD. *Social Stratification: A Comparative Analysis of Structures and Process*. New York: Harcourt, Brace and Co., 1957. An excellent analysis of social stratification.

BECKER, GARY S. *The Economics of Discrimination*. Chicago: University of Chicago Press, 1957. A good discussion of the economic bases and costs of discrimination.

BENDIX, RICHARD, and LIPSET, SEYMOUR MARTIN. *Class, Status and Power: A Reader in Social Stratification*. Glencoe, Ill.: Free Press, 1953. Probably the best source book on social stratification.

BLOCH, CHARLES J. *States' Rights—The Law of the Land*. Atlanta, Ga.: Harrison Co., 1958. The theory of states' rights as argued by the opponents of desegregation.

BUCKLEY, WALTER. "Social Stratification and the Functional Theory of Social Differentiation," *American Sociological Review*, 23, No. 4:369-75, August, 1958. A careful analysis of most of the theories of social stratification and social differentiation.

CENTERS, RICHARD. *The Psychology of Social Classes*. Princeton, N.J.: Princeton University Press, 1949. How Americans rate themselves by classes and the basis for their ratings.

COLE, G. D. H. *Studies in Class Structure*. London: Routledge and Kegan Paul, 1955. Especially good materials on British class structure.

DAHRENDORF, ROLF. *Class and Class Conflict in Industrial Society*. Stanford, Cal.: Stanford University Press, 1959. Examination of class conflict and bases for it.

DAVIS, KINGSLEY. *Human Society*. New York: The Macmillan Co., 1949. Good chapter on caste, class, and stratification.

DOLLARD, JOHN. *Caste and Class in a Southern Town*. New Haven: Yale University Press, 1937. A good community study of the etiquette of caste and class relations in a southern community.

DUBIN, ROBERT. *The World of Work*. Englewood Cliffs, N.J.: Prentice-Hall, 1958. Considerable data on occupational status and mobility.

FLOOD, J. E.; HALSEY, A. H.; and MARTIN, F. M. *Social Class and Educational Opportunity*. London: William Heinemann, 1956. How class influences educational opportunity, especially in Great Britain.

FRAZIER, E. FRANKLIN. *Black Bourgeoise: The Rise of a New Middle Class in the United States*. Glencoe, Ill.: Free Press, 1957.

GLASS, D. V. (ed.). *Social Mobility in Great Britain*. Glencoe, Ill.: Free Press, 1954. One of the better things on mobility trends in Great Britain.

GROSS, EDWARD. *Work and Society*. New York: Thomas Y. Crowell Co., 1958. Some good things on class and occupation and occupational mobility.

HOLLINGSHEAD, A. B. *Elmtown's Youth: The Impact of Social Classes on Adolescents*. New York: John Wiley and Sons, 1949. A particularly fine piece of work showing how social class influences the behavior of youth in a community.

HOLLINGSHEAD, A. B., and REDLICH, FREDERICK C. *Social Class and Mental Illness*. New York: John Wiley and Sons, 1958. Empirical study of the relationship between social class and mental illness.

HURVITZ, NATHAN. "Sources of Middle-Class Values of American Jews," *Social Forces,* **37**:117-23, December, 1958. Where middle-class American Jews derive their value systems.

KAHL, JOSEPH A. *The American Class Structure*. New York: Rinehart and Co., 1957. Carefully done study of the most important aspects of American class structure.

KOHN, MELVIN L. "Social Class and Parental Values," *The American Journal of Sociology,* **64**:337-51, January, 1959. An empirical study showing how working class values center around qualities that assure respectability and middle-class values around internalized standards of conduct.

MARTINDALE, DON. *American Social Structure*. New York: Appleton-Century-Crofts, 1959. Chapter XVI is devoted to "The Principles of Social Stratification," and Chapter XVII to "The Status Community in the United States."

MILLS, C. WRIGHT. *White Collar*. New York: Oxford University Press, 1951. Careful analysis of the American middle class in both its historical and contemporary aspects.

———. *The Power Elite*. New York: Oxford University Press, 1956. An unmasking of popular illusions about democratic checks on power.

PACKARD, VANCE. *The Status Seekers*. New York: David McKay Co., 1959. A best seller on the quest for status in America and means of achieving it.

REISSMAN, LEONARD. *Class in American Society*. Glencoe, Ill.: Free Press, 1959. A very good statement of the phenomena of social class and stratification in the United States.

ROGOFF, NATALIE. *Recent Trends in Occupational Mobility*. Glencoe, Ill.: Free Press, 1953. Occupational mobility in American society in recent years.

WARNER, W. LLOYD. *Social Class in America*. Chicago: Science Research Associates, 1949. How class structure may be examined.

———. "The Study of Social Stratification," *Review of Sociology: Analysis of a Decade,* ed. Joseph B. Gittler. New York: John Wiley and Sons, 1957. Rather careful resume of stratification research in the United States.

WARNER, W. LLOYD, and LUNT, PAUL S. *The Status System of a Modern Community*. New Haven: Yale University Press, 1942. One of the pioneer studies of community class structure in America.

# 16. ECOLOGICAL PATTERNING

IN THE OPENING CHAPTER of this book we indicated that each social system has a habitat which acts as a locus for its functioning. The people making up the unit seek not only to make adjustments within the system but also to the habitat of the system. For instance, the number of people in the social system and the separation of one system from another, such as the separation of one family from another, will be influenced by the surroundings—the food supply, the topography, the climate, and perhaps altitude factors.

## THE FIELD OF ECOLOGY

All living creatures seek to make adjustments to their surroundings. Squirrels will migrate with the supply of nuts and other available food. During an extended period of dry weather the leaves of a corn plant will curl to reduce the surface area exposed to the hot sun. The plant growing away from the sun- light will grow in the direction of the light. In preliterate societies, in order for individuals to survive they had to have a definite knowledge of their habitats.

*The systematic study of the adjustment of living things to their habitat constitutes the field of ecology.* Odum defines ecology as "the study of the structure and temporal processes of populations, communities, and other ecological systems, and of the interrelations of individuals composing these units." [1] The word "ecology" was apparently first used by the German biologist Ernst Haeckel in 1869. The term itself is derived from the Greek word *"oikos,"* meaning "house" or "place to live." There are three main fields of ecology: animal, plant, and human, or population. Human ecology is a rather recent field, and a limited number of books have been developed in this field to date.[2] Human ecology is a part of sociology, whereas animal and plant ecology is a division of the biological sciences.

An important part of the science of ecology is the pattern of distribution and relationships that living creatures develop as they scatter themselves over the surface of the earth. Human settlements are related to ecological factors of rainfall, temperature, and other natural resources. It is not an accident that urban communities develop first along rivers and coast lines and that most of the great cities of the world are found in zones where temperatures range between 45° F. and 70° F. and rainfall ranges from 20 to 60 inches.

On the Navajo reservation in Arizona and New Mexico there are few natural communities, although there are trading posts. One of the reasons for this is that, on the nonirrigated lands, it requires 23 acres of land to graze one sheep. The Navajo family, therefore, must live in the middle of a large area if it owns a hundred sheep and a few horses. Among the Pekangekum Ojibwa Indians in northwestern Ontario, where there is subsistence hunting and fishing and trapping for furs, there are about 12 square miles of poorly drained forest and muskeg per person. In contrast, the writer has been told of an intensively cultivated and irrigated region of Israel which contains 1,000 acres, yet furnishes a living for 25,000 people. Manhattan Island during the day is one of the most densely populated areas in the United States. This is partly because of the strong supporting rock structure of the island, plus its excellent port facilities.

Within the same city one may find a Negro belt, a Chinatown, a section inhabited largely by Puerto Ricans, and another by Italians. At one point there may be a concentration of retail stores, at another several wholesale houses, and at another a medical arts center with attendant hospital and other service facilities near by. In residential districts people may pretty well separate themselves into areas by income grades or classes. These areas are the result of accommodation and the ecological processes. They are distinctive and defined and have cultural characteristics of their own. Such areas are called *natural areas*. They are so called because they developed naturally and are not the product of zoning or land-use plans.

## ECOLOGICAL RELATIONSHIPS

Ecological patterning, or the presence of natural areas, does not develop by accident. This development is an answer to the quest of living organisms for adjustment. Animals will seek to locate where temperature, rainfall, and food factors are adequate. People will try to locate, all things being equal, in those parts of a community where they think they can make the best possible adjustment if there are no obstacles in the way. Two biological relationships found in nature influence their patterns of settlement and their groupings: *symbiosis* and *commensalism*. Where people of unlike race, culture, and interests exist to-

[1] Eugene P. Odum, *Fundamentals of Ecology* (Philadelphia: W. B. Saunders Co., 1953), p. 4.

[2] The development of this field has been traced in two excellent books in human ecology: James A. Quinn, *Human Ecology* (Englewood Cliffs, N.J.: Prentice-Hall, 1958), and Amos H. Hawley, *Human Ecology* (New York: Ronald Press, 1950).

gether in an area and work together for certain mutual ends, the relationship is called *symbiosis*. Some examples will suffice. Management and labor working together in the same plant indicates a symbiotic relationship. In a retail section of a downtown business district may be found theaters, restaurants, retail stores, hotels, and the offices of certain professional people. Each may contribute to the success and economic well being of the other. This is done in a relationship which is symbiotic, or mutually helpful. Doctors of medicine may house themselves in a medical arts building, near hospitals and drugstores, in order to be near each other for purposes of consultation, and near other resources which they and their patients may need.

Another ecological relationship is called *commensalism* and means literally "eating at the same table." Races, nationality, and interest groups that are physically and functionally alike may occupy the same area and live and work together. In this type of relationship one grouping may benefit more by the relationship than another grouping. The race or nationality benefiting is the commensal. People of a like culture may settle in the same area because they feel that they are similar and may

aid each other. All things considered, members of a race tend to seek out members of the same race and locate near them. This is another reason for people clustering into natural areas. Again these patterns of settlement are in response to the quest for adjustment.

Thus far we have drawn upon the fields of plant and animal ecology for illustrations of ecological relationships. As Odum points out, in human ecology—

. . . we must go beyond the principles of general ecology because human society has served very important characteristics which make the human population unit quantitatively, if not qualitatively, different from other populations. In the first place, man's flexibility in behavior and his ability to control his surroundings are greater than those of other organisms. In the second place, man develops culture which, except to a very rudimentary degree, is not a factor in any other species.[3]

A distinguishing characteristic of human groupings over plant and animal groupings is the degree of dominance which man is capable of exerting. Although not completely dominant, his intelligence and his culture building power free him from domination by his environment more than is true of plants and animals.

## SOME ASPECTS OF ECOLOGICAL PATTERNING

One aspect of ecological adjustment is related to the size of communities. In hunting and fishing cultures, unless the food supply is abundant the settlements are likely to be small, usually not more than 50 families. If one culture makes contact with another culture and is able to increase its food supply through barter or trade, then the farmers may increase the size of their settlements. If new food species are introduced by man, or wild species are domesticated, or if new methods of production of food supplies are developed, such as irrigation agriculture or dry land

farming, the size of settlements, indeed, the entire human population may increase.[4]

The time comes when settlements cannot grow purely on the basis of an adequate food supply. Culture enters the picture in other ways. There must be sanitation. There must be work for people to do which they can exchange for food. The people must be able to trade whatever goods they have in surplus.

Another aspect of ecology to which we have

---

[3] Odum, *op. cit.*, p. 344.

[4] For a good study of relationship between the flora and fauna of an area and its human population and social systems, *see* Laura Thompson, "The Relations of Men, Animals and Plants in an Island Community (Fiji)," *American Anthropologist*, 51:253-67, April-June. 1949.

*United Press International Photo*

*Areas of High and Low Density. Each is a response to many natural and cultural factors. Lebanon, Kansas, above, and Wilmington, Delaware, below.*
*Brooks Studio, Wilmington, Del.*

*Table 28*

DENSITY OF POPULATION UNDER DIFFERENT KINDS OF ECONOMIES

| Per Square Mile Density | Type of Economy |
|---|---|
| 0-8 | Hunting and fishing |
| 8-26 | Grazing and forestry |
| 26-64 | The beginnings of agriculture |
| 64-192 | Agriculture |
| 192-256 | Beginnings of industry |
| 256-381 | Agriculture and industry |
| 381-512 | Industry predominates |
| 512-2,560 | Industrial towns or suburbs |
| 2,560-5,120 | Centers of small cities |
| 5,120-12,800 | Centers of moderate cities |
| 12,800-25,600 | Centers of large cities |

Source: H. Weichel, quoted in William E. Cole, *Urban Society* (Boston: Houghton Mifflin Co., 1958), p. 152.

already referred is *density*. After a study of many kinds of cultures, H. Weichel showed that hunting and fishing cultures might have had a density of more than eight persons per square mile. Grazing and forestry cultures might have densities up to 25 persons per square mile, whereas the centers of large cities might have up to 25,000 people per square mile (Table 28). Density depends upon many factors. Among these are the supporting power of the economy, the ratio of population to land, the size of structures upon the land, the standard of living of the people, and the capacity of the means of transportation for moving food in and out of an area.

The *grain* or *texture* of an area is another ecological characteristic. This is more than a matter of topographical features. It relates also to the size of structures in an area and to the size of farms and other functional features within an area. As one flies over Manhattan Island, one is impressed by the coarse grain of Manhattan. Close by is Brooklyn with a much finer grain.

A mill village of small houses will have a finer grain or texture than an estate area of large lots and dwellings. Cities with water

bodies and with many parks and playgrounds have surface textures different from those that have few open spaces.

Modern cities tend to have more functional differentiation than older cities. Residence areas are now separated from commercial, industrial, and institutional areas, whereas once they were pretty close together. This means that functionally speaking cities are more coarsely textured now than they were historically.

If one flies over the Nile Delta he finds the farms smaller, many of them under five acres, than in the Kansas wheat country. The scarcity of land in the Nile Delta in ratio to the population is a partial answer to the smallness of the farms. In Kansas the ratio of land to people in the rural farm area is large.

Another ecological characteristic is the *shape of a settlement.* Settlements in valleys

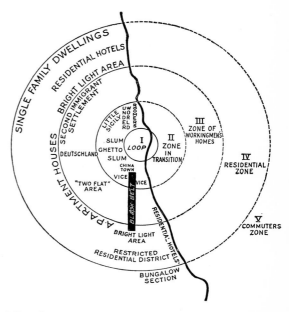

FIG. 27.   CONCENTRIC ZONES AND NATURAL AREAS IN THE GROWTH OF THE CITY OF CHICAGO

SOURCE: Robert E. Park, Ernest W. Burgess, and Roderick D. McKenzie, *The City* (Chicago: University of Chicago Press, 1925), p. 55.

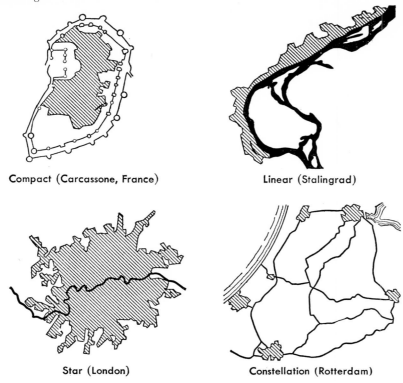

Compact (Carcassone, France)          Linear (Stalingrad)

Star (London)          Constellation (Rotterdam)

FIG. 28.  FOUR COMMON SHAPES OF CITIES

Geographic factors, size of boundaries, and transportation routes are perhaps the most important factors in determining the shapes of cities.

SOURCE: Kevin Lynch, "The Form of Cities," *Scientific American,* 190 (April, 1954), 54-63.

tend to follow the valley rather than flow across the hills, so that the settlement pattern becomes linear. Settlements along coasts or rivers likewise tend to be linear. This shows adjustment to topography which is an ecological feature.

Growth of cities in recent years tends to extend in the direction of transportation routes. This gives modern cities a characteristic star-shaped effect. With the building of interregional highways in this country, it is likely that urban growth along such highways will take on a linear pattern, at least the tentacles of growth of existing cities are likely to be extended. As we have already shown in the accompanying sketch of natural areas in Chi-

cago, cities before the days of rail and motor transportation grew by slow accretion outward from the center through a series of concentric rings (see Fig. 28). Growth patterns are now more by sectors and along major transportation routes. A commercial area may develop somewhere along the transportation route, usually on a highway. At some other point there will be a residential sector.

Another illustration of ecological patterning relates to the influences of environment upon the age composition of a population. Sunshine cities draw the elderly and the retired. The city draws the young adult and the middle-aged. The village frequently attracts the retired and the aged.

## THE ECOLOGICAL PROCESSES

Ecological patterning both in animal, plant, and human societies takes place through well-defined ecological processes. These again are the result of the attempt of living organisms to adjust themselves to their environment. In sociology we are interested largely in human ecological adjustments and the ecological processes involved in such adjustments.

### Centralization and concentration

Living creatures tend to centralize at locations which are favorable to them. A community of plant species may develop in a favorable location. On the desert or in the forest, colonies of animals may develop at spots where they can find food supply and compete with other animal species. Of course, man may interfere with this distribution.

Human settlements tend to develop in favorable locations, and people tend to gravitate to these settlements. After a while, as in the cities, the concentrated settlement may show great growth in density, as the table earlier in the chapter shows.

Legal and social pressures may force people to concentrate in certain areas of a city. For instance, zoning regulations may not permit a supermarket in a residential area but will require that it locate in a commercial zone. Social pressures may force a Negro population to remain in a certain section of a city. Restrictions may force a condition of overcrowding upon the area. The high cost of housing in desirable areas may force poor people to settle in slums, just as the cost of land may prohibit a wholesale warehouse on Main Street. Urbanization of population is itself a centralizing process. The development of shopping centers within a city brings about a polynucleolation of retail activities, which within itself is a centralizing tendency, although it may represent dispersal away from the downtown area of a city.

### Decentralization

The ecological process of decentralization is common in nature. Many plants have mechanisms for distributing their seeds over wider surfaces than they occupy. The seed pods of some plants burst. Some seeds, like those of the thistle, have appendages attached so that they float easily in the air. The seeds of many water-borne plants float upon the surface of the water and are dispersed in this way. Other seeds stick to the coats of animals and are dispersed. Animals, of course, are mobile and able to disperse themselves. Man is much more mobile because of his culture and has a greater opportunity for selecting the places where he will locate.

At the human level, when problems begin to develop out of centralization and concentration, the reverse process of decentralization, or dispersal, begins. We have spoken of suburbanization and fringe growth—a decentralizing movement—in the chapter on place groupings and in the one on urbanization and suburbanization. When the houses in an area begin to deteriorate and the area is not good for human habitation, there is likely to be a movement out of the area. Poorer and less discriminating families may move into the deteriorated area where rents are lower.

As congestion increases at the center of cities many firms may seek locations outside the central zones of the city. Rather than building new, larger stores in the central business districts, they may decentralize and build one or more branch stores in the suburbs. All over the country shopping centers are developing in suburban and fringe areas—an indication of decentralization. In England new towns are being built in an attempt to decentralize the population of London. Just as there is a decentralization of population and commercial enterprises, there is also a lesser decentralization of industries. Some industrial corporations have well-defined policies of expanding through the construction of branch plants, away from large centers of population, where the disadvantages of operation are less. In other words, such firms have developed a rather well-defined policy of industrial decentralization.

## Segregation

In the animal, plant, and human world segregated communities of plants, animals, and people tend to grow where conditions of life are favorable to their survival and development. Colonies of small animals may be found at one altitude where there is one set of food conditions, but not at another altitude where the food conditions are different. A lakeside may reveal one kind of segregated plant community, whereas a half mile away from the lake the fauna may be entirely different. People of low economic class may dwell in a slum area adjacent to a high-cost apartment area occupied by an upper, middle, or lower economic class. In rural areas the upper reaches of a mountainside may be farmed by the poorer farmers, whereas the wealthier classes occupy the bottom lands.

One great difference between plant and animal communities and human communities is that the former are made up of many species, whereas human communities are made up of one. Within human residential communities we have segregated units of population, such as races and nationalities and religious groupings. In addition to residences, the activities of people tend to pattern themselves in clusters. One area is a retail area, another wholesale, and another industrial.

Frequently people segregate or cluster by racial groups. In the cities of the South we find Negro clusters, whereas in the cities of the North we find well-defined "black belts" such as those in Detroit, St. Louis, Chicago, or New York City. In New York City, San Francisco, or Los Angeles there are Filipino and Spanish-American communities and Chinatowns in addition to segregated Caucasian and Negro groupings. Sometimes clusters of the same nationality or religious faiths are found in a city. Thus we may have Polish or Italian areas and Jewish settlements where the populations of these religious and ethnic groups are large.

Modern communities require segregation of economic activity. Thus we have segregated land-use areas given over to retail, wholesale, light industrial, or heavy industrial activities. In the professions there may be a medical arts center or a professional building for lawyers. In the case of land-use areas these are usually set up by city governing bodies. The economic use of the areas is confined to those enterprises which are permitted in such areas. For instance, a stockyard cannot be located in a retail district or a commercial garage in a plush residential area. With respect to churches and schools, cities are more lenient, permitting them in most land-use areas.

Why segregation? Part of the answer to this question lies in the quest for adjustment. As Professor Franklin Giddings of Columbia University pointed out some years ago, people appear to develop a feeling of "consciousness of kind" toward other people. This means that, all things being equal, one will seek out people of his own race, nationality, and culture with whom to associate and live. This is an example of commensalism. Perhaps this is done because people feel that they can compete and adjust best with people of their own kind.

Differences in land values may force segregation. Land along main streets in a city is expensive, too expensive, as a rule, to be used for either residential or industrial sites. Such lands are usually used for commercial retail sites. In rural regions the best farm lands are used for cash crops, whereas poorer lands are best adapted to forests or recreation. Lower economic groups will tend to gravitate to the areas of a city where housing is cheap. These areas will then tend to be segregated from the areas of better housing.

Legal restrictions and quasi-legal restrictions may force people into segregated areas.[5] Zoning restrictions are examples of legal restrictions; they will force people to use land-use zones for the purposes they are restricted to. In South African cities it is not unusual to find provisions in zoning made for each of three groups: native whites, native blacks, and Asiatics.

Deed restrictions, property owner compacts, and real estate codes may tend to force segregation. Both in the South and North it is common to find housing segregation and clauses in deeds restricting resale of real estate to members of the same race as the present owner. While restrictive covenants of this type have not stood up in the higher courts, they have the power of social pressure back of them. Segregation, therefore, may be of two types, voluntary and involuntary. We have said more about this in Chapter 14 on social stratification and its functioning.

*Invasion*

Invasion is in some respects the most spectacular ecological process. The movement of an unlike species, race, or activity into an area is invasion. Invasion is commonplace throughout nature. The home owner who has a good blue grass lawn may watch with some dismay the creeping crabgrass or Bermuda grass as it invades his lawn during the hot summer months. One species of animal may move out of an area as another species moves in.

A block occupied by one racial, nationality, or religious group may resort to legal measures and even physical conflict to keep out an invading group of unlike race, religion, or culture. No less emotional may be the opposition to a petition to rezone an area from residential to commercial in order to keep down commercial invasion of a residential area. A public university may invade a residential area because there is no other direction in which it can move. Through the use of the right of eminent domain, which is the power to condemn land for public use, the university may acquire, in spite of protest, the land it needs for expansion. In human ecology, invasion of unlike races, culture groups, or commercial interests into an area sets in motion a chain reaction of emotional responses that may result in anything from litigation to overt physical conflict.

Invasion may be the only way in which a "bottled up" population may expand. Areas must at times be changed from one type of land use to another. This requires an orderly process of change in land use. Space may be needed for expanded industries which again may require that areas be changed from agricultural and residential to industrial in order to let invasion take place.

*Succession*

The cycle of change through which an area may go in the replacement of one type of occupant or land use by another is called succession. A field may be cleared of trees, planted to crops, and after a while be abandoned to go back to trees. An urban area which at one time is commercial may become residential and then, under a slum clearance or urban renewal program, be changed back to commercial use. Under such programs land which at one time was used as a playground or athletic field, after several generations of residential use may be returned to playgrounds. Invasion and succession may proceed together, with invasion being the initial stage of the succession cycle.

In studying population movements away from the loop section of Chicago in the direction of the periphery of the city, Burgess has found that they formed a pattern of successive waves. He says:

[5] *See* Herman H. Long and Charles S. Johnson, *People vs. Property: Race Restrictive Covenants in Housing* (Nashville, Tenn.: Fisk University, 1947).

Succession as a process has been studied and its main course charted as (1) *invasion,* beginning often as an unnoticed or gradual penetration, followed by (2) *reaction,* or the resistance mild or violent of the inhabitants of the community, ultimately resulting in (3) the *influx* of newcomers and the rapid abandonment of the area by its old-time residents, and (4) *climax* or the achievement of a new equilibrium of communal stability.[6]

## RESHAPING ECOLOGICAL PATTERNS

One thing that upsets plant and animal ecological patterns is man. The force that changes the ecological patterns of human beings is man's culture. Man may destroy one kind of plant community, say trees, and replace it with another, say corn, cotton, or wheat. He may destroy a community of wild animals and replace it with a community of domesticated animals. He may poison the rough species of fish in a lake and replace them with game species. Man may perfect a system of irrigation of an area and literally revolutionize the flora and fauna of the area. He may level hills so that a settlement takes on a different form than it would take if the hills were left. He sets up land-use zones in a city limiting each zone to a particular land use. The courts of the land may render legal decisions which declare illegal segregated school systems, segregated transportation and recreation, and segregated public housing. Through such decisions the historical ecological process of segregation is upset.

## SUMMARY

The field of ecology has both its structural and functional phases. The adjustment of living creatures to their environments, especially their spatial arrangements in their environment, is known as ecology. Human ecology is but one phase of a larger ecology. Many adjustments and spatial arrangements are the results of two biological relationships found throughout nature—symbiosis and commensalism. At the plant and animal levels these relationships are largely between different species, whereas at the human level they are relationships within the same species—man. Within this same species there is, of course, a wide range of subraces and cultural and interest groups which form the basis for ecological patterns and processes in communities.

Biological relationships show up in many ways. They influence the size and density of settlement. They influence the texture and shape of settlement.

In ecological patterning, distinctive and fairly clearly defined ecological processes are discernible. Among these are centralization and concentration and their corollaries, decentralization or dispersal, segregation, invasion, and succession. Whether these processes are in animal, plant, or human communities they may be greatly influenced by man and the culture he seeks to impose by implementing or preventing the processes. Man passes laws and invokes policies and practices which change the ecology.

[6] Ernest W. Burgess, "Residential Segregation in American Cities," *Annals,* **140:**105-15, November, 1928. The quotation is from page 112.

THINGS TO DO AND TO DISCUSS

1. Select and compare several concepts of ecology, selecting what is to you a suitable concept.
2. What are ecological areas? What ecological areas are found in your community?

3. Explain the difference between symbiosis and commensalism. Give examples of each.

4. What are some of the factors that may influence the form of settlement of a community? The size of settlement and the density of settlement?

5. Define each of the ecological processes and give examples from your own community. Study one process going on in a community with which you are acquainted, and prepare a brief written or oral report on it.

6. How does man shape ecological areas and alter his ecological relationships?

FOR FURTHER STUDY

ALIHAN, MILLA AISSA. *Social Ecology*. New York: Columbia University Press, 1938. One of the earlier books on ecology containing a good discussion of ecological theory, natural areas, and ecological processes.

CLARKE, GEORGE LEONARD. *Elements of Ecology*. New York: John Wiley and Sons, 1950. Standard text in fundamentals of ecology.

COLE, WILLIAM E. *Urban Society*. Boston: Houghton Mifflin Co., 1958. Chapters on urban ecology, suburbanization, and metropolitan areas.

CRESSEY, PAUL. "Population Succession in Chicago," *American Journal of Sociology*, 44:59-69, July, 1938. One of the earlier and better articles on succession.

DICE, LEE R. *Man's Nature and Nature's Man: The Ecology of Human Communities*. Ann Arbor, Mich.: University of Michigan Press, 1955. The relation of human patterning to natural resources.

DUNCAN, OTIS DUDLEY, and DUNCAN, BEVERLEY. *The Negro Population in Chicago*. Chicago: University of Chicago Press, 1957. Growth, composition, and distribution of the Negro population in Chicago.

DUNCAN, OTIS DUDLEY, and LIEBERSON, STANLEY. "Ethnic Segregation and Assimilation," *The American Journal of Sociology*, 64:364-74, January, 1959. The two social processes studied in association with each other.

GIBBS, JACK P., and MARTIN, WALTER T. "Toward a Theoretical System of Human Ecology," *The Pacific Sociological Review*, 2:29-36, Spring, 1959. An attempt to construct a theoretical system of human ecology.

HAWLEY, AMOS H. *Human Ecology*. New York: Ronald Press, 1950. Basic discussion of ecology and human ecology, the human aggregate, ecological organization, and ecological change and development.

ISARD, WALTER. *Location and Space-Economy*. New York: John Wiley and Sons, 1956. The relation of space economy to land use.

KUPER, LEO, *et al. Durban: A Study in Racial Ecology*. New York: Columbia University Press, 1958. The ecological processes in race patterning amply treated.

LEE, ROSE HUM. "The Decline of Chinatowns in the United States," *American Journal of Sociology*, 54:422-32, 1948-49. Good treatment of the decline of Chinatowns as a natural area.

LYNCH, KEVIN. "The Form of Cities," *Scientific American*, **190**, No. 4:54-63, April, 1954. One of the few things written on the form or shape of cities.

ODUM, EUGENE P. *Fundamentals of Ecology.* Philadelphia: W. B. Saunders Co., 1953. Basic text in plant and animal ecology, with some interesting contrasts between human and animal ecology.

PARK, ROBERT E.; BURGESS, ERNEST W.; and MCKENZIE, RODERICK D. *The City.* Chicago: University of Chicago Press, 1925. Basic work on ecological zones of cities.

PARK, ROBERT E. *Human Communities: The City and Human Ecology.* Glencoe, Ill.: Free Press, 1952. Valuable discussion of the ecological aspects of human communities.

QUINN, JAMES A. *Human Ecology.* Englewood Cliffs, N.J.: Prentice-Hall, 1950. The field of ecology, the structure and planning of ecological areas, processes underlying areal change, and the interpretation of ecological data on urban pathology and institutions.

SCHMID, CALVIN F.; MACCANNELL, EARLE H.; and VAN ARSDOL, MAURICE D., JR. "The Ecology of the American City: Further Comparison and Validation of Generalizations," *American Sociological Review,* **23,** No. 4:392-401, August, 1958. An attempt is made to test the stability, reliability, and comparability of data concerning the ecological structure of American cities, as revealed in the 1940 census data.

SMAILES, A. E. *The Geography of Towns.* London: Hutchinson's University Library, 1953. Good basic discussion on the origin, location, and morphology of towns.

STORER, JOHN H. *The Web of Life.* New York: Devin-Adair Company, 1954. The "balance of life" theme strongly stressed by plant and animal ecologists.

TAYLOR, GRIFFITH. *Urban Geography.* New York: E. P. Dutton and Co., 1946. A study of site, evolution, ecological patterning, and contrast of villages, towns, and cities.

THEODORSON, GEORGE A. (ed.). *Studies in Human Ecology.* Evanston, Ill.: Row, Peterson Co., 1961. An excellent source book in human ecology.

VANCE, RUPERT J., and DEMERATH, NICHOLAS J. (eds.). *The Urban South.* Chapel Hill, N.C.: University of North Carolina Press, 1955. Contains a good chapter showing how urban ecological areas in the South are different from those of cities in other parts of the nation.

# 17. URBANIZATION AND SUBURBANIZATION

AN IMPORTANT FACTOR in society is the distribution and redistribution of population. As this has taken place in the United States and Europe, and lately in most parts of the world, the redistribution pattern has become one of centralization and concentration of people into cities. We speak of this trend in population redistribution as urbanization. Urban growth has also been accompanied by a movement of people into the suburbs and fringe areas of cities. This trend is called suburbanization. Just as Wirth called urbanism, which is a kind of culture dominance by cities, a way of life,[1] so Fava calls suburbanization a way of life.[2] More about this toward the end of the chapter.

## THE BEGINNINGS OF URBANIZATION

At the end of the Neolithic Period and the beginning of the Metal Ages, around 4500 to 4000 B.C., in Mesopotamia and Egypt and elsewhere in the Middle East, fairly large settlements of people began to develop. Some of the Neolithic or New Stone Age villages had as many as 50 houses, while the Metal Age villages and towns were much larger. Childe claims that the changes brought about by the Metal Ages constituted the beginning of the *urban revolution.*[3]

What were the major changes that took place during the beginning of the Metal Age period which made it possible to concentrate large populations together in compact settlements? First of all, during the Neolithic and early Metal Age period in the Middle East

[1] Louis Wirth, "Urbanism as a Way of Life," *American Journal of Sociology*, 44:1-24, July, 1938.

[2] Sylvia Fleis Fava, "Suburbanism as a Way of Life," *American Sociological Review*, 21:34-37, February, 1956. *See also* Robert M. Adams, "The Origin of Cities," *Scientific American*, 203, No. 3:153-68, September, 1960.

[3] V. Gordon Childe, *Man Makes Himself* (New York: New American Library of World Literature, 1951), and *What Happened in History* (New York: Penguin Books, 1948).

there was the domestication of plants and animals, the use of the metal plow, and the development of irrigation agriculture in the valleys along the Nile, the Tigris, and the Euphrates rivers. These developments in agriculture greatly stabilized and increased the food supply and made it possible for surpluses of foods to be produced for people who did not work the land.

Apparently considerable strides in the knowledge of how to prevent and cure diseases were also made by the Egyptians, the Babylonians, and the early Greeks. These developments without a doubt made it possible to reduce the health hazards of fairly large, compact settlements. However, it was not until water purification, inoculation for major contagious diseases, environmental sanitation, and food sanitation came into practice that the health hazards of cities were greatly reduced. Many of these improvements did not take place until the eighteenth and nineteenth centuries.

The Metal Age skills and products gave rise to the development of new kinds of crafts and craftsmen. Crafts not only enlivened trading and commerce, but gave a new source of livelihood to people who lived in villages, towns, and cities, and who did not engage in agriculture, fishing, or hunting.

Apparently the sailing ship was developed during the Metal Ages. The wind-driven ship supplemented the galley ship and smaller vessels, and added greatly to the development of ocean-going commerce. Substantial port development took place where there were breaks between ocean and land transportation. The metal-rimmed wheel also was a great improvement in overland transportation.

The exact size of these early cities is not known. Places of 7,000 to 20,000 were apparently not unusual during the early Metal Age period, with a few cities like Babylon and Nineveh reaching populations approximating 100,000. It is also true that, as these developments were taking place in the Middle East, substantial urbanization of people into villages

and towns was taking place in the Oriental world.

Sorokin has traced the emergence of 355 cities having populations of over 100,000 population. The dates and number of cities are summarized in Table 29. As we will see, over 60 per cent of the cities studied developed after the eleventh century began.

*Table 29*

THE PERIOD OF EMERGENCE OF SOME IMPORTANT WORLD CITIES

| *Period of Emergence* | *Number* | *Per Cent* |
|---|---|---|
| B.C. to 5th Century A.D. | 67 | 18.8 |
| 6th to 10th Century | 69 | 19.4 |
| 11th to 15th Century | 75 | 21.2 |
| 16th to 20th Century | 144 | 40.5 |
| Totals | 355 | 99.9 |

Source: Pitirim Sorokin, *Society, Culture and Personality* (New York: Harper and Bros., 1947), pp. 528-29.

It remained for the Industrial Revolution to develop a culture which would bring about the mass urbanization of populations. Not only did the Industrial Revolution develop the factory system, which required people who worked in the factories to live close to where they worked, but it also developed a tremendous economy around trade, finance, and the services necessary for the people employed on industrial jobs. The Industrial Revolution in England roughly covered the period 1750 to 1850. The change to steam power came in the eighteenth century after James Watt developed the steam engine. Two key inventions, Arkwright's spinning frame (1769) and Edmund Cartwright's power loom (1785), helped to establish the pre-eminence of England as a textile center. Coal mines and iron helped to establish its pre-eminence in heavy industries.

The Industrial Revolution, of course, spread rapidly to the other European countries, especially Germany and Belgium, and finally to the United States.

*America has many faces. Above, a quiet country road leads through farmland while, opposite, millions of lights make a great city glisten.*

## CAUSES OF URBAN GROWTH IN THE UNITED STATES

Against the preceding background of general causes of urbanization, the United States has had its own peculiar factors in urban development.

In the first place, the United States was settled during periods of great economic and social change. Europe, being as accessible as it was, made possible tremendous borrowing of knowledge. A heavy immigration from Europe meant that many peoples with many skills already developed were among those seeking new opportunities in America. In a land with abundant natural resources in ratio to popu-

lation, and with people skilled in the utilization of resources, it was inevitable that urbanization would move rapidly ahead.

From 1820, the date when data on immigration were first available for the country as a whole, down to the present, almost 50 million immigrants have been officially admitted to the United States. The mere numbers of immigrants would have added greatly to the urban population, even though they were distributed between rural and urban areas. However, the United States never developed an adequate policy for distributing immigrants.

As a result, millions were unloaded at seacoast towns mostly in the East, where they remained. While a considerable percentage of immigrants were people with rural backgrounds, they remained in the cities because there were no adequate national plans for distributing them to the rural areas.

The United States had not only abundant resources for industrial development, but also abundant natural ports and waterways for the development of water transportation. This was later supplemented by great extension of railroads. Wherever breaks in transportation developed, settlements tended to grow and many of these later grew into cities. The relationship between breaks in transportation and the growth of cities was pointed out by an eminent early American sociologist, Charles H. Cooley.[4]

Not only did the United States have a rich industrial base for the development of industry, it also had a rich resource base for the development of a productive agriculture. The acres of land available for tillage were extensive. There was great regional variation in land, temperature, soil, and rainfall factors, thus making for tremendous variation in agriculture. Phosphate, lime, and potash deposits

[4] Charles H. Cooley, *Sociological Theory and Social Research* (New York: Henry Holt and Co., 1930).

gave an adequate supply of fertilizers, nitrogen being the chief element lacking, and this was available through Chile and, later, through synthetic production in this country.

With a rich base for the development of an agricultural technology, it was possible for the United States to develop systems of agriculture which did not need all the people available on farms. This surplus of labor, plus poor crop and price years in agriculture, caused many people to migrate from the farms to cities. One-half or more of farm youth in the nation leave the farm for permanent work and residence in nonfarm areas. So rural-urban migration has become a major factor in urbanization of population. Whereas the farm population of the United States was 25 million in 1950, four years later, it was 21.8 million, even though the population had increased 10 to 12 million; and by 1960 it had fallen to 20 million on the basis of comparable definitions.

Education has also been a factor in rural-urban migration because cities offered rural boys and girls opportunity to sell their developed talents on the labor market. Urban conveniences have also been of considerable importance, along with economic opportunity and prestige of the city, in inducing off-farm migration to cities.

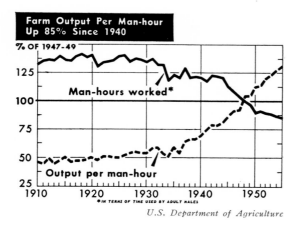

FIG. 29. INCREASE IN PRODUCTION PER MAN HOUR ON FARMS, 1910–1955

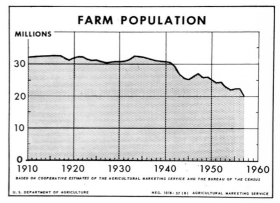

FIG. 30. FARM POPULATION IN THE UNITED STATES, 1910–1957

Migration of Negroes out of the rural regions of the South to cities of the South, the North, and East has been particularly heavy. Economic reasons and the fact that the Negro believed he could share better in civil rights in cities have been in large measure responsible for this migration.

Migration from the possessions, especially Puerto Rico, to certain cities like New York, has been a factor in urban growth. The growth factor has, of course, been inconsequential as compared to the minority problem created in the particular part of the city where these migrants have settled.

An individual city may grow as the result of migration from another city. There is a substantial amount of intercity migration taking place. While this country was perhaps settled with strong rural biases existing in our leaders, probably now urban biases are just as strong. The major channels of mass media of communication—the radio, television, the press—are for the most part operated from cities. In education, urban biases and values seem to be more widely taught than are rural biases. In this situation the city is at the hub of attention and prestige. People seek what the cities have to offer in preference to what rural areas have to offer. In this situation, the prestige of the city looms high as an element in urban growth.

*Table 30*

BIRTH RATES, DEATH RATES, RATES OF NATURAL INCREASE, AND NET MIGRATION PER 1,000 OF THE POPULATION, FOR THE UNITED STATES: 1950 TO 1958

| Fiscal Year (July 1 to June 30) | Rate of Natural Increase | Birth Rate | Death Rate | Net Civilian Immigration per 1,000 of the Population |
|---|---|---|---|---|
| 1957-1958 | 15.1 | 24.8 | 9.7 | 1.5 |
| 1956-1957 | 16.0 | 25.2 | 9.3 | 1.8 |
| 1955-1956 | 15.4 | 24.8 | 9.4 | 2.0 |
| 1954-1955 | 15.8 | 25.0 | 9.2 | 1.6 |
| 1953-1954 | 15.8 | 25.0 | 9.2 | 1.5 |
| 1952-1953 | 15.2 | 24.8 | 9.6 | 1.3 |
| 1951-1952 | 15.0 | 24.6 | 9.7 | 2.1 |
| 1950-1951 | 14.8 | 24.5 | 9.7 | 2.5 |
| Annual average, 1950 to 1958 | 15.4 | 24.8 | 9.5 | 1.8 |

Source: U.S. Bureau of the Census, *Current Population Reports, Population Estimates*, Series P-25, No. 182, September 3, 1958.

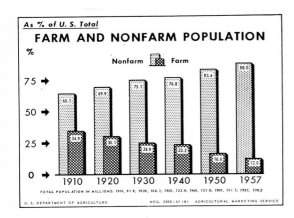

FIG. 31A. TRENDS IN FARM AND NONFARM POPULATION

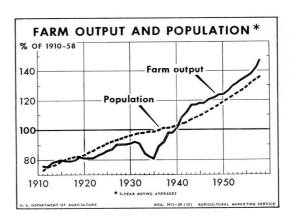

FIG. 31B. RELATION OF FARM OUTPUT TO FARM POPULATION

Currently American cities are growing as a result of natural increase. We discussed this point in Chapter 8. For instance, in the calendar year 1957 the number of births in the United States was 4.3 million, whereas deaths numbered 1.6 million. These figures mean that during that year the nation had a very great natural increase in population, the cities sharing in this increase along with the rural areas.

Table 30 shows the rates of natural increase between 1950 and 1958. As the data show, the average annual rate of natural increase during this period was 15.4 per cent.

While cities have shown a long-range decline in birth rates, they have also shown a more rapid decline in death rates. With the upswing in birth rates during the 1940's and 1950's, and the continued decline in the death rates, substantial increases in the population have taken place as a result of natural growth.

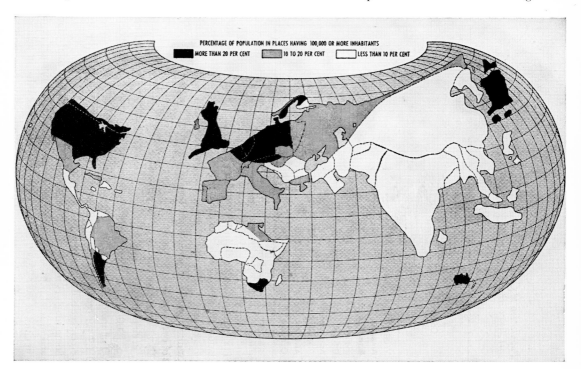

FIG. 32.  COUNTRIES OF THE WORLD WITH SPECIFIED PORTION OF THE POPULATION IN CITIES OF OVER 100,000

SOURCE: W. S. Woytinsky and E. S. Woytinsky, *World Population and Production: Trends and Outlook* (New York: Twentieth Century Fund, 1953), p. 119.

## THE EXTENT OF URBANIZATION

Urbanization is a world-wide trend.[5] Since definitions of urban vary from country to country, the only reliable way of showing the extent of world urbanization is by indicating the percentage of the world's population living

[5] For data on this point *see* William E. Cole, *Urban Society* (Boston: Houghton Mifflin Co., 1958), pp. 12-40.

in cities of different sizes. This is done in Table 31. As the table indicates, whereas 2.4 per cent of the world's population lived in cities of 20,000 or more in 1800, in 1950 20.9 per cent of the population lived in cities of 20,000 or more. The percentage of the population living in cities of over 100,000 increased

Table 31

PER CENT OF WORLD'S POPULATION
LIVING IN CITIES

| Year | Cities of 20,000 or More | Cities of 100,000 or More |
|------|--------------------------|---------------------------|
| 1800 | 2.4 | 1.7 |
| 1850 | 4.3 | 2.3 |
| 1900 | 9.2 | 5.5 |
| 1950 | 20.9 | 13.1 |

Source: Kingsley Davis, "The Origin and Growth of Urbanization in the World," *American Journal of Sociology*, **60:**429-37, March, 1955.

during the same interval from 1.7 per cent to 13.1 per cent. The distribution of the world's population by degree of urbanization is indicated in Figure 32.

The United States Census has changed its definition of urban at intervals. From 1910 to 1940 inclusive, *urban* referred to people living in the following places:

1. Cities and other incorporated places of 2,500 or more.
2. Unincorporated places of 10,000 or more and a population density of 1,000 or more per square mile.
3. Townships in the states of Massachusetts, Rhode Island, and New Hampshire containing a village of 2,500 or more, either by themselves or where combined with other villages, and comprising more than 50 per cent of the population of the township.[6]

A significant change was made in the concept of *urban* in the 1950 census, urban including the people living in the following places:

1. Places of 2,500 or more incorporated as borough cities or villages.
2. Incorporated towns of 2,500 or more, except in New York, Wisconsin, and New England where "towns" are minor civil divisions of counties.

[6] U.S. Bureau of the Census, *Statistical Abstract of the United States, 1948* (69th ed.; Washington, D.C., U.S. Government Printing Office, 1948), p. 2.

Table 32

POPULATION IN URBAN AND RURAL
PLACES, 1790-1960

| Date | Urban | Rural |
|------|-------|-------|
| 1960 | 69.9 | 30.1 |
| 1950 new definition | 64.0 | 36.0 |
| 1950 old definition | 59.0 | 41.0 |
| 1940 | 56.5 | 43.5 |
| 1930 | 56.2 | 43.8 |
| 1920 | 51.2 | 48.8 |
| 1910 | 45.7 | 54.3 |
| 1900 | 39.7 | 60.3 |
| 1890 | 35.1 | 64.9 |
| 1880 | 28.2 | 71.8 |
| 1870 | 25.7 | 74.3 |
| 1860 | 19.8 | 80.2 |
| 1850 | 15.3 | 84.7 |
| 1840 | 10.8 | 89.2 |
| 1830 | 8.8 | 91.2 |
| 1820 | 7.2 | 92.8 |
| 1810 | 7.3 | 92.7 |
| 1800 | 6.1 | 93.9 |
| 1790 | 5.1 | 94.9 |

Source: U.S. Bureau of the Census, *U.S. Census of Population, U.S. Summary, Number of Inhabitants,* PI-A, 1952. The 1960 data are from the *U.S. Summary: Number of Inhabitants,* 1961.

3. Unincorporated places of 2,500 or more outside any urban fringe.
4. The densely settled urban fringe, including both incorporated and unincorporated places around cities of 50,000 or more inhabitants.[7]

In 1850, only 19 million people in the United States lived in urban places. In 1900 the urban population had increased to 30 million. By 1950 urban dwellers had increased to 96.4 million, and by 1960 to 125.2 million. Percentagewise the population which was urban changed from 5.1 per cent in 1790 to 64.0 per cent in 1950 (see Table 32) and to 70 per cent in 1960.

[7] U.S. Bureau of the Census, *1950 Census of Population, Advance Reports,* 5 Series PC-9, No. 3, June 9, 1952.

By 1960 the population of the United States reached 179.3 million, and by 1975 may reach 225 million. The urbanization of population will doubtless continue, but it is likely that farm population will decline and rural non-farm population will increase.

## THE GROWTH OF METROPOLITAN AREAS

The great new kind of urban settlement is the metropolitan area. As we indicated in the chapter on place groupings, a metropolitan area is one made up of a city of at least 50,000 population plus the contiguous or connected counties economically integrated around the city. In 1950, the U.S. Census Bureau recognized 168 metropolitan areas in the United States and, in the census of 1960, it recorded 215 such areas.

Each metropolitan area has a central city. Between 1940 and 1950, central cities of such areas had a growth of 14 per cent, whereas the outlying parts of such areas had a growth of 36 per cent. Of all growth that took place in the population between 1940 and 1950, four-fifths took place within metropolitan areas. Data on the growth of metropolitan areas between 1950 and 1955 indicate that central cities grew 3.8 per cent during the period, whereas other parts of the metropolitan areas grew 27.8 per cent. Collectively, the five largest metropolitan areas of New York, Chicago, Los Angeles, Philadelphia, and Detroit contain 29 million people. New York has outranked all other American cities since the census of 1790; at that time, Philadelphia was the largest.

The metropolitan area is one of the outgrowths of improved transportation and communication plus a number of accompanying social and economic changes.

|  | 1960 population | | 1950 population | |
|---|---|---|---|---|
|  | (rank) | (total) | (rank) | (total) |
| New York | 1 | 7,710,346 | 1 | 7,891,957 |
| Chicago | 2 | 3,492,945 | 2 | 3,620,962 |
| Los Angeles | 3 | 2,448,018 | 4 | 1,970,358 |
| Philadelphia | 4 | 1,959,966 | 3 | 2,071,605 |
| Detroit | 5 | 1,672,574 | 5 | 1,849,568 |
| Houston | 6 | 932,680 | 14 | 596,163 |
| Baltimore | 7 | 921,363 | 6 | 949,708 |
| Cleveland | 8 | 869,867 | 7 | 914,808 |
| Washington | 9 | 746,958 | 9 | 802,178 |
| St. Louis | 10 | 740,424 | 8 | 856,796 |
| Milwaukee | 11 | 734,788 | 13 | 637,392 |
| San Francisco | 12 | 715,609 | 11 | 775,357 |
| Boston | 13 | 677,626 | 10 | 801,444 |
| Dallas | 14 | 672,117 | 22 | 434,462 |
| New Orleans | 15 | 620,979 | 16 | 570,445 |
| Pittsburgh | 16 | 600,684 | 12 | 676,806 |
| San Antonio | 17 | 584,471 | 25 | 408,442 |
| Seattle | 18 | 550,525 | 19 | 467,591 |
| San Diego | 19 | 547,294 | 31 | 334,387 |
| Buffalo | 20 | 528,387 | 15 | 580,132 |
| Memphis | 21 | 491,691 | 26 | 396,000 |
| Denver | 22 | 489,217 | 24 | 415,786 |
| Cincinnati | 23 | 487,462 | 18 | 503,998 |
| Atlanta | 24 | 485,425 | 33 | 331,314 |
| Minneapolis | 25 | 481,026 | 17 | 521,718 |
| Indianapolis | 26 | 470,464 | 23 | 427,173 |
| Kansas City | 27 | 468,325 | 20 | 456,622 |
| Columbus | 28 | 465,151 | 28 | 375,901 |
| Phoenix | 29 | 430,459 | 98 | 106,818 |
| Newark | 30 | 396,252 | 21 | 438,776 |
| Louisville | 31 | 385,688 | 30 | 369,129 |
| Portland, Ore. | 32 | 370,339 | 29 | 373,628 |
| Oakland | 33 | 361,082 | 27 | 384,575 |
| Fort Worth | 34 | 353,388 | 38 | 278,778 |
| Birmingham | 35 | 338,569 | 34 | 326,037 |
| Long Beach | 36 | 323,996 | 41 | 250,767 |
| Oklahoma City | 37 | 317,542 | 45 | 243,504 |
| Rochester | 38 | 316,074 | 32 | 332,488 |
| Toledo | 39 | 315,643 | 36 | 303,616 |
| St. Paul | 40 | 313,209 | 35 | 311,349 |
| Omaha | 41 | 300,674 | 40 | 251,117 |
| X-Honolulu | 42 | 289,864 | X | 248,034 |
| Akron | 43 | 287,592 | 39 | 274,605 |
| Miami | 44 | 282,600 | 42 | 249,276 |
| Norfolk | 45 | 272,908 | 48 | 213,513 |
| El Paso | 46 | 272,239 | 75 | 130,485 |
| Tampa | 47 | 270,610 | 84 | 124,681 |
| Jersey City | 48 | 269,621 | 37 | 299,017 |
| Tulsa | 49 | 258,563 | 51 | 182,740 |
| Dayton | 50 | 258,196 | 44 | 243,872 |

X—not ranked as part of U. S. state cities in 1950

*U.S. Bureau of the Census*

FIG. 33. FIFTY MOST POPULOUS CITIES OF THE UNITED STATES, 1960

## SOME CONCOMITANTS OF URBAN GROWTH

Prior to discussing some major problems associated with urban growth in the United States, something should be said about the positive value of cities in an economy like that of the United States.

Cities provide a wide range of occupations so necessary in a democracy where the theory prevails that each individual has special aptitudes, that he should be trained to develop these aptitudes, and that he should then have an opportunity to exchange these developed aptitudes on the labor market for financial and other kinds of rewards. Rural regions are limited in the number of occupations available. In some rural areas there may be only a dozen different kinds of occupations, whereas

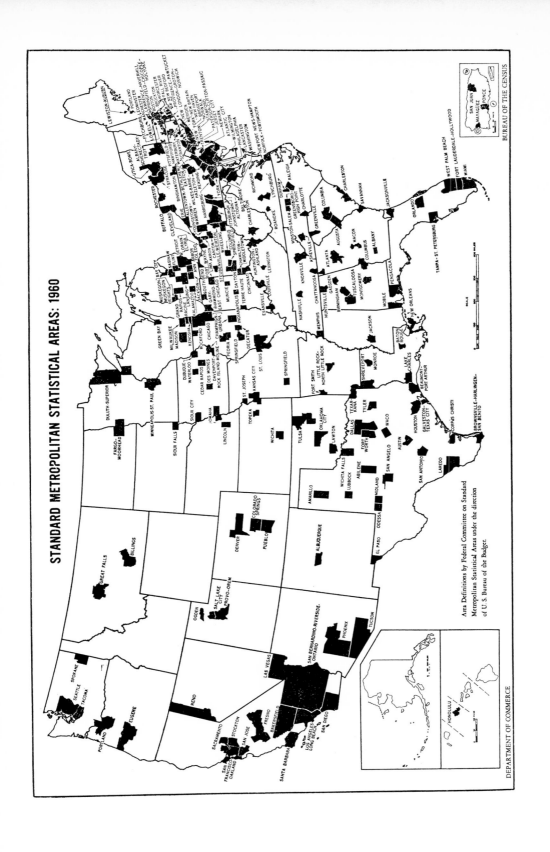

# STANDARD METROPOLITAN STATISTICAL AREAS: 1960

BUREAU OF THE CENSUS

Area Definitions by Federal Committee on Standard
Metropolitan Statistical Areas under the direction
of U.S. Bureau of the Budget.

DEPARTMENT OF COMMERCE

a large city may offer several thousand different jobs.

Cities are very important to the accomplishment of another kind of freedom. Cities offer freedom, at least for a favored minority, from the sometimes too-close personal relationships found in small communities. One can usually find in cities others of his own race, religion, and economic and professional interests. There will also be those of one's social class.

As we indicated in the chapter on ecology, there is a lot of mutual helpfulness in cities. A good example is in the medical profession where different specialists, druggists, clinical facilities, and other aids may be available to assist other medical practitioners. Symbiosis and commensalism characterize relationships between personal, professional, and economic interests in many areas of urban life. The city is not so cold and impersonal as many would have us believe.

Cities furnish a great consuming public, thus encouraging the development of a productive agriculture. Cities are also innovators of social change and therefore usually reflect a climate of liberalism and a progressiveness which most rural areas do not have. Part of this results from the young adult and middle-aged population which they largely attract.

Some of the concomitants of urban growth are urban problems. We shall discuss a few of these without going into great detail on any single problem. The interested student may want to pursue some of the problems of city life in more detail in the standard works on urban society cited in the bibliography.

1. *Urban dominance.* As cities have grown, and especially as metropolitan areas have developed, they have extended their dominance over practically all phases of American life. This means that our culture has taken on an urban bias which is reflected in the attitudes,

## Age Distribution of Dwelling Units in 1950

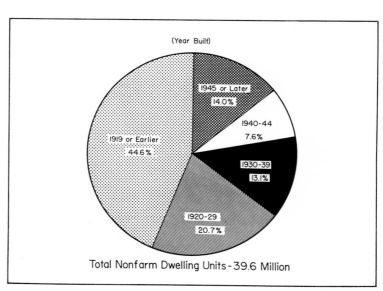

*U.S. Housing and Home Finance Agency*

FIG. 34. HOUSING—A MAJOR URBAN PROBLEM

The above chart shows when houses were built.

values, and occupational choices of people. This urban bias is perhaps reflected less in legislative bodies than in most other institutions. This is so because the system of representation in legislative bodies favors strongly rural populations.

We do not decry urban dominance, but we should point out that love for land, interest in growing things, interest in natural resources for purposes other than exploitation, participation in the primary group relationships of small communities, have declined in favor of the more mechanistic, rationalistic, and less personal life of cities. Another thing: the great dependence of city people upon jobs is such as to make urban populations vulnerable to economic depressions and, particularly, unemployment. Of course, rural farm people are vulnerable to depressions but many do have the land they can fall back upon.

2. *Political problems.* While cities have many political problems, we shall mention only three. One problem is the fact that the population of most cities, and especially of the large metropolitan areas, is out of harmony with the existing boundaries of governmental units. A metropolitan area, such as New York or Memphis, may cut across parts of two or three states, a half-dozen counties, and a dozen or more governmental units. No single unit of government may represent it fully or officially. Some attempts have been made to overcome this difficulty by consolidating government functions throughout a metropolitan area. Consolidated utilities and welfare and educational services are examples. Planning bodies, with jurisdiction over a whole county, or over a whole metropolitan area, may do much to simplify the problems of physical planning for such areas.

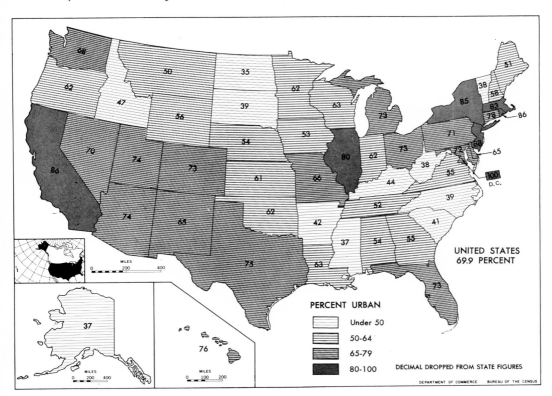

FIG. 35. PER CENT OF POPULATION URBAN, BY STATES: 1960

Cities are frequently discriminated against by laws and policies of state and county legislative bodies dominated by rural-minded legislators. Although many states have been expected to reapportion their representation in state legislative bodies at intervals, some have failed to do so. This has meant that small, sparsely populated rural county or parish areas may have the same representation as a large urban county. Rural blocs in legislative halls are frequently strong enough to defeat legislative measures which would be in the interest of cities.

As cities have become larger, they have also become technically more complicated to govern and to operate. Often the decisions that are to be made are much too complicated and involved for the quality of personnel employed by cities to make such decisions. This means that political decisions are often made when technical decisions are warranted by the gravity of the problems involved. What this statement adds up to is that professional competency in the operation and management of cities has not kept pace with the magnitude and nature of the managerial and technical problems at hand.

3. *Density and congestion.* A group of problems from which cities seem to have not been able to escape are those centering around density of population and congestion. This has often meant land overcrowding but, above all, has meant congestion of movement and all kinds of traffic problems. In many cities there is an acute shortage of space. The suburbs are, at their best, a questionable refuge. Commuting is expensive in money, time, and patience. Many of the suburbs are institutional deserts and others are halfway respectable slums, becoming more and more crowded.

While many remedial measures are being tried, ranging all the way from parking meters to limited access streets and highways, the problems of congestion will require more revolutionary movements than those employed to date. Ultimate solutions may require the planning of new towns, limited in maximum size, and designed particularly to meet the needs of the motor and air age.

4. *Vulnerability.* In an age of intercontinental ballistic missiles with atomic warheads, any city of considerable size in the world is vulnerable to attack. Of course, it is just possible that weapons are now so tremendously destructive that their use may be systematically and internationally outlawed. This fact does not offset the possibility that urban populations can be decimated by the impact of atomic explosions, the fire storms that they could ignite, and the fallout from which unprotected persons would perish. There are the ever-present problems of evacuating or feeding inhabitants in case of water scarcity—already critical on the West Coast and likely to occur in more and more cities; the breakdown in rail transportation and of key bridges or tunnels; power failure and danger of extensive damage from war or other causes.

5. *Human problems.* While the above problems are largely technical in nature, they involve human costs. However, there are other human problems which are concomitants of urban growth. Smog seems to be related in cities, where it is bad, to cancer and heart disease. The stress diseases appear to be more prominent as a cause of death in cities than in rural areas. For the bulk of the urban population, there is much regimentation, manipulation, economic exploitation—particularly of the lower economic classes, and an increasing loss of the sense of individual importance. As cities get bigger, thicker, and closer together, these disadvantages seem likely to increase.

While the foregoing groups of problems have accompanied the urbanization of population, there is no immediate indication that the urbanward trend will greatly slow up. Countries now only slightly urbanized are likely to become more so where conditions are favorable for urban growth. Industrialized countries, like the United States, are likely to continue to increase in urban growth until they reach a point where 80 or 85 per cent of their populations live in cities. This has been true of a number of European countries. Urban growth may not be geographically distributed in the future as it has been in the past. Some areas of this nation will obviously urbanize much more rapidly than others, unless there is planned dispersion of people and their enterprises into the areas now predominantly rural-farm. The South and West are likely to show greater percentages of urban increase in the next 50 years than are the New England states, the Middle Atlantic and the eastern North Central states, all of which are already heavily urbanized.

## SUBURBANIZATION

In Chapter 10 we said something about the development and types of suburban communities. We referred to the fact that, out of the nation's 150 million population in 1950, about 90 million lived in cities and 20 million in suburban and fringe areas. From 1950 to 1960 population growth in suburbs was almost 50 per cent as contrasted with the national growth of 18.5 per cent.

The rapid suburban trend in the growth of the population is indicated in Table 33.

The suburbanization of population, as indicated by ring growth, has been greater than central city growth in all geographical regions since 1900 except in the South. Urban growth's being delayed longer in the South than in the other sections of the nation is the reason why central city growth was greater between 1900 and 1950 than ring growth. During the past 20 years, however, ring growth has outpaced central city growth in the South.

The suburban trend in population is largely a response to better means of transportation and communication—the railway, the automobile, the bus, the truck, and the telephone. This response has been greater for families seeking new homesites than for economic institutions and industrial workers. While the percentage of all industrial workers in suburban and fringe areas is somewhat greater today than 25 years ago, it is not conspicuously greater.

While improved transportation has been the means whereby people move back and forth between suburbs and central cities, there have been other reasons for seeking the suburbs. Builders construct homes there because land at moderate prices is available. Many people seek the suburbs because they consider them a better place to rear children. They are cleaner and less congested. Lots are larger as a rule than in cities, land is cheaper, and taxes lower.[8]

Suburbs have many problems. One problem is the lack of subdivision control and planning in suburban areas. Another problem is the lack of adequate public transportation and the transportation problems for families that may have but one car, especially if the husband uses the car for transportation to work. Another problem is that of obtaining servants and other kinds of help and the general problem of services of one kind or another. The social

*Table 33*

RATES OF POPULATION INCREASE OF CENTRAL CITIES AND RINGS, BY REGIONS, 1900 TO 1950

| Region | Central City Per Cent | Ring Per Cent | Ratio: Ring Growth Rate to Central City Rate |
|---|---|---|---|
| Northeast | 103.6 | 138.5 | 1.34 |
| Midwest | 148.6 | 222.7 | 1.50 |
| South | 276.1 | 210.5 | 0.76 |
| West | 357.7 | 861.9 | 2.29 |

Source: Adapted from Leo F. Schnore, "Patterns of Decentralization" (Unpublished doctor's dissertation, University of Michigan, 1954).

[8] *See* William E. Cole, *op. cit.*, pp. 164-81; *also* William Dobriner (ed.), *The Suburban Community* (New York: G. P. Putnam's Sons, 1958).

services are often in short supply in suburban communities, as are also institutional facilities —especially schools and churches. The problem of commuting to and from work also becomes a major task and expense.

As a result of problems and difficulties of living in the suburbs, there is some movement back to the cities from the suburbs. Many of those returning are people whose children have grown up and left home. They find the upkeep of a home in the suburbs a burden, and commuting tiresome. They have kept their friendships in the city and welcome their return to the conveniences and privacy of the city.

## SUMMARY

One of the most influential trends taking place in society is the urbanization of population. While our concern is primarily with the urbanization of population in the United States, urbanization is a world-wide trend.

While roots of urbanization were laid in the cultural changes that took place in the New Stone and Metal Age periods, it took the impact of the Industrial Revolution to bring it to full fruition. Wherever industrialization has taken place it has been accompanied by urbanization.

Part of the urbanization complex is the suburbanization of population and the fringe growth that is now taking place around American cities. Many of the problems of cities are associated with this suburban trend.

While any place of 2,500 or more population is counted by the U.S. Bureau of the Census as urban, the great factor in urban development has been the growth of metropolitan areas, those places of 50,000 or more with the contiguous counties economically integrated around them.

While urbanization has brought into being many economic opportunities and much opportunity for freedom of expression and association, it has also been accompanied by personal regimentation and many problems. High on the list of urban problems which the sociologist must evaluate are urban dominance, a long series of political problems, problems of density and congestion, and vulnerability of attack by air-borne missiles and the fallout from atomic warheads and atomic industrial waste products. In spite of the fears created by this vulnerability, there is little reason to suspect that urbanization will greatly decrease in rapidity of growth, in fact a rapid increase seems most likely.

Another important reverse trend to that of centralization brought about by urbanization is suburbanization. Around 50 million people now live in suburbs. They have settled there because contractors have built houses there, because transportation facilities are available to them, and because they feel that suburbs have opportunities and conveniences, especially for their children. Although suburbanization continues at a rapid pace, having developed somewhat later in the South than in other sections of the country, there is now a counter trend back to cities from the suburbs led by people whose families have grown up and by persons seeking the conveniences and privacy of the city.

THINGS TO DO AND TO DISCUSS

1. During what period did the urbanization of population begin?
2. What inventions took place during the Neolithic and early Metal Age periods that accelerated the development of cities?
3. In what ways did the Industrial Revolution hasten the urbanization of population?

4. What are some of the peculiar causes of urban growth in the United States?
5. Why would cities tend to attract Negroes from the South more than would rural regions?
6. What is the current concept of "urban" as the term is employed by the U.S. Census Bureau? What is a metropolitan area?
7. What are some of the positive values of cities to our economy and to the democratic way of life?
8. What are some of the major problems arising out of the growth of cities? Which of these are in the category of human problems?
9. What have been some of the major causes of the growth of suburbs?
10. Why the movement back to cities from the suburbs?

FOR FURTHER STUDY

ADAMS, ROBERT M. "The Origin of Cities," *Scientific American,* **203,** No. 3: 153-68, September, 1960.

ANDERSON, NELS. *The Urban Community.* New York: Henry Holt and Co., 1959. A sociology of modern urban communities within international perspective.

BERGEL, ERNEST EGON. *Urban Sociology.* New York: McGraw-Hill Book Co., 1955. Standard general text in urban sociology.

COLE, WILLIAM E. (ed.). *Dynamic Urban Sociology.* Harrisburg, Pa.: Stackpole Co., 1954.

———. *Urban Society.* Boston: Houghton Mifflin Co., 1958. General urban text stressing the adjustment of people and institutions to cities and of cities to urban growth.

DOBRINER, WILLIAM (ed.). *The Suburban Community.* New York: G. P. Putnam's Sons, 1958. Comprehensive analysis of the structure and problems of suburban communities.

ERICKSEN, E. GORDON. *Urban Behavior.* New York: The Macmillan Co., 1954. Emphasis upon the impact of cities upon urban social systems and behavior.

HATT, PAUL K., and REISS, ALBERT J. *Cities and Society.* Glencoe, Ill.: Free Press, 1957. The best source book of readings on urbanization and urbanism.

HAUSER, PHILIP M. (ed.). "World Urbanism," *The American Journal of Sociology,* **60:** No. 5, March, 1955. The growth of world urbanization objectively treated.

LEE, ROSE HUM. *The City.* Philadelphia: J. B. Lippincott, 1955. Urban text with good chapters on cities of several countries.

LIEPMANN, KATE K. *The Journey to Work: Its Significance for Industries and Community Life.* New York: Oxford University Press, 1944. The significance of the journey to work.

LYNCH, KEVIN. *The Image of the City*. Cambridge, Mass.: Technology Press of Massachusetts Institute of Technology and Harvard University Press, 1960. An excellent treatment of how city people perceive their cities.

MARTIN, WALTER T. *The Rural-Urban Fringe*. Eugene, Ore.: University of Oregon Press, 1953. One of the better studies of adjustment to suburban living.

MARTINDALE, DON. *American Social Structure*. New York: Appleton-Century-Crofts, 1959. One of the few excellent books on social structure, with good chapters devoted to the regional, rural, urban and status community.

MUMFORD, LEWIS. *The City in History: Its Origins, Its Transformations, Its Prospects*. New York: Harcourt, Brace and World, 1961. A very useful survey of the development of cities and the changes they have undergone.

QUINN, JAMES A. *Urban Sociology*. New York: American Book Co., 1955. Good text with a strong ecological bent.

REDFIELD, ROBERT. *The Primitive World and Its Transformations*. New York: Dryden Press, 1951. Develops a good discussion of differences between folk societies and urban industrial societies.

ROGERS, EVERETT M. *Social Change in Rural Society*. New York: Appleton-Century-Crofts, 1960. A good resumé of changes taking place in rural society including many changes brought about by urbanization.

SEELEY, JOHN R., et al. *Crestwood Heights: A Study of the Culture of Suburban Life*. New York: Basic Books, 1956. Good case study of a suburban community.

VANCE, RUPERT B., and DEMERATH, NICHOLAS. *The Urban South*. Chapel Hill, N. C.: University of North Carolina Press, 1954. The most comprehensive thing that has been written on the urbanization of the South.

WIRTH, LOUIS. "Urbanism as A Way of Life," *The American Journal of Sociology*, 44: 1-24, July, 1938. A classical statement of the urban way of life.

# 18. COMMUNI-CATION

PREVIOUSLY we have defined communication as the transmission of meanings through the use of symbols. When we communicate we are trying to obtain information from others or we are seeking to share information, an idea, or an attitude with others.

## COMMUNICATION IN SOCIETY

Communication is basic in social interaction and social organization. Contacts are meaningless unless attitudes and ideas are communicated. If one person influences another person to respond, meanings must be communicated. The receiver must comprehend the meanings, at least enough to respond, if the circle of communication is to be complete. One frequently responds to symbols in behavior that he does not comprehend completely because complete comprehension is not necessary for response. If one is ordering a meal in a Spanish restaurant and the waiter does not understand English and the customer knows little Spanish, through gestures and some words the diner may finally "get through" to the waiter. The waiter responds with the correct meal and the cycle of communication has been completed. Diagrammatically, the cycle of communication is indicated in Figure 36.

Not only is communication necessary for the basic process of interaction in a social system, such as a group, an audience, or a social institution; it is also necessary in a society for the development of consensus. *Consensus* is understanding of basic symbols, ideas, attitudes, and values, and, as such, becomes necessary for the unification of a social system such as a group, an association, or a society. For consensus to be established, people must not only have a working knowledge of what symbols to use, but they also must know the meaning of the symbols.

The basic need for the members of social

systems to be able to communicate with each other, which means that they be able to understand each other, is ably put by Sapir:

While we often speak of society as though it were a static structure defined by tradition, it is, on the more intimate sense, nothing of the kind, but a highly intricate network of partial or complete understanding between the members of organizational units of every degree of size and complexity, ranging from a pair of lovers or a family to a league of nations or that ever increasing portion of humanity which can be reached by the press through all its transitional ramifications.[1]

## SOME MEANS OF COMMUNICATION

### Gestures

One does not know what means of communication were used first by man.[2] It seems reasonable to assume that gestures were among the original forms of communication. Insects, especially bees, communicate through gestures, sounds, and odors. Bees wiggle back and forth and run up and down the honeycomb to indicate the presence of nectar.[3] At the human level, the uplifted hand, the closed fist, the bowed head, and the extended thumb, so common on American highways, are all important gestures of communication. Frequently a group has its own subculture in the use of gestures. The Catholic religion has its own distinctive set of religious gestures decidedly different from those of Judaism. Trading in grain futures, as transacted in the trading pit at the Chicago Board of Trade, is carried on almost entirely by the use of gestures.

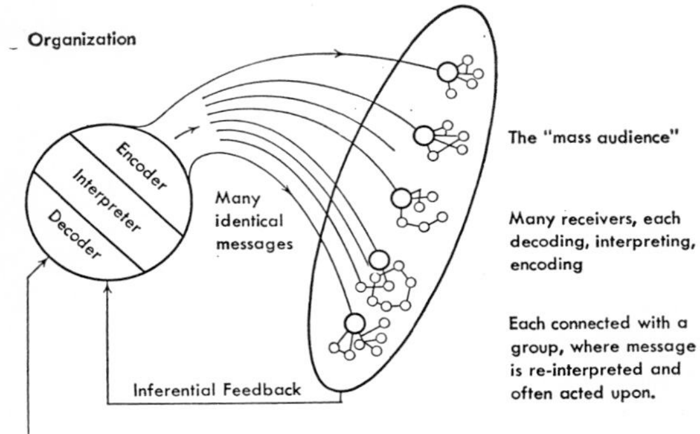

### Symbols

A *symbol* is an object, a behavior trait, or a cluster of traits which stand for something else. A symbol may be a physical object, a sound, or a gesture.

On the Navajo Indian Reservation in Arizona and New Mexico, along the paths and roads one finds piles of stones, with one stone carefully laid upon another. These have been placed there by Indians and other travelers to wish the traveler a safe and happy journey. Whether or not the traveler "reads" or understands the "message" of these symbols depends upon his understanding of what the stones are intended to convey. Otherwise they are simply piles of stone.

The early Indians in the United States used a system of smoke signals as one means of communication. They monitored their signals by the use of blankets, meticulously spelling out their messages. In the later development of the nation, when railroads were built, the telegraph, with its system of symbolic dots and dashes, became an important means of communication, supplanting, in instances, the pony express.

Languages are made up of symbols which we currently call "the alphabet." The charac-

FIG. 36. DIAGRAMMATIC SKETCH OF THE CYCLE IN MASS COMMUNICATION

SOURCE: Wilbur Schramm (ed.), *The Process and Effects of Mass Communication* (Urbana, Ill.: University of Illinois Press, 1954), p. 21.

[1] Edward Sapir, "Communication," in *Encyclopaedia of the Social Sciences* (New York: The Macmillan Co., 1931), IV, 78.

[2] For an interesting account of the development of means of communication, *see* Lancelot Hogben, *From Cave Painting to Comic Strip* (New York: Chanticleer Press, 1949).

[3] For an interesting account of how bees communicate, *see* Karl Von Frisch, *Bees, Their Vision, Chemical Senses and Language* (Ithaca, N.Y.: Cornell University Press, 1951).

Whether used in conversation, trade, science, or worship, symbols are important. The mathematician at right uses symbols almost exclusively to express his meaning.

Brokers in the New York Stock Exchange, at left, know the meaning of the many symbols used to report the buying and selling of shares of stock.

ters used in the Chinese language are greater in number and much more complicated than those in the English alphabet.

In the development of writing it is believed that the use of pictures or drawings came first. Later followed a series of pictures, called a picture narrative, which was designed to present a message. Following this, a set of symbols having sounds and meanings was developed by the Phoenicians. Back of this was a rich heritage of the use of hieroglyphics or symbol writing used by the Egyptians and other peoples of the Mediterranean area.

## Language

From all we know, sounds have always been a means of communication. Perhaps they originally developed along with gestures. Man, of course, is set apart from the animals by his ability to use speech. It is the great intellectual capacity of man that makes it possible for him to develop and use a language. Here the key is perhaps man's capacity to memorize and to imitate.

A language is a body of words, sounds, and combinations of sounds and words characteristic of a people. It is sometimes called a tongue. While speech is universal to mankind, languages vary from country to country, sometimes from tribe to tribe. In some countries, such as the United States, a common language, in our case English, may be universally used, whereas in other countries a number of languages may be spoken. For instance, the Swiss use French, German, and Italian. Within a country the range of vocabulary may vary from person to person. A first-grade student may have a vocabulary ranging from 5,000 to 50,000 words, whereas that of a college graduate may exceed 200,000 words.[4] Current dictionaries for college students in the United States may contain as many as 550,000 words. The learning of a language is, of course, an important part of the socializing process.

Within a country having a common language, there may be considerable variation in dialects and expressions. The variety of terms used to cover familiar objects is indicated in an interesting article by a student of the subject who feels that as communication improves in a country like the United States, and as English taught in schools becomes better standardized, increasingly regional expressions will disappear but he doubts if they will disappear entirely. Kurath says:

Local and regional expressions are not likely to disappear entirely from our language. Most of them survive because they stand for local or regional phenomena. It is very doubtful, for example, that we shall ever have a nationally accepted term for griddlecakes made of corn meal. For one thing, they are rarely served in the Wheat Belt. It is difficult to detect any trend toward a national name for them; they are still known by a wide variety of expressions, such as Johnnycakes, Johnnikins, corn cakes, corn dodgers, hoe cakes, ash cakes. A similar situation exists with regard to wheat cakes. The term pancakes is generally known throughout the Eastern states, but in Eastern New England they are almost always called griddle cakes, around Philadelphia hot cakes, west of Philadelphia flannel cakes and south of the Potomac batter cakes or batty cakes.[5]

Many attempts have been made to establish an international language. One of the most vigorous attempts in this direction was made by a Russian, Dr. L. L. Zamehof, in 1887. He attempted to develop a language, Esperanto, based on the words common to the chief European languages. Of all attempts during the nineteenth century to develop a universal language, only Esperanto has had any degree of acceptance, and it is fast disappearing.

Semantics lies at the basis of poor communication in the use of language. *Semantics* is the study of meaning and is sometimes extended to include the relation between meaning and behavior which is oftimes referred to as *general semantics*.

---

[4] *See* L. Carmichael (ed.), *Manual of Child Psychology* (New York: John Wiley and Sons, 1946).

[5] Hans Kurath, "The American Languages," *Scientific American*, **182**:48-51, January, 1950.

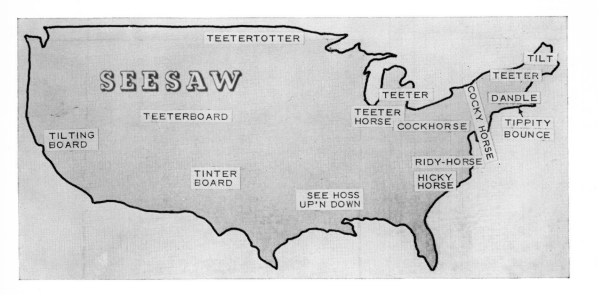

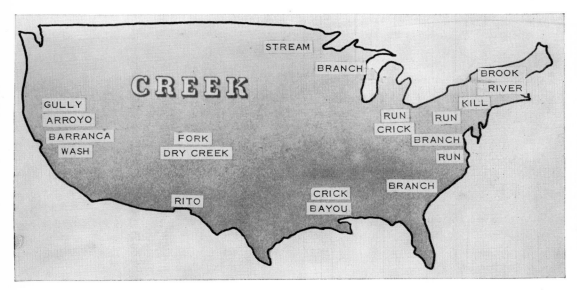

*These two linguistic maps of the United States locate certain regional expressions used to refer to common objects.*

SOURCE: Adapted from Gledhill Cameron, "Some Words Stop at Marietta, Ohio," *Collier's*, June 25, 1955, p. 78. Reproduced by permission of the publisher and the artist.

Stuart Chase has effectively pointed out the power of words.[6] He also shows that many of the problems that plague us are due to communication failure and that certain words as "liberty," "security," "co-existence," "bureaucracy," and "welfare state" mean different things to different people.[7] Some are "fighting" words. Some words are also omnibus words. "Freedom" is such a word. The word does not mean much until it is analyzed in the context of "freedom for what" or "freedom to do what." "Aggression" is such a word. It means different things in different cultures and must be analyzed for specificity before it means much. Language has been referred to as a map and a tool. The culture determines the use of the map and the map can mean different things to the people of different cultures. All that we are doing here is attempting to show the importance of semantics and suggesting that better translation of meaning of words and that better contacts and discussions are necessary if the key problems of semantics are to be solved.

### Subliminal communication

Psychologists have used subliminal perception or communication for many years to effect a mood, an attitude, or to help establish an idea. Its use is based on the human ability to absorb sights and sounds that cross the threshold of the subconsciousness but which, because of their fleeting nature, are not detected consciously.

From what we know, subliminal communication came to public view in the fall of 1957 when a machine was invented, by a person working in the field of motivational research, to flash brief advertisements on television or motion picture screens. The machine was first used in a motion picture theater to request the patrons to purchase coca cola and popcorn. Afterwards, we are told, popcorn sales increased 58 per cent and coca cola sales 18 per cent.[8] Since then this method of advertising has been used considerably in television and motion picture advertisement. There are those who say that subliminal communication has many political possibilities, especially in creating "subliminal awareness" of the names of politicians, and political issues at stake.

Subliminal communication could well be used for purposes of manipulation and exploitation of the public, just as other methods of communication may be so used; however, there seem to be few arguments against its valid use. While some people have put subliminal stimulation on the same level as hypnosis, its use would appear to lie in the area of illusion, which even has a legitimate use in communication. In the meantime, the full possibilities and limitations of subliminal stimulation in communications would seem to lie in further research.

## MASS MEDIA OF COMMUNICATION

Whatever the method of communication, and all three in various combinations are in current use, much communication today takes place through what are called mass media. The term *mass media* is used in two ways. First, it is used to denote a mechanism of impersonal reproduction and transmission between the speaker and the audience (Fig. 37). Radio, television, movies, books, periodicals, and newspapers are common examples. Second, mass media may refer to media of communication which reach the masses. Although no minimums have been set for determining what proportion of the population must be reached before a medium is called a mass medium, certain comic books would be so classified since they reach more than 90 per cent of American children between eight and 14 years of age. Because they reach masses of people, television and radio are mass media. Mass media, then,

[6] Stuart Chase, *Power of Words* (New York: Harcourt, Brace and Co., 1954).

[7] Stuart Chase, *The Proper Study of Mankind* (New York: Harper and Bros., 1956), p. 277.

[8] Richard P. Barthol, "The Subliminal Rabbit," *The Nation*, 187:356-58, November 15, 1958.

are those mechanical devices used to decode and transmit the spoken word, music, songs, and pictures from the sender to the listener, greatly amplifying the audience in communication, as indicated in Figure 37. These media are in contrast to face-to-face discourse, such as the lecture, the concept, or the spoken word, in which no intervening mechanism is used between the sender and the audience, and where the audience is much more restricted.

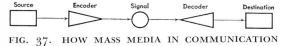

FIG. 37. HOW MASS MEDIA IN COMMUNICATION OPERATE

SOURCE: Wilbur Schramm (ed.), *The Process and Effects of Mass Communication* (Urbana, Ill.: The University of Illinois Press, 1954), p. 4.

1. *The availability of mass media.* From time to time the United Nations Educational, Cultural, and Scientific Organization makes an inventory of major forms of mass media communication facilities for which data are obtainable. Table 34 shows the extent of such facilities in 12 important nations of the world. Data on the percentage of illiteracy in the populations of the selected countries are also given.

While Table 34 shows unevenness in the distribution of mass communication facilities as between different countries, growth of facilities in most countries has been rapid. In many parts of the world where mass media are not as accessible as in the United States, there is no way of telling how many people may use a single facility. In some Greek villages, for instance, where there are only one or two television sets, on certain nights many families will congregate around the sets to watch the shows and hear the news.

2. *Mass media in the United States.* As of January 1958, 75 per cent of all households had telephones, 83 per cent had one or more television sets, and 97 per cent of all households had one or more radios. Telephones per 1,000 population increased from 162 in 1930 to 281 in 1950 and to 379 in 1958.

The percentage of households with tele-

vision sets increased from 80 per cent in 1957, to 83 per cent in 1958, and to 86 per cent in 1959. There are, of course, regional differences in the availability of communication facilities. For instance, the percentage of households in 1959 having television sets was 92 per cent in the Northeast, 88 per cent in the North Central states, 79 per cent in the South, and 86 per cent in the West.

The net circulation of daily newspapers was 52.2 million in 1948 and 59 million in 1958. New books copyrighted in the United States numbered 177 million in 1940 and 227 million in 1958.[9] We have indicated the increasing educational attainment of the population in Chapter 6.

The availability of mass media is one thing; their use is something else. On the basis of some 7,000 interviews in 48 states, the extent of the use of mass media of communication is indicated by the following data developed by one of the leading marketing analysis firms.

There were 123,262,000 people in the United States over 12 years during the week September 8-14, 1957. This is how they spent their time—

81.8% (100,828,000) spent 385.6 million hours reading newspapers

63.3% (78,025,000) spent 1438.5 million hours watching television

55.1% (67,917,000) spent 919.7 million hours listening to radio

46.1% (56,864,000) spent 237.9 million hours attending movies

29.2% (35,993,000) spent 170.8 million hours reading magazines.[10]

[9] U.S. Bureau of the Census, *Statistical Abstract of the United States, 1958* (79th ed.; Washington, D.C.: U.S. Government Printing Office, 1958 and 1959). *See also* Alfred Politz Research, Inc., *The Importance of Radio in Television Areas Today* (New York: Henry J. Christol Co., 1953), Appendix 34, and Bernard Berelson, *The Library's Public* (Manuscript of study prepared for the Public Library Inquiry of the Social Science Research Council, November, 1948), p. 3.

[10] Data compiled by Sindlinger and Company, Analysts, Ridley Park, Pennsylvania. Copyright 1957, Sindlinger and Company, and reported in *Broadcasting-Telecasting*, September 23, 1957, p. 40. For a good discussion of the magazine industry and its impact, *see* Theodore Peterson, *Magazines in the Twentieth Century* (Urbana, Ill.: University of Illinois Press, 1956).

*Table 34*

## POPULATION, ILLITERACY, AND MASS COMMUNICATION FACILITIES IN TWELVE SELECTED COUNTRIES, 1955

| Country | Popu- lation (Rounded Millions) | Per Cent Illit- erate | No. Radio Receivers | No. TV Receivers | No. Cinemas | No. Daily Papers | Daily Newspaper Circulation |
|---|---|---|---|---|---|---|---|
| China | 583 | 50-55 | 1,500,000 | — | 800 | 776 | 8,000,000 |
| India | 372 | 80-85 | 695,000 | — | 2,933 | 330 | 2,500,000 |
| USSR | 209 | 7-10 | 20,000,000 | 700,000 | 39,961 | 7,800 | 44,000,000 |
| USA | 160 | 2-3 | 127,000,000 | 35,000,000 | 19,000 | 1,786 | 55,000,000 |
| Japan | 87 | 2-3 | 11,263,000 | 35,000 | 3,750 | 179 | 34,500,000 |
| Brazil | 56 | 50-55 | 2,500,000 | 120,000 | 2,850 | 254 | — |
| United Kingdom | 51 | 1-2 | 13,873,000 | 4,156,000 | 4,500 | 137 | 31,000,000 |
| West Germany | 51 | 1-2 | 12,170,000 | 100,000 | 5,300 | 671 | 16,000,000 |
| France | 43 | 4-5 | 8,853,000 | 125,000 | 5,300 | 132 | 10,280,000 |
| Mexico | 28 | 40-45 | 1,500,000 | 100,000 | 2,062 | 162 | 1,300,000 |
| Turkey | 22 | 65-70 | 647,000 | — | 275 | 116 | 700,000 |
| Egypt | 22 | 75-80 | 405,000 | — | 365 | 46 | 500,000 |

Source: Compiled from United Nations Educational, Scientific, and Cultural Organization, *World Communication* (Paris: UNESCO, 1956), p. 362.

From the preceding data it is obvious that Americans possess and utilize mass media of communication on a very substantial basis. The extent of possession and use indicates the great possibilities mass media have for forming opinions and influencing the tastes of the population. Such data have implications for our democratic system and for the high degree of freedom which should be exercised in the management of facilities of mass media.

We must, however, use such data as the above, and those in Table 34, with caution. We must also use caution when we compare the data on the availability of mass media in India and the United States. One battery radio, in an Indian village, operated two hours a day, may be of greater influence for social change and social control than a radio in every house in the United States. A documentary or propaganda film coming to such a village in an underdeveloped country can have an influence which the film as an escapist or amusement device in America does not possess. And the less developed countries are increasingly using such mass media as devices for expanding political movements and for social control and education as well as for the dissemination of news.

### SPECIFIC ADVANTAGES OF CERTAIN FORMS OF MASS MEDIA

Each form of mass media in communication has its own distinct advantages. Television, for instance, has the advantage of both the spoken word and visual aid, supported by whatever sounds and props are necessary to develop the telecast into an effective communication medium.

Klapper summarizes the peculiar advantages of key means of communication:

(1) *Print* permits the reader to govern the pace and occasions of exposure, permits successive re-exposure, and allows for treatment at any length. Of all mass media, print is apparently the least reluctant to give expression to minority views, and

publications specially designed for such expression are extremely effective persuasive agents.

(2) *Radio* reaches an audience not often reached by the other mass media, and tending to be more poorly cultured and more suggestible than the audience of other media. Radio affords the spectator some degree of participation in the actual event being broadcast, and thus approaches face-to-face contact. Radio has been alleged to possess unique persuasive capabilities because of its often being the first medium to communicate given material to the audience, and because of a group feeling alleged to be experienced by the audience. These last two allegations are neither supported nor disproved by existing empirical evidence.

(3) The *screen* is believed to enjoy unique persuasive and pedagogical advantages by virtue of its presenting concrete visual material. These concrete settings and other factors are believed by some investigators to render the films taking "emotional possession" of children. While it is established that children tend to accept without question information presented in films, the pedagogical and persuasive implications of this trust have not been made clear, nor has it been shown that other media do not achieve similar effects.[11]

Face-to-face discourse, as in personal conversation, which is decreasing percentagewise, has many virtues over other means of communication. It is here that heretical ideas have most freedom. It is a flexible means of communication. Immediate responses or failure to respond may be detected. The personal qualities of the relationships involved may weaken or strengthen the process.

Effectiveness of means of communication depends not only upon the method but upon the state of mind or condition of the receiver and the social situation in which the receiver finds himself. The response to a television show may be different in the quiet of a home than it would be in a crowd at a bar. The response to music when one is accompanied by his best girl may be different than when one is alone. Response to the same martial music is different in wartime than in peacetime.

### THE IMPACT OF MASS COMMUNICATION

By impact of mass media we mean some of the social functions served by mass media and some of the influences of mass media upon cultural and social life.

1. *Speedy transmission.* One of the major social effects of mass media of communication has been the increase in speed of transmission of news, music, and pictures. This, of course, means that time and distance have been nearly erased by mass media. Speedy transmission means that vast audiences know of incidents moments after they occur. Thus to a culture already extremely time-conscious another element of consciousness of time in communication is added. Millions of people listen to their radios in order to get news before the items appear in newspapers.

2. *Completeness of coverage.* At one time conversation and the printed page were the chief means of communication. Mass media communication was limited to those who could read. Of course, there was a verbal spread of items appearing on the printed page from the reader to other receivers. Now the volume of communication facilities and media in communication have increased so that coverage has greatly broadened. A factor in completeness of coverage is the growing sensitivity of mass media to audience response. In this lie dangers of contributing to the baser tastes and credulities of the consuming public. Radio and television have audiences greater than any single printed document. A single telecast may reach 30 million people. People who cannot read watch television and listen to the radio. Broadcasts are frequently interpreted into two or more tongues. People who never read a book purchase radio and television sets.

Certain broadcasts and telecasts make special appeal to a particular group, such as housewives. Certain age groups are appealed

[11] Joseph T. Klapper, *The Effects of Mass Media* (New York: Columbia University, Bureau of Applied Sociology, October, 1950), pp. II, 28-29.

to by comic books, magazines, radio, and television programs. Mass media programs, designed to appeal to minorities or to a single sex, are also common, as are special newspapers and magazines. What this discussion adds up to is completeness of coverage by the various mass media of communication.

3. *Propaganda potential.* The completeness of coverage of mass media, and the speed with which transmission takes place, means that the potential for the use of mass media for propaganda purposes is tremendous. Incidents, propaganda, or false reports may be used to incite revolts or demonstrations of a segment of a population. A political clique may control a communication facility. As an illustration, in 1958 the vice-president of the United States scheduled a series of visits to South American countries. The news of his contemplated visits was relayed to Communist groups in the countries he visited, where carefully timed demonstrations were held. Incidents of race conflict in Little Rock, Arkansas, in 1957 and 1958 were effectively used as anti-American propaganda. The prospect of the use of mass media for propaganda purposes raises the very important problem of who controls the mass media.

4. *Relaxation and escapism.* There is substantial literature on the contribution made by mass communication to relaxation and escapism. Anxieties and tensions are fairly routine in life. Music and some forms of drama tend to relieve such tensions and anxieties. Reading may also serve a similar purpose, as do broadcasts and telecasts of sports events, although these may have their moments of tenseness. Whatever the media, emotional release is provided the receiver by diverting him from his own problems and anxieties. There are perhaps four ways in which communications serve escapist functions: [12]

(a) by providing for relaxation
(b) by providing compensation and prestige to the individual

[12] Adapted from *ibid.*, p. III-7.

(c) by serving as a safety valve for physical and social tensions
(d) by serving as a source of advice and information

5. *Source of serious information.* Mass media of communication serve as a source of serious information and for providing assistance in the interpretation of public affairs. From the data available, newspapers, news telecasts, and radio broadcasts best serve this purpose. The newspaper is widely used as a buying and selling guide as well as a theater guide. Persons seeking jobs peruse the help wanted columns. It was found in a study made during a newspaper strike in New York that missing the newspaper gave a sense of insecurity to many readers. [13]

6. *Status value.* Communication facilities and programs give status to people and events. A single telecast or broadcast of an unknown song may put it on the "hit" list. For weeks it may be a best seller, thus giving status to the song, its singer, and perhaps its composer. People who are at the center of the mass media stage are likely to have status just because they are performing artists.

Events likewise are given status. Newscasts now pick up on-the-scene news events and personalities and telecast and broadcast them to mass populations, thus adding status and importance to places, people, and events in the news.

7. *The improvement of tastes.* While people tend to select largely the radio and television programs and the books and periodicals they are interested in, there is some evidence that the tastes of people are improved by exposure to music, drama, and written material above the level of their accustomed consumption and tastes.

After summarizing the studies available on the subject of taste and mass media of communication, Klapper arrives at the following

[13] Bernard Berelson, "What Missing the Newspaper Means" in *The Process and Effects of Mass Communication,* ed. Wilbur Schram (Urbana, Ill.: University of Illinois Press, 1954), pp. 36-47.

conclusions, which are neither very positive nor negative:

The essential value of these data for our present purpose lies in its strong indication that mass media in general cater to existing standards of taste, bringing the better material to those who like better material and the poorer material to those of lesser taste. The media tend to reinforce rather than alter already established taste patterns. We have thus far been speaking, however, only of tendencies, of what has been in most cases. None of these data thus far adduced suggests that mass media cannot or never do alter established tastes.[14]

Suchman found that radio did contribute significantly to the improvement of musical tastes among listeners. Lazarsfeld reports a study which arrives at a similar conclusion.[15] No doubt record players or phonographs and television contribute to the improvement of music tastes. Record sales of quality musical selections indicate this, as do research studies of the subject.

8. *The development of knowledge, attitudes, and opinion changes.* The problem of evaluating the influence of mass media upon changes in knowledge, attitudes, and public opinion is difficult. People are exposed to many sources of stimulation.[16] They may not know precisely where their knowledge and attitudes toward a subject come from. If they change their opinion they may not know precisely what led them to change.

The acceptance of new ideas is a complicated process. Gallup indicates that the incorporation of a new idea into the thinking process is more pronounced in groups than in individuals. The most important factors in acceptance are the complexity of the idea, the susceptibility of the idea to proof and demonstration, the extent to which the idea is opposed, the degree to which there is a felt need

for the idea, and the frequency with which the public is reminded of the idea.[17]

Studies show that the presentation of factual material by communities increases the listeners' knowledge in the areas dealt with. The predictions of commentators, as in the prediction of the outcome of elections, change audience opinion in the direction of the expressed predictions.[18]

9. *The development of consensus.* One of the greatest social values of mass media of communication, and yet one of its greatest dangers, lies in the use of mass media for the development of consensus.[19]

Consensus is necessary for a society. It is also necessary for the smooth functioning of social systems. We have explored this topic in Chapter 5. There are many ways of establishing consensus. Consensus, of a type, may be established through force and the power of authority. It may be established through the transmission of common elements in the cultural heritage, through identification with great heroes and leaders, and through the symbols and ideas, including propaganda, associated with great leaders. Persuasion, arbitration, diplomacy, and bargaining constitute other bases for forming consensus.

In a democracy we place much emphasis upon the development of public opinion in the development of consensus. "Public opinion is formed in the course of living, acting, and making decisions on issues."[20] Clashes over issues, and sometimes personalities, frequently precipitate the formation of public opinion. The dynamic effect of public opinion lies in its power to influence decision-makers in social systems. Consensus, in the sense that it is used

14 *Ibid.,* I-26.
15 *Ibid.,* pp. I-33-34.
16 *See* C. R. Wright, "Evaluating Mass Media Campaigns," *International Social Science Bulletin,* 7:417-30, 1955.
17 George Gallup, "The Absorption Rate of Ideas," *Public Opinion Quarterly,* 19:234-42, Fall, 1955.
18 Howard E. Freeman, H. Ashley, and Walter J. Wirtheimer, "New Commentator Effect: A Study in Knowledge and Opinion Change," *Public Opinion Quarterly,* 19:209-15, Summer, 1955.
19 These potentials have been well explored in a lively article by Louis Wirth entitled, "Consensus and Mass Communication," *American Sociological Review,* 13:5-12, February, 1948.
20 *Ibid.,* p. 439.

in democracies, does not mean complete agreement, but often agreement on the most critical issues and frequently an expression from a minority of people.

As Wirth so well points out, when once established—

Consensus is supported and maintained not only by the ties of interdependence and by a common cultural base, by a set of institutions embodying the settled traditions of the people, and the norms and standards they imply and impose, not merely by living together, and dealing with one another, but also, and not least important, by the continuing currents of mass communication, which in turn

rest for their meaningfulness and effectiveness upon the pre-existence of some sort of a society, which hold that society together and mobilize it for continuous concerted action.[21]

The reach of mass communication to all kinds of societies in all parts of the world enlarges greatly the scope of its use in the formation of consensus, as well as in driving wedges of separation between peoples. It also raises the very grave problem of the quality and level of materials transmitted in communication, as well as the more serious problem of control of mass media. The latter problem we shall explain presently.

### THE ISSUE OF SOCIAL CONTROL

In 1959, 4,466 broadcasting TV and radio stations were on the air in the United States. Added to these were other important mass media. Increasingly, we are dependent upon mass media to hold societies together. In fact, the human race depends more and more upon mass communication to hold it together. As Wirth says: "Mass communication is rapidly becoming, if it is not already, the main framework of the web of social life."[22]

Hitler showed how, by controlling the content of the social heritage transmitted for a generation, a false concept of a superior Aryan race could be built up in a new generation. By controlling mass communication, both in media and content, he developed not only a tough, hating, fighting machine, but also a tough, hating public to support him. The democracies, especially the United States and Great Britain, for two decades have had a tough time counteracting propaganda made possible by controlled mass communication channels from communist countries to the more undeveloped countries.

Many years ago, the actor Orson Welles threw the Atlantic seaboard into panic by broadcasting a convincing dramatization of

the invasion of the earth by warriors from the planet Mars.[23]

The above discussion, plus the data on the scope and availability of means of communication in the modern-day world, are enough to point up the critical problem of control. The congressional hearings on the fixing of television quiz shows held in 1959 point to the need of controls to prevent the "rigging" of telecasts.

Perhaps in the near future the United Nations may move more freely into the problem of communication facilities, channels, and control. To date it would seem to have godlike responsibilities for social control but mouselike abilities to meet them. This is a problem worth exploring by the interested student.

There are those who greatly favor the governmental ownership and control of broadcasting facilities, both radio and television, in the United States. These advocates often point to the British Broadcasting Corporation, to its experiences in airing programs without detracting commercials, and to its successful experiments in bringing good art, music, and high cultural values to selected audiences.

21 *Ibid.*, pp. 441-42.
22 *Ibid.*, p. 442.

23 For an interesting account of the panic created by this broadcast, *see* Hadley H. Cantril, *Invasion from Mars* (Princeton, N.J.: Princeton University Press, 1940).

Recently the movement for paid television was undemocratically squelched by powerful pressure groups. Obviously, governmental regulation of a type which will preserve many of the advantages of private ownership and control of communication facilities, and yet give us some of the advantage of government-owned facilities, is very difficult in a country where pressure groups are so strong, and where money talks so effectively and convincingly. Perhaps a little more socialism might pay off in the control of the broadcasting services. There are many local examples of merchants, turned politicians, who use their commercial broadcasting programs for political propaganda, apparently with little or no censorship or control.

We, in general, accept the principle of freedom in mass communication. Some suppliers will misuse this freedom until such time as an enlightened public requires an improved quality of the kinds of communication transmitted via mass media. In the meantime, the following avenues of control are open in mass communication:

1. *Governmental regulation.* It is obvious that radio networks, television channels, and telephone and telegraph operations cannot successfully operate without some federal coordination of channels, wave lengths, and so on. On this point there is little argument.[24] It is beyond such controls that arguments develop.

2. *Police powers.* State and local units of government have wide discretionary use of police powers, which give them the right to establish censorship and review boards to examine and, if necessary, ban broadcasts, unwholesome movies, telecasts, books, comics, and newspapers. Licenses are usually issued to firms dealing in communication media. The power to license and tax also means the power to control the taxable media, at least to some degree.

3. *Trade control.* The motion picture industry perhaps does one of the best jobs of trade control of its productions of any medium of communication. Television and radio broadcasters and newspapers have standards which they try to achieve in their productions. Lately, the publishers of comic books have attempted trade control. Trade control has much in its favor over other methods of control in that it institutes controls at the source where the communicating document, film, or telecast originates.

## SUMMARY

Communication is fundamental in any social system or system of interaction. It is, therefore, fundamental in society as a means of establishing consensus and bringing about social unity and organization.

In the communicating process usually two or more means of communication are combined. The leading combinations are made up of gestures, symbols, sounds, and language. Language, of course, is the major means of communication. While there have been some attempts to establish an international language, the attempts have not been successful.

Where a mechanical device or mechanism is used between the speaker and the audience in communication, the term "mass media" is used to cover the device. Important mass media are the telephone, telegraph, phonograph, tape recorder, radio, television, and the newspaper. In general, there is a great upswing in the use of most forms of mass media throughout the world, with the populations of the United States and England being widely served by the principal forms of mass media.

Each form of mass medium has its peculiar advantages. Many forms are used in combination with one another to give an effect superior to any one form.

The impact of mass media is tremendous.

24 *See* Elmer Lewis (ed.), *Radio Laws of the United States* (Washington, D.C.: House of Representatives, 1954).

Speedy transmission of music and news and completeness of coverage of different segments of population are provided. Mass media may serve propaganda advantages, relaxation, and escape. They serve as sources of serious information, adding status to people and events, improving tastes, increasing knowledge, and changing public opinion.

THINGS TO DO AND TO DISCUSS

1. What is communication? Why is it fundamental in social interaction and in establishing consensus in a society?
2. What are the more important means of communication?
3. What are some of the reasons for linguistic differences within the English language in the United States today?
4. What are mass media of communication? Give examples.
5. From the data presented, what countries are best supplied with communication facilities?
6. Give the peculiar advantages of (1) the printed page, (2) radio, (3) television, and (4) subliminal stimulation as media of communication.
7. In your community, what has been the major social impact of mass media of communication?
8. What are some of the most effective methods of control over mass media of communication? What methods are effective in your community?
9. What are the pro and con arguments for governmental ownership of broadcasting facilities as contrasted with privately owned and operated facilities?

FOR FURTHER STUDY

ALLPORT, GORDON W., and POSTMAN, L. *The Psychology of Rumor.* New York: Henry Holt and Co., 1947. How rumors originate, spread, and decline.

CHERRY, COLIN. *On Human Communication.* New York: John Wiley and Sons, 1957. Comprehensive, general treatment on communication.

EMERY, EDWIN; AULT, PHILIP H.; and AGEE, WARREN K. *Introduction to Mass Communications.* New York: Dodd, Mead and Co., 1960. A good description of the Mass Communications industry and its role in modern society.

GALLUP, GEORGE. "The Absorption Rate of Ideas," *Public Opinion Quarterly,* **19**:234-42, Fall, 1955. One of the better things on the ability of the public to absorb new ideas.

KLAPP, ORRIN E. "The Concept of Consensus and Its Importance," *Sociology and Social Research,* May-June, 1957, pp. 336-42. Good treatment on consensus and how it is formed.

KLAPPER, JOSEPH T. *The Effects of Mass Media.* New York: Columbia University, Bureau of Applied Social Research, October, 1950. Mimeographed. The social impact of mass media well treated.

NAFZIGER, RALPH O., and WHITE, DAVID M., eds. *Introduction to Mass Communications Research.* Baton Rouge, La.: Louisiana State University Press, 1958. Good treatment of methodology in communications research.

PACKARD, VANCE. *The Hidden Persuaders.* New York: David McKay Co., 1957. How the public is manipulated in an age of mass communication.

PETERSON, THEODORE. *Magazines in the Twentieth Century.* Urbana, Ill.: University of Illinois Press, 1956. The role of magazines in communication.

ROSENBERG, BERNARD, and WHITE, DAVID MANNING. *Mass Culture.* Glencoe, Ill.: Free Press, 1957. The impact of mass culture and the role of communications in forming it.

SCHATZMAN, LEONARD, and STRAUSS, ANSELM. "Social Class and Modes of Communication," *American Journal of Sociology,* **61**:329-38, January, 1955. Class selectivity in communication.

SCHRAMM, WILBUR. *The Process and Effects of Mass Communication.* Urbana, Ill.: University of Illinois Press, 1954. How communication takes place and some of its broad social effects.

STEINBERG, CHARLES S. *The Mass Communicators.* New York: Harper and Bros., 1958. Major sources of mass communication well treated.

UNITED NATIONS ECONOMIC AND SOCIAL COUNCIL. *World Communications.* Paris: UNESCO, 1956. The best source of data on world communication facilities.

WIRTH, LOUIS. "Consensus and Mass Communication," *American Sociological Review,* **13**:5-12, February, 1948. An excellent article on consensus, how it is formed, and the importance of communications in forming consensus.

WRIGHT, C. R. "Evaluating Mass Media Campaigns," *International Social Science Bulletin,* **7**:417-30, 1955. Some answers to the effectiveness of mass media campaigns.

# 19. SOCIAL MOVEMENTS

FROM TIME TO TIME there appears in the structure and functioning of a society an idea or a trend which fires the imagination of a lot of people and finally develops a following. If this idea or trend in thought and action brings about some fundamental change in the economic, political, or social thinking of the people, then it has the earmarks of a social movement. A social movement must not be confused with a social fad or craze.

## THE MEANING OF SOCIAL MOVEMENTS

A social movement is defined by one student of the subject as follows: "A movement is a type of collective behavior by means of which some large segment of a society attempts to accomplish adjustment of conditions in its culture which it thinks are in maladjustment." [1]

Another authority defines a social movement as a concerted and persistent effort on the part of a grouping of people to institute a social order, to resist change, or to perpetuate a social order, or parts of it. [2]

A group or structural concept of a social movement states that "... a social movement will be understood to be a group venture extending beyond a local community or a single event and involving a systematic effort to inaugurate in thought, behavior, and social relationships." [3]

The term "social movement" implies a certain amount of mobility and a certain amount of fluctuation. On the whole, social movements must be for and against something. [4] They are, after inception, wide-scale in follow-

[1] Carl C. Taylor, *The Farmers' Movement, 1620-1920* (New York: American Book Co., 1953), p. 1.
[2] Logan Wilson and W. L. Kolb, *Sociological Analysis* (New York: Harcourt, Brace and Co., 1949), p. 828.

[3] C. Wendell King, *Social Movements in the United States* (New York: Random House, 1956), p. 27.
[4] Seba Eldridge and Associates, *Fundamentals of Society* (New York: Thomas Y. Crowell Co., 1950), p. 428.

ing, in that they must enlist the support of many people. A nation-wide movement would, of course, have the support of many more people than a community, state, or regional movement. The movement must entail making some fundamental changes in one or more segments of the thinking and behavior of the people of the area in which it develops. For instance, the labor movement, which started in England and which suffered delayed development in the United States because of immigrant slave labor and the vastness and rapid development of the country, had as a major purpose the organizing of labor in order to strengthen its bargaining power. Another purpose of the labor movement was to establish a favorable attitude toward labor and its prob-lems in the minds of the public. It brought about fundamental changes in labor legislation, in working conditions, and in the labor market in that collective bargaining, that is, bargaining by craft and industry, was substituted for the process of individual bargaining.

Scope and purpose are important identifying characteristics of a social movement. They are important in differentiating a social movement from a social trend, the latter being a social or cultural change in the direction of a central tendency. Scope and purpose are also important in differentiating a social movement from social change, which is only a deviation from the past in one or more aspects of a people's culture. Cultural change is a broad enough concept to include social change.[5]

## DISTINGUISHING CHARACTERISTICS OF SOCIAL MOVEMENTS

*Desire for change* is one of the crucial characteristics of a social movement. While this desire may not be deep-seated or articulate at the time of the inception of a movement, this is one of the things that social movement leaders try to accomplish.

The desire for change must become strong enough, or the character of the change appealing enough, to attract a following. How large a following is necessary to constitute the nucleus of a movement depends upon the scope of the movement. A simple reform in a country of 175 million people would need support only from those people who would be concerned with bringing about the reform. Mass change in a society would require a larger following.

Obviously, a social movement has to have a *geographical setting*. It is concerned with the people of an area. Some social movements are world movements in that they have appeared persistently and recognizably in dozens of dissimilar countries. Among these are militarism, nationalism, feminism, industrialism, literacy campaigns, public health campaigns, Christianity, communism, socialism, and liberalism.

As we tried to indicate in the previous chapter on communication, with the world-wide influence of mass media, it is entirely possible that social movements may spread much more rapidly today, and in the future, than in the past. It is also possible that more movements may reach world-wide proportions in the future than in the past. At least, they are likely to reach world-wide proportions faster.

Nationalism and socialism are social movements at their peak in that they propose to effect changes in national economies. Of course, they may spread from one country to another. Democracy as a social movement has had similar spread. Other movements are regional. An example is the recent States' Rights and White Citizens' Council movements which developed in the South to oppose integration in the public schools. Other movements may be state-wide in scope. In short, there are various kinds of societies, ranging from national to community. A social movement may encompass one or more societies.

In its inception a social movement is amorphous, without organization and without a

[5] For more on how a social movement differs from a social trend or tendency, *see* Rudolf Heberle, *Social Movements* (New York: Appleton-Century-Crofts, 1951), pp. 1-19.

leader. One of the sources of social power is organization. A social movement has to have *organization,* and part of organization is a directing force or hand. A successful movement has to have an organization adequate to develop, nourish, and sustain the movement. The degree of complexity and formality of the organizational machinery will depend upon the nature and scope of the movement. For instance, the Women's Christian Temperance Union (W.C.T.U.), spearheading the movement for temperance and abolition of the use of alcoholic beverages throughout the United States and its possessions, had not only to do an educational job on the ill effects of alcohol, but had also to seek to make the state and nation "dry" through local, state, and national legislation. This meant an elaborate organization was necessary all the way down from the national to the community level. A more intellectual or religious movement would perhaps need less elaborate organization than the

W.C.T.U. with its printing presses, brochures, extensive release of films, publications and newspaper articles, and individual leaders. As a social movement progresses it becomes collective, rational behavior to the extent that it has an ideology, a well-defined goal, a set of rules limiting the behavior, and a division of labor within the movement.

Finally, social movements have a *persistence.* They endure. The growth of an articulate Farmers' movement in this country was traced by Taylor from 1620 to 1920—a period of 300 years. This movement was made up of many submovements, such as the Grange movement, the Farmers' Alliance, the Farmers' Union, and the Nonpartisan League.[6] The movement for racial segregation in the South has had a longer life than has the counter-integration movement. Liberalism as a movement has required many centuries, whereas the National Christian Crusade dates from 1948 when the "crusade" or "party" was formed.

### CONDITIONS FAVORABLE TO THE DEVELOPMENT OF SOCIAL MOVEMENTS

#### Social heterogeneity

King holds that social heterogeneity in the structure and organization of a society, plus cultural confusion and individual discontent, tend to provide conditions favorable to the growth of social movements.[7] We are willing to accept these views, but would like to add a fourth, and that is a tolerance for social movements. Thus, as we see it, there are four important conditions favorable to social movements:

1. social heterogeneity
2. cultural confusion
3. individual discontent
4. tolerance for change.

Since ideas are an important part of a social movement, new ideas are more likely to develop in a heterogeneous society, where there

6 Taylor, *op. cit.*
7 King, *op. cit.,* pp. 13-17.

are many diverse peoples and interests, than in a homogeneous society. For instance, it would require a biracial society for segregation-integration movements to spring up. Anti-Semitism would hardly develop on an organized basis except in a culture containing Jews and non-Jews. Farming interests and crop regions have been so diverse in the United States that they have spawned many kinds of farmers' movements. This diversity has even been so great as to make it difficult for farmers of all sections to support any single movement.

#### Cultural confusion

Social movements are often the result of cultural confusion and lag. If widespread in a society, social confusion makes for turmoil and uncertainty and creates a favorable soil in which social movements may develop. For example, until the period following World

*Acme Photo*

*A social movement must have a following. Adolf Hitler, who whipped to destructive flame and to psychic illness the National Socialist movement in Germany, speaks to one of his mass meetings. This movement had many features of the Fascist movement developed in Italy under Mussolini.*

War I, the pattern of racial segregation was well established in the South. The principle of separate but equal facilities had been upheld by the U.S. Supreme Court in 1896 (*Plessey vs. Ferguson,* 1896). From 1915 to 1959 there was a series of Supreme Court decisions declaring segregation unconstitutional in land zoning, in transportation, in colleges, in recreation, and finally in public schools.[8]

To challenge the Supreme Court decisions there were many attempts in the South to pass legislation to maintain segregation in the schools or to postpone the integration of the schools. Such laws in general were declared unconstitutional or the federal courts refused

[8] For a good discussion of the rise and decline of segregation, *see* Guy B. Johnson, "Freedom, Equality and Segregation," *The Review of Politics,* **20**:147-63, April, 1958.

to hear them. The result was further conflict. In some states the Ku Klux Klan was reorganized. In other states the White Citizens' Council developed. Only time will tell how permanent the movements developed during this period will prove to be.

Cultural confusion often results from the fact that the goals sought by people are not clear or are unattainable through the institutions and by the methods with which the people are accustomed to obtaining goals. A case in point was the great depression of the 1930's. Twelve million men were out of work. The ordinary channels for obtaining jobs did not produce them. The impact on the public was so severe and the public so confused that the whole social security movement skyrocketed. Anyone who had a panacea for unemployment received a hearing. Finally the Social

Security Act was passed and social security as a responsibility of government is now widely accepted.

The depression gave rise to such movements as the Townsend movement, which was a movement to obtain federally and state-supported pensions of substantial amounts for all aged people.

### Individual discontent

If the discontent of a society cannot make itself articulate in the thinking of people, especially through the leadership of the people, it is not likely to be a strong force in generating a social movement. A precondition of a social movement is an issue, something to incite the people to action. If no discontent exists, then there is not likely to be enough demand for change to inspire a social movement. If the discontent exists and does not find expression in the thought and action of leaders, then the chances are good that a social movement will not develop. Discontent in a population which cannot find expression in a peaceful social movement may find expression in revolution. The French Revolution is an example.

Warner and Lunt have pointed out that "ideas of progress, of freedom, of democracy, and other values which are highly cherished in . . . the United States all sanction certain kinds of change, particularly technological, but they facilitate to lesser degree changes in social organization." [9]

### Tolerance for change

Whether or not discontent becomes articulate in a population and spawns leaders depends upon another factor favorable to social movements. This is tolerance for change. As Taylor says: "If a society is so structured that public manifestations of discontent are forbidden, then either revolutions are staged or the maladjustments continue. In a society which believes in democratically initiated change, movements are to be expected." [10]

## TYPES OF SOCIAL MOVEMENTS

Different authorities classify social movements differently. Blumer speaks of three broad classes: general movements, like the public health and the labor movements; specific movements, which he subdivides into reform and revolutionary movements; and expressive movements. While expressive movements originate out of tension and unrest, unlike others they do not attempt an objective change in the basic social systems of the social order. Religious movements and fashion movements are examples.[11]

For our purposes we will classify social movements into four generalized types: revo-lutionary, reform, coordinated, and uncoordinated movements.[12]

### Revolutionary movements

A revolutionary movement is one designed to bring about extensive changes in depth in the economy or in the political or social life of a society. A change in government from one form to a radically different form would be revolutionary in character, especially if it took place rapidly. It would likely be a widening of scope as well as a change in depth. We mean by depth changes, changes in the basic character of an institution or some aspect of society. A movement leading to such revolutionary change could be very gradual and could develop over a long period of time. The chances are, however, that it would be revolutionary in

[9] W. Lloyd Warner and Paul L. Lunt, *The Social Life of a Modern Community* (New Haven: Yale University Press, 1942), pp. 25-26.

[10] Taylor, *op. cit.*, p. 2.

[11] Herbert Blumer in Alfred M. Lee, *New Outline of the Principles of Sociology* (New York: Barnes and Noble, 1946), pp. 199-214.

[12] King, *op. cit.*, pp. 27-30.

character, being rapid in changing fundamental practices and perhaps value systems. Marxism is a revolutionary movement; so is socialism in some countries.

In many revolutionary movements agitation may be perpetuated among those who are distressed or exploited. Attempts are made to establish a strong following among such classes. Often, then, revolutionary movements operate among the underprivileged and the oppressed. The Cuban counterrevolutionary movement against dictator Batista in the winter of 1958-59 was a good example of such support.

## Reform movements

Social movements may be of reform type. We might even say that revolutionary movements are reform-seeking, but their methods and scope are different from reform movements. Rather, these are designed to accomplish, usually through peaceful means, reforms in some aspect of the economy or the political and social life, not usually extensive in scope or revolutionary in character. The labor movement, although at times rugged in character and full of conflict, could hardly be called a revolutionary movement. Rather, it has been a reform movement, seeking reforms in methods of collective bargaining, working conditions, wages and compensation, and treatment of those who are injured on the job, and reasonable insurance against the hazards of unemployment and old age.

An unusual kind of movement, which may well be discussed as a reform movement, is anarchy. This is so because most instances of anarchy are aimed at basic reforms or improvement in economic or social conditions.

*Anarchism* is the theory that the state should be abolished and replaced by the free association of individuals working through groups. Both the state and private property are looked upon as intrinsic evils. Socialism may be differentiated from anarchism in that it accepts certain kinds of private property and

believes in a strong state as a controller, operator, and owner of some forms of property.

The literature on anarchism is extensive, some works going back to Greek and Oriental philosophers who lived prior to the time of Christ.[13] According to the principles of anarchism codified by the Pittsburgh Congress of American Anarchists in 1883, anarchists emphasize the following principles in their reform movements:

[The fact that] (1) our unbearable social and moral evils cannot be cured, or even alleviated, by the state, which is necessarily an instrument of domination and exploitation. (2) Human nature is essentially good, if not corrupted by the state and its institutions. (3) All reforms from above are worthless and can only augment our present misfortune. Only the principle of federalism, beginning with the humblest of human relations and ascending to the highest international cooperation, can establish the new society. (4) This new society can only be the result of a revolutionary action (in the soul or in the social-political life) which will destroy the state. (5) Such a revolution, however, would be a complete failure if it built up a new government or any coercive system whatever. (6) The new society of anarchism will not be the product of an inevitable evolution (as is taught, for instance, by Marxist socialism) but will emanate from the natural tendencies of the human soul led by reason and justice and aided by scientific experimentation.[14]

Prince Kropotkin, who may be styled as an anarchist believing in complete communism, held that the state should be replaced by the free village commune. Modern socialistic movements, especially communism in its current forms, places, as we have indicated, a strong emphasis upon the need for the state.

The critics of anarchism point to the need of a coercive organization in any human society if unity and organization is to be achieved. They reason that only through violence can the state be destroyed and that, when

[13] For a lead to the exploration of such literature, *see Encyclopaedia of Social Sciences* (New York: The Macmillan Co., 1930), II, 46-53.

[14] *Ibid.*, p. 46.

once destroyed, a new state will replace the old. The use of violence and other "immoral" means to destroy the state would also destroy many of the good human impulses and tendencies upon which anarchism would build its new society.[15] Perhaps the moral of this discussion thus far is that democratic societies should try to make a major effort to curb those movements which might result in an excessive polarization of government in favor of movements which would stress the decentralization of governmental power and functions and the intensification of autonomous life in social systems. It is said that the United Nations is having to do its necessary and great work with practically no powers of governmental coercion, that is, within a framework of anarchy. An accepted law of good administration makes responsibility commensurate with power. The United Nations, credited with many excellent achievements administratively, obviously is an exception to this rule.

### Coordinated and uncoordinated movements

Social movements may also be classified as coordinated or uncoordinated. An uncoordinated movement spreads and may develop a big following and considerable influence, yet does not reflect careful coordination. In general, the over-all Farmers' movement, as Taylor describes it, has been of this type, although some of the farmers' organizations within the movement have been rather carefully coordinated. Up to now the Ku Klux Klan movement in the South has had poor coordination, as was true of a movement in the 1950's to elect states' rights candidates to the Congress and to governorship of the states.

In both revolutionary and reform movements there is class consciousness.

The reform movement, while usually existing on behalf of some distressed or exploited group, does little to establish its strength among them. Instead, it tries to enlist the allegiance of a middle-class public on the outside and to awaken within them a vicarious sympathy for the oppressed group. Hence, generally, it is infrequent that the leadership or membership of a reform movement comes from the group whose rights are being espoused.[16]

Although Heberle identifies the growth and development of democracy as a social movement its growth has not been well coordinated.[17] Totalitarian movements such as communism, fascism, and Nazism have, in the main, had better coordination. The Christian Science movement has evidenced considerable coordination, whereas the Townsend movement has not.

## STRUCTURAL ELEMENTS

Heberle conceives social movements as one form of group structure.[18] They may be looked upon as a form of social system with both structure and function.[19] They must first of all have certain *goals* which the movement is trying to accomplish. These goals may be of ideological nature or they may be highly practical and concrete, such as elections by secret ballot or old-age pensions. Goals may be short-range or long-range, may be defined in ideological concepts, or may be materialistic and empirical. Whichever they are, the ideology of a movement must be accepted, so *ideology* is a second structural element. The achievement of goals or the results obtained may be one factor in cohesion, as well as the character of the leadership which the movement has.

Cohesion and goal attainment imply *organization* at least adequate to sustain the movement and lead it to achievement, so organization becomes another structural element. In an attempt to perfect an organization and to achieve its goals, each movement develops its own set of *tactics*. For example, the labor movement developed strikes, boycotts, slowdowns, and legislative programs only to have management counter with lockouts, right-to-work laws, shutdowns, and other reprisals.

15 *Ibid.*, p. 52.
16 Blumer, as quoted in Lee, *op. cit.*, p. 213.
17 Heberle, *op. cit.*, pp. 38-62.
18 *Ibid.*
19 *See* Chap. 1.

*The Ku Klux Klan represents an uncoordinated type of social movement.*

*The Ku Klux Klan movement, which originated in Giles County, Tennessee, in 1865, was one of several organizations developing out of cliques of veterans who had returned home following the Civil War. Other groups in the South were the Constitutional Union Guards, The Pale Faces, and the Order of the White Rose. At first the functions of the Klan were fraternal, recreational, and its ritual burlesque. The name was derived from the Greek word "kuklos," meaning "circle" or "cycle." Later it became violently anti-Negro.*

*See* Edward James Pack, "The Sociology of a Social Movement, the Ku Klux Klan" (Master's thesis, University of Tennessee, Knoxville, 1950).

## LIFE HISTORY OF SOCIAL MOVEMENTS

Much more has been written about the life history of revolutions than of social movements. King identifies three phases in the internal development of a movement: *the incipient phase, the organizational phase,* and *the stable phase.*[20] In the external development of the career of a social movement he identifies three stages: *innovation, selection,* and *integration.* We are most concerned with the internal stages of the career of the movement. Regarding this we would accept King's three stages but would add a fourth, *a period of decline or senescence.* A social movement starts, then develops an organization and program which shows growth if the movement is successful. It may finally reach a point of stability and then decline.

## THE ROLE OF SOCIAL MOVEMENTS

Dawson and Gettys indicate two very important roles of social movements. They are

... symptoms of unrest and disorganization and ... possible tendencies which may cumulate to establish trends of change toward a new order of life.[21]

Movements then may reveal flaws in the social-economic complex and may serve to correct these. They may spearhead changes and trends, reflective not only of need but of the period in which they develop. They, of course, also afford opportunity for leadership and followership in a democracy.

## SUMMARY

Social movements are designed to bring about fundamental changes or reforms in some phase of the society supporting them. They develop out of desire for change, and to be successful must attract attention of enough people to effect the changes. They have a geographical or territorial setting, although this may be ill-defined. Some movements are worldwide. They have longevity or persistence in time, longevity depending in part upon the length of time it takes to get the movement launched and established and results accomplished.

Conditions giving rise to movements, or creating an atmosphere for movements, are heterogeneity of culture and interests, confusion, individual discontent, and tolerance for movements.

Social movements generally fall into two categories: revolutionary and reform types, and uncoordinated and coordinated movements. A special, and somewhat universal, type of reform movement is anarchy.

Social movements are social systems which have their own distinctive set of structural elements. These are, in the main, goals or objectives, a system of values or ideals built around the goals, and cohesion, organization, and tactics designed to achieve the goals. Finally, as social movements live out their lives they tend to reflect well-defined steps in their careers. They rise, have periods of growth and stability, and then most of them decline. This is so because most social movements are tied to an interval or to a period in history which reflects a distinctive set of problems.

Social movements serve the role of revealing discontent and unrest in a society and of attempting to correct this discontent. They serve also as outlets for both followership and leadership.

[20] C. Wendell King, *op. cit.*
[21] Carl A. Dawson and Warner E. Gettys, *An Introduction to Sociology* (New York: Ronald Press Co., 1948), p. 678.

THINGS TO DO AND TO DISCUSS

1. Have there been any social movements in your community? In your state? Identify these.
2. Make a study of a social movement and prepare a report on it. If possible, select one from your state or community. If this is not possible, the following topics may be suggestive:

> The Labor Movement
> The Growth of Liberalism
> Sectionalism and the South
> Sectionalism in New England
> National Socialism in Germany (Nazism)
> The Nature of Fascism in Italy
> The Development of Marxism
> The Social Psychology of Social Movements
> The Grange Movement
> The Rise of the Farm Bureau
> The Rise of the Ku Klux Klan in the South
> The Communist Movement
> The Nature of Totalitarianism
> The Nature of Anarchy

3. What is the difference between a social movement and a social trend? Between a social movement and a social change?
4. Analyze a social movement to determine if the structural elements set forth in this chapter are sound. Point out any variation which may exist.
5. Why would a tolerance for change likely be conducive to the development of social movements, whereas a repugnance for change could conceivably lead to revolution?
6. Evaluate the theory of anarchy as an especial kind of social movement.
7. What useful purposes do social movements serve?

FOR FURTHER STUDY

BUCK, SOLON. *The Agrarian Crusade.* New Haven: Yale University Press, 1920. The growth of agrarianism.

CANTRIL, HADLEY. *The Psychology of Social Movements.* New York: John Wiley and Sons, 1941. The psychological bases for the beginnings and continuation of social movements.

*Communism in Action.* House Document No. 754, 79th Congress, 2nd Session. Washington, D.C.: U.S. Government Printing Office, 1946. What appears to be an authoritative statement on communism in action.

DULLES, FOSTER RHEA. *Labor in America.* New York: Thomas Y. Crowell Co., 1949. Some good things on the growth of the labor movement in America.

EBENSTEIN, WILLIAM. *Today's Isms.* New York: Prentice-Hall, 1954. Good discussion of communism, fascism, socialism, and "democratic capitalism."

FINER, HERMAN. *Mussolini's Italy.* London: Victor Gollancz, 1935. A popular account of the growth of fascism in Italy under Mussolini.

GREEN, ARNOLD W. *Sociology.* New York: McGraw-Hill Book Co., 1956. A good general treatment on social movements; also Chapter 26.

GREER, THOMAS H. *American Social Reform Movements.* New York: Prentice-Hall, 1949. Good historical account of the growth of reform movements.

HEBERLE, RUDOLF. *Social Movements.* New York: Appleton-Century-Crofts, 1951. A scholarly sociology of social movements.

HITLER, ADOLF. *Mein Kampf.* London: Paternoster Library, 1936. Some of the key means that Hitler used to launch and sustain fascism in Germany.

HORTON, PAUL B., and LESLIE, GERALD R. *The Sociology of Social Problems.* New York: Appleton-Century-Crofts, 1955. Touches upon various social movements as solutions to social problems.

KING, C. WENDELL. *Social Movements in the United States.* New York: Random House, 1956. Good description of representative social movements in the United States.

LAIDLER, HARRY W. *Social-Economic Movements.* London: Routledge and Kegan Paul, 1949. Various social and economic movements analyzed.

LESSA, WILLIAM A., and VOGT, EVON Z. *Reader in Comparative Religion: An Anthropological Approach.* Evanston, Ill.: Row, Peterson and Co., 1958. Some anthropological bases of religious movements analyzed.

LODA, N. "Interpretazioni Del Fascismo," *Studi Politici,* 3:555-72, December, 1954. A good analysis of fascism.

McCLOSKY, HERBERT, and TURNER, JOHN E. *The Soviet Dictatorship.* New York: McGraw-Hill Book Co., 1960. The ideology and organization of the Soviet dictatorship.

MILLIS, HARRY A., and MONTGOMERY, ROYAL E. *Organized Labor.* New York: McGraw-Hill Book Co., 1945. Good discussion of the growth and scope of the labor movement.

PACK, JAMES EDWARD. *The Sociology of A Social Movement: The Ku Klux Klan.* Unpublished master's thesis, The University of Tennessee, Knoxville, 1950. A good account of the growth and operation of the Ku Klux Klan.

TAYLOR, CARL C. *The Farmers' Movement, 1620-1920.* New York: American Book Co., 1953. The most scholarly work on the growth and development of farmers' movements in the United States.

*The Townsend Crusade.* New York: The Twentieth-Century Fund, 1936. The growth of the Townsend movement, a plan for old-age pensions, which was important in the 1930's.

VANDER ZANDEN, JAMES W. "Resistance and Social Movements," *Social Forces,* 37:312-15, May, 1959. Discussion of social movements and resistance to some popular movements.

WASSERMAN, LOUIS. *Modern Political Philosophies and What They Mean.* (2nd ed.). New York: Garden City Books, 1951. A readable account of current political movements.

WILSON, LOGAN, and KOLB, W. L. *Sociological Analysis.* New York: Harcourt Brace, and Co., 1949. Chapter 23 discusses social movements as a means of bringing about social change.

# 20. CULTURAL AND SOCIAL CHANGE

SOMEONE has wisely observed that the only permanent thing is change. Changes in the physical world are usually slow, changes in the biological world are more rapid, but most rapid of all are the changes in the social and cultural world.

Cultural and social changes are in progress all the time, with the rate of change varying greatly in different societies and in different facets of the same society. Changes in the religious life of a people may be much slower than changes in their economy. Changes in an ancestor-ridden society would probably be much slower than in a society where these are related more to the material culture of a people and where belief in change has an important place in the ideology and value systems of the people.

## THE MEANING OF CULTURAL AND SOCIAL CHANGE

Sociology involves not only man's relationship with other men, but also man's relationship with nonhuman objects. There is little, if anything, in sociology worth considering where social relations are not intimately bound up with culture. In the past, as someone has said, there has been a tendency to try to develop a "sociology of the angels," a sociology of just people floating in a void. We have tried to stress the relationship between people and their culture.

Cultural and social changes are related to each other. Distinction between cultural and social change is somewhat artificial. This is so because changes in social forms and relations are also part of the larger area of cultural change. The term "sociocultural change" is often used instead of the two terms we are about to discuss.

*Cultural change* is a deviation from the past in cultural traits, trait complexes, and value systems of a people. *Social change* is a deviation from the past in the structure, organization, and composition of social systems and in

*297*

*Few phases of culture have more variations than do styles. These coeds on The University of Delaware campus reflect the current emphasis on the wearing of leotards.*

the structure and functions of the society of which the social systems are a part. There is a trend in the United States toward the use of automobiles with automatic transmission and a trend toward smaller cars. This trend is a cultural change, as is the smoking of filtered cigarettes.

Changing patterns of race relations in the South as a result of legislation declaring segregated facilities for Negroes invalid is social change. The decline of the legal validity of segregation laws involves a change in the social relationships of people. The long-range decline in the size of families is social change, as is also the decline of ratio of males to females in the population of the nation. Again, we wish to stress that these changes are part of the larger picture of cultural change. The distinction here is one designed solely for clarity of discussion.

## THE CONCEPT OF SOCIAL PROGRESS

While change is a deviation from the past, *social progress* is change in a direction believed to be socially desirable. In determining what is progress, the problem here is one of agreement. Not all people will agree on what changes are socially desirable. Yardsticks for measuring progress often give way to value judgments. For instance, not many people would argue that the decline in the death rate and the lengthening of the expectation of life are not an index of progress. Most people would agree that the growing availability of cultural items and opportunities to people is an index of progress. Goods and services and opportunities for health and education are generally more available to people of the world today than formerly. This greater availability of goods and services we would call progress, but someone else might not agree. On the international front, the peaceful discussion of issues between nations in international bodies, such as the World Court and the United Nations, is, to us, an indication of progress. When management and labor arbitrate and mediate disputes rather than resort to strikes, boycotts, shutouts, and walkouts, we would say that progress has been made in the relations between these two important divisions of the economy.

The concept of progress is highly subjective in that much of it deals with values. The evidence for or against progress is a matter of honest dispute among respectable scientists. Such controversy is not only inevitable but, indeed, desirable. In our times of dizzy social change, controversy and heresy are the very grammar of progress. Much more objectivity is needed in measuring and assessing progress, some of which we are beginning to get into the health and education fields. Detached scholarship and philosophical assessments, though indispensable, are not enough to meet the standards of education for "progress" or even survival.

## THE SOURCES OF CHANGE

Some of the sources of change were discussed in Chapter 2.

Many changes have their origin in *new inventions* and their use. For example, the use of the radio and motorcar has produced many profound social and economic changes in the population. Travel time is greatly diminished. Communication time has almost vanished. Knowledge of events span the world in seconds. Radio and television have speeded up the transmission of news and music and have influenced greatly the buying habits and the recreational habits of people. Automation, as well as the rapidly increasing energy per capita, has had some influence on the size of the working population needed in many industrial processes and on farms and may, in the long run, influence the length of the workday and the work week. All of these, in turn, change society and the culture.

Some inventions may well be called social inventions. They are equally as important as scientific and engineering developments. As the accompanying illustration shows, some of the social inventions which constitute part of our culture are very old. Among the social inventions which greatly influence us today are public schools, insurance—including social insurance, guilds and labor unions, patents, political parties, and modern corporations. These may be called social inventions because they are the result of ideas, require widespread or mass effort, and are widespread in influence.

Another source of change lies in *innovation*. A basic invention may, of course, be adapted to many uses. New uses for prevailing inventions and discoveries we call innovations.[1] For example, radioactive materials are now used

[1] *See* E. Rose, "Innovations in American Culture," *Social Forces,* **26:**255-72, 1948.

*Social inventions of the pre-Christian era, dating from about 2500 B.C., are documented in cuneiform writing on these clay tablets.*

*Catastrophes are frequently a source of change. This is a dust storm in the West during the 1930's.*

*TVA*

*Nothing has brought comfort and convenience to rural families more than has rural electrification.*

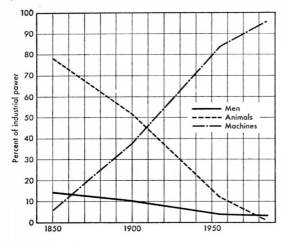

FIG. 38.   MEN, ANIMALS, AND MACHINES AS
SOURCES OF POWER

SOURCE: George A. Lundberg, Clarence C. Schrag, and
Otto N. Larsen, *Sociology* (Rev. ed.; New York: Harper
and Bros., 1958), p. 702.

as tracers in plant fertilization, as tracers in
the human body, and as treatment for many
diseases. Radiation may be used in one way
to treat a cancerous thyroid or in another way
to preserve beefsteak. The use of biologicals is
as important in preventing infections as in
curing them.

*Cultural borrowing* is a source of change.
For instance, many forms of Latin American
dances are now having a run of popularity in
the United States. Latin American styles in
clothing are also copied here.

Another source of change lies in the *change
of generations*. There is the ever-present
change in germ plasm or chromosomes. Heredity and environment are always interacting.
A generation ages and dies out and is replaced by a younger one. The young generation modifies the culture of the past generation.
Even as the aging of a generation takes place
its needs and its cultural requirements are
modified. Several years of a high national birth
rate develops an interest and an emphasis in
children, reflected not only in educational institutions but also in economic institutions.

*Ideas* are a source of change. They may be

looked upon as nonmaterial innovations and,
in instances, a form of invention. The changes
growing out of new ideas are often not immediate but may take place at a later date. As
an example, someone develops the idea of a
world court, a world parliament of powers,
an atomic bomb, or a regional development
plan perhaps well ahead of their realization.

*Education* and *learning* are sources of
change. One studies community development
and settles in a locality and proceeds to change
the community because he knows the potentialities of community organization and has
technical knowledge of how it may be brought
about. One studies and develops proficiency in
the field of medicine and microbiology and
progresses in his research to the point of developing a vaccine against polio. One learns
home decoration and is able to redecorate the
home in good taste. One studies in the field of
institutional care of children and revolution-
izes the system of child care in a child-care
institution. One becomes proficient in city
planning and changes the physical make-up of
a city. A generation schooled to national socialism becomes fanatical in its support.

Many changes are purposefully instituted
or developed. Sometimes these develop out of
new inventions and innovations. For instance,
changes in automobile styling and engineering
are not all the result of public response but
are often designed to attract new customers
and to start a revival in automobile purchasing. An educational system may literally be
transplanted into an underdeveloped culture
and be designed to perpetuate democracy or
communism depending on the ideology of the
host country and that of the nation implanting
the system. The new system would bring about
a series of changes, with the whole system
being designed to perpetuate the ideology of
the supporting governments. Communism in
China has put an end, we are told, to many of
the Great Family traditions, to feudalism and
to landlordism, and has won over the huge
mass of Chinese peasants to its doctrines.
Many of the changes we have discussed are in

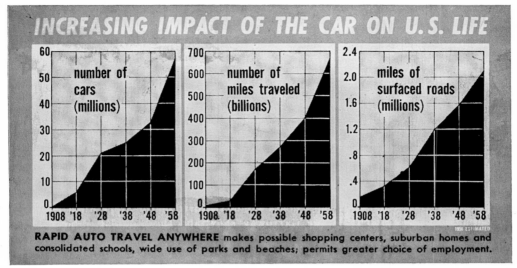

*E. I. du Pont de Nemours & Co., Inc.*

FIG. 39. CHART SHOWING SOCIAL AND ECONOMIC CHANGES BROUGHT ABOUT BY THE AUTOMOBILE

the nature of planned change. *Planned change* has been defined as "change which derives from a purposeful decision to effect improvements in a personality system or social system and which is achieved with the help of professional guidance." [2]

*Catastrophes* and *disasters* are sources of cultural and social changes. A series of grade-crossing accidents will cause people to do something about the crossing. A disastrous war may cause several countries to combine their efforts to seek a lasting peace. Distress among the aged may cause the leaders of a state or nation to secure legislative and other measures which will reduce the plight of the aged.

Closely associated with change are *changes*

in the natural environment or resource base. An area may be mined out or timbered out, thus producing basic changes in the economy. The lowering water table of a Western state may result in nonirrigable sections being abandoned for farming.

*Fear* is perhaps a cause of change. The use of poison gas was never common in war because of humanitarian feelings and the fear of reprisal. It is just possible that the fear of atomic weapons may cause leading world powers to cooperate in the control of these weapons. It is also said that *curiosity* and/or laziness frequently lead to invention. If this is so, then they, too, may be looked upon as sources of change.

## WHAT CHANGES IN A CHANGING SOCIETY?

Our discussion of change has already indicated something of what changes in a changing society. Cultural traits change. For instance, the cigarette lighter replaces the match.

[2] Ronald Lippitt, Jeanne Watson, and Bruce Westley, *The Dynamics of Planned Change* (New York: Harcourt, Brace and Co., 1958), p. vi.

Culture complexes change. As an example, the length of a worship service may be shortened, as are also funeral services under the streamlined supervision of present-day morticians. Social institutions change in a changing society. The family becomes smaller, home ownership increases, the planning of family size becomes an established practice, and the marriage rate increases.

In a changing society the population changes. The size and composition of the population changes. As an illustration, the foreign-born element in the American population is declining, the percentage of persons over 65 and under 18 is increasing, and the ratio of males to females is declining. We are told that today Americans are taller than they were generations ago, which may be attributable to improved diet. The American Negro is rapidly losing his distinctive Negroid characteristics and is becoming a distinct type. This again shows the reciprocal reaction between heredity and environment.

The personality of people may change in a changing society. We are told that obedient, docile, Chinese children changed rapidly to disobedient, aggressive children as communism spread in China and as the children were indoctrinated away from the Great Family traditions and ancestor worship of their family systems.

## SEQUENCE OF CHANGE

Sequence in change is not always easy to chart. The development of many culture traits and complexes, such as new inventions, is paced by ideas or concepts of the new trait or complex. Long before the development of airplanes men had ideas that they could fly through the air, as indicated by the large number of drawings and writings speculating upon space flights.

Material changes often pace nonmaterial changes. On the whole, material changes take place more rapidly than do social and spiritual changes and changes in value concepts.[3] This results partly from the ease with which the superiority of material items can be demonstrated. Much research, advertising, and promotion go into the development of material changes. More dollars are spent on promoting the sale of new lipsticks than on the improvement of governmental practices. More money goes into restyling automobiles than into the restyling of educational systems.

Social changes may follow the use of material cultural items. Television programs apparently hold people at home more than radio programs do. How television has influenced the visiting habits of members of the family is not clear. Certainly television has altered such practices as meal preparation and attendance at movie theaters. The automobile makes possible the dispersal of family members.

Material changes often pace or precede nonmaterial changes to a point where there is a lag between one phase of culture and another. For example, the development of atomic energy has moved rapidly ahead, whereas the international control of atomic weapons has lagged. Our knowledge of best practices in education, government, and social work has fallen behind the quality of administration usually shown in administering such services.[4] In many communities the theories of democracy and the lip service given democracy are far in advance of democratic practices.[5]

Frequently conflicts arise in habits and behavior of men, some of these as a result of lack of adjustment between the material culture and behavior. Today, in American culture, such conflicts are in evidence between work and leisure, custom and change, and the traditional lag in government over and against the need of government, not only to modernize its operations but also to plan for its future.

---

[3] *See* Cora Du Bois, "The Dominant Value Profile of American Culture," *American Anthropologist*, **57**:1232-39, 1955.

[4] For a good discussion of the concept of cultural lag, *see* William F. Ogburn, *Social Change* (New York: Viking Press, 1950).

[5] *See* W. Lloyd Warner, *American Life: Dream and Reality* (Chicago: University of Chicago Press, 1953).

*The following of economic trend lines is essential to the planning and success of large corporations.*

## PATTERNS OF CHANGE

Some changes take place in a cyclical manner, that is, they are rhythmic in pattern (Fig. 40). Seasonal change in employment, for instance, follows a cycle, employment usually declining during winter months and picking up during summer months. Styles tend to move in cycles. At one stage of the cycle hemlines drop, and at another time they may rise. At one stage in a cycle necklines will plunge, and at another stage they will heighten and cling to the neck.

A change may be cyclical but cumulative in character. For instance, the percentage increase in population will vary from year to year but will be cumulative in increase as long as the population grows. The number of new automobiles purchased will vary from year to year, but since World War II the change has been cumulative. The percentage of the population belonging to churches fluctuates from year to year but the trend in church membership is a cumulative one.

Many cultural and social changes follow a pattern of rise, plateau, and decline. During periods of floods in a river valley there will be a rise of enthusiasm for river development. As the floods recede the enthusiasm wanes and finally dies. A war accelerates the interest in peace, but the public's interest tends to subside during the period of peace. Aggressive

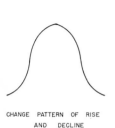

CYCLICAL PATTERNS OF CHANGE

CYCLICAL BUT CUMULATIVE

CHANGE PATTERN OF RISE
AND DECLINE

CYCLICAL BUT DECLINING

FIG. 40.  PATTERNS OF CHANGE

patriotism picks up in wartime and wanes with the coming of peace. Wartime inventions in potential war weapons increase greatly during war and cold-war periods, but decline during peace when inventors turn their attention more to the peacetime use of discoveries.

Some patterns of change are declining patterns. To illustrate, the use of horses and wagons on farms has declined as trucks and tractors have increased. Mechanical energy on farms shows growth as the use of human energy on farms has declined. Family prayer and worship have evidently declined in the American home, indicating a change from the past.

## THE ACCELERATION OF PLANNED CHANGE

Planned change, which we have already defined, is becoming important and widespread in societies. We have already indicated instances of planned change upon the political ideologies of a people. Attempts to institute planned changes in agriculture, conservation, and industry are common in underdeveloped countries. In psychiatric treatment and in institutions for offenders, attempts to institute planned change are common.

The phases in the development of planned change have been well stated by Lippitt and others. These are: [6]

1. The development of a need for change
2. The establishment of a change relationship

3. The clarification or diagnosis of the client system's problem
4. The examination of alternative routes and goals; establishing goals and intentions of action
5. The transformation of intentions into actual change efforts
6. The generalization and stabilization of change
7. Achieving a terminal relationship

The above steps may involve largely an "unfreezing" process which is designed to develop a feeling of need for change, a "moving" process designed to move in the direction of the change desired, and a "freezing" process designed to put the changes into action or practice.[7]

## SUMMARY

Change is essentially a deviation from the past, whether it be a change in culture items or a change in composition, structure, and function of social systems. The distinction between cultural and social change is partially an artificial one and is made for purposes of clarification only.

Social progress is change in a direction believed to be socially desirable. Perhaps the best test of whether or not there is progress is indicated by the consensus of the people who assess it.

The sources of change are many. One source of change lies in new inventions. Cultural borrowing may be a source of change as is a change in generations—which is the dying out of one generation and the rise of a new one.

Some changes have their inception in the implementation of great ideas. Education and learning are sources of change. A generation trained in the ideology of a great change, say a change in political ideology of a society, will be a powerful force in the perpetuation of the ideology. Instances of this are found in Germany and Italy, where German and Italian youth were trained in national socialism and fascism, respectively. Currently, the second and third generations of Russian youth are being trained in the principles of communism, and first and second generation Chinese youth are being similarly trained to communism. Finally, catastrophes and disasters are important sources of cultural and social change.

[6] Lippitt, Watson, and Westley, *op. cit.,* pp. 129-43.

[7] For more on this point, *see ibid.,* pp. 145 ff.

Any phase of the cultural or social life of a people is subject to change. Cultural traits and complexes, behavior patterns, and many aspects of a population may change.

While in general, material changes in a culture may pace other aspects of the culture, there seems to be no uniformity of sequence in change. It is often true that change originates out of ideas. On the other hand, ideological changes may follow the application of some invention or discovery.

THINGS TO DO AND TO DISCUSS

1. What is the distinction between cultural and social change?
2. How does social change differ from social progress?
3. What are some of the important sources or causes of cultural and social change?
4. What changes in a changing society?
5. Is there a well-defined sequence to change? If not, why not?
6. What are some of the different patterns which change may follow?
7. From a knowledge of your own community, make a list of the important changes that have taken place there in the last five years.
8. Why must the concept of social progress necessarily be subjective?

FOR FURTHER STUDY

ALLEN, F. R.; HART, H.; MILLER, D. C.; OGBURN, W. F.; and NIMKOFF, MEYER F. *Technology and Social Change.* New York: Appleton-Century-Crofts, 1957. A comprehensive compilation devoted to the impact of technology in bringing about social change.

BARNETT, HOMER G. *Innovation.* New York: McGraw-Hill Book Co., 1953. A scholarly treatment of the role of innovation in cultural change.

COTTRELL, FRED. *Energy and Society.* New York: McGraw-Hill Book Co., 1955. The increase of energy; new sources of energy and the social impact of energy.

DAVIS, KINGSLEY. *Human Society.* New York: The Macmillan Co., 1949. Chapter 22, on the meaning of social change, is excellent.

KEESING, FELIX M. *Culture Change: An Analysis and Bibliography of Anthropological Sources to 1952.* Stanford, Cal.: Stanford University Press, 1953. An excellent bibliography on culture change.

LIPPITT, RONALD; WATSON, JEANNE; and WESTLEY, BRUCE. *The Dynamics of Planned Change.* New York: Harcourt, Brace and Co., 1958. How planned change may be brought about.

NORDSKOG, JOHN ERIC. *Social Change.* New York: McGraw-Hill Book Co., 1960. An examination of basic sociological principles of change and an examination of several areas of change including institutional change.

OGBURN, WILLIAM F. *Social Change.* New York: Viking Press, 1950. A reissue of one of the classic works on culture change.

REDFIELD, ROBERT. *A Village That Chose Progress: Chan Kom Revisited.* Chicago: University of Chicago Press, 1950. A picture of change in a selected community.

REDFIELD, ROBERT. *The Primitive World and Its Transformations*. Ithaca, N.Y.: Cornell University Press, 1953. One of the better things on the transition from primitive to contemporary societies.

ROSE, E. "Innovations in American Culture," *Social Forces,* **26:**255-72, 1948. Some of the more important innovations in American culture up to 1948.

SPICER, EDWARD H. (ed.). *Human Problems in Technological Change*. New York: Russell Sage Foundation, 1952. A casebook of how technological change caused the rise of human problems in different cultural situations.

WARNER, W. LLOYD. *American Life: Dream and Reality*. Chicago: University of Chicago Press, 1953. The expectations of American life and the extent to which they have been realized.

WHITE, LESLIE A. *The Evolution of Culture*. New York: McGraw-Hill Book Co., 1959. Part Two, made up of five chapters, is devoted to the agricultural revolution and its consequences.

ZELOMEK, A. W. *A Changing America: At Work and Play*. New York: John Wiley and Sons, 1959. Major changes in the world of work and play of Americans.

# 21. ATTEMPTS AT SOCIAL CONTROL

SOCIAL CONTROL and attempts at social control are among the most important functions of a society. During periods of militant revolution there are attempts to restore control and stability to a society. During periods of peace the agencies and methods of social control exert their influence in all kinds of social systems from simple groups to national societies. Even internationally, forms of control are exerted through agreements, treaties, and international law. Different ideologies battle for the control of men's minds.

## THE MEANING OF SOCIAL CONTROL

The term "social" control is used in many ways. In the sense that we use the term, *social control* is the sum total of the means whereby society secures conformity to expectations on the part of constituent groups and individuals. Fairchild defines social control as "the sum total of the processes whereby society, or any subgroup within society, secures conformity to expectation on the part of its constituent units, individuals, or groups." [1] He indicates that there are two main forms of social control: those in which coercion is used and those in which persuasion is used. We shall say more about these later. Persuasive methods may be quite subtle and doctrinaire.

Social control may emanate from any social system such as a group, an association, or an institution. Primary groups and social institutions are very effective in their control functions. As an example, a family (a group) may train, persuade, or coerce its children to conformity. A church or a government (an institution) may seek through teaching, through its services, and through law, conformity to expectations. A retail trade organization (an association) may establish certain regulations regarding credit standards or methods of competing in business.

[1] Henry Pratt Fairchild (ed.), *Dictionary of Sociology* (New York: Philosophical Library, 1944), p. 279.

## THE PROBLEM OF SOCIAL DECISION PECULIAR TO
## A DEMOCRATIC SOCIETY

By social decisions we mean decisions made by groups or by a collective society, expressed through public opinion.

One of the problems peculiar to social control in a democracy, particularly in the making of group decisions, is that these decisions theoretically are to be made in such a way as to allow the fullest possible freedom to the individual in decision-making. In other words, major social decisions regarding laws are not to be made by the state or a small group representing the state without consideration for the welfare of the people. Elections are not supposed to be rigged in a democracy and ballots are secret, with the qualified citizen being permitted to vote for the candidates of his choice. Officials are elected with the idea that they will be responsive to the electorate. Under democratic principles, control is to be responsive to individual rights and desires, and social decisions are to be made in response to, and with the participation of, the people affected by the decisions. It is obvious that such decisions cannot always have the unanimous support of the people. Therefore, agencies of social control often have to operate on the basis of what is good for the majority. Social decisions also have to be made through voting, or through polls, on the basis of majority expressions. At the same time, our democratic philosophy holds that minorities shall not be eliminated. They are supposed to be tolerated, respected, and listened to.

These are some of the problems in social control and decision-making that exist to lesser degree under totalitarian regimes, where decisions for the masses are made by a dictator and a small group immediately surrounding him. Who makes the decisions becomes an important sociological matter in social control.

Another social problem related to social control is the increase and growth in strength of pressure groups, not only in the United States but throughout the world. Such groups exert much pressure upon institutions, particularly upon government. Pressure groups make use of many methods of social control, some of which the public may not readily recognize or understand and is often ill-prepared to deal with.

## THE NECESSITY FOR SOCIAL CONTROL

There is no argument about the necessity for social control; the only argument is over methods and the degree to which controls are applied.

Wherever people come together in any considerable number, and for whatever purpose, two problems of control arise—the control of relations and the control of conditions. The control of relations is involved in the interaction of person to person, person to group, and group to group. As an example, even in small social units, such as individual families, some members lose their temper, they may fight their parents or their brothers and sisters, or otherwise create problems of relations which have to be controlled. In some simple societies where a member of one family commits a crime against a member of another family, the offender may be disciplined by members of his own family or by the opposing clan. This punishment may extend even to death. All social institutions develop systems of social control in relations between people. Government is an excellent example. States and the national government define certain forms of conduct as criminal, and proceed to prohibit them. Not all criminal acts are offenses against people. Some are crimes against property. To put it another way, some crime involves conditions as well as relations. A crime against property, as, for example, theft, involves conditions.

*In a democratic society somewhat of a balance has to be developed between ordered relations and freedom. A democracy places emphasis upon the ordering of relations rather than the control of relations.*

Another problem in social control involving conditions applies to the habitats in which people live. For instance, automobile traffic has to be controlled or else traffic conditions would become so bad that the flow of traffic would neither be orderly nor safe. If people living in cities were not required to dispose of their garbage adequately, sanitary conditions would become unbearable and the health of the populace would suffer.

Even the best-controlled society will have mental and behavioral deviates who have to be controlled. Many mental deviates have to be institutionalized to prevent them from harming other people. Most motorists are reasonable in traffic; however, the deviate, the law violator, is so common as to require traffic control. Most urban citizens will treat the property of others with respect; for those who will not, control measures are necessary.

## SOME IMPORTANT METHODS OF SOCIAL CONTROL

There are many methods of social control, not all of which we shall discuss. These methods may be classified in various ways. We indicated earlier in the chapter two categories of methods—coercive and persuasive. Force is a coercive method, whereas ethical appeal is a persuasive method. Anarchy, which we discussed in the chapter on social movements, is somewhat the antithesis of coercion by the state.

Bernard classified social control methods as exploitive and constructive.[2] Among exploitive controls he listed pacification, punishment reprisals, intimidation, fraud, deception, intolerance, censorship, and repression. As constructive social controls he listed regimentation, standardization, supernaturalism, ethics, custom, law, legislation, social reform, and

[2] L. L. Bernard, *Social Control* (New York: The Macmillan Co., 1939).

education. Control measures may also be classified as formal and informal. We shall discuss these categories briefly.

### Informal social control

The simpler societies make use of many informal methods of social control.[3] As societies develop from simple to more complicated stages, there is a tendency for informal controls to weaken in influence and for them to be replaced by more formal methods of control.

Among the informal methods of social control are tradition, the story, the legend, the ballad, the song, and the dance. These may be used to drive home a lesson in conduct, to heighten group loyalty, to develop a feeling of patriotism in a group, or for various kinds of motivation. As an example, one of the stories used by the Navajos to develop good behavior in their children is very effective. In one of the canyons of the Navajo reservation there is a tall, needlelike rock known as Spider Rock, which extends from the canyon floor. The top of the rock is figured and white from weathering. The Navajos tell their children that if they are naughty a huge spider which lives on the rock will descend and carry them away to the top of the rock where it will "pick their bones." The Navajos say the story is effective in disciplining children.

As we have indicated in Chapter 14, The Development of Statuses and Roles, role expectations are more easily defined and understood in simple than in complex societies. In simple societies children know at an early age what conduct is expected of them and what roles they are likely to fill when they become adults. Teaching programs are tailored to train them specifically for these roles. Since parents and community leaders are better known to the young, personal example becomes an effective means of control. In all societies group opinion, or, on a wider scale, public opinion, is an effective method of social control. Many primitive peoples have systems of primitive law.[4]

In complicated societies like those of modern metropolitan central cities, standards of conduct are variable. Children may have little idea of what they will be doing when they grow up. Value systems are highly variable, varying not only with individuals but also with different economic, ethnic, and religious groups. Many people are self-directed in urban cultures and beyond the pale of control by their parents, their kin, and church and community influence. In such environments informal social control methods are no longer adequate, and more formal methods of social control are necessary. Of course, informal methods of control have some influence in all societies.

The arbitrary division of controls into formal and informal categories is beset with difficulties. For instance, people buy in response to mass advertising, and are otherwise influenced by public opinion and mass appeals of one type or another. However, it is a little difficult to know whether these means of control are formal or informal. Other communications are planned in such a way as to constitute a formal means of control, although the response to them may hardly be informal in nature.

### Formal controls

There are many formalized methods of social control which influence people in modern societies. We shall indicate only a few of the more important ones:

1. *Regimentation.* The regimentation of people in modern societies is a type of formal control in which various phases of life may be regulated to achieve a given goal. During wartime, rationing, the regulation of the use of

---

[3] *See* Robert Redfield, *The Little Community* (Chicago: University of Chicago Press, 1955), and Robert Redfield, "The Folk Society," *American Journal of Sociology,* **52**:293-308, 1947. *See also* S. M. Seymour, *Native Law in South Africa* (Capetown, South Africa: Juta Company, 1953).

[4] For a good discussion of these, *see* E. Sidney Hartland, *Primitive Law* (London: Methuen and Co., 1924).

*Bill Crowell photo, North Carolina Motor Vehicles Dept., North Carolina State Highway Patrol*

*The "law" represents a form of institutionalized control backed by the power of government. In most communities the police constitute the grass-roots contact of the people with the law.*

materials and equipment, and the regulation of behavior are directed to the end of winning a war or carrying on a successful military operation.

Totalitarian philosophies of government tend to impose restrictions and regimentation upon the various phases of life of a people in order to perpetuate the totalitarian regime. In Germany, under Hitler, youth organizations were developed and German youth were carefully trained and steeped in Nazi propaganda to carry out the National Socialist Movement. Even the anthropology of the German people was rewritten to try to convince them that they were a "chosen" people whose superior qualities warranted war and other militant methods in order to give them opportunities for dominance. Private property was

regulated in response to Hitler's demands and the whims of the clique which surrounded him. In order to achieve and to continue a revolutionary social and economic doctrine like national socialism, fascism, or communism, the regimentation of many phases of life of the people is almost invariably resorted to. It is also possible for people in a family, a church, a school, or a business to have one or more aspects of their life regimented by the social systems of which they are a part.

2. *Law.* Laws are, collectively, an important means of formal control. Most laws are statutory, having been enacted by national, state, and local legislative bodies. Cities have ordinances of great variety designed to control various aspects of the residence, work, and movement of urban dwellers.

Laws may be designed to encourage the performance of a favorable type of behavior as, for example, safe driving. Other laws are designed to discourage disapproved types of behavior, for example, murder, thievery and armed robbery, or drunken driving.

Laws vary greatly from community to community in the extent to which they are effective in control. This is true of laws applying to the same offenses in various parts of the country. The people of communities vary widely in education and economic status, as well as in their regard for law enforcement. It is perhaps the certainty that laws will be enforced that makes them effective rather than the severity of punishment provided by the laws. Enforcement varies widely from place to place. As an illustration, Canadians enforce their laws better than most of the American states do, and their crime rates are much lower. Only under extreme pressure from law enforcement officers will a population obey an unpopular law. Indeed, the unpopularity of a law may be so great that enforcement officials cannot possibly enforce it. This was true of the attempt to legislate prohibition in this country through passage of the Eighteenth Amendment to the Constitution of the United States. Finally, because of the unpopularity of the national prohibition laws, especially the Volstead Act, prohibition was repealed by the passage of the Twenty-first Amendment in 1933, thus putting the enforcement of liquor laws largely under state and local control, except for the manufacture of alcoholic beverages.

3. *Propaganda*. It is difficult to place propaganda techniques in a category of methods of social control. But since so much propaganda is planned, it perhaps merits discussion as a formal means of control.

Propaganda is designed especially to bring favorable results to the propagandists or the causes they represent. It may be directed to placing the propagandists and the interests they represent in a favorable public light. It may be directed at placing a competitor in an unfavorable light, thus serving also the propagandists' interest.

Skilled propagandists use various methods to achieve their ends. They may use false information or they may "skew" their information by withholding unfavorable information regarding themselves or their products, presenting only the information which places themselves and their interests in a favorable light.

Propagandists frequently use glittering generalities and downright lies which sound good but which, when they are analyzed, mean very little. Testimonials or personal experiences are often used, especially in the promotion of products.

Name-calling and card-stacking techniques, whereby a "case" is built up for or against an issue or an individual using false information, are also used by propagandists against competitors and their products to place them in an unpopular or unfavorable light. For instance, to call someone a radical in a conservative society is to place the tagged person in an unfavorable position.

The power of words as a propaganda device is well illustrated by Sutherland, Woodward, and Maxwell:

The power of word-symbols to arouse emotion and to glorify a cause on the one hand or damn it on the other is tremendous. "Name calling" has long been a potent device for ruling out the opposition without bothering to examine their arguments, and each culture has its "bad names" to call out opprobrium. Today we use such terms as Fascist, "red," Communist, rabble-rouser, wrecker, troublemaker, Tory, "do-gooder," high-brow, and public enemy to stigmatize those we dislike and by inference the things they stand for. We arouse favorable response for our own program through such "glory words" as liberty, democracy, America, "social justice," progress, and brotherhood and by such appealing adjectives as practical, redblooded, patriotic, common-sense, and Christian. Labels like these make the cause holy, and we do not need to examine the evidence to see whether the vague and general aims implied can actually ever be achieved through the proposed program. Publics need be given real information only in homeo-pathic doses if they are fed on word-slogans or aroused by the use of symbols like the national flag, the hammer and sickle, or the swastika. Once a citizen has developed an approving attitude toward the moral principles and the general aims professed and has acquired confidence in the standard bearers, it is relatively easy to convince him about details of the program. He will take the details "on faith." [5]

In every society there are social trends and conditions which propagandists try to ferret out and take advantage of. For instance, if there is a conservative trend in a society propagandists will try to take advantage of it. The exploitation of prejudice is a popular strategy in the power struggle. This procedure is known as mounting the band wagon or "band-wagon techniques." We have had recent examples in the South, where many politicians have put an antisegregation plank in their platforms in order to take advantage of the rising opposition to desegregation of schools. This is not to deny that many of these candidates are sincere, but some have simply made political hay of the desegregation issue.

As we indicated in Chapter 18 on communication, the wide availability of mass media of communication, such as newspapers, radio, and television, make the public especially vulnerable to propagandists. Unless there is enough regulation of radio, television, motion pictures, and the press to keep them from being abused by propagandists, the public may be victimized by them. Such controls as those exerted by the pure food and drug laws and ordinances are necessary to keep persons from being victimized by the sale of fraudulent or dangerous products.

4. *Brainwashing*. Apparently an old method of social control with a new name is "brain-washing." [6] Closely akin to indoctrination but

different from "brain change" which [...] some past period in a person's life, [...] "brainwashing" became popular d[...] after the period of United Nation [...] action against the Chinese Comm[...] Korea.

United Nations soldiers captured in battle were exposed to a technique of social control known as "brainwashing." This was done in an attempt to get them to reveal military secrets, to abandon their democratic ideology, and to collaborate with the Communists in propaganda broadcasts and in "re-educating" captured United Nations troops to the merits of communism.[7]

Brainwashing is a collective term. The technique consisted of alternating periods of harsh treatment and leniency with emphasis upon flogging, starvation, and ample meals. Informal and formal groupings in prison camps were broken up by divisive techniques. Particular attention was given to undermining the prisoner's democratic beliefs, his attitudes, and his values. Collaboration with Communist officials was encouraged through a system of rewards and punishment. The full use of interrogation, indoctrination, and propaganda was made. While most soldiers did not succumb to control by brainwashing, a few did and those few became influential tools in the Communist cause.[8]

5. *Rewards*. Rewards are an effective means of social control. Parents and schools often use them as a basis for approval of good behavior. Approval for a desirable kind of conduct is a reward within itself. In social systems, such as business and educational institutions, promotions in salary or rank are often given to those whose behavior and contributions receive the

---

[5] Robert L. Sutherland, Julian L. Woodward, and Milton A. Maxwell, *Introductory Sociology* (4th ed; New York: J. B. Lippincott Co., 1952), p. 531.

[6] *See* William Sargant, *Battle for the Mind* (Garden City, N.Y.: Doubleday and Co., 1957). This volume has a good reference list on the subject.

[7] *See* E. H. Schein, "Some Observations on Chinese Methods of Handling Prisoners of War," *Public Opinion Quarterly*, **20:**321-27, 1956.

[8] *See* Edward Hunter, *Brainwashing in Red China* (New York: Vanguard Press, 1951). *See also* William E. Daugherty, *A Psychological Warfare Case Book* (Baltimore: Johns Hopkins University Press, 1958); Eleutherius Winance, *The Communist Persuasion* (New York: P. J. Kenedy and Sons, 1959).

approval of their superiors. In such situations behavior of employees is often tailored to please superiors.

Another interesting example of the use of rewards as a means of control is the current crop control restrictions imposed by the federal government to limit the production of certain cash crops and to accelerate conservation practices. Restrictions on crop acreage are accompanied by support prices as rewards. Such products as butter are supported in the trade by minimum support prices rather than by placing it in open competition with vegetable fats in order that it might seek its own price level. Under current soil bank and con-

servation policies, farmers are paid to take their lands out of cultivation and return them to grass or timber. It is inconceivable that many farmers would take land out of cultivation and plant it to trees or to grass without some reward.

In closing this discussion of formal methods of control we should say that government has at its command some of the most effective methods of formal social control. A few of these are: the power to legislate, the power to license and to tax, the wide constitutional powers to use police force, and the power to reward for approved kinds of services and practices.

## PANIC AND THE LOSS OF CONTROL

The subject of panic [9] has been neglected by the writers of introductory college texts in sociology.

Ordinarily, the group activities of people and the behavior of individuals show a certain amount of organization and integration. Panic is the antithesis of this. It is a fear reaction and is characterized by nonrational behavior and loss of self-control, especially flight or running. While such behavior is not peculiar to panic, it is nonetheless an everpresent feature whenever panic occurs.

Certain conditions give rise to panic. The

fear of being entrapped is one of the most common conditions causing panic. Whenever an individual or a group has a feeling of helplessness or of being isolated or cut off from others in a crisis, panic may result.

Another feature of panic is the loss of group control, with the individuals depending strongly upon their own resources and their own habit patterns while seeking to flee. Thus panic represents a situation in which the usual self-controls present in an individual may no longer function, and where group controls break down.

## SUMMARY

The control of behavior through group or collective action is social control. There are many ways in which social control methods may be classified. In this chapter we have organized our discussion largely around informal and formal controls, rather than basing our classification upon their exploitive or con-

structive nature. Social control may emanate from any social system, but especially effective are the small group and the social institution controls.

The major problem in a democracy is to maintain enough social controls for social stability without excessively curbing individual initiative and freedom. This concern is much less in dictator countries. Whatever the kind of society, the necessity for control of relations and conditions always exists. In simple societies informal methods of control are effective, but usually give way to more for-

[9] For a good treatment of the subject, *see* E. L. Quarantelli, "The Nature and Conditions of Panic," *The American Journal of Sociology,* **60**:267-75, November, 1954. *See also* Anthony F. C. Wallace, *Human Behavior in Extreme Situations,* Committee on Disaster Studies Report No. 1 (Washington, D.C.: National Academy of Sciences, National Research Council, 1956).

*Panic often drives people to give up their usual controls in a social situation. Here, guests in a hotel dining room panic during the San Francisco earthquake. The scene is taken from a movie on the subject.*

malized controls such as laws, police forces, and regulations as societies grow in complexity. Whatever the methods of control, the ends are much the same—the control of the behavior and ideology of people in response to the wishes or expectations of the controlling social systems and the individuals making them up.

THINGS TO DO AND TO DISCUSS

1. What do we mean by social control?
2. What are some of the peculiar problems of social control in a democratic society?
3. Why is social control necessary in social systems?
4. What are some important methods of informal social control?
5. What are some leading formal methods of control?
6. What methods of control are in common use in your community? Is propaganda used, and in what way?

7. In what ways is regimentation a control means?

8. Why is anarchy, which was discussed in Chapter 19, somewhat an antithesis of control by the state?

9. What is brainwashing, and how is it done? Evaluate it as a means of control.

10. What are some of the characteristics of panic? Why is social control difficult under conditions creating panic?

11. In the future, is panic likely to be more or less of a problem? Why?

FOR FURTHER STUDY

ALBIG, WILLIAM. *Modern Public Opinion*. New York: McGraw-Hill Book Co., 1956. One of the better works on the nature and development of public opinion and its use as a method of social control.

BERNARD, L. L. *Social Control*. New York: The Macmillan Co., 1939. One of the better texts on social control.

BREED, WARREN. "Social Control in the Newsroom: A Functional Analysis," *Social Forces*, 34:328-31, May, 1955. The development of newspaper policies and the development of staff conformity to newspaper policy.

CARTWRIGHT, DORWIN, and ZANDER, A. F. *Group Dynamics*. Evanston, Ill.: Row, Peterson and Co., 1953. Control as a necessary aspect of group dynamics.

DAUGHERTY, WILLIAM E. *A Psychological Warfare Casebook*. Baltimore: Johns Hopkins University Press, 1958. Instances of psychological warfare and how it is waged.

GEORGE, ALEXANDER L. *Propaganda Analysis*. Evanston, Ill.: Row, Peterson and Co., 1959. A study of inferences made from Nazi propaganda in World War II.

HUNTER, EDWARD. *Brainwashing in Red China*. New York: Vanguard Press, 1951. How the Chinese Reds brainwashed prisoners of war.

KATZ, ELIHU, and LAZARSFELD, PAUL F. *Personal Influence*. Glencoe, Ill.: Free Press, 1955. The rise of personal influence as a control measure.

LaPIERE, RICHARD T. *The Theory of Social Control*. New York: McGraw-Hill Book Co., 1954. One of the better statements of the theoretical aspects of social control.

MOORE, HENRY ESTILL. *Tornadoes Over Texas*. Austin, Tex.: University of Texas Press, 1958. Good study of panic and the reactions to destruction created by tornadoes.

QUARANTELLI, E. L. "The Nature and Conditions of Panic," *The American Journal of Sociology*, 60:267-75, November, 1954. The nature of panic and the conditions under which people panic.

SARGANT, WILLIAM. *Battle for the Mind*. Garden City, N.Y.: Doubleday and Co., 1957. The battle of opposing ideologies for the control of the mind.

SCHRAMM, WILBUR. *The Process and Effects of Mass Communication*. Urbana, Ill.: University of Illinois Press, 1954. Some aspects of communication relating to control are given.

STEWARD, JULIAN H. *Theory of Cultural Change.* Second Printing. Urbana, Ill.: University of Illinois Press, 1958. A good survey of theories and methods of cultural change.

SUTHERLAND, ROBERT L.; WOODWARD, JULIAN L.; and MAXWELL, MILTON A. *Introductory Sociology.* New York: J. B. Lippincott Co., 1952. Good chapter treatment on social control.

"Unofficial Government: Pressure Groups and Lobbies," *The Annals,* 319: September, 1958. How lobbies and pressure groups exert social control.

WINANCE, ELEUTHERIUS. *The Communist Persuasion.* New York: J. P. Kenedy and Sons, 1959. The personal experience of a missionary and college professor who underwent 18 months of brainwashing in Red China.

WIRTH, LOUIS. "Consensus and Mass Communication," *American Sociological Review,* 13:1-14, January, 1948. How consensus is reached; the relation of communication to its development, and a clear statement of the importance of consensus in relation to control.

# PART IV  SOME PRODUCTS OF SOCIETY

Thus far in the text we have discussed how society developed, how society is structured, and what's going on in society. The last division of the book has to do with some of the products of society's structure and functioning.

In connection with social structure and social processes we have treated other social products. For example, culture is a social product, but part of it is also social structure and organization. The social processes are cultural products but they comprise much of the functional mechanisms of society.

Chapter 22 treats personality development and personality types. In this chapter the concern is largely with "normal" personalities and their development. Chapter 23 is devoted to human deviation and some of its implications. Chapter 24 has to do with attempts at social integration and equilibrium in society.

Part IV of the text rounds out the primary objectives we are trying to achieve in the introductory course in sociology. There are four of these objectives: to show how society developed; to indicate something of the structure of society; to indicate what goes on in a society, and what is coming out of it. In all phases of the book our emphasis has been on the American society and its counterparts.

# 22. PERSONALITY DEVELOPMENT AND PERSONALITY TYPES

*omit*

*for several reasons!*

PEOPLE are more than simply the offspring of a biological process. Their personalities, their likes and dislikes, are the products of their social systems and of the distinctive cultures in which they live.

Inheritance, maturation, and the biological structures and processes shape the human form and physiological functions of human beings.

Among the constitutional determinants of personality are age, sex, stature, pigmentation, and the fact that the individual is born helpless. After birth the culture transmits its value systems, and approves and disapproves certain role expectations and personality characteristics, all of which make the human personality in part the product of culture.

## THE MEANING OF PERSONALITY

We have previously discussed various aspects of personality, especially the biological basis of personality, how culture influences personality, and the development of social roles.

A restricted concept of personality is that *personality is an individual's social stimulus value*. Social stimulus value is measured by the responses other people make to a person. The sum total of the reactions which others make to a person becomes the gauge of his personality.

A more sociological and comprehensive con-

cept of personality is that it is the totality of a person's physical features, attitudes, behaviors, and value systems. Using this concept, a series of personality characteristics become the basis on which the total personality of the person is evaluated. The first of these are physical traits. Our initial judgment of a person on first acquaintance may be largely determined by physical characteristics or "looks." Another series of traits are physiological functions, having to do with speech, walk, and other physiological habits. After one observes a person's speech, walking, or eating habits he may be assigned a personality rating other than that assigned on the basis of physical traits. One's personality rating is influenced by dress. Mental condition or state of mind reflect one's personality, as do also the products of one's labor. Thus total personality is revealed through looks, physiological functions, state of mind, dress, and work. To some extent one also reveals his personality through the friends or associates which he selects.

Personality is not a static thing. Even one's physical features are not static. One may grow fat and slouchy in his habits. One may slenderize, and one does age. One's attitudes and values may change with training and experi-ence. An unhappy event or a series of circumstances in the life of a person may change his personality. Maturation, biological changes resulting from growing older, change the personality. Note, for example, the changes a young person undergoes during adolescence.

One's associates may influence one's personality. An obedient teenager may become a belligerent rebel under the influence of his teenage associates. A carousing juvenile delinquent may develop all the habits of a gentleman under training from his school or group contacts, or the inspiration of a devoted girl friend. Thus the impact of maturation and socialization upon personality.

## THE DEVELOPMENT OF THE SELF

By the *self* we mean one's own concept of his personality or one's own awareness of himself. The child at birth does not have a self. He makes no distinction between himself and things other than himself. He is not conscious of himself. As the child develops he begins to discover himself and to develop a self-perception. He discovers his body and realizes that if he makes responses other responses will be made to him. This involves not only what one thinks of himself but what he thinks the attitudes of others are towards himself. These concepts of what we believe others think of us involves what W. I. Thomas, American sociologist, called "the definition of the situation." In other words, if one believes that certain people dislike him, whether they do or not, the situation of being disliked is real to him.

Freud introduced three terms that enter into the concept of self. These terms were *id, ego,* and *superego.*[1] The *id* is the sum total of biological drives and impulses. The *ego* represents the social self at work and play. The *superego* is equivalent to the conscience. The *id* develops out of biological needs and impulses, whereas the *ego* and the *superego* develop as part of the socialization process. Both vary greatly with different personalities, even in children brought up in the same family.

If there were an adequate number of child isolates, or feral children, brought up under conditions of isolation from human beings, these would furnish some data to contrast with what is known about the socialization and personality development of children reared under conditions of normal association in family and peer groups.

Much of the information available about feral children falls into the category of folklore rather than science. As an example of this, Ogburn made an on the spot investigation of the wolf boy of Agra, reported by an Indian newspaper. The child was reported to have been carried away by wolves and remained in their care for four and one-half years. When found, the boy was supposed to have lapped up water as a wolf might. The child could not talk and had wild habits. Apparently the child had been lost and, upon discovery, was returned to his parents who, to their own satisfaction, identified him. It seems that the part of the story relating to the child's sojourn with wolves was a myth and Ogburn presents it as such.[2]

[1] Sigmund Freud, *The Ego and the Id* (London: Hogarth, 1927).

[2] William F. Ogburn, "The Wolf Boy of Agra," *The American Journal of Sociology,* **64**:449-54, March, 1959.

Probably the most famous story of feral children was one about Amala and Kamala,[3] the wolf girls of Midnapore, India. After being reported as having lived with wolves, these children, when discovered, were said to run on all fours, had wild looks, including matted hair from applying saliva to their bodies, and would regularly bare their teeth like wolves. They could not speak when captured, and were sometimes thrown into panic by the presence of others.

No doubt some children may be put into isolation by their parents because they are feeble-minded. This was possibly true of the wild boy of Aveyron.[4] There is considerable evidence that Amala and Kamala had been abandoned or had been lost in the forest. Possibly the story that they had been reared by wolves was folklore.

Davis reports the well-documented case of Anna, a child born out of wedlock, who was isolated at birth in an upstairs room because her grandfather disapproved of the mother's act. Anna was found at the age of six. As reported by Davis:

> ...Anna could not talk, walk, or do anything that showed intelligence. She was in an extremely emaciated and undernourished condition, with skeleton-like legs and a bloated abdomen. She was completely apathetic, lying in a limp, supine position, and remained immobile, expressionless, and indifferent to everything. She was believed to be deaf and possibly blind. She, of course, could not feed herself or make any move in her own behalf. Here, then, was a human organism which had missed nearly six years of socialization. Her condition shows how little her purely biological re-

sources, when acting alone, could contribute to making her a complete person.[5]

The instance of Anna shows how the self and the personality fail to develop without the opportunity for socialization. Bettelheim indicates that autistic, excessively withdrawn, and introverted children may show characteristics similar to those reported for feral children. Some autistic children may mat their hair with saliva, may keep their face hidden, may panic in the presence of others, may consume food and drink like an animal might, and may show unusual kindness and interest in animals. Such children may also show mutism and regression to a crawling stage. Bettelheim, in comparing feral and autistic children, says:

> Study of the so-called feral children, and comparison of them with known and well-observed wild autistic children, suggests strongly that their behavior is due in large part, if not entirely, to extreme emotional isolation combined with experiences which they interpreted as threatening them with utter destruction. It seems to be the result of some persons'—usually their parents'—inhumanity and not the result, as was assumed, of animals'—particularly, wolves'—humanity. To put it differently, feral children seem to be produced not when wolves behave like mothers but when mothers behave like non-humans.[6]

The above statement shows how emotional isolation may impede the personality development of a child in much the same way that physical isolation impedes such development. The self under such conditions does not develop as an approved self but takes on some of the characteristics of wild children.

[3] Reported by J. A. L. Singh and R. M. Zingg, *Wolf Children and Feral Man* (New York: Harper and Bros., 1940).

[4] J. M. C. Itard, *The Wild Boy of Aveyron* (New York: Century Co., 1932).

[5] Kingsley Davis, *Human Society* (New York: The Macmillan Co., 1949), pp. 204-5.

[6] Bruno Bettelheim, "Feral Children and Autistic Children," *The American Journal of Sociology*, 64:455-67, March, 1959.

## *PERSONALITY TYPES*

There are numerous ways in which personality types may be characterized. Perhaps the simplest and most common classification is to categorize personality types as introverts, extroverts, and ambiverts. As early as 1923, Jung used the classification introverts and extroverts.[7] During times of emotional stress and conflict the introvert tends to withdraw into himself and, as a rule, prefers to be alone and work alone. The extrovert under usual circumstances will lose himself in the company of others and often shows more interest in others than in himself. The ambivert, on the other hand, tends to balance his relationships, thoughts, and concerns between himself and others. Ambiverts have periods of introversion and extroversion, but do not reach extreme states of emotionalism for extended periods of time.

Most sociologists and psychologists would agree that extroversion and introversion are not characteristic of two distinct personality types but merely extremes on a scale of personality traits.[8] It is assumed that the middle of the scale of distribution would be made up of ambiverts, whereas extrovert and introvert personalities would occupy positions at the extreme ends of the scale.

Sheldon and his associates rejected the thesis that individuals can be divided into distinct

*Table 35*

GENERAL PERSONALITY TRAITS REVEALED THROUGH
FACTOR ANALYSIS OF INDIVIDUAL RATINGS

| *General Traits Resulting from Factor Analysis* | *Individual Traits Revealed by Ratings* |
|---|---|
| Social adaptability | Cheerful–depressed   talkative–silent, introspective adventurous–cautious   adaptable–rigid   placid–worrying, anxious |
| Emotional control | Unshakable–easily upset   self-sufficient–dependent placid–worrying, anxious   limited–marked overt emotional expression |
| Conformity | Readiness to cooperate–obstructiveness   serious–frivolous trustful–suspicious   good-natured, easy-going–self-centered, selfish   conscientious–not conscientious |
| The inquiring intellect | Broad interests–narrow interests   independent-minded–dependent-minded   imaginative–unimaginative |
| Confident self-expression | Assertive–submissive   talkative–silent, introspective marked overt interest in opposite sex–slight overt interest in opposite sex, frank expressive–secretive, reserved |

Source: Adapted from D. W. Fiske, "Consistency of Factorial Structures of Personality Ratings from Different Sources," *Journal of Abnormal and Social Psychology,* **44:**329-44, 1949.

[7] C. G. Jung, *Psychological Types* (New York: Harcourt, Brace and Co., 1923).

[8] Ernest R. Hilgard, *Introduction to Psychology* (New York: Harcourt, Brace and Co., 1958), pp. 407-33.

physical personality types. They do conclude, however, that individuals distribute themselves along a physical type continuum which is made up of three components: endomorphic, mesomorphic, and ectomorphic. Endomorphic people have prominent stomachs or paunches, indicating excess viscera. Mesomorphic people are long and muscular, wide-shouldered and narrow-hipped, what is called the athletic type. The ectomorphic type is tall, thin, and often stoop-shouldered, with a tendency to fair skin and a sensitive nervous system.[9]

On the basis of analyzing personality factors through the use of individual personality ratings, Fiske classifies personalities according to five general traits (Table 35): social adaptability, emotional control, conformity, the inquiring intellect, and the degree of confidence revealed through self-expression.

Relative to the general evaluation of common personality traits, Hilgard concludes:

Trait theories avoid the extremes of type theories by recognizing that a trait is at best merely one of the dimensions of personality. How successful are trait theories as alternatives to type theories?

1. The trait approach is a straightforward one lending itself readily to experimentation. As a starting point there is scarcely any alternative to a trait approach; even contemporary type theories begin with trait appraisal. Hence the methods of trait appraisal are legitimate and merit additional careful investigation.

2. The trait profile that emerges from the scores of an individual is not an adequate description of his personality, even though it may be a true one. When behavior is fragmented into traits, we do not know how the traits are ordered in the goal-seeking behavior of the individual. Thus a person characterized by the trait of compulsiveness may occupy himself merely with useless repetitive rituals, or, on the contrary, he may show dogged determination to stay with a productive task.

The trait profile, while it tells something about

personality patterning, is not dynamic enough to show the interrelationships of the traits in the individual. One method of meeting this objection is by the use of *profile analysis*. It consists of appraising the trait patterns as well as the individual traits, and by using it we may learn something more from the set of scores.

3. An individual's traits are his ways of behaving under environmental provocation, and they depend upon this interaction between person and environment for their existence. There is some objection to assigning traits to an individual as though they were something he *possessed*. He does not possess shyness or forwardness: he acts (and feels) shy under some circumstances and acts forward (and does not feel shy) under other circumstances. Care is needed lest traits, like types, divert attention from the importance of the cultural surroundings in which behavior occurs.[10]

There are democratic and tolerant personalities and there are status-minded, authoritarian personalities. Since the publication of *The Authoritarian Personality*,[11] the term "authoritarian personality" has been much discussed in the literature.

The authoritarian personality is made up of a number of characteristics which form a personality syndrome, a number of symptoms of mental or personality deviation occurring together. This type personality is likely to be conventional, have strong in-group attitudes and feelings, strong prejudices and antagonisms.[12] Authoritarian personalities are likely to have hostility toward people who are not conventional.[13] Authoritarian parents are likely to be status-minded and sometimes have weak egos. Their children have been shown to be more prejudiced than the children of democratic parents.

9 W. H. Sheldon, S. S. Stevens, and W. B. Tucker, *The Varieties of Human Physique* (New York: Harper and Bros., 1940).

10 Hilgard, *op. cit.*, pp. 419-20.

11 T. W. Adorno, *et al.* (New York: Harper and Bros., 1950).

12 Peter Heintz, "Zur Problematik Der Autoritaren Personlichkeit," *Kolner Zeitschrift fur Soziologie Und Socialpsychologie*, **9**:28-49, 1957.

13 Walter C. Kaufman, "Status, Authoritarianism and Anti-Semitism," *American Journal of Sociology*, **62**:379-82, January, 1957.

## *FACTORS IN PERSONALITY DEVELOPMENT*

We need not labor the point of how personality traits are biologically rooted. We have referred to this point in Chapter 2 and earlier in this chapter.

Part of the biological make-up of the human organism are the human drives or motives. These are directing tendencies within the organism. The most dependable human drives, those that have a definite physiological basis, are hunger, thirst, and the sex drive, the drive for sleep and rest. Garrett speaks of emotional motives as drives and lists anger, fear, grief, and love as emotional motives.[14] He also indicates a category of social motives—those which have their origin in social conditioning—and lists self-assertion or mastery, social approval, and gregariousness as examples.[15]

In the development of the personality and the self there is a complex reciprocal reaction between heredity and environment. The two great groups of influences keep competing and cooperating with each other and kicking back at each other from the cradle to the grave. Thus it is that no two people, even Siamese twins, can have the same environment because each one is constantly selecting his effective environment, that part of his surroundings to which he pays attention. It is generally conceded that temperament traits have a biological base, which, of course, may be modified by cultural and social conditioning. For instance, one may be born with a set of biological characteristics which would make for a small body build. But whether or not he is sensitive to his size will depend greatly upon his social conditioning, especially the kind of treatment he receives in his group associations. One may be born with a sensitive neural system but the degree of sensitivity and nervousness would be influenced by food and social and cultural factors acting upon this neural system. As we have said, even "looks" are greatly modified

by the culture. Individuals vary widely in potential mental capacities. This being true, people will react differently to the same cultural conditioning influences. One would not expect the same cultural response from a person with an I.Q. of 70 as from a person whose I.Q. is 140. Perhaps simple responses, such as crossing the street on a green light, would be the same for the person with the low I.Q. as with the high one.

Personality, then, is conditioned by biological factors. Second, personality is modified by the culture. For instance, in the Navajo culture the development of a quiet, obedient child is a cultural emphasis in child training. In most non-Indian cultures in this country an aggressive child is the ideal. A mountain child, dominated by his parents, may be less assertive than an urban child who has more freedom. Value systems, which are learned from the culture—especially the institutions of the culture—influence aggressiveness, the attitude toward the young and the old, and the extent of striving and the goals striven for. In our culture we go to much trouble to teach a child to walk. In the Alarese culture the child receives no help when learning to walk. Alarese children are shy. They do not expect the affectional responses that children in our own culture expect. They may readily fly into tantrums when molested. Not being able to obtain desires in a direct way, as the children of our own culture do, they resort to foraging and stealing.[16]

In Chapter 14, The Development of Statuses and Roles, we have indicated how role development, and many of the personality requirements entering into these roles, is conditioned by the culture. A Moslem woman may veil her face and cover the rest of her body, whereas an American girl may publicly display much of her physical charm. The American girl may hope for a professional or business career and

[14] Henry E. Garrett, *General Psychology* (New York: American Book Co., 1955), pp. 245-55.

[15] *Ibid.*, pp. 255-63.

[16] E. Adamson Hoebel, *Man in the Primitive World* (New York: McGraw-Hill Book Co., 1958), p. 588.

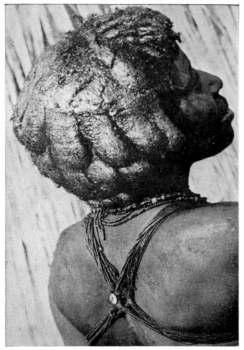

*Personal grooming is shaped by culture. Above, at left, is an old-style Congo hairdo, carefully set with a mixture of palm oil and clay. The young girl at right shows how native women wear their hair now. Below, at a celebration marking the independence of the new Republic of Congo on July 1, 1960, the audience is adorned with paint and feathers.*

train for it accordingly, whereas the Moslem woman may largely confine herself to home activities. The American male may liberally share the household activities with his wife, but an upper-class Hindu male would likely consider such work woman's work or servant's work and beneath his dignity.

Every general culture exerts its pressures toward conformity to certain role expectations. Every general culture, such as the American culture, has many subcultures, which in turn exert their own peculiar pressures upon individual personalities, particularly in role and personality relationships. Some of these cultures may deviate greatly from the general culture. For instance, cultural islands, such as the Amish communities in Ohio and Pennsylvania, require a type of dress, religious conformity, behavior, and travel and household methods much in contrast to those of the people who live around these islands.

Some cultures place much emphasis upon success and personality development. This is true of American culture. Some cultures may tend to develop abnormal personality traits. Erich Fromm raises the whole question of the sanity of American culture. He indicates that man has won for himself great freedom from various kinds of authority. He shows that Western man has devoted himself strongly to developing a great industrial and economic machine, but that there is still the possibility of man achieving a state of humanity which corresponds to the vision of some of the great humanitarians.[17]

As adequate as it is, some writers indicate contradictions in the American culture which tend to give rise to neurotic personality traits. For instance, Horney indicates[18] contradictions between competition and success, on the one hand, as against brotherly love and humility on the other. She discusses also the contradiction between the stimulation of needs and wants and the attempts to satisfy them, and the great freedom enjoyed by Americans and the restrictions placed upon them.

In neurotics, contradictions may be intensified to a point where an unsatisfactory adjustment is made to them and no satisfactory solution is found for them. The normal personality as a rule absorbs most contradictions and adjusts to them with perhaps no greater stress than worry or irritation.

Frustration of drives, whether social or biological or emotional, may be factors in personality development. For instance, the person habitually frustrated may become embittered, or militant, or he may tend to the opposite extreme of being a shy and withdrawn personality.

A Negro in a biracial community, dominated by whites, may be forced to develop personality characteristics, such as submission to domination and cautiousness, in expressing his displeasures against discrimination, whereas a white person in the same community may be more aggressive in his expressions.

The nature of individual experiences within a culture may influence personality. A brilliant child growing up in an adequate family is likely to have personality characteristics different from a child of equal intelligence brought up in an institution without the careful guidance of substitute parents, or without the intimate attention of biological parents.

The personality adjustment of the child is related to the social status of his family and to his own status in the family.[19] In the socialization and conditioning of young children, two types of family experiences may also influence personality characteristics. These are very unhappy crisis situations and very happy experiences. Indeed, throughout one's lifetime these two types of situations may become factors in personality development and performance. Many people cannot withstand a trau-

---

[17] Eric Fromm, *The Sane Society* (New York: Rinehart and Co., 1955).

[18] Karen Horney, *The Neurotic Personality of Our Time* (New York: W. W. Norton and Co., 1937), pp. 281-90.

[19] William H. Sewell and Archie O. Haller, "Social Status and the Personality Adjustment of the Child," *Sociometry*, 19:114-25, 1956.

matic experience without mental or physical disorganization. Other people can contain a traumatic experience and react to it without marked influence upon the personality. Some people can adjust to an illness, a loss of money or property, or the absence or loss of relatives, and others cannot.

E. I. du Pont de Nemours & Co., Inc.

*The American culture places much emphasis upon success and personality development.*

## SUMMARY

The human personality is society's greatest product. Personality may be thought of as a person's social stimulus value or as the total characteristics and behavior of a person. Personality is not a fixed thing but may change as a person matures, as he is socialized, and as he is influenced by contacts, situations, and events.

A key to personality is a person's self and his concept of his own personality. This involves also what he believes others think of him. The concept of one's self perhaps results more from one's early socialization and from one's individual experiences while growing up than from any other group of factors. Many attempts have been made to classify personality types into, for instance, introvert, extrovert, and ambivert. A more meaningful classification characterizes personalities by variation in general traits, such as adaptability, emotional control, inquiry or curiosity, and degree of self-expression. Into the development of personality go many groups of factors, chief of which are biological factors, maturation, socialization, and individual traumatic and joyful experiences.

### THINGS TO DO AND TO DISCUSS

1. Give several concepts of personality. Select the one you prefer.
2. What is the self and how does it develop?
3. How does one reveal or express his personality?
4. What is the distinction between introvert and extrovert personalities?
5. What are some major characteristics of authoritarian personalities as compared to tolerant, democratic personalities?
6. How does Fiske classify personalities?
7. What groups of factors go into the development of a personality?
8. Are there characteristics in American culture which you feel have a tendency to develop neurotic tendencies in personality?

### FOR FURTHER STUDY

ALLPORT, G. W. *Personality*. New York: Henry Holt and Co., 1937. One of the better standard works on personality.

COOLEY, CHARLES H. *Human Nature and the Social Order*. New York: Charles Scribner's Sons, 1902. An original discussion of primary group influences on personality development.

DAVIS, KINGSLEY. *Human Society*. New York: The Macmillan Co., 1959. The nature of socialization and how it influences personality development is well discussed.

FARIS, ROBERT E. L. *Social Psychology*. New York: Ronald Press, 1952. Good treatment of social conditioning upon personality development.

FISKE, D. W. "Consistency of Factorial Structures of Personality Ratings from Different Sources," *Journal of Abnormal and Social Psychology*, **44**: 329-44, 1949. Empirical study of personality traits as revealed through ratings.

GARRETT, HENRY E. *General Psychology*. New York: American Book Co., 1955. A good discussion on biological, social, and emotional drives.

HILGARD, ERNEST R. *Introduction to Psychology*. New York: Harcourt, Brace and Co., 1953. Good discussion of drives.

KLUCKHOHN, CLYDE, and MURRAY, H. A. (eds.). *Personality in Nature, Society, and Culture*. New York: Alfred A. Knopf, 1948. How culture influences personality roles and expectations.

McCLELLAND, D. C. *Personality*. New York: William Sloane Assoc., 1951. General treatment of personality.

SHELDON, W. H., *et al. The Varieties of Human Physique*. New York: Harper and Bros., 1940. Physical personality types examined.

# 23. SOCIAL DEVIATION AND DEVIATES

AMONG THE PRODUCTS of the structure and functioning of a social system are social deviates and deviation. Deviates and deviation are present in all societies but are more prevalent in some cultures than in others. For example, native Italian or Japanese families have much less juvenile delinquency than American families or Italian or Japanese families in America do. There is less delinquency and dependency in Mormon communities in Utah than in Utah communities populated by non-Mormons. Urban communities show more mental defectiveness than rural communities do, some of which may be because of better detection in urban communities. The data show that sex deviation is more of a problem in urban than in rural communities. Here again better data are available for urban areas.

## THE CONCEPT OF DEVIATION

Deviates and deviation are in a real sense relative terms. Deviation is a variation from individual or group norm or standard. Deviation denotes a behavior or condition already developed or in process of developing. Norms are sets of ideas or standards on how a person or group should behave in a given situation or under specified circumstances. The term "deviate" denotes a state of being, a condition, or a variation from norm already achieved or developed. A delinquent is one whose behavior has been defined as delinquent. In other words, he has the status of delinquent and represents a deviation from norm in conduct. Predelinquency is delinquency in process of development, representing one who is in the state of becoming delinquent.

Deviation may be a relatively static or dynamic condition or state. A person may be six feet, eight inches tall. He is a deviate in height. Such deviation may or may not greatly influence his behavior. Deviation in height is a static condition unless one is in process of growing. On the other hand, a manic depressive may be in dynamic state. His condition is behavioral, influencing his own per-

*334*

## DEGREE OF MENTAL RETARDATION VARIES WIDELY

**It is estimated that 3 percent of the total population have an intelligence quotient of 75 or less, but the potentialities within this group are large**

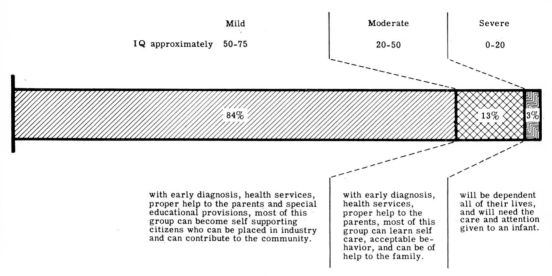

FIG. 41.  HOW MENTAL RETARDATION VARIES
SOURCE: U.S. Children's Bureau Publication No. 363.

spective and outlook and the relationships between himself and others. His mental state varies from time to time.

We have said that deviation is a relative term. A feeble-minded person in a community of feeble-minded, or an illiterate in a community of illiterates, would be of less concern as a deviate than in a community of literate, adequate persons. There are sections in the United States, we are told, where moonshining, a form of illegal behavior, is not looked upon by the participants as illegal. In the mind of a confirmed Catholic a sin is a sin, whereas a Protestant may look upon a kind of conduct as sinful only if popular opinion defines it as sinful. What we are saying is that the standards of a culture or a subculture may define one type of personality as a deviate and a given pattern of behavior as deviation, whereas in another culture each would be

accepted as normal or at least within the limits of tolerance. Deviation is, therefore, a relative term. More about the cultural definition of deviation in a later division of the chapter.

The student of sociology should understand that not all kinds of deviation are bad and that not all forms of deviation are disapproved. Feeble-mindedness is an undesirable kind of deviation, whereas genius is not. A seven-foot giant of a man might be desirable as a basketball player but hardly as a jockey. Absentmindedness is not a particularly undesirable quality among scholars but it might be suicidal to a controls operator and his fellow workers in an explosives plant. A community which is strongly frontier in its law enforcement attitudes may approve of piety in religious matters. Both may be forms of deviation. In a community torn by race hatred a prejudiced person may not be looked upon as a deviate to the extent that he would be in a more democratic, tolerant community. A degree of freedom of speech will be tolerated in peacetime which will not be tolerated in wartime. Bohemian conduct in a neighborhood made up of the beat generation would perhaps not be defined as undesirable, whereas in another community it would be.[1]

Lundberg, Schrag, and Larsen show graphically the concept of approved and disapproved deviations of which we have spoken. As Figure 42 shows, deviates, such as the poor, the criminals, the sick, isolates, and vandals, are disapproved, whereas the wealthy, the learned, esthetes, and the virtuous are approved deviates.

## SOME IMPORTANT CAUSES OF DEVIATION

We have already indicated some of the important causes of social deviation. Some of these we shall again summarize in this section of the text.

### Sex differences and differentiation in sex roles

One of the basic causes of deviation in the population is that there are two sexes and that each has its distinct sex roles which differentiate one sex from another.

While the urge to have children is perhaps culturally learned, the physiological equipment for having children is present only in the human female. Males are physically more aggressive than females, because of their greater strength and because of the fact that our culture favors greater aggression in males. In moral conduct, especially sex relations, men will tend to deviate more from mean tendencies than women will. This is true for both premarital and marital sex relations. The explanation here is that our culture holds women more to the moral norms.

Women mature slightly earlier than men and have a higher basal metabolism. Mortality rates are higher for men. Men marry women younger than they. Women live longer, hence the problem of widowhood which is very serious among women. In aptitude, women are generally superior to men in verbal ability, memory, perceptual speed, and dexterity in

[1] See Gene Feldman and Max Gartenburg, *The Beat Generation and the Angry Young Men* (New York: Citadel Press, 1958).

the performance of small tasks. In matters of spatial judgments, mechanical tasks, mathematics, and reasoning men tend to be superior to women. In intelligence there is little significant differences except that men are more variable. There is some evidence that women possess more ability to survive physical deprivation, exposure, and starvation than men.

### Differences in capacity or potential intelligence

Differences in capacity lie at the base of much deviation. Feeble-mindedness itself is an important form of deviation, as we shall see later. In Mongolism, significant genetic causes, possible through the mother, are found. Although intelligence is as much a problem in crime as the lack of it, the lack of ability is at the base of much truancy and delinquency, especially in girls. Many misdemeanants, such as those that comprise the jail population, are inadequate persons. Often this inadequacy extends back to a basic lack of ability. Sex offenders, both men and women, rank among the lowest in intelligence of all criminals.

### Disease and crippling

Much deviation has its origin in disease and crippling. For instance, there is a relation between encephalitis and mental disease and mental retardation. It is also related to the lack of mental development. Many people are born crippled, and others become crippled through disease and accidents. Prematurity,

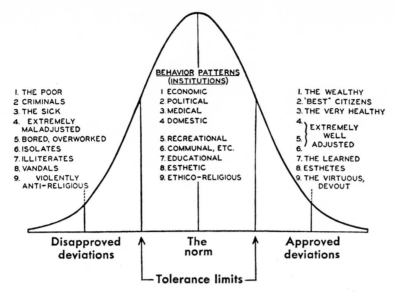

FIG. 42. HOW PEOPLE MAY BE DISTRIBUTED ACCORDING TO DISAP-
PROVED, TOLERATED, AND APPROVED TYPES

SOURCE: George A. Lundberg, Clarence C. Schrag, and Otto N.
Larsen, *Sociology* (Rev. ed.; New York: Harper and Bros., 1958),
p. 349.

birth injury, or neonatal asphyxia may be causes of mental retardation. Until recently, polio was a great crippler of children and adults and the cause of much physical deviation. Rheumatic fever has an important relation to heart defects. Syphilis may cause mental deterioration. Glandular defects may lead to lack of biological development, including mental development. The overfunctioning of some glands may lead to overdevelopment in physical growth.

### Culture conditioning

We have said that the kind of conditioning required in one culture, which produces a personality whose behavior is defined as normal in that society, may produce a deviant in another culture. Hoebel cites the instance of a healthy Ojibwa Indian boy who was sent to the psychiatric ward of the University of Minnesota Hospital because he believed that spirits existed and that people could be killed by

shooting them with magic-charged shells of mollusks. These mysteries the child had been taught by his grandfather, his beliefs and his behavior being completely normal in the Ojibwa culture.[2]

In speaking of attitudes toward the homosexual, a type of deviate in our own culture, Hoebel says:

In our society the habitually homosexual male is looked upon with emotionally intense hostility. His rejection by the normal elements of our world is often complete and devastating. His conflicts of guilt, remorse, and frustration may be enough to turn him into a psychopath no matter how healthy his early personality may have been. Homosexuality usually accompanies a rejection of the normal social roles fixed for the two sexes.[3]

In certain nomadic Arab cultures homosexuality was not looked upon as a deviation.

As the above quotation indicates, cultures

[2] E. Adamson Hoebel, *Man in the Primitive World* (New York: McGraw-Hill Book Co., 1958).
[3] *Ibid.*, p. 589.

greatly in the degree to which they tol-
e deviation. In most groups in American
iety a "conscientious objector" would be
wned upon. In a Quaker society whether
or not one would fight in war, register or enlist for noncombat duty, or fail to participate
at all in military activity, is left to the individual as a matter of conscience, with general
approval of the pacifistic tendency.

To provide a way out for a male who could
not fulfill the role of warrior, the Plains Indian institutionalized *berdache,* or transvestite.
The young male, under berdache, took up a
woman's role, performed a woman's work, and
wore women's clothes. The choice in role was
supposed to be the outcome of a vision; therefore, no blame was attached to the role or the
person in it. In fact, berdaches were looked
upon with awe by the Plains Indian children.
They were respected and their advice widely
sought by young men, especially in love-mak-
ing. Such deviates were not looked upon as
abnormal personalities because the culture
supported them.[4]

### An inadequate culture and inadequate opportunities

Many otherwise normal persons are made
deviates by the culture in which they live and
the lack of opportunity to develop normally.
A child, born normal, may become a deviant
because his parents are inadequate or because
his home and community do not furnish
wholesome outlets for his interests and abilities. A nagging, uninteresting, or cruel teacher
or a deficient program of studies may "drive"
a student to truancy and predelinquency and,
finally, to delinquency.

On the other hand, a culture may have adequate resources but a person may not have
adequate opportunities to share in the culture.
For example, one may have a rheumatic heart
or polio and may not have access to modern
medical or treatment facilities. As a result he
becomes a cripple. A child may live next door
to a good high school but his parents are ill
and he has to leave school, secure a work permit, and go to work to support his family.
Throughout the years he may live and work
as an inadequate individual because of lack of
education and training. A blind boy may be
sheltered and pampered in his home and grow
up as a deviate because his parents failed to
take advantage of the educational opportunities offered by an excellent state school for the
blind. A harmless sex deviate may develop into
a wild sex killer because he had no social treatment in childhood to help him overcome his
deviation. A predelinquent, truant girl may
develop into a professional prostitute because
the school system had inadequate personnel
and resources to give her predelinquency attention. Again, in some societies sex experience of single girls is approved and is not
looked upon as a form of deviation but rather
as a useful preparation for mate selection and
marriage.

## SOME SIGNIFICANT KINDS OF DEVIATES AND DEVIATION

There are many forms of deviation. Space
in any introductory sociology is necessarily
limited to a few significant kinds.

### Deviates in intelligence

Among the significant kinds of deviation
found in people are basic differences in poten-

[4] *Ibid.,* p. 589.

tial intelligence, or the capacity to learn. Such
differences are not only significant within
themselves but are causes of other kinds of
deviation, such as illiteracy and inadequacy.
The ability to respond to learning situations
and to a culture varies greatly with the capacity of the individual to learn.

Of the 4,200,000 children born annually in
the United States, about 3 per cent, or 126,000,

will never develop the intellect of a 12-year-old child; 0.3 per cent, or 12,600, will remain below the seven-year intellectual level; and 0.1 per cent, or 4,200, if they live at all, will be helpless imbeciles.[5] These data, of course, are always tentative, subject to much more research on the subject.

As indicated by the accompanying normal curve of potential mental capacities, people distribute themselves as to mental abilities along a normal curve of distribution. Some 2.14 per cent are typed as retarded, 13.59 per cent as slow, 68.26 per cent as average, 13.59 per cent as superior, and 2.15 per cent as gifted. The range of I.Q. scores on the scale is between 50 and 150.

[5] Richard L. Masland, Seymour B. Sarason, and Thomas Gladwin, *Mental Subnormality* (New York: Basic Books, 1958), p. 3.

At the lower end of the curve of potential intelligence are idiots. The next highest group are imbeciles, and the next highest below normal intelligence are morons. These three kinds of mental deficiency constitute the greatest problems as far as inadequacy is concerned.

Idiots usually have an intelligence quotient below 25 and must have the protective care of an institution or home. The following sketch indicates something of the behavior and capacity of an idiot.

Female, age twenty. Has been in institution fourteen years. Has a mental age of about one year. When admitted (at the age of six) she could hardly walk, could not care for her own bodily needs, said only a few words, would play with her doll a little. Since, she has scarcely improved. Learned to string a few beads and to say a few sentences. The attendants say she never sleeps;

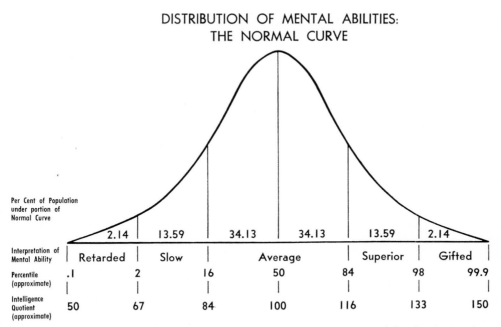

DISTRIBUTION OF MENTAL ABILITIES: THE NORMAL CURVE

| Per Cent of Population under portion of Normal Curve | 2.14 | 13.59 | 34.13 | 34.13 | 13.59 | 2.14 |
|---|---|---|---|---|---|---|
| Interpretation of Mental Ability | Retarded | Slow | Average | | Superior | Gifted |
| Percentile (approximate) | .1 | 2 | 16 | 50 | 84 | 98 | 99.9 |
| Intelligence Quotient (approximate) | 50 | 67 | 84 | 100 | 116 | 133 | 150 |

*How people distribute themselves according to mental capacities is shown in this normal curve of distribution.*

SOURCE: William E. Cole and Charles S. Montgomery, *High School Sociology* (Boston: Allyn and Bacon, 1959), p. 49.

does not understand commands; eats garbage. Very little known of her condition, which is congenital.[6]

Imbeciles have I.Q.'s from 25 to 50. If physically fit they may do labor which is not complicated, including simple kinds of farm labor and housework. The following description is of an imbecile with an I.Q. of about 40.

Man, age thirty-four. Has mental age of six years. At ten, when admitted, speech was defective, memory poor, could not dress himself, was unclean, dangerous with fire, brutal, vulgar, profane and difficult to manage. Has improved under institutional discipline and is now strong and healthy and a good worker in the institution driving coal teams. Has quarrelsome, cranky spells, is somewhat sober, willing and tries to help, and is usually obedient. But he is not truthful or honest, is quick tempered and forgetful.

Father and two uncles feeble-minded. One of his mother's brothers was also feeble-minded and had several feeble-minded grandchildren. Grandmother was feeble-minded. Cousin is also feeble-minded and in the same institution.[7]

At the other extreme are mental deviates of high intelligence such as the following boy with an I.Q. above 180.

At the age of eight, Edward was above the norm in height and weight. While average children of his age are in the third grade, Edward was in the sixth grade. At age twelve Edward entered college, his score on the freshman entrance test being the second highest of 483 boys who average six years older than himself. Edward graduated in four years and was elected to Phi Beta Kappa. He is reported to have had at least a working knowledge of twelve languages. Edward took the Ph.D. degree in the early twenties and embarked upon a career in the ministry.[8]

As we shall see later, people with differences in mental capacities or developed abilities will react differently to their social and cultural environments. For some, adjustments will be adequate, whereas others will make an inadequate adjustment to the same culture, as do the idiot and the imbecile. Cronbach summarizes from various sources what kinds of tasks students at various I.Q. levels may perform.[9]

## Mental defectiveness

At the beginning of the year 1958 there were 664,029 patients on the books of hospitals for mental disease. Admissions during the year numbered 291,843, of which 180,042 were first admissions and 99,896 were readmissions. The remainder of admissions were transfers from other hospitals. During the year 1958, there were 291,693 separations from mental hospitals, of which 224,828 were discharges. During the same year about 53,000 patients died in mental hospitals.

It is significant that about 56 per cent of first admissions to public mental hospitals are men. Also significant is the fact that 30 per cent of all first admissions are under 34 years of age.[10]

Like the feeble-minded, mental defectives do not represent a separate species. Rather, they simply show a greater degree of disturbed behavior or exaggerated forms of the same kinds of behavior found in normal people. It is normal for a person to be suspicious of some people but suspicion does not reach the exaggerated form that it does in a paranoic who believes that his destruction is being planned, or that he is being persecuted because he is a "great person."[11] It is normal for a person to daydream and think well of himself, but when he develops delusions of grandeur, thinking he is Christ, or Napoleon, or Josephine, wife of Napoleon, deviation has

[6] H. H. Goddard, *Feeble-mindedness: Its Causes and Consequences* (New York: The Macmillan Co., 1914), pp. 224 and 434.

[7] *Ibid.*

[8] Henry E. Garrett, *General Psychology* (New York: American Book Co., 1955), p. 477.

[9] L. J. Cronbach, *Essentials of Psychological Testing* (New York: Harper and Bros., 1949), p. 124.

[10] U.S. Bureau of the Census, *Statistical Abstract of the United States: 1959* (80th ed.; Washington, D.C.: U.S. Government Printing Office, 1959), pp. 80-81.

[11] For more on this point, *see* Garrett, *op. cit.*, pp. 586-89.

reached a point of abnormality or a stage where the illness is a problem to the paranoic and his family.

As Garrett indicates:

Within our society a normal person may best be thought of, perhaps, as one who is well adjusted to and happy in his station in life. Ordinarily a normal man works steadily at his job, pays his bills, marries and rears a family, and is regarded as a responsible and trustworthy member of the community. Normality is, to be sure, conditioned by the culture in which one is born and reared. Habits and customs (of dress and of eating, for example) normal to the Australian aborigine or the Eskimo might be considered highly abnormal in a mid-western American town.[12]

On the fringe between normal behavior and mental defectiveness are an ill-defined group of mental disorders known as *neuroses*. The writer has a friend who has a phobia against dirt. Phobias constitute neurotic conditions, many of which are temporary in character. This friend washes his hands in disinfectant. He opens doors by using his coat pocket as a shield against germs on the door knob. He protects his pipestem from contamination by carrying it in his tobacco can when it is not in use.

Neuroses represent mild disturbances in the personality. Such persons are said to be neurotic. They often reflect feelings of inadequacy and inferiority, anxiety, worry, and fatigue. For example, a person may have an anxiety about his health which reaches a stage of neurosis.

While neurotics are problems to themselves and others, they seldom need institutional treatment. They do, as a rule, need help from counselors, clinical psychologists, and psychiatrists. What percentage of the population is neurotic we do not know exactly. A good range would be 15 to 20 per cent of the population.

The more serious mental illnesses are called *psychoses*. Psychotics perhaps make up about 1 per cent of the population. It is known that about 1 million people in the population have serious personality deviations.

Psychoses fall into two categories: *organic* and *functional*. Organic psychoses develop from diseases or physical degeneration. At one time syphilis was the cause of a major mental illness known as *paresis*. Encephalitis, which is an infection of the brain, often leads to an organic psychotic condition in children. Because of the aging processes an elderly person may develop a psychotic condition, especially *senile dementia*. The habitual alcoholic may reach the stage of *alcoholic psychoses*. Functional psychoses have no known physiological base. They have their origin in some phase of the culture, especially in the area of interpersonal relationships. A person may suffer from the trauma of disappointment in courtship or the loss of a loved one through death. One may lose his health or property or be subjected to some other kind of crisis situation which causes him to become disorganized.

Some common types of functional psychoses are schizophrenia, paranoia, and manic-depressive psychosis. Garrett describes each of these three forms of psychoses.

The psychosis known as *schizophrenia* takes at least four forms, all marked by disassociation (splitting of the personality). The schizophrenic is highly introverted and shut into himself, shows little real emotion, often experiences auditory hallucinations, and lives in a dream or fantasy world of his own making. Movement is often jerky; other characteristics are giggling and grimacing, and sometimes stupor and catalepsy. Schizophrenia is the most prevalent form of insanity, patients suffering from this psychosis making up 50 per cent of the hospital population. The disease is commonly found in adolescence and early adulthood; in fact, it is often called *dementia praecox* or "youthful sanity." Interest in the treatment of schizophrenia has been revived of late as a result of the introduction of various forms of shock therapy. When the schizophrenic patient is thrown into a shock or coma by means of electricity or drugs, in many cases marked improvement follows.[13]

[12] *Ibid.*, p. 587.

[13] *Ibid.*, pp. 596-97.

The use of lobotomy operations, controversial, of course, as to use, sometimes gives sensational improvements with some dementia praecox patients.

The *manic-depressive psychosis* is characterized by extreme fluctuations of emotional mood. At one time the patient is exhilarated and excited (manic phase), swears, shouts, and talks incessantly; at another he is gloomy and sad (depressed phase) cries, refuses to eat, and accuses himself of various sins. In *paranoia,* delusions of persecution and/or delusions of grandeur are typical. Paranoia is often complicated by schizophrenia.[14]

We have placed considerable emphasis in this chapter upon mental deficiency and defectiveness. Most deviates are sociopaths in that they suffer from status and role impairment and that a large percentage of them are dependent upon relatives and upon public and private agencies for support and custodial care. This fact, plus the fact that much deviation is sociogenic in origin, makes deviation a real concern of the sociologist.

[14] *Ibid.*, p. 597.

### The juvenile delinquent

Another significant deviate in American society is the juvenile delinquent. To phrase the problem another way, one of the significant forms of deviant behavior in society is delinquency. Delinquency is strongly a product of society and the social systems making up the society.

In 1950 there were 140,315 juveniles in correctional institutions. During the year 1957, 254,000 children under 18 years of age were arrested by police, as compared to 35,000 such arrests in 1950.

Of 2,340,000 arrests in 1,586 cities of over 2,500 in 1958, 284,215, or 12.1 per cent, were under 18 years of age; 19.7 per cent under 21 years of age, and 29.3 per cent were under 25 years of age.

Although youths under 18 accounted for only 12.1 per cent of all persons arrested in the cities indicated in 1958, this age group made up 64.1 per cent of all arrests for auto theft, 49.9 per cent for burglary, 48.5 per cent for larceny, 30.9 per cent for receiving stolen

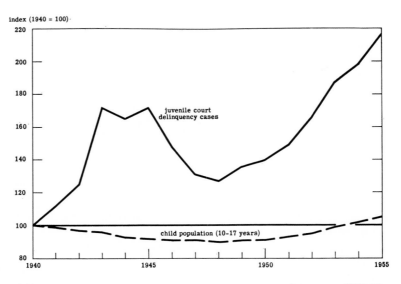

FIG. 43. TRENDS IN JUVENILE DELINQUENCY IN THE UNITED STATES, 1940–1955

SOURCE: U.S. Children's Bureau Publication No. 363.

property, and 22.8 per cent for robbery.[15] These figures are enough to point to the youthfulness of offenders, especially in crimes against property. In addition, there is the large volume of juvenile offenses such as truancy, sex offenses, and loitering.

[15] Federal Bureau of Investigation, *Uniform Crime Reports, 1958* (Washington, D.C.: 1959), p. 94.

Who is a delinquent and what is delinquency is defined by statute. Usually a delinquent is a person under 18 who commits offenses specifically prohibited by statute. Major offenses include habitual truancy from school; vagrancy; malicious mischief; stealing; sex offenses, in girls especially; traffic violations; auto theft; breaking and entering, often

## WHAT IS A DELINQUENT?

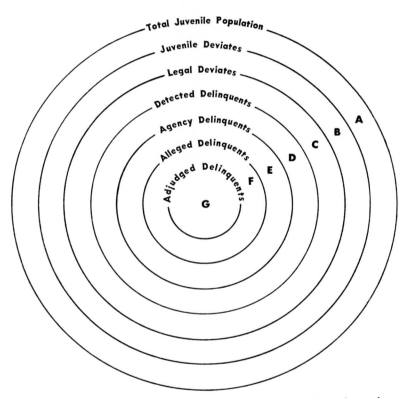

Total Juvenile Population

Juvenile Deviates

Legal Deviates

Detected Delinquents

Agency Delinquents

Alleged Delinquents

Adjudged Delinquents

**Legend:**

A. All children in given area, below given age.

B. All children showing deviant behavior, whether or not anti-social.

C. All deviants committing anti-social acts as defined by law.

D. All anti-social deviants detected.

E. All detected anti-social deviants reaching any agency.

F. All apprehended anti-social deviants brought to court.

G. All court anti-social deviants "found" delinquent.

FIG. 44.   DELINQUENCY CHART

SOURCE: Based on Lowell J. Carr, *Delinquency Control* (New York: Harper and Bros., 1950), p. 59. The chart is from the National Education Association.

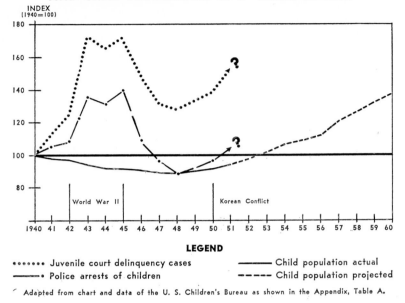

**DELINQUENCY CASES DISPOSED OF BY 210 JUVENILE COURTS,
POLICE ARRESTS OF CHILDREN UNDER 18 YEARS OF AGE,
AND CHILD POPULATION 10-17 YEARS OF AGE**

LEGEND

•••••• Juvenile court delinquency cases ———— Child population actual
———• Police arrests of children        ----- Child population projected

＇ Adapted from chart and data of the U. S. Children's Bureau as shown in the Appendix, Table A.

FIG. 45. JUVENILE DELINQUENCY AND THE COURTS

referred to as burglary, and being ungovernable. Unless he commits a capital offense like murder, the juvenile is usually dealt with in special courts. In the courts, and during periods of treatment, the juvenile offender receives special kinds of care and treatment by virtue of the fact he is a juvenile rather than an adult offender.

Carr uses the accompanying chart to show how classes of juvenile delinquents and juvenile deviants are differentiated.[16]

In the preceding definitions each category, from one to seven, becomes smaller. Adjudged delinquents will be fairly small as compared to the total category of detected delinquents.

One of the great concerns of American society is the large volume of delinquency and

[16] Lowell J. Carr, *Delinquency Control* (New York: Harper and Bros., 1950), p. 59. The chart is from the National Education Association. *See also* Milton L. Barron, *The Juvenile Delinquent in Society* (New York: Alfred A. Knopf, 1954).

the amount of adult crime committed by young persons, especially young adult men. In a given year alleged delinquents will comprise slightly more than 1 per cent of the child population 12 to 16 years of age, inclusive. Annually, about 3,000,000 juveniles reach the courts; 500,000 are detained in jails and other detention institutions; and about 36,000 are committed to 300 state and private training schools. It is not uncommon for these schools to be so crowded that the buses taking a "new crop" of juveniles to the schools will need to make the same number of releases to make room for the new offenders.

*The adult offender*

At the end of the year 1957 there were 195,000 persons in federal and state prisons. During the year there were 154,000 admissions and 148,000 discharges from prisons. In addition there were many more persons in jails

*"I said people don't seem to like me for some reason—*
*open your ears, fathead!"*

SOURCE: *Saturday Evening Post,* May 16, 1953. Reproduced by permission of the artist.

and workhouses than were in state and federal prisons.

Some of the volume of crime is indicated by Table 36, as well as the leading offenses per unit of population. As indicated in this table, crimes against property greatly exceed crimes against the person. Aggravated assault leads all crimes against the person, followed by forcible rape and murder. The volume of crime varies from month to month and, of course, from year to year. Crime trends are reported annually in the *Uniform Crime Reports* by the U.S. Federal Bureau of Investigation.

An adult offender, or criminal, is a person over juvenile age who commits an offense against the state. Such offenses are prohibited by law. Such cases are prosecuted in courts of law by a representative of the state. Technically, a person is not a criminal until a court has found him guilty of violating a criminal statute. Criminality is, of course, a form of deviation and is strongly a social product. If criminality was essentially a biological product, then the incidence of crime would not vary as much as it does from nation to nation, state to state, and community to community.

*Table 36*

ESTIMATED NUMBER OF OFFENSES
COMMITTED AND NUMBER OF
OFFENSES PER 100,000 POPULATION,
UNITED STATES, 1958

|  | Estimated Number of Offenses | Number of Crimes Per 100,000 Population |
|---|---|---|
| Total | 1,553,922 | 896.9 |
| Murder | 8,182 | 4.7 |
| Forcible rape | 14,561 | 8.4 |
| Robbery | 75,347 | 43.5 |
| Aggravated assault | 113,530 | 65.5 |
| Burglary | 679,787 | 392.4 |
| Larceny over $50 | 391,550 | 226.0 |
| Auto theft | 270,965 | 156.4 |

Source: Federal Bureau of Investigation, *Uniform Crime Reports, 1958* (Washington, D.C.: 1959), pp. 3-4.

Minor criminal offenses are known as *misdemeanors*. They are usually punishable by fine, probation, or imprisonment for less than a year. *Felonies* are more serious offenses and are usually punishable by imprisonment for more than a year, or, in the case of murder or other capital offenses, may be punishable by death. *Treason* is an offense against the foundations of government or security of a state, and is usually punishable by death, long term imprisonment, or exile. An attempt to overthrow a government by revolt, spying, or the selling of secret information is usually classed as treason.

The total volume of crime is not known because many offenses are never detected nor reported. Many crimes known to police are never reported, and of course many offenders, even though guilty, are reported who are never convicted. The American system of criminal justice also leans over backwards to keep from convicting the innocent.

During World War II there was a decline in major crimes and commitments to state prisons in the United States. Beginning with 1944, crime rates and commitment rates began to increase, and increased faster than the civilian population.

## SUMMARY

Deviation is a variation from a standard or norm. In every society certain kinds of personalities and behavior are defined as normal. Variations from these are called deviations. In one sense of the word "deviate" or "deviation" are relative terms. Behavior defined as normal in one culture or subculture may be defined as abnormal in another culture or subculture.

In every society certain deviates and certain forms of deviation are disapproved, while other forms of deviation are approved.

While some deviation is genetic and biological in origin, much of it is sociogenic, having its origin in the culture and especially in the systems of interpersonal relationships maintained in a culture. Lack of access to what a culture has to offer may be a cause of deviation, as well as features of the culture which encourage deviation.

THINGS TO DO AND TO DISCUSS

1. What is a social deviant? What is deviation?
2. What is meant by approved and disapproved deviation?
3. How may deficiency in potential capacity be a cause of deviation?
4. Show how an inadequate culture may cause deviation.
5. Give examples of deviation caused by disease.

6. From knowledge of a community known to you, give the major causes of social deviation.
7. Distinguish between an idiot, an imbecile, and a moron.
8. What is the distinction between mental deficiency and mental defectiveness?
9. What are the essential differences between neuroses and psychoses?
10. What are some of the characteristics of a normal personality?
11. What is the difference between an organic and a functional psychosis?
12. Who is a juvenile delinquent? An adult offender?
13. What conditions in your community are conducive to the development of juvenile offenders? Of development of adult offenders?

FOR FURTHER STUDY

AUSUBEL, DAVID P. *Drug Addiction.* New York: Random House, 1958. One of the better treatments of this form of deviation.

BARNES, HARRY ELMER, and TEETERS, N. K. *New Horizons in Criminology.* New York: Prentice-Hall, 1951. Good standard text in criminology.

BARRON, MILTON L. *The Juvenile Delinquent in Society.* New York: Alfred A. Knopf, 1954. One of the better standard texts in juvenile delinquency.

BROWN, JULIA S. "A Comparative Study of Deviation from Sexual Mores," *American Sociological Review,* 17:135-46, April, 1952. Sex deviations in various societies and punishment for some. The data are from the Human Relations Area files.

CLINARD, MARSHALL B. *Sociology of Deviant Behavior.* New York: Rinehart and Co., 1957. One of the better comprehensive treatments of deviancy.

COHEN, ALBERT K. *Delinquent Boys: The Culture of the Gang.* Glencoe, Ill.: Free Press, 1955. Juvenile gang culture explored and explained.

DAVIES, STANLEY POWELL. *The Mentally Retarded in Society.* New York: Columbia University Press, 1959. Comprehensive and readable study of retardation.

DAVIS, KINGSLEY. *Human Society.* New York: The Macmillan Co., 1949. Chapter 9 contains a good discussion of personality integration, as Chapter 10 does of personality disorganization.

FEDERAL BUREAU OF INVESTIGATION. *Uniform Crime Reports,* 1958. Washington, D.C., 1959. The best source of data on national crime rates and trends.

GLUECK, SHELDON, and GLUECK, ELEANOR. *Unraveling Juvenile Delinquency.* New York: Commonwealth Fund, 1951. Basic study of the causes of juvenile delinquency.

HIGGINS, LOIS LUNDELL, and FITZPATRICK, EDWARD A. *Criminology and Crime Prevention.* Milwaukee: Bruce Publishing Co., 1958. Standard criminology text with emphasis on crime prevention.

KLUCKHOHN, CLYDE, and MURRAY, HENRY A. *Personality in Nature, Society and Culture.* New York: Alfred A. Knopf, 1953. How certain cultures make for deviancy in behavior.

LINDESMITH, ALFRED R. *Opiate Addiction.* Bloomington, Ind.: Principia Press, 1947. A good source of information on addiction.

MASLAND, RICHARD L., *et al. Mental Subnormality.* New York: Basic Books, 1958. Comprehensive volume on causes and treatment of mental subnormality.

McCARTHY, RAYMOND G., (ed.). *Drinking and Intoxication: Selected Readings in Social Attitudes and Controls.* New Haven: Yale Center of Alcohol Studies, 1959. A good summary of drinking practices, the effects of alcohol, and attempts at control of alcoholism.

MORRIS, TERRENCE. *The Criminal Area: A Study in Criminal Ecology.* London: Routledge and Kegan Paul, 1957. Good study of the spatial distribution of crime.

MYERS, JEROME K., and ROBERTS, H. BERTRAM. *Family and Class Dynamics in Mental Illness.* New York: John Wiley and Sons, 1959. Relation of family and class status and situation and mental illness.

VAN NYE, F. *Family Relationships and Delinquent Behavior.* New York: John Wiley and Sons, 1958. The nature of family relationships in relation to delinquency.

VOLD, GEORGE B. *Theoretical Criminology.* New York: Oxford University Press, 1958. The leading theoretical schools of criminology; theories of individual deviancy in relation to criminal behavior; theories concerning culture influences and crime and the use of criminological theory in relation to research and to penal practices.

WAUGH, COULTON. *The Comics.* New York: The Macmillan Co., 1947. A good treatment of consumers of comics and the impact of comics upon behavior.

# 24. DISORGANI-ZATION, EQUILIBRIUM, AND INTEGRATION

Except in a society torn by revolution, or some other equivalent disorganizing crisis, the products of a society are heavily weighted on the favorable side of the ledger. What we mean is that normal personalities are in the majority over abnormal personalities in our society, and that the disorganizing processes of conflict, excess competition, and intolerance are overridden by the processes of cooperation, mutual aid, accommodation, and toleration. In short, individual and group norms observance, the processes of organization, unity, equilibrium, and integration are more in evidence in social systems than those of disorganization, disunity, and norm violation and deviation.

## THE WEB OF RELATIONSHIPS

In every society the web of relationships always involves forces of disorganization and forces of unity. We tried to point up this fact in Chapter 13. Alongside the inadequate person may be eight or ten adequate persons. The adequate and the inadequate may be separated or segregated from each other. In the same community where there is adequacy of people and their social systems, there may be some inadequacy and pathology. On the other hand, the worst crime-ridden and delinquency-ridden communities will have a high percentage of law-abiding people.

The concept that the student should acquire is that societies are not all black or all white. There are black and white products and processes but they are part of the matrix of the same society. Black and white operate back and forth in a complicated maze of reciprocal relationships. There are also shades of gray. Societies, along with other social systems, such as groups and institutions, always have the task of keeping the forces of disunity and disorganization reduced to a point where they are subordinate to those of unity and organization. Eventually, of course, out of crisis a

*349*

greater social unity and stability may come. This was true of the French Revolution, the American Revolution, the Civil War, World Wars I and II, and the great depression of the 1930's.

The student of sociology must consider the probability, with Fromm, that when an individual, group, or other form of social system makes an unsatisfactory adjustment in society, it may be the society that is neurotic or insane.[1] In answer to the question "Are we sane?" Fromm assembles considerable data comparing homicide, suicide rates, and alcoholism rates of various countries. In the comparisons the United States emerges with a high rate of pathology, even in spite of the fact that it is the most prosperous country in the world.[2] The point he makes is that our material ways lead to boredom and that suicide and alcoholism are "pathological ways" of escape from boredom. Fromm furthermore raises the question of what would happen should our

escape mechanisms, such as movies, radio, and television, fail to function for a period of only four weeks. If this should happen, what would be the consequences for the American people thrown back upon their own resources? The resulting disunity we can well imagine. The point is well made that society can be sick, can be sociopathic, and may contribute to the deviation and disorganization of both individuals and groups. Horney discusses this same thesis at length.[3] Also, most of the books on social disorganization and personal deviation give ample space to sociocultural factors and conditions which contribute to deviation.[4]

Numerous studies of juvenile delinquency show a relationship between the weakening of social controls, community disorganization, and delinquency. As a rule, such studies go further and show that delinquency areas have a special subculture in which delinquency is learned as cultural behavior.[5] This is true of drug addiction and other forms of deviancy.

## DISORGANIZATION

Social disorganization, like progress, is subjective and not easy to define. An aggressive feminist and a rigid fundamentalist would have different convictions about the increase in divorce. We would agree that an improvement in health is a sign of progress. In the same way there are some criteria of disorganization where there would be considerable agreement among experts. For example, signs of disorganization might include an increase of fear, hate, suspicion, isolation, and conflict, and a decrease of cooperation.

Social disorganization is also a relative term. For instance, the depression of the 1930's is said to have been a period of disorganization, yet the economic status of the majority of the people of the world is worse today than the economic status of most Americans during the

depression. The point on the organization-disorganization continuum at which the community becomes disorganized, because of conflict, unemployment, illness, crime, delinquency, or other forms of lawlessness, is not easily determined. In fact, the definers of disorganization would not be in accord. A degree of lawlessness which the Ministerial Association might define as bringing disorganization to the com-

[3] Karen Horney, *The Neurotic Personality of Our Time* (New York: W. W. Norton and Co., 1937), especially Chapter I, "Cultural and Psychological Implications of Neuroses," also Chapter X, "The Quest for Power, Prestige, and Possession."

[4] For a good resumé of important literature on social disorganization, *see* Albert K. Cohen, "The Study of Social Disorganization and Deviant Behavior," in *Sociology Today*, ed. Robert K. Merton, Leonard Broom, and Leonard S. Cottrell, Jr. (New York: Basic Books, 1955), pp. 461-84.

[5] Sheldon and Eleanor Glueck, *Unraveling Juvenile Delinquency* (New York: Commonwealth Fund, 1950). *See also* Marshall B. Clinard, "Criminological Research," in *Sociology Today*, ed. Robert K. Merton, Leonard Broom, and Leonard S. Cottrell, Jr. (2nd ed.; New York: Basic Books, 1960), pp. 509-36.

[1] This thesis is developed in Erich Fromm, *The Sane Society* (New York: Rinehart and Co., 1955), especially in Chapter 2, "Can A Society be Sick? The Pathology of Normalcy."

[2] *Ibid.*, pp. 8-9.

munity might not get much response from the sheriff and his deputies, all of whom might see nothing unusual about the community's crime situation.

Social disorganization has been defined as "any disturbance, disruption, conflict, or lack of consensus within a social group or given society which affects established social habits of behavior, social institutions or social controls, so as to make relatively harmonious functioning impossible without some significant intermediate adjustments."[6]

To recapitulate, when customary social controls are no longer effective, and when the usual norms and ways of behaving are no longer adequate, social disorganization may result. For example, when, through the usual process of obtaining jobs, jobs are not available, disorganization may result. When the usual social controls of law, public opinion, value systems, morals, and personal example no longer control the population, disorganization may result. When governmental officials are thrown out of office, and a crisis pending the establishment of a new government develops, political and economic disorganization and disruption may follow.

## EQUILIBRIUM

Perhaps it would be nice if all disorganizing influences could be eliminated from a society. On the other hand, such extremes of stability might be deadening. The elimination of disorganizing influences is nevertheless not possible. In all societies an attempt is made to establish at least an equilibrium between the forces of organization and those of disorganization. The quest for equilibrium becomes a social process and equilibrium itself becomes a goal and a product. Let us be more specific. For example, the quest for equilibrium seeks to balance the number of jobs available with the people needing work. To maintain equilibrium, officials try to see that the forces of law enforcement and treatment of offenders at least are adequate to cope with lawlessness. Of course, attempts are made to reduce the amount of crime.

The idea of equilibrium goes further. In every society there are elements, such as sentiments, values, and ends, which give unity to a society. There are also technological and economic activities and ideologies and political and religious-moral beliefs and values which sustain sentiments and help to achieve ends.

In every society there are normative prescriptions in the form of folkways, mores, laws, and institutions which give continuity, stability, and order to the society. The balance between these elements, along with sustaining activities, such as economic activities, determines the nature and amount of equilibrium. As Davis points out, this equilibrium not only resists deflection but is, in part, self-restoring.[7]

The equilibrium normally present in the variables mentioned above may be altered by forces outside the society and over which the society itself has little or no control. The lack of equilibrium in one set of variables may upset the equilibrium of another set. For example, the economic equilibrium of a country may be thrown into disorganized state by the cessation of trade with a large importing country. Equilibrium between trade and production would, in this case, be destroyed by such action on the part of a major importing country. If successful in finding new markets, equilibrium would be restored in the economy of the exporting nation.

The people of a country may precipitate a state of affairs within the nation which destroys equilibrium, as the Indonesians did against the Dutch during their revolt against colonial domination. Even up to the present time a new state of equilibrium has hardly been

---

[6] Henry Pratt Fairchild, *Dictionary of Sociology* (New York: Philosophical Library, 1944), pp. 280-81.

[7] Kingsley Davis, *Human Society* (New York: The Macmillan Co., 1949), pp. 633-34.

reached by the Indonesians. Even though they have freed themselves from Dutch domination and rule, there are competing factions in the government seeking control. Conflicting philosophies exist about the direction in which the emancipated country should move. In trade they have difficulty disposing of their raw products, especially rubber, and they are not equipped as yet to manufacture consumable goods from their raw products. In time, no doubt, equilibrium may be restored.

Equilibrium, then, may be destroyed by forces outside a society or forces from within a society. A catastrophe might disorganize a community or even a small nation. Conflicts over ideologies, such as religion, integration of schools, or political doctrines, may likewise destroy the equilibrium of a society, as would a people's revolt or the overthrow of a government. These might not only alter the structure but also the function of a society.

## INTEGRATION IN SOCIETY

In the last chapter we spoke of the normal personality in contrast to a deviant one. We should, at this point, say something of personality integration, since the most important product of an integrated society is integrated personalities.

In evaluating the personality profiles of individuals, Garrett scores them on the basis of calmness, good nature, deliberativeness, cooperativeness, responsibleness, resolution, and constancy of mood.[8] It is the pattern of these traits which counts. It is assumed, furthermore, that consistency of desired traits in a person is a mark of an integrated personality.

Krech and Crutchfield describe an integrated personality as follows:

An integrated personality is one in which the needs, demands, and goals—instead of functioning as separate, segmented parts of the behavior—work together optimally in a way that is self-consistent, mutually reinforcing, and non-conflicting. And this integration is mainly possible through the individual's system of values, ideals, and ideology.[9]

We see from the above statement that an integrated personality is composed of more than simply the absence of conflict. It is a personality which has unity of elements and in which values, ideals, and behaviors are integrated.

Sociologically, one of the most important factors in the integration of a person is a person's value system or system of value orientation. Each value system may vary greatly from person to person. This accounts, in part, for the great variation in behavior of people. Haak indicates that people have ten significant areas of orientation which make up their value systems. These are religion, science, mystery, aesthetics, humanitarian orientation, economic and political orientation, militaristic, sensate, and status orientation.[10] Within each of these there may be wide variation. For instance, a person in his religious orientation may view religion from a humanitarian, an aesthetic, a mystical, or a scientific viewpoint.

In speaking of conflicts within an orientation and between orientation areas, Haak says:

The individual does not have perfect freedom to choose which of these various orientations and arrangements of value systems he will accept; for he will be either well or poorly adjusted, depending on whether or not his values are generally accepted by the society in which he lives. He is faced with the disharmony between groups and also the disharmony between actions and words.

If, for instance, his values are organized around the aesthetic or even around the militaristic, he

[8] Henry E. Garrett, *General Psychology* (New York: American Book Co., 1955).

[9] David Krech and Richard S. Crutchfield, *Theory and Problems of Social Psychology* (New York: McGraw-Hill Book Co., 1948), p. 68.

[10] Leo A. Haak, "Conflicting Value Systems," *Basic Values and Human Relationships* (East Lansing: Michigan State College, The Basic College, 1948), pp. 60-64.

*The United Nations is a symbol of the attempt to minimize disorganization and to effect unity and equilibrium among nations.*

will be a member of a minority group and thus the object of some criticism and scorn. One of the most powerful means of putting pressure on a person is by ignoring him; this would be relatively ineffective in the case of a mystic. But a different problem arises in the case of a religious or humanitarian orientation. Much has been said in favor of these but actions are frequently not consistent with words. During the Inquisition non-Christians were killed . . . and, more recently, it has been reported that large numbers of internationally minded humanitarians have been purged in various European countries. Differences in values have been and probably will again become bases of conflict.

An individual is in a favorable situation if his values are those which are in the ascendancy. Evidence of continued change and conflict are about us all the time and can be recognized by the discerning observer. We are being torn by the rival claims of these various ways of life and must take two sides. The conflict is in the world in which we live; groups to which we belong are affected by it; it is even within us.[11]

It has been pointed out that one of the problems of modern societies is the integration of differentiated activities, such as occupations, into some kind of a coordinated whole. It is the degree specialization and differentiation of occupational roles that constitutes one of the major differentiations between urban-industrial and folk type societies. It has been shown, for instance, that suicide rates in a society vary inversely with the degree of occupational integration.[12] In modern urban-industrial societies, where bureaucratic structures have grown, especially in government and economic institutions, bureaucratic structures serve integrating as well as differentiating functions.[13]

An integrated society is much like a society in equilibrium. The various parts are in harmony and functioning. There is adherence to core value systems. On major issues on which the people express themselves there is concensus.

Social integration has also been defined "as a measure of the degree to which the norms are accepted by and serve as guides to action for a group or a society."[14] Often the term "social cohesion" is used interchangeably with social integration.

Social integration and group cohesion may be measured or otherwise determined. For instance, Durkheim found that the suicide rate varied with the degree of integration in social structures, such as the church, family, political party, or national state.[15] In social structures where controls were close and frequent, and where existing norms were accepted by the large majority of people making up the social structure, suicide rates were lower than where opposite conditions existed in social structures. Group cohesiveness may also be measured in terms of group likes and dislikes, the group sources from which one selects one's friends, prestige feelings for groups, dependency upon groups and services received from the group, frequency and length of contacts, and feeling toward dissolving the group structures one has contacts with, or at least dissolving contacts with such groups.[16]

In an integrated society there would be a low incidence of pathology, deficiency, and dependency, and a high incidence of adequacy. Whatever pathology exists, the adequate in an integrated society would seek to reduce it. In a test of moral integration in American cities, Angell used such indices as satisfaction with the community, level of personal conduct, participation in civic affairs, relations among groups, effort to support schools, recreation,

11 *Ibid.*, p. 64.

12 Elwin H. Powell, "Occupation, Status, and Suicide," *American Sociological Review*, 23:131-39, April, 1958.

13 For more on this point, *see* Walter I. Wardwell, "Social Integration, Bureaucratization, and the Professions," *Social Forces*, 33:356-59, May, 1955. *See also* Peter M. Blau, *Bureaucracy in Modern Society* (New York: Random House, 1956).

14 Charles Y. Glock, "The Sociology of Religion," in *Sociology Today*, ed. Robert K. Merton, Leonard Broom, and Leonard S. Cottrell, Jr. (2nd ed.; New York: Basic Books, 1960), p. 157.

15 Emile Durkheim, *Suicide*, trans. George Simpson (Glencoe, Ill.: Free Press, 1951).

16 *See* L. Festinger and A. Zander, *Group Dynamics* (Evanston, Ill.: Row, Peterson and Co., 1952).

libraries and museums, the health and welfare services, and the crime index.[17]

It is perhaps possible that a society can be so integrated or cohesive that it would be highly resistant to change. Mead reports that the Tiv culture of Nigeria is so tightly integrated that any change threatens the whole of the culture. Other cultures, like that of the Palaunas in Micronesia, are characterized by such "bounce" and patterns of manipulating events that it is easy to introduce change without disturbing the whole of the culture.[18] It is hardly possible that a modern urban-industrial society would be so closely integrated that it would resist change. Rather the reverse is likely to be true, namely, that the culture is so flexible and changeable that integration is difficult.

## SUMMARY

In every society there are social processes making for unity and organization and those making for disorganization. The perpetual task a society faces is to keep the forces of disorganization as a minor element compared to the forces of unity and organization.

Disorganization in a society exists when disruption, conflict, and lack of consensus are great enough that the usual forms of social control do not operate and institutions cannot perform their customary services and functions.

Disequilibrium in a society is a stage that is reached before disorganization takes place. The lack of equilibrium implies the lack of balance between the various elements making up a society and not necessarily always disorganization. For instance, it is often remarked that the religious-moral element in American society does not keep pace with the technological and the economic elements. This is disequilibrium but not necessarily disorganization such as might result from a civil war, a religious war, or a major depression. Conflict over desegregation in a community might reach a point where the community is disorganized and might be the culmination point of an attempt to establish a stronger equilibrium for minorities in education.

An integrated personality is one in which the various elements are substantially in balance. An integrated society has a similar meaning. There is not only substantial balance as between the various components of the society but there is consensus and agreement as to what social values are important. For instance, unless there is general agreement in the United States upon the important goals of our society and the means of achieving them, there is not likely to be the amount of consensus necessary to maintain stability and integration in the society.

[17] *See* Robert Cooley Angell, *The Moral Integration of American Cities* (Chicago: University of Chicago Press, 1951).

[18] Margaret Mead, *Cultural Patterns and Technical Change* (New York: New American Library, 1955), pp. 96-125.

THINGS TO DO AND TO DISCUSS

1. Why is it important that the processes of unity be greater than those of disunity in a society?
2. What is meant by social disorganization?
3. What is meant by a state of equilibrium in a society?
4. How may events outside a society precipitate disorganization in a society?
5. What is an integrated society? How may the nature of a society tend to develop deviation?

6. Why is the orientation of a person an important part of personality integration?

7. Show how the orientation of a person toward religion may vary.

8. What are some of the more important areas of integration that a person may have? Show how the variation in one of these areas may result in personal integration or the lack of it.

9. Is it possible for a society to be integrated to a point where it resists the changes that are necessary for progress?

FOR FURTHER STUDY

ANGELL, ROBERT COOLEY. *The Moral Integration of American Cities*. Chicago: University of Chicago Press, 1951. Series of indices testing integration in American cities.

———. *Free Society and Moral Crisis*. Ann Arbor, Mich.: University of Michigan Press, 1958. Conflicts between freedom and crisis.

DAVIS, KINGSLEY. *Human Society*. New York: The Macmillan Co., 1949. Has a good chapter on personality integration and a good discussion of equilibrium and social change.

DIXON, WILLIAM G. (ed.). *Social Welfare and the Preservation of Human Values*. Vancouver, B.C.: J. M. Dent and Sons, 1957. How social welfare contributes to preserving human values.

FAIRCHILD, HENRY PRATT. *Dictionary of Sociology*. New York: Philosophical Library, 1944. Good source of terms used in sociology.

FROMM, ERICH. *The Sane Society*. New York: Rinehart and Co., 1955. How a society may contribute to deviation and disorganization, is discussed in the chapter, "Some Roads to Sanity."

GARRETT, HENRY E. *General Psychology*. New York: American Book Co., 1955. Good treatment of patterns of traits involved in personalities.

GRAHAM, SAXON. *American Culture*. New York: Harper and Bros., 1957. An excellent analysis of American culture.

HAAK, LEO A. "Conflicting Value Systems," *Basic Values and Human Relationships*. East Lansing, Mich.: Michigan State College, The Basic College, 1948. Good treatment of the various aspects of individual orientation and how the personality is influenced by them.

HAINES, C. GROVE (ed.). *European Integration*. Baltimore: Johns Hopkins Press, 1957. The integration of European society examined against some of the disrupting influences.

HORNEY, KAREN. *The Neurotic Personality of Our Time*. New York: W. W. Norton and Co., 1937. A good analysis of neuroses at the time the book was written and especially good on how culture contributes to neuroses.

KRECH, DAVID, and CRUTCHFIELD, RICHARD S. *Theory and Problems of Social Psychology*. New York: McGraw-Hill Book Co., 1948. Some good things on the disorganized personality.

MERTON, ROBERT K.; BROOM, LEONARD; and COTTRELL, LEONARD S., JR. (eds.). *Sociology Today*. New York: Basic Books, 1959. Has a good analysis of the status of literature on social disorganization.

OGBURN, WILLIAM F. *Social Change.* New York: Viking Press, 1938. The original formulation of the "cultural lag" hypothesis.

OPLER, MARVIN K. *Culture and Mental Health.* New York: The Macmillan Co., 1960. A compendium of cross-cultural studies in mental health around the world.

PERSONS, STOW. *American Minds: A History of Ideas.* New York: Henry Holt and Co., 1958. Good on the historical aspects of American ideals.

# INDEX OF SUBJECTS

# INDEX OF NAMES